# Scotland and France
# in the Enlightenment

# Studies in Eighteenth-Century Scotland

General Editor: Richard B. Sher
New Jersey Institute of Technology and Rutgers University, Newark

*Studies in Eighteenth-Century Scotland* publishes multi-author volumes dedicated to particular themes. Published in association with the Eighteenth-Century Scottish Studies Society, the series aims to produce lively, interdisciplinary scholarship on a wide variety of topics having to do with the thought and culture (in the widest sense of that term) of eighteenth-century Scotland, including Scottish connections and relations with other parts of the world.

TITLES IN THE SERIES

*Scotland and France in the Enlightenment.* Ed. Deidre Dawson and Pierre Morère. 2003.
*Nation and Province in the First British Empire: Scotland and the Americas, 1600–1800.* Ed. Ned C. Landsman. 2001.

TITLES PUBLISHED BY ECSSS

*William Robertson and the Expansion of Empire.* Ed. Stewart J. Brown. 1997.
*The Glasgow Enlightenment.* Ed. Andrew Hook and Richard B. Sher. 1995.
*Sociability and Society in Eighteenth-Century Scotland.* Ed. John Dwyer and Richard B. Sher. 1993.
*Ossian Revisited.* Ed. Howard Gaskill. 1991.
*Scotland and America in the Age of the Enlightenment.* Ed. Richard B. Sher and Jeffrey R. Smitten. 1990.

www.departments.bucknell.edu/univ_press

# Scotland and France
# in the Enlightenment

### Edited by Deidre Dawson
### and Pierre Morère

Lewisburg
Bucknell University Press
London: Associated University Presses

Associated University Presses
2010 Eastpark Boulevard
Cranbury, NJ 08512

Associated University Presses
Unit 304, The Chandlery
50 Westminster Bridge Road
London SE1 7QY, England

Associated University Presses
P.O. Box 338, Port Credit
Mississauga, Ontario
Canada L5G 4L8

The paper used in this publication meets the requirements of the American National Standard for Permanence of Paper for Printed Library Materials Z39.48-1984.

Library of Congress Cataloging-in-Publication Data

Scotland and France in the Enlightenment / edited by Deidre Dawson and Pierre Morère.
   p.   cm. — (Studies in eighteenth-century Scotland)
   Includes bibliographical references and index.
   ISBN 0-8387-5526-7 (alk. paper)
   1. Enlightenment—Scotland.   2. Scotland—Intellectual life—18th century.   3. Enlightenment—France.   4. France—Intellectual life—18th century.   I. Dawson, Deidre, 1958–   II. Morère, Pierre.   III. Series.
B1402.E55S38   2004
941.107—dc21                                                    2003004615

To the memory of Hélène Boucé
and
to Richard Sher,
in appreciation of his friendship and of his many
contributions to this project.

# Contents

# List of Illustrations

# Preface

BUILDING ON THE PIONEERING LITERARY STUDIES OF PROFESSOR HENRI Gibault, "Scottish Studies" has existed as a separate entity at the Université Stendhal in Grenoble since 1979. In that year the university established the Centre d'Études Écossaises, with a focus on literature and the history of ideas from the eighteenth century to our time. Under the leadership of its illustrious director, Professor Pierre Morère, the Centre has encouraged research on Scottish topics, integrated Scottish studies into the curriculum, entertained a varied international collaboration among scholars from Scotland, England, Germany, the United States, and Canada, and established its pedigree as a research center by attaining recognition by the Centre National de Recherche Scientifique (CNRS). The Grenoble research center publishes a review, initially entitled *Écosse, littérature et civilisation* but known since 1992 as *Études Écossaises*. Concerning the eighteenth century specifically, it has been particularly interested in the notion of historicity, that is, this historic substratum, real or imagined, that perpetuates itself in Scottish literature and thought in a constant reaffirmation of an identity that was, until the reopening of the Scottish Parliament in 1999, nearly lost politically, but which has always been culturally alive. It is worth mentioning that the Grenoble research center also includes a branch devoted to the twentieth century, directed by Professsor Keith Dixon, which has been particularly active in producing French translations of contemporary Scottish novels.

With such an active Scottish Studies presence, Grenoble was the perfect place to host an international conference on the theme "France and Scotland in the Enlightenment," jointly organized by the Eighteenth-Century Scottish Studies Society (ECSSS) and the Centre d'Études Écossaises in July 1996. The conference marked the tenth anniversary of the founding of ECSSS, which had grown from a handful of North American scholars at the time of its establishment to more than three hundred members around the world. As a longtime friend of Pierre Morère and the Grenoble research center, Deidre Dawson, then chair of the Department of French at Georgetown University and now associate professor of French in the Department of Romance and Classical Languages at Michigan State University, was an ideal choice to join Pierre in organizing the conference. With fine French food and wine, and Chartreuse liqueur from the nearby monastery of that name, the participants were well fortified for four days of intellectual stimulation.

It is only fitting that Deidre and Pierre, who were chiefly responsible for the success of the Grenoble meeting, have continued their collaboration by editing this collection of revised papers from that conference—the seventh volume in ECSSS's Studies in Eighteenth-Century Scotland series, and the second to be published by Bucknell University Press. The book's fourteen essays address a wide range of topics in literature, the arts, encyclopedias, natural history, philosophy, and political thought. Their authors represent a half dozen academic disciplines and reside in France, Scotland, England, the United States, Hungary, and Israel. In its multidisciplinary, international approach, this volume is characteristic both of its sponsoring society and of the Enlightenment itself.

As if their hospitality at the time of the conference was not enough, the Scottish Studies group at Grenoble also provided a generous publication subsidy, for which ECSSS is extremely grateful.

Richard B. Sher, Executive Secretary—ECSSS

# Introduction: A New Incarnation of the Auld Alliance: "Franco-Scottish Studies"

DEIDRE DAWSON AND PIERRE MORÈRE

## FRANCE AND SCOTLAND: FROM POLITICS TO CULTURE

RELATIONS BETWEEN FRANCE AND SCOTLAND GO BACK TO ANCIENT times, and were initially founded on a common mistrust of England. However, with the Union of the Crowns in 1603, and especially with the Act of Union in 1707, Scotland found itself more closely associated with its powerful neighbor in the south. Yet if these historical developments removed the edge from Franco-Scottish affinities of a strictly political nature, there remained a kind of affection nourished by memories of the past (such as the Auld Alliance), sometimes even bordering on myth. In this important and durable sense, cultural exchanges between France and Scotland have been continuous, but they reached their apogee in the Age of Enlightenment.

In politics, the first solid links between France and Scotland were established when the two countries united their efforts to thwart the influence of the Plantagenets. This alliance materialized through the support of Pope Boniface VIII and the French king at Balliol. But Scotland's fate took a turn for the worse when France lost the battle of Courtrai in 1302 and when William Wallace, the national hero, was taken prisoner by the English and executed in London. One could also mention Robert the Bruce's turbulent reign, which began inauspiciously, to say the least. Bruce was initially forced to seek refuge in the Highlands before being able to regain the upper hand and inflict one defeat after another upon the English. Recognized as king of Scotland by France, excommunicated by the Pope until 1328 but supported by his own clergy, he succeeded in establishing his authority and in assuring the existence of Scotland as an independent kingdom.

13

What is commonly referred to as the "Auld Alliance" is considered a legend today, but it was a historical reality between 1371 and 1492. Its consequences for the French influence in Scotland were far from negligible. The Auld Alliance was initially characterized by the numerous extended stays of Scottish clergymen in France, where they went to put the finishing touches to their training. During the "Great Schism" that gave rise to two rival papacies in Rome and in Avignon, Scotland aligned itself with France, which had naturally taken the side of Avignon. During those years, Scotland and France often found themselves fighting together against common enemies, in particular English enemies, to the point where Charles VII established the "Garde Écossaise," or Scottish Guard. When France equipped itself with a regular standing army, called "Gens d'Ordonnance," a permanent company composed entirely of Scottish soldiers was included. Inevitably, cultural exchanges were woven into this political tapestry. Thus, in the first French "novels," known as the *Cent Nouvelles Nouvelles*, the Scottish soldier always has a good role. Similarly, the founding of St. Andrew's University coincided with the beginning of the Auld Alliance, and that university followed the same principles as the Sorbonne in Paris.

The nature of relations between France and Scotland started to change quite noticeably with the Reformation. France remained an important Roman Catholic power, while Scotland could not remain untouched by the political and religious upheavals that marked England at the time of the Renaissance and throughout the seventeenth century. John Knox, the founder of the Presbyterian Church of Scotland, belonged to the Anglophile party, and suffered at the hands of the French, who held him prisoner for a time. Significantly, Knox chose the English language in his translation of the Bible and as the official language of the church service (*The Book of Common Order*, inspired by Geneva). In the political arena, the Treaty of Leith between France and England put an official end to the military presence of France in Scotland in 1560. Meanwhile, Scotland was affected by the great movement of ideas that marked England in the seventeenth century. The Civil War had repercussions in Scotland from the moment it became evident that affinities existed between the "Round Heads" of the south and the "Covenanters" of the north. The Puritans' rise to power was accompanied by new political concepts. France continued to be the incarnation of absolute monarchy and repressive Catholicism, and if the Edict of Nantes, which granted religious freedoms to the Huguenots in 1598, suggested the emergence of a more tolerant regime, those hopes were dashed by the revocation of the edict by Louis XIV in 1685. The Calvinists of England and Scotland, on the contrary, were evolving toward a constitutional monarchy, and some of them did not hide their republican feelings.

The Act of Union was supposed to join Scotland to England in a durable manner, even if it appears in retrospect that England was the primary beneficiary. During the eighteenth century, political relations between France and Scotland necessarily passed through England. Of course, some people thought wistfully of the Stuart family, of the "Old Pretender" taking refuge at the court of Versailles, and especially of the fantastic epic of "Bonnie Prince Charlie," whose complete failure with the tragic defeat at Culloden in April 1746 signaled the end of a dream. Once peace had returned to the Continent, even France, out of political realism, distanced itself from the Stuarts, who ended their lives in sad and desperate wandering.

Aside from the last maneuvers of the Stuarts, and later the disruption caused all over Europe by the French Revolution, it is not so much in the political as in the cultural domain that the renewal of relations between France and Scotland must be situated. The Act of Union created a new kingdom, but it raised at the same time the problem of the permanence of Scottish identity. This identity lived on to some degree in the three fundamental institutions of law, the Church, and the educational system. Nevertheless, the cultural domain lacked a secure foundation. In a century of cosmopolitanism, it was unimaginable to look for inspiration by falling back on provincialism. Besides, the vernacular Scots of the Lowlands lacked unity and did not benefit from any cultural recognition, and the three components of Scottish institutional identity expressed themselves in English. This identity had to affirm itself, and beyond that, create itself, in the language of the big neighbor to the south. Paradoxically, Anglicization was brought about as much by the Scots themselves as by the inevitable influence of the English, as shown by several works by Scottish authors that invited their countrymen to rid themselves of the self-consciously provincial expressions known as "Scotticisms."

Is it possible, then, to speak of the emergence of a Scottish cultural inferiority complex during the eighteenth century, as some scholars have suggested? At first, one feels compelled to reply in the affirmative. England had become a model. Nevertheless, the desire to affirm oneself in the politically dominant language does not necessarily signify a renunciation of one's own cultural identity. The Enlightenment principle of cosmopolitanism would enable Scotland to make a rich, original contribution to the literature and ideas of the age. With David Hume, Adam Smith, and other great thinkers, Edinburgh became the Athens of the North. The novels of Tobias Smollett, and above all James Macpherson's brilliantly counterfeited poems of Ossian, would assure for posterity the literary renown of Scotland, distinct from that of England. Cultural relations between France and Scotland in the eighteenth century were carried out in a reciprocal manner: David Hume stayed in Paris and met the Encyclopédistes; his friendship with Rousseau ended in a well-publicized tempest. At the same time, the tenets of a more traditional empiricism with religious overtones were also well known in France through the writings of Thomas Reid and others. In the Age of Enlightenment, it seemed as if the intellectual and cultural affinities between Scotland and France compensated for the ups and downs of history, almost as if the strength of the intellect shielded, against all obstacles, a cultural communion that time cannot erode. The cultural affinities between France and Scotland had banished political factors from the past.

In the nineteenth century, Victor Cousin attempted to reconcile commonsense philosophy with the new principles of German transcendentalism. In literature, the poems of Ossian invaded Europe like a breaking wave, and became one of the beacons of the Romantic movement. James Beattie's poem *The Minstrel* (1771–74), composed in Spenserian verse, should also be mentioned, for it served as a link between postclassicism and preromanticism. Beattie's distinction between the notions of "genius" and "imagination" prefigured the celebrated theory of poetic creation elaborated by Wordsworth in his *Prelude,* and continued by Coleridge in light of German philosophy (for example, the difference between "fancy" and "imagination"). It is not surprising, then, that in such a context Chateaubriand would be so inflamed by the impulsive emotions felt by the hero of *The Minstrel*, Edwin, and that he would render a magnificent French translation of book 1 of the poem, so admired by Sainte Beuve. Finally, in politics, the repercussions caused by the French Revolution were similar in Scotland and England. In the north as in the south of Great Britain, the first movements of the Revolution were often favorably received because they seemed to signify the fall of an archaic regime, and to indicate that the French were embracing British "Revolution Principles" of 1688–89. Here and there in Scotland people planted trees of liberty, and some voices were raised against the nobility. But the excesses of the Terror overshadowed the initial enthusiasm, and Scotland soon joined in the universal condemnation of Napoleonic France as an arrogant, conquering nation. Relations between the two countries were once again blurred and became engulfed within relations between the two states of France and Great Britain. The ascendancy of politics was reaffirmed. Yet a common political and cultural memory, embellished by legend and myth, remained intact, and continues to be a fertile source of a continually evolving renaissance.

## Scotland and France in the Enlightenment

The essays in *Scotland and France in the Enlightenment* reflect these varied resonances. The cross-fertilization that occurred between the two countries was particularly rich in literature and the arts, which forms the subject of part I. Politics and history often played a role in the creation and reception of both Scottish and French works dealing with Scotland or Scottish themes. Paul-Gabriel Boucé situates Smollett's *Present State of All Nations, 1768–69* within the context of Smollett's other works of an encyclopedic nature, such as the *Complete History of England* and *The Universal History, The Modern Part*. Smollett's systematic method of categorization places him well within the tradition of the encyclopedic compilation of knowledge that was already a hallmark of the eighteenth century. Boucé's meticulous and often humorous comparison of the accounts of Scotland and France in the *Present State* reveals some interesting attitudes on Smollett's part. Smollett's account of France is rife with anti-French stereotypes and reflects what might have been the typical attitude of a Briton in the wake of the Seven Years' War against France. Notwithstanding Smollett's personal revulsion at the atrocities committed by Cumberland's army in the aftermath of the Battle of Culloden, the account of England is remarkably evenhanded. There is hardly any mention of the long history of Franco-Scottish alliances. Boucé's analysis of the *Present State* reveals that whereas Smollett wrote his account of Scotland from a Scottish perspective, his account of France was written from a distinctly British one.

Sylvie Kleiman-Lafon's lively investigation of the publication, translation, and reception of Voltaire's play, *L'Écossaise*, presents us with a work in which French Jacobite sympathies were obscured by the author himself, who denied his own authorship by posing as a fictitious Scottish author distantly related to David Hume. The introduction of a satire of the French literary scene into a Scottish plot offers comic relief but detracts from the political drama. As Voltaire often noted, Parisians were a fickle lot, and while the adventures of Bonnie Prince Charlie and his supporters might have been the rage in the late 1740s, by 1760, when *L'Écossaise* was performed, the literary quarrel between the philosophes and Voltaire's nemesis Fréron was of much greater interest to readers and theatergoers in the French capital. Thus, although Voltaire wrote a play almost entirely inspired by the Jacobite rebellion, its success had little or nothing to do with the work's political content. In England, where the Jacobite themes of the play drew the attention of the censors, all references to Scotland and things Scottish were removed, and the play still enjoyed some success. In the cases of both the French and the Scottish reception of *L'Écossaise*, form, style, and wit eclipsed political content, in spite of the fact that the work owed its existence to the idea of an independent Scotland.

Indeed, the prevalence of Scottish themes and ideas in eighteenth-century French literature and art often owed more to aesthetics than to politics. Pierre Carboni examines the role of the literary critic, journalist, and academician Jean-Baptiste-Antoine Suard in introducing the poems of Ossian into France and in shaping the direction that French Ossianism would take in the last decades of the eighteenth and first decades of the nineteenth century. The particular character of French Ossianism, which came, via Suard, directly from the Scottish belles-lettres tradition, found in the work of James Macpherson's legendary bard a poetic structure and aesthetic that appealed to French classical tastes. Ossian's poems, before they were known to be forgeries, were an antidote to the artificiality of eighteenth-century French poetry, since they dealt with primitive simplicity and virtue while preserving a classical form. The themes of patriotism, violence, and secularism struck emotional chords in French readers during the Revolutionary and Napoleonic periods. In Carboni's analysis, "Ossian helped France find new settings and inspirations." Ossian and Ossianic criticism became a common cultural reference point between France and Scotland in the latter part of the eighteenth century. For Carboni, the popularity of Ossian in France was another manifestation of the "intellectual kinship between the Scottish Enlightenment and the French Lumières." Suard's "joint discovery of Ossian and Scottish belles-lettres therefore helped France to come to terms with her own inner cultural contradictions between 1760 and the outset of a self-styled French romanticism after 1820."

Andrew Hook picks up where Carboni leaves off, in 1820, and continues the discussion of the enormous impact that Scottish literature had on the development of French Romanticism. Hook persuasively argues that one should look to the French taste for Scottish Romanticism—in particular, to the French obsession with the novels of Sir Walter Scott—for the strongest example of a Franco-Scottish alliance: "There can be no doubt that in the decades 1820–30 Scotland and France were linked culturally in an embrace which was stronger than anything the politics of the 'Auld Alliance' had ever achieved." Throughout the eighteenth century, the Jacobite movement, which aroused much sympathy and political support in France, was a more recent incarnation of the historical "Auld Alliance" between France and Scotland against their mutual enemy England; conversely, during France's revolutionary war with England, some French politicians expressed the hope that Scotland would side with France, break from English control, and form a Scottish republic. And yet, while military alliances between France and Scotland either never materialized or else failed miserably, the cultural alliances between the two countries seemed to strengthen as the eighteenth century drew to a close. Hook notes that Scottish literary Romanticism initially encountered more obstacles in France than had Scottish philosophy, in part because conservative critics still believed that classicism and neoclassicism were more appropriate modes for expressing traditional French values. But eventually Scottish literary Romanticism triumphed during the early part of the nineteenth century because, on the one hand, these were years when Romanticism firmly established itself as the dominant cultural force throughout the Western world, and on the other hand, France itself was undergoing a time of cultural upheaval. Sir Walter Scott's novels inspired operas, paintings by Delacroix and Delaroche, plays, and literary fiction such as the novels of Stendhal; they also inspired fashion, furniture, and masked balls. In Hook's analysis, the popularity of Scott's Waverley novels "helped give identity to an existing French inclination that was waiting to be exploited" and in this way played a crucial role in the development of French Romanticism.

The rapport between Scott's fiction and France was symbiotic and reciprocal; French history left an indelible mark on the novels of Scotland's most famous writer. Susan Manning's analysis of Scott's late works with French themes brings to light an image of the author that is quite different from the familiar one of a stoic, conservative Tory, ending his days as resistant as ever to reform. Manning discovers a Scott who, far from being a moderate Hanoverian afraid of insurrection, was secretly drawn to it. In his writings on French subjects, she writes, Scott "created a France in which rage, anarchy, and violence could flourish, and thus found new creative energies at a low point in his personal fortunes." Manning draws a parallel between the writer's personal struggles and the historical struggles he depicted in his work. *Quentin Durward* (1823) and *Anne of Geierstein* (1829) deal with France in the age of Louis XI and are filled with descriptions of cruelty and torture. But the most striking example of this identification of the author with his subject is *The Life of Napoleon Buonaparte* (1827), begun when Scott was still prosperous and completed during the writer's financial collapse, in which Scott progressively linked his own fate with that of the emperor he had once opposed, and saw his own triumphant career ending in disgrace, confinement, and physical pain. By the end of the work it can be said that Scott understood, if not sympathized with, the emperor's violent torment. As Manning makes clear, "Scott's France is no land of Enlightenment. It is, rather, the battleground of the passions: anger and self-control, authority and freedom, policy and impulse and—perhaps most fundamentally—pain and imagination."

The new direction toward the psychology of human emotions in the moral philosophy of Adam Smith and other Scottish thinkers, and the emphasis on the expression of feelings in art, became a major area of Franco-Scottish exchange. Art historian Duncan Macmillan examines the impact of Scottish thought on the development of French art in the late eighteenth and early nineteenth centuries. Throughout his analysis, Macmillan presents art as a branch of Enlightenment thought. Beginning with a discussion of the moral philosophy of Adam Smith and its influence on Scottish painter Gavin Hamilton, and through Hamilton, of Jacques-Louis David, Macmillan traces the development of the link between sympathy and the expression of feeling, which reached its apex as a field of inquiry for French and Scottish painters and physicians in the opening decades of the nineteenth century. Thomas Reid's account of sensation influenced French physicians such as Cabanis, and the Scottish physician Charles Bell's *Essays on the Anatomy of Expression in Painting* provided inspiration for Géricault and Delacroix. The Scottish painter David Wilkie radically changed the definition of history painting, by suggesting that it should be constructed from the detailed observation of human behavior. The shift away from an idealist, academic art toward a natural art based on experience was one of the pivotal moments in the development of modern art and was rooted at least in part in Scottish empiricism.

An empirical and "commonsense" approach to philosophy and natural history informed the accomplishments of William Smellie, the printer and naturalist who was chiefly responsible for compiling the first edition of the *Encyclopaedia Britannica* (1768–71). Part II of this collection contains three essays on aspects of this subject. The *Britannica* was the first Scottish universal reference work of the arts and sciences organized alphabetically, the first such British work to call itself an encyclopedia, and one of the first British encyclopedias to stress long syntheses instead of short definitions. Notwithstanding these innovations, the French *Encyclopédie* was certainly the superior work in terms of depth, breadth, accuracy of coverage, originality of thought, and choice of up-to-date sources. Frank A. Kafker examines the economic, political, and editorial reasons for the greater success over time of the *Encyclopaedia Britannica* as compared with Diderot and d'Alembert's *Encyclopédie*. Much of the

*Britannica*'s success had to do with printing practices and marketing decisions. More importantly, the open and tolerant political and business environment in Britain and, in particular, Scotland, was a boon to publishing, since there was little or no censorship. In Catholic, absolutist France, Diderot and d'Alembert's *Encyclopédie* had suffered through more than fifteen years of censorship and suspension, and a government ban was placed on any future revised editions. The unparalleled success of the *Encyclopaedia Britannica*, which boasts of being the oldest continuously published encyclopedia still in existence, was directly related to the intellectual and political climate of the Scottish Enlightenment.

Some of the liberties enjoyed by British printers were temporarily suspended in reaction to the French Revolution. Pitt's government felt the need to squelch the possibility of seditious activity by suspending habeas corpus and passing acts against treason and sedition. Kathleen Hardesty Doig examines how the conservative majority of the ruling and professional classes, the press, and the Church of Scotland, joined by the conservative editors of the third edition of the *Encyclopaedia Britannica* (1788–97), Colin Macfarquhar and George Gleig, united in a strategic move to protect their freedoms and ward off political unrest. Under Macfarquhar and Gleig, the third edition and the *Supplement* became organs of anti-Jacobin propaganda in Britain. Entries dealing with the British social structure defend the "natural aristocracy of the country" and praise the liberty of British citizens. English institutions are presented as superior to all others, and the claims of British reformers are given no hearing. Articles that chronicle the events of the revolution in France are intended as anti-Jacobin propaganda; their purpose is clearly to convince the reader of the danger of undermining religion, overthrowing the nobility, and letting an undereducated populace run rampant. That the conservative Gleig, a minister of the Episcopal Church of Scotland, would hold such a view of the French Revolution is hardly surprising. The propagandistic and even apocryphal tone of some of the articles dealing with the Revolution suggests that he may have gone overboard in his anti-Jacobin fervor in an effort to preempt any government intervention in the *Encyclopaedia Britannica*. Doig notes appropriately that while Gleig never acknowledged his intellectual debt to the *Encyclopédie*, it is clear that he had accepted

"Diderot's principle that a repository of knowledge could also be a *machine de guerre* in political controversies and attempts to reform society."

In addition to his work as the editor of the first edition of the *Encyclopaedia Britannica*, William Smellie edited for a short time the *Scots Magazine* and the *Edinburgh Magazine and Review*, translated the first fifteen volumes of Buffon's *Histoire naturelle* (1780–85), and wrote an original *Philosophy of Natural History* (1790–99). Focusing particularly on the last of these accomplishments, Jeff Loveland examines Smellie's reaction to two important figures of the French Enlightenment, the naturalist-philosopher Buffon and the philosopher Condillac. This familiarity with French and continental natural history, combined with Smellie's firsthand knowledge of Buffon's work, make Smellie a focal point for exploring the reception of French thought in Enlightenment Scotland. Smellie's approach to science was typically British; he endorsed the empirical methodology of Bacon, Newton, and Locke, saw final causes throughout nature, and ascribed much of animal and human behavior to instinct. As a Scot, Smellie took objection to some of Buffon's ideas, agreeing with his compatriot Thomas Reid that innate instincts underlie thinking and behavior, and criticizing Buffon for failing to realize that behavior and knowledge are inborn and not simply learned. In this light, it seems surprising that Smellie would praise Condillac's *Traité des sensations*. Loveland suggests that Smellie "appreciated the *Traité* as a careful, detailed account of mental development" and as a refutation of idealism. Smellie's openness to Buffon and Condillac is characteristic of the general ethos of the Scottish Enlightenment, which sought to reconcile opposing philosophies rather than embrace one at the expense of all others.

The third part of the volume is devoted to Franco-Scottish connections in philosophy and political thought. Not surprisingly, it begins with the Scottish Enlightenment's foremost philosopher, David Hume. Hume's views on the philosophical and moral issues of his time, such as the relation between animal and human nature, were generally consistent with the eighteenth-century interest in the connections between the senses and human sensibility and the modern preoccupation with the ethical treatment of animals. A. E. Pitson situates Hume midway between the philosophical positions of Montaigne and Descartes. Descartes's view of animals as no more than machines or *automata* reflected his dualistic conception of a human being as a combination of mind and body considered as distinct kinds of substance. Descartes based his claim that animals possess neither mind nor soul on animals' inability to express themselves through language. Montaigne's Pyrrhonism, on the other hand, led him to believe that it was primarily human pride that supported humans' claims to be morally and intellectually superior to animals. The Renaissance philosopher who asked "que sais-je" questioned the infallibility of human knowledge, which only comes through the fallible senses, and saw some evidence of a similar capacity for reasoning and communication in animal behavior as in human actions. Rather than oppose reason in humans to instinctive behavior in animals, Hume avoided a binary opposition between reason and instinct and recognized that reason can function as a kind of instinct arising from past observation and experience. Although Hume saw animals as being motivated to avoid pain and to seek pleasure and, therefore, capable of communicating feelings to some extent, he did not believe that they could have any moral sense, owing to their inability to theorize and judge their actions. But even if animals could not be classified as moral agents, Hume believed that humans had a moral obligation to treat them kindly.

Harvey Chisick sets out to determine how the works of David Hume and Adam Smith were received in France, through a careful examination of their treatment in two prominent literary journals, the *Année Littéraire* and the *Journal Encyclopédique*. The duration of both journals was long enough to allow one to follow responses to Smith and Hume from the mid-1750s to the French Revolution, and both were successful ventures with sizable readerships. The *Année Littéraire*, published by Fréron, has traditionally been considered the more conservative of the two periodicals, while the *Journal Encyclopédique*, which was published outside of France, presented itself as allied with the progressive ideas of the French philosophes. In spite of their very different philosophical and political positions, both journals printed very positive reviews of Smith's treatise on ethics, praising Smith for rooting his ethics in human nature, and for retaining the connection between religion and morality. The treatment of *The Wealth of Nations* was quite different. Chisick notes that "even so progressive a periodical as the *Journal En-*

*cyclopédique,* while taking note of the importance of Smith's theory, was far from accepting it without reservation." The *Année Littéraire* was expressly forbidden from printing translated excerpts of *The Wealth of Nations* after the liberalization of grain prices, which had been mandated by minister Turgot and advocated by Smith, caused widespread rioting. Chisick's study of the treatment of Hume in the two French periodicals reveals that "during the second half of the eighteenth century, Hume was known in France primarily . . . as a historian, secondarily and significantly as an essayist concerned with economic, political, moral and literary issues, and rather incidentally as a philosopher." Although a French translation of Hume's works had appeared in 1756–60, both the *Treatise of Human Nature* and the *Enquiry Concerning Human Understanding* were completely ignored. Moreover, both journals express serious reservations about Hume's skepticism and his treatment of religion. The *Année Littéraire* for once was in agreement with its more progressive rival that Hume was a brilliant thinker and a fine writer with ideas which were a bit too radical for their tastes.

Understanding the origins of a moral sense in humans and the reasons for our moral actions was a major preoccupation of Scottish Enlightenment thinkers. For the Scots, moral actions derived from the ability of human beings both to identify with others and to distance themselves from a particular situation in order to reflect upon it. This ability was best exemplified by Smith's concept of the impartial spectator in his *Theory of Moral Sentiments*—a concept which, according to Smith, allows us to step back and judge the propriety or impropriety of our own or other people's actions. Of all the works by Scottish philosophers that were available in France in the latter half of the eighteenth-century, *The Theory of Moral Sentiments* was probably the best received. The first edition of 1759 was widely read in the original, and three French translations appeared by the end of the century. Smith's treatise on how sympathy or "fellow-feelings" for others informs an individual's moral actions cast new light on what it meant to be human, and struck a chord with a French public for whom sentiment and sensibility were essential components of the most popular literature of the day. Like Hume, who was affectionately dubbed "le bon David" by French salon society, Smith spent a considerable amount of time in France, and perhaps drew some of his inspiration for *The Theory of Moral*

*Sentiments* from his reading of French authors such as Marivaux, Riccoboni, and Du Bos, who had also explored the effects of sympathy on social interactions.

Deidre Dawson explores the French reception of *The Theory of Moral Sentiments* through the lens of Sophie de Grouchy, marquise de Condorcet. De Grouchy's translation of the seventh and last edition of *The Theory of Moral Sentiments* was published in 1798, along with her commentary on Smith's theory, the *Lettres à Cabanis sur la sympathie*. De Grouchy's writings on Smith reveal admiration for his ideas, but also great skepticism that sympathy alone, without the guidance of reason, can constitute a system of moral philosophy. She grounds her criticisms of Smith in her conviction, which she shared with her husband, the marquis de Condorcet, that inequalities in fortune and education prevented many individuals from experiencing fully the sentiment of sympathy, so essential to Smith's theory. She argues that reason enables one's compassion to be active, and that poverty and hard labor render peasants and menial laborers less capable of feeling sympathy or compassion for others. De Grouchy, an ardent feminist *avant la lettre*, also criticizes Smith for making almost no references to women, except for his negative portrayal of so-called "feminine" emotions. As a corrective to and extension of Smith's theory, Sophie de Grouchy advocated free, public education for all children and young people, male and female, rich and poor. The importance of public education in helping young people form the ability to make moral judgments was also stressed by Condorcet, in his *Second mémoire sur l'instruction publique*. Condorcet's insistence on the absolute equality of all French citizens, male and female, made him in many ways the most radical of all Enlightenment thinkers, French or Scottish. It is somewhat paradoxical that in spite of the emphasis on civility and sociability in Scotland, women played a very minor role in the Scottish Enlightenment compared with their sisters in Ancien Régime France.

Scottish reformers often occupied a different place in society from their French-speaking counterparts. B. Barnett Cochran offers a comparative analysis of Jean-Jacques Rousseau and Robert Wallace as two voices of provincial protest against "an increasingly imposing urban, courtly and enlightened culture." Both Wallace and Rousseau believed that civic values and virtue were crucial to preserving liberty, and looked to the ancient republican values of Rome and Sparta as models for a virtuous society. Both saw human society as having developed in stages, and both viewed the development of private property as the root of economic inequality, which was the source of poverty, crime, corruption, loss of patriotism, and many other evils. Wallace used the decline of Rome as a metaphor for modern society, and traced disruption and corruption of human desires, economic relationships, and political organization to the loss of constitutional equilibrium. By demonstrating what must be done to create a virtuous political order, Rousseau and Wallace denounced the injustice of modern life and exposed the inequalities of the modernizing, Enlightenment project. Despite these similarities, they were writing from within very different social and political contexts. Whereas the radical Rousseau had experienced severe social alienation both from his native Genevan society and from the circle of the French philosophes, Wallace was a social insider and a joiner, a model and early leader of the group of moderate clergymen around William Robertson. In keeping with the emphasis on sociability and social virtues so important to thinkers of the Scottish Enlightenment, Wallace "expressed horror at the image of that isolated, savage, and nonrational natural man. . . . For Wallace, earliest man was in society, but a barbaric society not worth emulating."

The fact that a Presbyterian minister with radical ideas was well integrated into Scottish society underscores a major difference between the thinkers of the Scottish Enlightenment and the French philosophes. Scottish civil society, with its emphasis on tolerance and sociability, was able to accommodate those thinkers whose views departed quite drastically from those of the majority, such as David Hume, who made no attempt to hide his unorthodox religious views, whereas in France and Geneva the philosophes labored under the constant threat of censorship, imprisonment, and exile. The heavy restrictions on intellectual freedom imposed on the philosophes no doubt contributed to the more provocative and combative tone in the writings of Rousseau, Diderot, Condorcet, and Voltaire, whose impassioned appeal to his correspondents, "écrasez l'infâme!" became the *cri de guerre* of the Enlightenment movement in France from the 1760s onward. And whereas in Scotland the national church, or kirk, was a key player in the Scottish Enlightenment, in France the Catholic church was the avowed enemy of freedom of religious, political, and philosophical expression.

Ferenc Hörcher proposes a rereading of the debate on capital punishment that surrounded Beccaria's *Treatise on Crimes and Punishments,* with a focus on its moral, philosophical, and political consequences, in an attempt to measure the difference between the enlightened reformism of eighteenth-century France and Scotland. Hörcher demonstrates that the reception in Europe of Beccaria's celebrated book was far from homogeneous, and even disagreement over its basic principles did not make one an ardent opponent of social progress. It was the social contract theory which prevented Beccaria from accepting capital punishment; since no citizen would willingly give up to others the authority to take his life, the death penalty was, according to Beccaria, "an act of war on the part of society against the citizen." Voltaire, in his famous commentary on Beccaria, praised the humanity of Becarria's *Treatise* and drew upon the social contract theory, natural law theory, and the principle of utility to argue against the brutality of the Ancien Régime. But Scottish philosophers did not share Voltaire's confidence that laws could be reformed through the use of reason. A fear of the socially dangerous outcome of the social contract theory led Kames and Smith to work out criminal theory more precisely, in the context of their own moral and social "theory of sentiments." Kames's idea of criminal jurisprudence is firmly based on a moral sense, and views the primary goal of capital punishment as "the accomplishment of justice, by the proper punishment of crimes that have been committed," rather than the deterrence of future crimes. Thus, the "impartial spectator" serves as a guide to the justification of punishment, since the ability to share the fellow-feeling of others includes the ability to administer justice or even revenge for a grievous offense. The positions of these moderately reformist Scottish philosophers reveal that it was possible even within the general movement of the Enlightenment to present arguments in favor of capital punishment if they were founded on theories of the origin and the aim of civil society as well as on general theories of morality.

A common theme that emerges from the wide-ranging essays in this volume concerns reception and receptiveness. Perhaps the most important factor in the continuation of strong cultural ties between Scotland and France has been each country's receptiveness to what could be offered by its sister "across the water," if a variation on the famous Jacobite toast may be permitted. The Scots were well read in all the major works published in France, as a cursory glance at the catalogues of Smith's or Hume's libraries will affirm, and they followed French political events very closely, though not always giving them their approbation. Likewise, French *gens de lettres* were open to the light emanating from their northern neighbor, and hastened to translate, critique, and interpret the work of Scottish literati in print and on canvas. Notwithstanding the very different political destinies that the French and the Scots have had over the last two centuries, they have always had in common a high regard for writers, literature, philosophy, the arts, and lively conversation, and have shared a belief in the pursuit of social progress through philosophy, not politics alone. It is hoped that this volume—a modest contribution to the vast body of literature on the Enlightenment—will in turn be well received by scholars from a wide range of disciplines.

# Scotland and France
# in the Enlightenment

# I
# Literature and the Arts

# Scotland and France in Smollett's
## *Present State of All Nations*, 1768–69

### PAUL-GABRIEL BOUCÉ

LITTLE IS KNOWN ABOUT THE COMPOSITION OR PUBLICATION OF THE eight octavo volumes of Tobias Smollett's compilation, *The Present State of All Nations* (abbreviated hereafter as *PS*). It was advertised in the press in May–June 1768 and, according to Lewis M. Knapp, "originally published in weekly six-penny numbers, the first of which was issued about June 25, 1768."[1] Four-page advertisements appeared in volume 38 of the *Monthly Review* in 1768.[2] Smollett mentions his work on *PS* only once in his correspondence, in his well-known and informative letter of 8 May 1763 to his American admirer, Richard Smith: "I had engaged with Mr. Rivington, and made some Progress in a work exhibiting the present state of the world, which work I shall finish if I recover my Health."[3] If, as seems likely, the "Mr. Rivington" mentioned in this letter was James Rivington, who had co-published Smollett's *A Complete History of England* in 1757–58, the engagement regarding *PS* must have been made before that bookseller emigrated to America in 1760. Despite Rivington's departure, Smollett lived up to the plan he articulated in his letter to Smith, and *PS* appeared in London under his own name ("T. Smollett, M.D.") in 1768 (volumes 1 and 2) and 1769 (volumes 3 through 8), printed for R. Baldwin, W. Johnston, S. Crowder, and Robinson and Roberts.[4]

There is only one known private critical reaction to the publication of *PS*, in one of Dr. John Armstrong's friendly letters to Smollett from London, dated 28 March 1769, while the latter was desperately trying to revive his badly failing health in Pisa, during his final visit to Italy from the autumn of 1768 until his death on 17 September 1771. In a somewhat joking mood, Armstrong—a fellow Scot who should hardly have been offended at Smollett's strictures on the uncleanliness of the Highlanders, and the nocturnal discharges of filth from the upper windows of the multistory houses in Edinburgh—writes: "Several people who have a particular regard and esteem for the reputed Author of the 'Present State of All Nations' are sorry to find, that he has too much exposed the posteriors of our brothers in the North, and made some undeserved compliments to their neighbors in the South, who have already a comfortable enough share of self-conceit, and that amongst other perfections he allows them to be the handsomest people in Europe; which they think a very disputable opinion."[5] Armstrong himself had exposed more than bare posteriors in his "versified sex manual for the uninstructed young, [which] inevitably received a mixed reception,"[6] that is, the often reprinted *The Oeconomy of Love*, first published in London in 1736. But Armstrong has at least the merit of raising the problem of Smollett's impartiality, in a social, historical, and literary climate of mutual hatred between the Scots and the English, when Scottophobia was still widespread, as Smollett personally experienced during the notorious mudslinging match between his *Briton* (29 May 1762–12 February 1763) and Wilkes's and Churchill's *North Briton*.[7] As far as modern scholarship is concerned, very little attention, apart from Louis L. Martz's pioneering and enduring work, cited below, has been paid to *PS*. The only scholarly article worth mentioning is one by John McVeagh, which proves conclusively that Smollett, or one of his unknown hacks, borrowed heavily, sometimes verbatim, whole paragraphs from Malachy Postlethwayt's *Universal Dictionary of Trade and Commerce* (1751) for his description of Africa in volume 8 of *PS*.[8]

Neither the title nor the genre of *PS* was original. Thomas Salmon published the thirty-two octavo volumes of his *Modern History or, The Present State of All Nations* in London between 1725 and 1739. From the late 1660s, Edward Chamberlayne (1616–1703), later assisted by his son John (1666–1723), published a yearly account of Britain entitled *Angliae Notitia or, The Present State of England*; and under John's editorship, *Magnae Britanniae Notitia or, The Present State of Great-Britain* regularly contained in its second part a section entitled *The Present State of Scotland*. Smollett himself was no newcomer to that genre of encyclopedic synthesis, a dominant cultural trait of the eighteenth century, with its insatiable hunger for the systematic study of vast fields of fast-developing knowledge in arts, science, or what was referred to as "natural history."[9] The word "history" figures in the full title of *PS: The Present State of All Nations. Containing a Geographical, Natural, Commercial, and Political History of All the Countries in the Known World.* Furthermore, the caption of the frontispiece to the first volume of *PS*, engraved by Charles Grignion the elder (1717–1810), reads "Frontispiece to Smollett's History of All Nations."

Smollett's immense contributions to encyclopedic compilation, forced by a chronic lack of funds, had certainly prepared him well for the composition of *PS*. The seven duodecimo volumes of *A Compendium of Authentic and Entertaining Voyages* appeared in 1756, followed by *A Complete History of England* (1757–58) in four quarto volumes and *Continuation of the Complete History of England* in five octavo volumes (1760–65). Smollett also performed Herculean labors on the *Universal History, The Modern Part* (44 volumes, 1759–66), which numbered thirty-eight volumes when he departed for France in June 1763, the thirty-ninth appearing in July of that year. In the excruciatingly busy years between 1760 and 1765, he also acted as joint editor of the thirty-five-volume annotated translation of Voltaire's *Works*. Smollett was certainly no idler.

In the six-page "Plan of the *Present State of All Nations*" (1:3–8), Smollett appears once again as a man deeply influenced by the contemporaneous Horatian tenet, *Omne tulit punctum qui miscuit utile dulci, / Lectorem delectando pariterque monendo* [He has gained every point who has mixed practicality with pleasure, / By delighting the reader at the same time as instructing him] ("Ars Poetica" ll. 343–44). He starts off with the usual complaints about "this frivolous age" (1:3), little inclined "to subjects of real utility," and extols "this laudable aim of mingling entertainment with instruction," although many media-saturated readers in our own day would find precious little entertainment in all the eight volumes of *PS*. What he proposes is "a general view of Nature," whether animal, vegetable, or mineral, "including every system of society, and specifying every invention of art for the support and enjoyment of life" (1:4). In view of Smollett's encyclopedic aims, the word "system" is certainly of nuclear importance, and it is buttressed by such a phrase as "methodizing the subject" (1:5). Throughout the eight volumes of *PS*, Smollett sticks, with more or less copiousness, to a systematic method in his accounts of the known countries of the world. The following points are dealt with in the same order: geography; description of the country (its topography, including lakes, rivers, waters), what he calls "the Face of the Country"; air and climate; nature of the soil and productions; constitution, government, laws; religion; the monarchy (if applicable), officers of the Crown (for England and Scotland); nobility, gentry, customs; people, persons, attire, disposition, manners; amusements and diversions; habitation and manners; plus, as the country under scrutiny may require, separate sections on its diseases, state of learning and liberal arts, architecture, commerce, duties, taxes, public debts, funds, and money. No project could be more overwhelmingly encyclopedic! His method was to move down from the polar regions to the southern climes. Thus, volume 1 starts at Spitzbergen and volume 8 ends with the Indian and Oriental Islands, Africa, America, its islands, closing with a couple of pages on Cape Breton, without any attempt at a general synthetic conclusion about the present state of all nations, which in any case would have been well-nigh impossible to write. In spite of his promise to indicate his sources at the end of each account, "so that the sceptical reader may occasionally have recourse to the fountain-head of intelligence, and decide for himself how far we have acted our part with candour, accuracy, and judgment" (1:8), no sources are mentioned at the end of the accounts of England, France, or the mainland of Scotland. They appear only at the end of the account of the Scottish isles (1:510), but they are neither complete nor accurate, as Martz has shown.[10]

Although a dozen years had elapsed since the anonymous first edition of *A Compendium of Authentic and Entertaining Voyages* in 1756, it is impossible not to notice striking similarities between the titles and the prefaces of the two compilations. The full title of the *Compendium* reads like a blueprint for *PS: A Compendium of Authentic and Entertaining Voyages. Digested in a Chronological Series. The Whole Exhibiting a Clear View of the Customs, Manners, Religion, Government, Commerce, and Natural History of Most Nations in the Known World.* A second edition, like the first in seven duodecimo volumes, was reprinted in 1766, two years before the appearance of *PS.* In the three-page preface, Smollett develops the same points as in the preface to *PS:* "We live in an age of levity and caprice, that can relish little besides works of fancy; nor do we listen to instruction, unless it be conveyed to us under the pleasing form of entertainment" (*Compendium*, 1:1). Perhaps in accordance with the bellicose spirit of the proposals for publishing the *Critical Review*[11]—which began to appear in March 1756, a month before the *Compendium*—Smollett launches a Gulliverian attack on the other compilations already available: "Besides they are generally so stuffed with dry descriptions of bearings and distances, tides and currents, variations of the compass, leeway, wind and weather, sounding, anchoring, and other terms of navigation, that none but meer pilots, or seafaring people can read them without disgust" (*Compendium*, 1:2).

Having provided this brief introduction to the background of *PS*, I turn now to the main theme of this chapter: a comparison of the accounts of Scotland and France. The first point to consider is authorship. According to Martz, the account of Scotland in *PS* was apparently "projected before 1760, was at least partially compiled by 1761, and, at the very latest, was completed before Smollett left England in June 1763."[12] The much less satisfactory account of France in the sixth volume is almost certainly not by Smollett, whereas the rich nexus of parallels and echoes, aptly analyzed by Martz, between *PS* and *Humphry Clinker* (1771), not to mention his characteristic style, strongly suggests that Smollett wrote, or at least closely edited, the description of Scotland. Only one faint biographical, or rather genealogical, allusion is to be detected in the accounts of the isles and mainland of Scotland. In one of the bays of the Isle of Mull, "the Florida, one of the largest ships of the Spanish armada, was blown up by one Smollet" (1:498). Smollett must have felt sufficiently proud of this gallant action to report it again in *Humphry Clinker*, in Matt Bramble's letter of 6 September from Cameron, with the additional information that the man was "one of Mr. Smollett's ancestors."

In the account of France in *PS*, a few sundry allusions are also to be found to the "late war," that is, the Seven Years' War of 1756–63, ending with the February 1763 Treaty of Paris between Great Britain, France, and Spain. Thus, "by the last treaty of peace concluded between France and England, and their respective allies, it was expressly stipulated, that all fortifications should be again demolished, and the harbour filled up; but whether this article hath yet been executed, in its full extent, is what we will not venture to affirm" (6:217–18). This pessimistic admission of ignorance reads rather strangely in the light of what Smollett himself writes in the fifth volume (1765) of his *Continuation of the Complete History of England* about the demolition of Dunkirk according to the stipulations of the Treaty of Paris. After recalling that such a clause had been shamefully evaded after both the treaties of Utrecht (1713) and Aix-la-Chapelle (1748), Smollett remarks: "but the remonstrances of the British ministry were so effective, that in November [1763] the nation had authentic information that the cunette of Dunkirk was entirely filled up, excepting a trifling part, for which there was no earth; and that near three hundred men were employed in demolishing the king's bason there."[13] Could such a contradiction between the fifth volume of the *Continuation* in 1765 and the account of France in the sixth volume of *PS* mean that the latter was completed before November 1763?

The placement and character of the respective accounts of Scotland and England on the one hand, and France on the other, are also significant. After dealing with Greenland, Norway, Iceland, Denmark, Sweden, and Russia in the first volume of *PS*, Smollett devotes twenty-five pages (1:404–29) to "the Islands of Shetland and Orkney," then the remaining eighty pages (1:430–510) of the volume to "The Hebrides, or Western Isles of Scotland." The account of the Scottish mainland, with a folding map by Thomas Kitchin, takes up the first 150 pages of the second volume, immediately followed by 327 pages on England (2:151–478), continued for another 346 pages (3:3–349) in the third volume. In all, Scotland rates 255, England 673, against a beggarly 159 pages (73–232) to France in volume 6 of *PS*. Italy, with 162 pages (6:325–487), and Spain, with 63 pages (6: 261–324), are also somewhat neglected.

The obvious imbalance in favor of Scotland, and especially England, is not only quantitative but markedly qualitative as well. Even though the systematic, heavily factual description of the shires of Scotland and England makes for dull reading, both accounts bear the mark of Smollett's deep attachment, not devoid of occasional strictures, for his native land. He waxes enthusiastic over the progress of agriculture, industry, and commerce in England, carefully refusing to return any of the contempt and hatred the English had for so long poured over Caledonia. As Martz rightly points out, the opening section (2:151–260) on England, "by one of the canniest observers of the age afford[s] a better introduction to eighteenth-century life than many longer and more famous accounts," while the largely original description of the Highlanders and their mode of living (1:431–39) would be difficult to surpass: "Indeed, it is doubtful whether a better account has ever been packed into so little compass."[14]

Unfortunately, no such praise may be bestowed on the perfunctory account of France, monotonously jejune, still distorted by post–Seven Years' War rankling bias and Gallophobic rancor, especially in religious matters. It is surprising that few or no traces of Smollett's authorship may be detected in the account of France, because he had recently visited that country (1763–65) and had carefully, if at times somewhat cantankerously, observed, described, and analyzed it in *Travels through France and Italy*, published in London in May 1766. Possibly because there was no dearth of travel books and detailed guidebooks to France, and especially Paris, the account of France in the sixth volume of *PS* soon degenerates into a dry, mechanical list of the "principal places," with the lame excuse that "our proposed brevity would not admit of our being more particular" (6:96). The "à la Prévert" catalogue effect is rampant throughout the account of France, compounded by vague, hasty generalizations, as in this typical description of Orléans:

> It is one of the largest cities in the kingdom, but meanly built, and most of the inhabitants are poor, tho' there are here several inferior courts of justice, with an university, at present of no great repute; a public library; a stately Gothic cathedral, and a great number of other churches, some of which are collegiate; a public walk, planted with several rows of trees; some sugar bakers; a manufacture of stockings and sheepskins; a seminary, in which divinity is taught; and a great trade in brandy, wine, spices, and several manufactures, which, with many other commodities, are conveyed from hence to Paris, and other places, by means of the Loire, and the canal, which takes its name from the city. Some of the trading people are very rich. (6:188)

This reads appallingly when compared, for instance, with the vivid and minute description of Edinburgh (2:112–24), approached by Smollett as though it were an unknown city to be discovered by ignorant and biased English readers in dire need of impartial information.[15] From the outset, therefore, it is a perilous task to compare the accounts of Scotland and France, because of the quantitative and qualitative imbalance in favor of Scotland. Moreover, as a close reading of the accounts of Scotland and England makes quite plain, these two countries are natural mutual referents, while France is not. Yet, because of *PS*'s systematic and encyclopedic methodology, some synthetic, if mostly negative, parallels may be drawn between Scotland and France as depicted in *PS*.

In view of the importance of natural history throughout the eight volumes of *PS*, I will first analyze some of the recurrent traits pertaining to the natural history of both Scotland and France, especially the climates and their influence on health and longevity, then the flora, fauna, and natural resources, with special attention to the quality of water, and finally a few considerations on the state of agriculture in both countries. From the start, the account of Scotland betrays Smollett's meteorological bias in favor of his native country. The gist of his argument is that Scottish weather, both in the isles and the mainland, although windy, drizzly, if not downright rainy, is basically healthy, and contributes to the shaping of a rugged, hardy and long-living breed of natives:

> The air of this kingdom is generally moist and temperate, except on the tops of high mountains covered with eternal snow, where it is cold, keen, and piercing. In other parts it is tempered by warm vapours from the sea, which environs it on three sides, and runs far up into the land by friths, inlets, and indentations. This neighbourhood of the sea, and the frequency of hills and mountains, produce a constant undulation in the air, and many hard gales, that purify the climate, which is for the most part agreeable and healthy. (2:5)

Obviously, Smollett, like the rejuvenated Matthew Bramble in *Humphry Clinker*, was an enthusiast for fresh air, advocating cold sea-baths for the cure of pulmonary disorders, a practice he repeatedly resorts to in his *Travels through France and Italy*. He backs up his positive view of the Scottish climate with the occasional testimony of famous foreigners, such as the Italian physician and philosopher, Girolamo Cardano (1501–76), professor of medicine at Pavia, who, coming to St. Andrews "to prescribe for archbishop Hamilton, declared it was the most healthful place in which he had ever resided" (2:83). With due respect to

Smollett's fondness for Scotland, a reader today will be some-what surprised to discover that at Inveresk, just east of Edin-burgh, the air "is esteemed so healthy that this village is called the Montpellier of Scotland" (2:125). One may wonder why Smollett, instead of traveling twice to the southern climes of France and Italy, did not take up residence in Inveresk, where he would have also benefited from the company of the local minis-ter, his old friend, Alexander Carlyle. Such is the influence of the healthy Scottish climate, that numerous instances of ex-traordinary longevity may be found both in the isles and on the mainland. Thus, in Jura, "One Gilouir Mackirain attained to the age of one hundred and fourscore: a woman of the isle of Scarba lived sevenscore years, and here are several persons turned of one hundred" (1:503; cf. 480–81). An avatar of the golden age myth may be detected throughout the account of the Scottish isles and some regions of mainland Scotland.

No such positive considerations are to be found in the pages devoted to France, where the general assessment of the climate takes up but two terse lines: "The air is temperate, neither so cold as in the northern kingdoms, nor so hot as in Spain and Italy" (6:74). In the ensuing descriptions of the various "govern-ments" (provinces and principalities), it is obvious that the au-thor of the account of France is no sun worshipper. About Upper and Lower Provence, he writes: "The air and soil differ widely in the two divisions; for in the former the air is temperate, but in the latter, so hot that it would be intolerable, especially up on the sea-coast, were it not qualified by certain winds" (6:131). Montpellier, dismissed in twenty-two lines, and its climate—so eagerly sought after by British invalids, including Smollett and Sterne—get but half a sentence, in passing: "The air of this city is accounted exceeding wholesome" (6:149). Roussillon hardly fares any better: "The heat here in summer is very intense, and the inhabitants, in consequence thereof, very meagre and swar-thy" (6:153). The implicit conclusion is that too much sun makes for an inferior race, as opposed to the vigorous Scots, case-hardened by their vivifying weather. It may be suspected that Smollett, whose Latinophobia suffuses his *Travels through France and Italy*, was a distant herald of the scornful British quip: "Wogs begin at Calais."

The same imbalance in favor of Scotland prevails in the de-scriptions of the flora, fauna, and natural resources of the two

countries. It would be interesting to know where Smollett derived his amazingly thorough information about this field. In
the Lowlands, for instance:

> Their farm-grounds are well-stocked with wheat, rye, barley, oats,
> hemp, and flax: their gardens produce great plenty of kitchen-roots,
> sallads, and greens, among which last, we reckon the colewort,
> known by the name of Scotch-kail: their orchards bear a variety of
> apples, pears, cherries, plumbs, strawberries, gooseberries, raspber-
> ries and currants: here also apricots, nectarines, peaches, and some-
> times grapes, are brought to maturity. In a word, there is nothing,
> whether shrub, fruit or flower, that grows in any part of South-Brit-
> ain, which may not, with a little pains, be brought to the same per-
> fection in the middle of Scotland. (2:7)

Obviously a land of plenty, but the phrase "with a little pains"
implies that the potentialities of Scotland are not yet exploited
to the full when compared with the development of England.
Hence, the recurrent use of the modal conditional "might" in
the account of Scotland, for instance when referring to the
abundance of juniper berries in some part of the Highlands, so
that "in the space of a few miles, many tones of the berries *might*
be yearly gathered" (2:7; emphasis added).

Furthermore, lakes, rivers, rivulets, and the coastal waters are
always teeming with fish, as the forests and moors are with
game. Smollett repeatedly insists on the abundance of fish and
the urgent necessity of developing Scottish fisheries. In the
coastal waters of the Hebrides, "cod, ling, mackarel, whiting,
haddock, and soles, are here caught in abundance," as well as
"two kinds of white fish, which seem to be peculiar to the coast,
known by the names of the lithe and cea, esteemed good eating:
but the greatest treasure the ocean pours forth, is the prodigious
quantity of herrings" (1:441)—"the silver darlings" of Neil
Gunn's 1941 novel of the same title. Salmon, of course, is repeatedly mentioned; for instance: "the water of Thurso, a small
river, so incredibly stocked with salmon which live there all the
year, that several horse-loads are taken at a time, either by nets
or baskets, which the natives call creels. . . . : above three hundred good salmons have been taken at one draught of the net,
by the fishermen of Thurso" (2:28).

Birds are granted particular attention throughout the accounts of the isles and the mainland. Three and a half pages are

devoted to the bird population of St. Kilda, and especially to the Solan goose, down to its cries: "When this bird perceives any noise at a distance, he calls softly *grog, grog*; but if he sees the fowler approaching, he cries aloud *bir, bir*, which the rest no sooner hear, than they take wing in a body" (1:447). And many more seabirds with their various names are duly mentioned, such as the scraber, puffin, or puffinet; assilag; guillem, guilla-mot, or lavy; falk or razorbill, bowger, coulterneb, or pope; guer-fowl and fulmar (1:448–49). In Sutherland "there is one bird pe-culiar to this shire, called knag, which resembles a parrot, and digs its nest with its beak, in the trunks of oaks" (2:29).

Mineral resources are systematically indicated in both the ac-counts of the isles and the mainland, down to "little bits of solid gold . . . gathered in brooks immediately after torrents" (2:6), while the purity of the water—a theme also recurrent in *Hum-phry Clinker*—is repeatedly extolled: "The water in Scotland is remarkably pure, light, and agreeable to the stomach" (2:5). Smollett never misses the opportunity of mentioning the many medicinal springs throughout the country, for instance at Mof-fat in Dumfrieshire, "a neat little town . . . famous for its medici-nal wells impregnated with salt and sulphur" (2:145), which is consonant with the lifelong balneological interests of the au-thor of the *Essay on the External Use of Water* (1752).

After such a detailed account of the Scottish isles and main-land, the description of France cuts a sorry figure. It is at best perfunctory, and usually quite inadequate. No such lavish atten-tion is paid to the flora, fauna, or natural resources, which are occasionally mentioned in passing when the various "govern-ments" or provinces are examined. The skimpy account of France is from the outset flawed by a pro-British bias, already rife in *Travels through France and Italy*. The pervasive theme, in-forming the deliberately slighting and occasionally scornful treatment of the country, holds that "France is not sufficiently improved, yielding, even in plentiful years, little more corn than is necessary for the subsistence of the inhabitants; so that a bad harvest is always attended with great scarcity, especially in time of war" (6:74).

The account of France voices concern for the influence of the climate on men and their activities. The quality of water, for in-stance, as in the famous description of the "London dainties" in *Humphry Clinker*, is deemed rather deficient in the French capital: "Its greatest defect, according to some, is the want of good drinking-water; but others tell us, that very fine water is brought by an aqueduct from the village of Arcueil, not far from Paris, but own the water of the Seine, and the city, is not good" (6:89). Mineral and medicinal springs are duly recorded, for example at Bourbon-Lancy (6:123), Barèges and Bagnères de Bi-gorre (6:166), Forges-les-Eaux (6:180), and Bourbon l'Archam-bault (6:195). Although the notations on the flora, fauna, natural resources, and agriculture of the French provinces are too often sketchy, they manage all the same to convey some idea of their wealth or poverty. Normandy is thus allotted half a dozen lines, which at least fulfill the function of reminding a modern reader of the changes which have intervened since the middle of the eighteenth century in the types of agricultural produce: "It is very fruitful in corn, flax, hemp, pasturage, and fruits of several sorts, particularly pears and apples, of which a great deal of cider and perry is made. Here is also plenty of wood, coals, cattle, madder and woad, together with fish, min-eral waters, iron, copper and other metals" (6:178). Burgundy receives scant attention: "It is very fertile in corn, wine; fruit and tobacco. . . . There are some noted mineral springs in it, with subterraneous lakes, and plenty of ochre" (6:121). Unfor-tunately for connoisseurs of fine Burgundy wines, this is the only mention of their relished, if nowadays expensive, pota-tion. Our ideas of what is valuable in nature have changed radi-cally with the advent of industrial progress: for the author of the account of Dauphiné, larchwood was obviously precious: "Near two thirds of the province are very barren and mountainous; but the mountains contain a variety of minerals, and in some places are covered with larch-trees, which are very valuable, as they not only yield a very durable wood, but also manna, ben-zoin, and agaric, the last of which is used in physic and dying scarlet" (6:125). And the present-day ecologist might also won-der at the man-wrought havoc on the fauna of Dauphiné: "On the mountains are also found several sorts of wild animals, as bears, marmots, chamois goats, and another species of goats, called by the French bouquettons, or chevrels, together with white hares, partridges, eagles, hawks" (6:125).

As in Smollett's creative works, whether novels or plays,[16] not to mention the *Travels through France and Italy*, the accounts of Scotland, England, and France in *PS* greatly contributed to the crystallization of national types, still more or less current today in the ethnic quasi mythology of nations. Whether explicitly or implicitly, such recurrent national traits, founded both on accurate observation and chauvinistic, sometimes obnoxious, prejudice, serve to underpin the deviously oblique judgmental values that inform the ethnic background of the accounts, through allusions to such historical events as national or international conflicts, religious wars, and persecutions of vanquished or oppressed populations. They are common in the sections of the accounts dealing variously with the natives of the Shetlands and Orkneys (1:414–17), the Hebrides (1:431–39), the Scottish mainland (2:9–22), and France (6:75–78).

The description of the sturdy inhabitants of the Hebrides is highly laudatory on the whole, stressing their vigorous health, golden age simplicity, humaneness, and hospitality to strangers, "whom they cultivate even with a religious veneration" (1:432).[17] But, because of their "martial turn, joined to a choleric disposition" (1:434), they may fall into bellicose excesses degenerating into clannish feuds. Likewise, they are addicted to "excessive drinking" of whisky, called "trestareg" (1:436, 464), which is three times distilled usquebaugh on St. Kilda. On the mainland, wedding festivities and funerals are signal occasions for prolonged drinking bouts, weddings being "generally concluded with drinking and debauchery," and funerals ending in a "deluge of drinking" (2:15). Smollett also reproaches the Highlanders with their notorious lack of hygiene: "These people are utter strangers to cleanliness; they are extremely sluttish in their houses, and nasty in their persons; and this impurity is, in all likelihood, one great cause of that inveterate itch, with which they are so generally infested" (1:439). The indictment of the Edinburgh inhabitants' lack of domestic and urban hygiene (2:115–16), later taken up in *Humphry Clinker*, vibrates with ferocious Smollettian indignation: "At ten of the clock every window is opened, and such a general deluge of these materials poured forth, that the whole air is impregnated with a most unsufferable odour, and the foot passenger in the most imminent danger of being overwhelmed with the most substantial part of the annoyance" (2:116). To make matters even worse, the ritual warning, "Gardez l'eau," is now dispensed with, and the pious scavengers, keeping the Sabbath, never clean the streets on Sundays!

This severe stricture on the Scottish disregard for cleanliness partakes of Smollett's strategy of impartiality, a point made clear by the final sentence describing the "gardez l'eau" ritual: "Their neighbours of England, it must be owned, have some reason to twit them in the teeth with these and other unsavoury practices" (2:116). Smollett also takes exception to some "ridiculously absurd"(2:38) mainland customs, for instance in Inverness where big, sturdy fishermen are carried to their boats on the backs of females wading to them, with their "petticoats tucked up to a very indecent height" (2:38), or the surprising spectacle, also in Inverness, of wenches trampling linen in tubs at the waterside "with their legs and thighs entirely bare" (2:38). It is a sort of festival; during which, they think themselves enfranchised from domestic slavery. Standing thus in their tubs, they deal in repartee, and merry altercation with passengers, or hold conversation with their sweet-hearts, who visit them on this occasion, and feast their eyes with the naked beauties of their mistresses" (2:38–39). The gloomy, misogynous John Knox and the austere Scottish Kirk had not quite managed to suppress all cheerful fun in Scotland, as Burns's *Merry Muses of Caledonia* bears witness. Smollett underlines the Scots' love of poetry and music, of which they are so fond "that one can hardly meet with an individual who cannot play upon some instrument: but their voices are generally harsh or husky" (2:13).

Finally, Smollett is careful to draw a distinction between the Highlanders and Lowlanders, whom he describes as "for the most part, sober, industrious, circumspect, shrewd and insinuating, well aware of their interest, which in foreign countries they prosecute with perseverance and success, even among people by whom they are envied and discountenanced" (2:10). The last clause is a probable, if devious, allusion to the Scottophobia that was rampant in England in the early 1760s. Smollett is also perfectly aware of the worldwide diaspora of Scottish "soldiers, sailors, merchants, scholars, physicians, surgeons, and apothecaries," to whom he might have added gardeners and engineers. He quotes the old proverb, attested as far back as 1662 in the *Oxford Dictionary of Proverbs*, whereby "in every corner of the earth, one may find a Scot, a rat, and a Newcastle grindstone" (2:10).

Once again, the assessment of the French national character, entitled "Character of the People, and Language," approximately one paltry page (6:75–76), can hardly compare with the detailed and subtly balanced discussion of Scottish national traits. It reads like a sketchy and mostly negative summary of his animadversions on the French in letters 6 and 7 of *Travels through France and Italy*. A close stylistic analysis of this section reveals that any positive trait is immediately counterbalanced by a string of negative judgments. Thus, and true to the mid-eighteenth-century apprehension of the French character by the British, the French are "a gay sprightly people, but vain, rash, fickle, and unsteady" (6:75). They boast of their courteous manners and good breeding, yet "their manners, notwithstanding, in many respects, are extremely offensive and shocking to persons of true taste, sound judgment, and uncorrupted morals" (6:75). They are abject flatterers and liars, "intolerably insolent, vain, arbitrary and imperious, in prosperity, and extremely litigious" (6:76). As in letter 7 of *Travels through France and Italy*, French women do not escape the Smollettian lash: they lack modesty and are flirtatious, with the smug connivance of their husbands. The section on the French character nevertheless ends on a positive note: "On the other hand, it must be allowed, that the French are very active, brave and ingenious, have a good address, and a genteel air" (6:76).

Yet even an apparent note of praise may be actually deciphered as an oblique criticism. For instance: "The art of war is no where better understood than in France, that part of it especially which relates to gunnery and fortification" (6:87). Does not this ambiguous compliment imply that the French are a bellicose nation, whose military forces, especially their navy, suffered heavy losses during the Seven Years' War? A typical patriotic "Rule Britannia" burden follows:

> Yet they have been extremely active since the peace, in restoring it [their navy]. But considering how low it was brought, it must require a great expence, and many years, to bring it to its former condition; and, indeed, as their trade, in consequence of the losses they suffered in the late war, is much less extensive than formerly, it cannot be supposed that this will be in their power, till they first find means to recover their losses, which, it is to be hoped, Great Britain will attentively guard against, as her prosperity and tranquility so much depend upon it. (6:87–88)

Smollett was no Jacobite, in spite of his moving poetic outburst, the now unfairly neglected ballad, "The Tears of Scotland," written immediately after the Battle of Culloden in 1746. No sentimental "Auld Alliance" myth is anywhere discernible in his historical writings, although he was painfully shocked at the gory havoc wrought by Butcher Cumberland's troops in Scotland after the last Jacobite rebellion was crushed. As in his *Complete History of England* (1757–58) and its *Continuation* (1760–65), in *PS* he strives for the apparent impartiality of a Briton, neither a Scot nor an Englishman. And like most Britons of his time, he could not abide the French.

Another recurring national theme in *PS* is Smollett's revulsion at superstition, or any form of religious intolerance and fanaticism, which is also a dominant theme in his novels, from *Roderick Random* (1748) to *Humphry Clinker* (1771).[18] The Scots, especially the inhabitants of the Orkneys and Hebrides, are severely taken to task for their superstitious beliefs, particularly the notorious "second sight." In the Orkneys, the islanders "are much addicted to superstitious rites; in particular interpreting dreams and omens and believing in the force of idle charms" (1:415). For instance, they will resort to a conjurer, or use charms and amulets, to cure diseases. One whole section of the description of St. Kilda, in the Hebrides, is entitled "Of the Second Sight" (1:460–63), "called taish in the Erse language, . . . a supernatural faculty of seeing visions of events before they happen" (1:460), of which various instances are duly given, partly borrowed from Martin Martin's *A Late Voyage to St. Kilda* (1698) and *Description of the Western Islands of Scotland* (1703).[19] Smollett rejects and condemns all varieties of superstitious belief, as did Voltaire and the Enlightenment as a whole. The picture of the golden age felicity of the Hebrideans is qualified and marred by "the horrors of superstition, to which they are miserably subject, such as signs, tokens, charms, omens, dreams, and a pseudophrotic [pseudoprophetic?] spirit, which they distinguish by the appellation of the second sight" (1:432), a theme taken up and developed at some length in the account of Scotland (2:19), denouncing such absurd beliefs and the cruel repression of suspected witchcraft. But "these cruel and absurd laws, however, have been happily repealed by the British legislature" (2:19), Smollett writes, referring to legislation of 1736.[20] Likewise, as in his novels, especially *Humphry Clinker*, Smollett denounces religious fanatics and their ignorant, obnoxious enthusiasm, although such "extravagancies of puritanical enthusiasm" (2:18) are believed to be on the wane among the more liberal younger clergy of the Kirk. But he still remains wary: "nevertheless, there is a sort of schism in the kirk, occasioned by some of the old leaven of fanaticism" (2:18).

Papist France, by contrast, is repeatedly accused of religious intolerance and protracted persecution of the native Protestants. The account of France never misses an opportunity, in spite of the catalogue-like description of the thirty-seven "governments" and their main towns, of pointing out all the historical occasions on which the Huguenots were persecuted, massacred, or banished from the kingdom. To give but a few instances of this pervasive reprobation: the Saint Bartholomew massacre, perpetrated in August 1572 "leaves an indelible stain on the people of France" (6:82), while the earlier Amboise massacre (1560) of hundreds of Protestants accused of conspiring against Francis II was triggered off in reality by "their design . . . only to obtain liberty of conscience, and to remove the Guises" (6:209). No mention is made of the edict of Amboise, signed in March 1563 by Catherine of Medici, granting the Protestants freedom of worship. The sieges of Protestant-held cities like La Rochelle by Richelieu in 1627–28 (6:169), Sancerre in 1573, resulting in cannibalism among the besieged (6:207), are duly mentioned. This intolerance is not confined to the Protestants, but also oppresses the Jews who, in Metz, "are confined to a particular quarter, along the bank of the Moselle, in which they may not only hire, but purchase houses [which was exceptional]. To distinguish them from others, they are obliged to wear yellow caps" (6:129)—a sinister chromatic touch and distant foreshadowing of the yellow star of David that Jews were forced to wear in Nazi Germany. The 1685 revocation of the edict of Nantes, under Louis XIV, is also mentioned, as well as the "still great numbers of Protestants in France, especially in the southern provinces. They never would admit the inquisition in this country" (6:76; cf. 6:150–51), which is true enough but somewhat reductive. In Strasbourg there are "a great many churches, most of which are now in the hands of the papists; yet the greater part of the burghers are Lutherans" (6:227). Oppression may be economic as well as religious and military: "In 1744, the protestant inhabitants of this town [Millau] had three troops of dragoons quartered on them for three months, by which they were entirely ruined" (6:161). It is striking that in every bishopric mentioned in the monotonous and often vague catalogue of the "places of note," the archbishops' or suffragan bishops' revenues are quoted with minute precision. The archbishop of Bordeaux "has a revenue of fifty-five thousand livres per annum, out of which his taxation to Rome is four thousand florins" (6:158), while in Grenoble the suffragan to the archbishop of Vienne "has a revenue of twenty-eight thousand livres per annum, out of which he pays a taxation to Rome of one thousand florins" (6:126). The implication is that the wealthy Gallican church is an intolerable financial burden shouldered by the wretched people of France, while money grubbing papal Rome exacts her share of the pelf.

As is made clear by his sometimes virulent criticisms of monarchic absolutism in *Travels through France and Italy*, and the disastrous poverty it induced in the reign of Louis XV (see letter 36), as well as his account of the Rochette and Calas affairs (1762) in his *Continuation* (5:69–76), Smollett could never brook any kind of tyranny, whether political, economic, or religious. The Protestant bias throughout the account of France is pervasive, both explicitly and implicitly. The French may be oppressed by the monarchy and the church, but they are also potentially fanatic oppressors, even to the detriment of their economy, or their learning. Saumur in Anjou is a case in point: "It was one of the cautionary towns [*places de sûreté*] given to the Protestants. While it was in their hands, the celebrated John Cameron [1579?–1625], a Scots divine, was, for sometime [c. 1618–20], professor of divinity in the university. . . . The town was much more opulent while it was in the hands of the Huguenots" (6:212). The late-seventeenth-century Huguenot diaspora to Britain and all over northern Europe, was—as is historically proved—an economic and intellectual disaster for France. At least the *parlement* of Bordeaux has enough sense, if only because of the city's ancient historical links with England, and also out of canny economic self-interest, to indulge foreign Protestant merchants "in the *private* exercise of their religion" (6:159; emphasis added). Is there a possible link between good claret and religious toleration? "In vino veritas!"

A close study of all the historical allusions in the accounts of Scotland and France, ranging from the Roman conquest to the late war of 1756–63, would demand a separate chapter. As in *Travels through France and Italy*, Smollett is fascinated by Roman remains, as well as those of earlier defunct civilizations. Hence his savage indignation at any kind of wanton vandalism ruining ancient monuments. Thus, in his description of Stirlingshire, he rails at the crass stupidity of a landowner in the vicinity of Falkirk who destroyed a Roman *sacellum*, or sanctuary, misleadingly known as Arthur's Oven, "the most intire and curious monument of Roman Antiquity that remained in Great Britain" (2:92). Here the same sincere ring of genuine antiquarian reverence as in *Travels through France and Italy* for the monuments and remains of the glorious Roman civilization may be detected: "Be that as it may, every lover of taste and antiquity must be seized with an emotion of grief and indignation, when he reflects that a few years ago this noble monument was demolished by the more than Gothic barbarity of the gentleman on whose ground it stood, that he might employ the stones in building a mill-head" (2:92–93). Notwithstanding Sterne's far-from-deserved nickname, "Smelfungus," Smollett, even though he could react like a splenetic traveler at times, was an enthusiastic admirer of classical antiquity. He could even display a grim sense of humor when recounting stories, or anecdotes, pertaining to the barbarism of the darker ages. Thus, he relates the exemplary, if self-mutilating, chaste behavior of the Coldingham (Berwickshire) nuns, "who, at the Danish invasion, by the advice and example of their abbess, defaced themselves by cutting off their lips and noses, that their beauty might not subject them to brutal violation. The good lady, whose name was Ebba has been canonized for this act of virtuous self-denial; and a neighbouring promontory is called St Ebb's head [St Abbs] in memorial of this transaction" (2:133). What would present-day feminists think of such drastic surgery, or of the extraordinary privilege granted to husbands by the founder of Villefranche in Beaujolais, Humbert II (1312–55)—incidentally, the founder also of Grenoble University in 1339—who "in order to draw inhabitants to it . . . gave the husbands leave to beat their wives till the blood run, without being liable to be punished for it, provided they did not kill them" (6:198)? Since both St. Ebba and Humbert II were pious Roman Catholics, one cannot help sensing, in the tumultuous, and often gory, stream of religious history as it is frequently alluded to in both accounts, a devious but strong undertow of anti-Catholicism. Such anecdotes fulfill a less than innocent emblematic function.

Although Smollett refrains, as he does in both his *Complete History* and *Continuation*, from launching any polemical attacks against the English, especially when alluding to the 1715 and 1745 rebellions, he never fails in his account of Scotland to mention the battles against the Sassenachs, whether lost or won by the Scots, for instance, Bannockburn (1314) and Falkirk, scene first of Wallace's defeat by Edward I in 1298, and then, on 17 January 1746, of a victory by the Young Pretender (2:91). Massacres, during the struggle of Edward I with William Wallace, swiftly succeed each other, as in Ayr (2:136). Forfeited estates and burnt castles, as a result of the various Jacobite risings, are systematically mentioned, for instance in Ross, the earl of Seaforth's in 1719, Macdonald of Glengarry's in 1715, and Cameron of Lochiel's in 1746 (2:33, 35, 36). But Smollett just states such events, and refrains from both gloating *Schadenfreude* at English defeats and polemical animadversions at Scottish setbacks and ensuing English repression. He strives to abide by his clearly announced spirit of "candour, accuracy, and judgment" (1:viii), the words with which his general preface closes. Thus, the crushing Jacobite defeat at Culloden on 16 April 1746 is mentioned in just six lines in the account of Inverness-shire, without any commentary. But the ferocious repression by Cumberland's troops, which Smollett had described powerfully in his *Complete History*, is more than once covertly hinted at, as in the following excerpt:

> Before the late rebellion, scarce a Highlander was to be seen without a curious iron pistol slung in his belt, a broad sword under his arm, and a large leathern purse, decorated with silver, hanging before him: but the British parliament hath thought proper to forbid this peculiarity of dress, which was supposed to keep up odious and dangerous distinctions among his Majesty's subjects, and maintain a martial spirit, to the prejudice of the public peace. Several regiments, however, composed of this people, still retain the ancient garb, which is not only agreeable to the eye, but admirably adapted to the use of a soldier. (1:433)

A few Franco-Scottish historical links are mentioned, most often in a derogatory or desultory fashion. The Lowlanders speak "an antient dialect of the English language, interlarded with many terms and idioms which they borrowed immediately from France, in a long course of correspondence with that kingdom" (2:3). Edinburgh's notorious and offensive "Gardez l'eau" nocturnal ritual was "taught, in all probability, by their polite allies, the French" (2:116), whose nasty influence on Scotland is thus evidenced! As in his novels, Smollett deplores the craze for French cookery, "prevailing universally among the great; but the people of middle rank still retain their old dainties" (2:13). French cooks, hairdressers, and dancing masters were all suspected by Smollett of constituting an effete fifth column, sapping the virility of Britain. Lacemaking in Perth does not fare any better: "a little piddling manufacture imported of old from France, where it still prevails" (2:53). Even French claret, of which the gentlemen of Scotland consume "annually a great quantity . . . sold at a very reasonable rate" (2:14), attracts patriotic reprobation: "The zealous patriots of the country have renounced this liquor; and, in order to encourage the British plantations, commit all their debauches with rum-punch" (2:14). Smollett was apparently a moderate drinker but, as evidenced in *Travels through France and Italy*, not averse to a bottle of good claret, and it is unclear whether he approves or disapproves of such a shift. Many present-day French readers will be surprised to learn that their revolutionary guillotine already existed as "the Maiden" in mid sixteenth-century Scotland, introduced by James Douglas, fourth earl of Morton, regent of Scotland, whose own head was cut off by it in 1581 (2:19–20). The mentions of Scottish links in the account of France are few and unimportant, and there is no attempt to trace a history of the ancient and complex historical relationships between the two countries.[21]

Finally, the same imbalance appears in a comparison of the treatments of the economy, industry, and commerce of Scotland and France. The underlying theme is that France was exhausted by the Seven Years' War, and that its industry and commerce would take a long time to recover. The account of France is less graphic and prophetic than Smollett's celebrated letter 36 in *Travels through France and Italy*, where his pessimistic, but not altogether unfounded, assessment of the wretched state of France in 1765 brings him to prophesy "a great change in the constitution."[22] On the contrary, the incipient economic growth of Scotland is duly and repeatedly stressed from the very outset of the account of the mainland: "A remarkable spirit of industry has of late years appeared very visibly in many parts of

Scotland" (2:23). Smollett emphasizes the improvement of agriculture in the Lothians and on the eastern coast, the development of Scottish textile manufactures (linen and wool), of fishing, and of cattle-breeding, so that: "In a word, this kingdom, though branded with the reproach of poverty and barrenness, might prove an inexhaustible source of wealth to the natives. . . . The inhabitants seem at length acquainted with their own interest: they understand the nature of commerce: they see the happy effects of industry: they take example by their southern neighbours and fellow subjects" (2:24). Scotland was no longer the "sink of the earth," as it was called after the '45, but a fast-developing country, characterized by rapidly expanding overseas commerce and urbanization.[23] It thus appears that Smollett's optimistic account of Scotland's economic development is historically well founded, as was his quasi-prophetic assessment of pre-Revolutionary France in *Travels in France and Italy*. But, in comparison with the minutely detailed account of Scotland, the perfunctory hackwork on the state of France fails to provide a relevant and substantially comparable picture.

The view of manufactures, trade, and revenues in the account of France is not entirely negative. "With regard to manufactures, France has made great improvements" (6:78) is the opening sentence of the section which mentions the Gobelins tapestries, filigree, sculpture, silk in Lyons, wool in Abbeville ("not . . . greatly inferior to the English or Dutch"), textiles of all descriptions, arms (already!), and leather ("their artisans, however, in most of these articles, are surpassed by the English"). French foreign trade is deemed "still very considerable," especially to the West Indian colonies. Yet because of the "very mortifying restrictions" (6:79) imposed on the French by the Peace of Paris in 1763, their East Indian, African, North American trade has been all but ruined, so that "they will, probably, never be in a condition to dispute the empire of the ocean" with the British. The ordinary revenue of France, arising from various taxes, customs, and duties, is "computed at about ten millions sterling" (6:86), while no figure is quoted for Scotland. But the Treasury is often empty, or "involved in prodigious debts, and the people, by endless exactions, reduced to the last degree of wretchedness. . . ; and this is said to be pretty much the case at present, the late war having not only greatly disordered their finances, but stopped up some of its principal resources" (6:87).

Such a state of wretchedness, at least of the lower classes, had already been emphasized graphically in *Travels through France and Italy*, where it acted as a foil to British prosperity. As is implied throughout the account of France in *PS*, the arrogant, warlike French had merely received their due for attempting —with disastrous results—to crush Britain's power, especially Britain's vital maritime trade. Hence, not the slightest trace of compassion is to be detected in the account of France. Even after the Peace of Paris, and as the Revolutionary and Napoleonic wars sadly proved between 1789 and 1815, France was "the natural and inveterate enemy and rival of Great Britain" (2:222).

In *PS*, twenty years after Johnson's *The Vanity of Human Wishes* (1749), Smollett fulfills the Great Cham's all-encompassing injunction: "Let observation with extensive view, / Survey mankind from China to Peru." But this Smollett does with a very variable energy of implication. If he is, in spite of his apparently respected stance of declared impartiality, vibrantly energetic in his presentation of his beloved Scotland, the same can hardly be said about the disappointing pages of hackwork devoted to France, soon degenerating into a wearisome catalogue of the "principal places" in the thirty-seven "governments." Nevertheless, the account of France, with its grudging admiration for French arts, architectural achievements, and manufactures, is far from devoid of interest when its contemporaneous context is scrutinized, such as its Protestant bias, its rejection of absolutism, and its diffuse Gallophobia. In spite of the Treaty of Paris, the "late war" of 1756–63 was still going on in the minds of British observers like Smollett. From the outset, the account of France is hopelessly biased against the French people. Whereas the islanders and mainland Scots are nearly always presented as sturdy, virile, and resistant, the French "are not so large and strong as their neighbours, but nimble and active; they generally wear their own hair in a queue or bag: their complexions are none of the best, which, no doubt, gave rise to the custom of painting their faces, so common among the ladies" (6:75).

Such sweeping generalizations are potentially dangerous, as they both reflect current ethnic prejudice and help to strengthen and spread its poisonous venom. The Scots, as Smollett himself knew all too well, were also for centuries the victims of such obnoxious prejudices. Henry Thomas Buckle (1821–62), in the third volume of his *History of Civilization in England* (1857–61), which is at times, in its lengthy chapters devoted to seventeenth- and eighteenth-century Scotland, stridently Scottophobic, could still view the rebellions of 1715 and 1745 as "the last struggle of barbarism against civilization. On the one side, war and confusion; on the other, peace and prosperity."[24] "Sancta simplicitas!" Such Manichean dichotomies make for deep-rooted national hatreds, which may be skillfully nursed into hysterical and bellicose phobias by such demagogues as Smollett's archenemy in the early 1760s, John Wilkes. As Linda Colley has observed, in words that amply confirm the context of Smollett's mistrust of the French: "Right until the end of the nineteenth century, in fact, most politicians, military experts and popular pundits, continued to see France as Britain's most dangerous and obvious enemy and for good reason. France had a larger population and a much bigger land-mass than Great Britain. It was its greatest commercial and imperial rival."[25] As André Maurois so aptly puts it: "L'histoire est un perpétuel recommencement."

## NOTES

1. Lewis M. Knapp, *Tobias Smollett, Doctor of Men and Manners* (1949; New York, 1963), 274.

2. James G. Basker, *Tobias Smollett, Critic and Journalist* (Newark, Del., 1988), 156. Unfortunately, the advertisements are not to be found in most bound sets of the *Monthly Review*, as they were cut off by the binders.

3. *The Letters of Tobias Smollett*, ed. Lewis M. Knapp (Oxford, 1970), 113.

4. The *English Short-Title Catalogue* records no reprints of *PS*, though in 1768 a second, more current edition appeared of volumes 1 and 2, which will be used here for all references to that volume. Unless otherwise indicated, all parenthetical page references in the text refer to *PS*.

5. *The European Magazine* 45 (1804): 258.

6. Clive Hart and Kay Gilliland Stevenson, "John Armstrong's *The Oeconomy of Love*: A Critical Edition with a Commentary," *Eighteenth-Century Life* 19 (1995): 39.

7. On contemporaneous Scottophobia, see Linda Colley, *Britons: Forging the Nation, 1707–1837* (London, 1992), 105–32.

8. John McVeagh, "Smollett and the Sceptical Reader," *N & Q*, n.s. 27 (1980): 34–40. See also James P. Carson, "Britons, 'Hottentots,' Plantation Slavery, and Tobias Smollett," Philological Quarterly 75 (1996): 471–99, a critically illuminating analysis of the crucial role of such compilations as the *PS*

in the progressive but contradiction-ridden construction of Britishness in the eighteenth century.

9. The thirty-five volumes of Diderot and D'Alembert's *Encyclopédie* were published between 1751 and 1776, while William Smellie's first edition of the *Encyclopaedia Britannica* came out in 1768–71. See Frank A. Kafker, "The Achievement of Andrew Bell and Colin Macfarquhar as the First Publishers of the *Encyclopaedia Britannica*," *British Journal for Eighteenth-Century Studies* 18 (1995): 139–52, and Kafker, ed., *Notable Encyclopedias of the Late Eighteenth Century: Eleven Successors of the* Encyclopédie (Oxford, 1994), especially his two contributions: "William Smellie's Edition of the *Encyclopaedia Britannica*," 145–82, and "The Influence of the *Encyclopédie* on the Eighteenth-Century Encyclopedic Tradition," 389–99. See also Louis L. Martz, *The Later Career of Tobias Smollett* (New Haven, Conn., 1942), 1–5.

10. Martz, *Later Career*, 113–15. "The list is chiefly sham" (113).

11. See Knapp, *Tobias Smollett*, 171–72. The proposals for the monthly publication of the *Critical Review* appeared in the *Public Advertiser* for 30 December 1755.

12. Martz, *Later Career*, 108. On Smollett's sources for his account of Scotland—a problem that will not be examined here—see 108–18.

13. Tobias Smollett, *Continuation of the Complete History of England* (London, 1760–65), 5 vols., 5:264.

14. Martz, *Later Career*, 122, 117.

15. On the "discovery" of Scotland by eighteenth-century British travelers, see Marie-Hélène Thévenot-Totems, *La Découverte de l'Ecosse du XVIIIe siècle à travers les récits des voyageurs britanniques* (Paris, 1990).

16. See Paul-Gabriel Boucé, *The Novels of Tobias Smollett* (London, 1976).

17. Martz, *Later Career*, considers the lively description of the Highlanders' manners and customs in *PS* to be "largely original with Smollett: here, in eight pages, Smollett presents the most succinct and vivid description of the Scottish Highlander and his life which had thus far appeared" (117).

18. On the opening page of *Roderick Random*, a seer is consulted to interpret a dream of Roderick's mother during her pregnancy. In *Humphry Clinker*, see Matthew Bramble's letter to Dr. Lewis from Manchester, 15 September, on Scottish superstitions and the second sight.

19. On Smollett's use of Martin Martin's works in *PS* and *Humphry Clinker*, see Martz, *Later Career*, 113–16, 139–41, 143–45.

20. David M. Walker, "Witches and Witchcraft," in *Oxford Companion to Law* (Oxford, 1980).

21. See 6:171–72, Châtellerault conferred on James Hamilton, second earl of Arran, by Henry II, "as a reward for resigning the regency of Scotland" in 1554, thus becoming duke of Châtellerault; 6:201, a chapel and palace built by John, duke of Albany, at Vic-le-Comte in Lower Auvergne. The duke, who served as an admiral in France, was regent of Scotland during the minority of James V of Scotland, between 1515 and 1524; 6:207, Aubigny in Berry: "Both town and castle were given, as some say, by Charles VII [1403–61] to John Stuart, constable of Scotland: but according to others, by Charles VIII [1470–98] to Bernard Stuart, captain of his guards, of the family of Lenox, in Scotland."

22. Tobias Smollett, *Travels through France and Italy*, ed. Frank Felsenstein (Oxford, 1979), 313.

23. Colley, *Britons*, 13, 123.

24. Henry Thomas Buckle, *History of Civilization in England* (1857–61; London, 1872), 3:157.

25. Colley, *Britons*, 24–25.

# Voltaire's *L'Écossaise*: The Story of a French and Scottish Fraud

### SYLVIE KLEIMAN-LAFON

WITH THE PSEUDODISCOVERY OF JAMES MACPHERSON'S OSSIANIC FRAG-
ments, the year 1760 marked the occasion of one of the most
famous literary forgeries, not only in the literary history of the
Scottish Enlightenment, but also, undoubtedly, in the literary
history of Europe. However, hardly any scholar seems to remember that 1760 also gave birth to another literary mystification, which, at the time at least, created an almost equal uproar
among the French literati. The turmoil was generated by a short
one-act play by Voltaire, entitled *Le Caffé ou L'Écossaise*. The
story of this tragicomedy can be read and told in the manner of
a detective story. Although not a single drop of blood was shed,
an intricate mystery, artfully sustained, surrounded the publication and staging of the play.

Between 6 and 12 May 1760, the printed text of the play, together with a foreword, circulated in the Parisian literary milieu.
Contrary to tradition, the text was printed and distributed without any prior or simultaneous plans for staging the play. The
original text was dated from London (it was actually printed in
Geneva), signed Hume, and supposedly translated into French
by an anonymous translator.[1]

It took quite a while before the public started to suspect Voltaire as the author. As a matter of fact, Diderot was first thought
to be the actual father of *L'Écossaise*. This is hardly surprising
since, as we shall see, Voltaire took great care and energy to deny
authorship, even in his correspondence with intimate friends
such as d'Argental.

The action in the play takes place in London and involves the
following characters: Lindane, the Scottish woman of the play;
her maid Polly; Fabrice, the French owner of the café and of a
few rooms upstairs, rented by Lindane, among others; Lord

Montrose, also a Scotsman; Lord Murray, son of Montrose's mortal enemy; Freeport, a wealthy London merchant; Lady Alton, who is secretly infatuated with young Lord Murray; and finally Frélon, a "gutter press" writer.

All the scenes take place in the café-auberge owned by Fabrice, where Lindane has retired from the world. The other tenant is Lord Montrose, who, we soon learn, is another exile from Scotland. The café is also frequented by the other characters, especially Frélon, who soon develops a strong interest in the young Scottish woman. The quite discreet Lindane quickly becomes the focus of attention. Lord Murray is also charmed by her, which arouses the jealousy of Lady Alton, who decides to wreak vengeance on Lindane with the help of Frélon. The latter says he can prove Lindane to be a Scottish spy plotting against the British crown, and intends to have her arrested. Thanks to Fabrice, all is well that ends well: Lindane agrees to marry young Lord Murray at the very moment when she identifies Montrose as her father, who had disappeared after the battle of Culloden, where her own brother had perished. Montrose finally befriends the son of the one who betrayed him. Frélon disappears and with him all rumors of a plot.

The story told in *L'Écossaise* is by no means original—it is quite simple and seems rather harmless. Yet, it generated a fierce and passionate debate. On 26 July 1760, while the controversy was already at its height, the play was staged for the first time. On the eve of the first performance, one Jérôme Carré, from Montauban (being, of course, Voltaire), presented himself as the translator of the play in a letter addressed to "Messieurs les Parisiens."[2] The letter was printed separately and is posterior to the original 1760 edition of the play. Its full title is "Requête de Jérôme Carré aux Parisiens à la veille de la représentation de l'*Écossaise*." It did not appear in the first two editions of the play but was soon added to all the subsequent editions after 1761.[3] The aim of this letter was to put an end to the rumor which attributed *L'Écossaise* to Voltaire and—rightly—saw the character of Frélon as a mockery of Fréron, the archenemy of Voltaire and the Encyclopédistes.[4] Toward the end of 1760, a new edition of the play appeared, in conformity with the text used by the Comédiens-Français Ordinaires du Roi. At the special request of the censor Crébillon, it substituted the anglicized name of Wasp for the original Frélon, considered defamatory for the director of *L'Année Littéraire*.[5] In this edition, the name of Voltaire appeared for the first time, not as the author but as the translator.

The violent joust opposing Voltaire to Fréron, much more than the unexceptionable plot, accounts for the enormous success of the play in France. It was staged 134 times between its creation in 1760 and the year 1794, and went through no less than thirteen editions during the year 1760, followed by an impressive number of editions or reprints, including editions in 1761, 1763, 1764, and 1765.[6] As early as 1760, *L'Écossaise* was also rendered in rhyming verse by Monsieur de Lagrange, and this new version was staged on 20 September 1760 at the Comédie Italienne and subsequently published in Paris the following year.[7] A few days earlier that same year, on 4 September 1760, *L'Écosseuse*, a parody of *L'Écossaise* also appeared on stage. *Les Nouveaux Calotins*, another parodical play by Harny de Guerville, A. R. Lesage, Fuzelier and d'Orneval—staged for the first time on 19 September 1760—was in fact less a proper parody than a set of commentaries and reactions written around Voltaire's play.[8]

If the quarrel between Fréron and Voltaire—and later between Palissot and the *philosophes*[9]—seems enough to have guaranteed the success of the play in France, it certainly does not account for its incredible fortune abroad. Beyond its strictly French polemical content, *L'Écossaise* is in fact the very center of a whole network of plays, all directly or indirectly inspired by the sentimental stylings of Richardson's *Pamela*, which had drawn effusive praise from Diderot and did not fail to impress Voltaire.[10] It therefore appears as a European play *par excellence*, owing its success to a general theme which was highly fashionable at the time.

Thanks to Colin Duckworth's studies,[11] we now know that Voltaire was doubly inspired by Richardson when he wrote *L'Écossaise*. In 1749, he had published *Nanine*, an adaptation of *Pamela* for the French stage, and ten years later, he very carefully read another *Pamela*, a play by his niece Madame Denis, which was never played or published. Madame Denis's *Pamela* was not directly inspired by Richardson's work of the same title. It is in fact the adaptation of Goldoni's *Pamela Nubile*, which already contained some elements later to be found in *L'Écossaise*. Lord Murray originally appears in *Pamela Nubile* as Comte Auspingh, who went into exile after the Jacobite risings of 1715, and not after Culloden as in *L'Écossaise*. By a strange looping phenomenon, a play by Goldoni entitled *La Scozzese*, directly inspired by Voltaire's *L'Écossaise*, was published in 1799. It marked the ultimate achievement for a play which would not only be translated into English but also into German, Danish, Italian, and Dutch.

Madame Denis's *Pamela* upsets the chronology established by Goldoni. The original Comte Auspingh is thus renamed d'Astaingue and becomes a Jacobite hero of 1745: "un rebelle qui souleva l'Écosse contre l'Angleterre, pour soutenir le parti du prétendant."[12] Thanks to his niece's play, Voltaire became aware of the dramatic potential of the Culloden massacre. He also added to it the story of one of his close friends: Suzanne de Livry. A second-rate actress, who had formerly been Voltaire's passion, she was actually given shelter in London by the French owner of a café. Much like the heroine of the play, she was poor and ended up marrying a rich man before a final reconciliation with her family in France.

Such is the French context of *L'Écossaise*. More remains to be said about the detailed Scottish background of the play, especially since nothing has yet been written on that particular aspect. Let us first go back to the fraud itself, that is to say the fallacious attribution of the play to Hume.

It seems likely that the play's first signature was misinterpreted, so that, at least for a while, the Hume of *L'Écossaise* may have been thought to be David Hume the philosopher and not John Home the playwright, whose name was pronounced the same way. An identical mistake was made in the catalogue of the Bibliothèque Nationale, where the play is to be found under David Hume's name. Voltaire did not seem particularly eager to encourage this mistake, although from the first line of the letter by the so-called Jérôme Carré, the very identity of Hume/Home is discussed. It may almost be said that the entire letter was meant less to answer Fréron's attacks than to give extra credit to the literary fraud through an excess of details. Thus, the author writes:

Il [Mr. F . . . , that is to say Fréron] appelle Mr. Hume *Mr. Home*; et puis il dit que Mr. Hume le prêtre, auteur de cette pièce, n'est pas parent de Mr. Hume le philosophe. Qu'il consulte seulement le *Journal Encyclopédique* du mois d'Avril 1758 . . . il y verra cette annonce page 137: "L'auteur de *Douglas* est le ministre Hume, parent du fameux David Hume, si célèbre par son impiété." . . . J'avoue à ma honte que je l'ai cru son frère; mais qu'il soit frère ou cousin, il est toujours certain qu'il est l'auteur de *L'Écossaise*. Il est vrai que dans le journal que je cite, *L'Écossaise* n'est pas expressément nommée; on n'y parle que d'*Agis* et de *Douglas*: mais c'est une bagatelle.[13]

The confusion as to the exact nature of the family link between David Hume and John Home is indeed Voltaire's, since this very mistake may be found in his correspondence, in the letter to d'Argental dating from 6 July 1760: "Mr Aliboron, dit Fréron, est un ignorant bien imprudent de dire que le poëte prêtre Humes [*sic*], n'est pas le frère de Humes l'athée. Il ne sçait pas que Humes le prêtre a dédié une de ses pièces à son frère" (Besterman, D9043). A few months later, Voltaire wrote in a letter to Madame du Deffand on 10 October 1760: "Il est, comme vous sçavez le cousin de l'auteur de *l'Écossaise*" (Besterman, D9297). The way Voltaire spells "Hume" adds to the confusion, since he does not make any distinction between Home and Hume, using the same—erroneous—spelling for both (Humes). He also suggests they have the same activity, since he writes in his preface: "ces deux philosophes font également honneur à l'Écosse leur patrie."

Voltaire is equally precise in the preface he writes for the first Amsterdam edition of the play. It was not until 1761 that he added a footnote to this same preface: "On sent bien que c'était une plaisanterie d'attribuer cette pièce à Mr. Hume."[14] Throughout 1760, Voltaire kept denying the authorship of *L'Écossaise*, even though he made a first move toward disclosure in July, when he acknowledged having translated it. This acknowledgment allowed him to pay himself a fair number of compliments, which he obviously relished integrating into his preface to the July edition:

La comédie intitulée *L'Écossaise* nous parut un de ces ouvrages qui peuvent réussir dans toutes les langues, parce que l'auteur peint la nature, qui est partout la même: il a la naïveté et la vérité de l'estimable Goldoni, avec peut-être plus d'intrigue, de force, et d'intérêt. . . . Cette pièce paraît un peu dans le goût de ces romans anglais qui ont fait tant de fortune; ce sont des touches semblables, la même peinture des mœurs, rien de recherché, nulle envie d'avoir de l'esprit, et de montrer misérablement l'auteur quand on ne doit montrer que les personnages. . . .[15]

Several reasons may be cited to explain why Voltaire chose John Home as the putative author of his play. Voltaire is far too insistent upon the family bonds existing between Home and Hume for this duo—a philosopher and a playwright—not to be, in his mind at least, the transposed image of what he sees himself as: a philosopher and a writer of imaginative literature. Voltaire's selection of John Home is not arbitrary either. At the time, Home was famous across Europe for his tragedy *Douglas*, which has now fallen into quite undeserved oblivion. A Scottish spectator at the Edinburgh premiere of *Douglas* even exclaimed: "And where's yer Willie Shakespeare noo!" In his preface, Voltaire is careful to emphasize the fame of Home, whom he presents (somewhat inaccurately, since Home was a Church of Scotland minister but never a minister in Edinburgh) as "pasteur de l'église d'Édimbourg, déjà connu par deux belles tragédies jouées à Londres."[16] Still, Voltaire's pride is not the sole reason for that choice. In fact, he was also paying back Home for having drawn some material in *Douglas* from his play *Mérope* (first staged in London in 1748),[17] the play's mainframe being drawn from the Scottish ballad *Gil Morrice*.[18]

However, on the precise question of Scotland, a huge gap seems to separate John Home and Voltaire. At the time of the Jacobite rebellion of 1745, Home took part in the conflict—on the government's side—and was imprisoned by the Jacobites after the battle of Falkirk. On this subject, Voltaire's opinion is perfectly clear. Unlike Home, he was in favor of the pretender and found in the writings of Home's illustrious "cousin" the ideological support and main motif for *L'Écossaise*. According to Jean Balcou, Voltaire took the Jacobite theme of his play from the *Histoire de Marie Stuart, Reine d'Ecosse et de France*, which his old enemy Fréron had published in 1742 with the Abbé Marsy.[19] However, in the catalogue of Voltaire's library at Ferney, Fréron's book is nowhere to be found. But, Voltaire did own a copy of the first London edition of David Hume's *History of Great-Britain*, covering at least the early part of the Stuart reign (1754), as well as a copy of Prévost's French translation of Hume's complete account of the Stuarts, *Histoire de la maison de Stuart*, which significantly appeared at the beginning of 1760, before *L'Écossaise* went into circulation.[20]

In his correspondence with Madame du Deffand, Voltaire confirms his interest in this painful episode in the history of Scotland. In response to one of her letters of 20 September 1760, where she writes: "J'ai été très contente de l'histoire des Stuart, elle est un peu fatigante, mais il y a des morceaux sublimes" (Besterman, D9248), Voltaire wrote back on 10 October of the same year, confirming that the book in question is indeed by David Hume: "vous avez bien raison, madame, d'aimer l'histoire de mon ami Hume. Il est comme vous sçavez le cousin de l'auteur de *l'Écossaise*. Vous voyez comme il rend dans cette histoire le fanatisme odieux"(Besterman, D9297).

*L'Écossaise* also echoes another historical work: Voltaire's own *Précis du siècle de Louis XV*. It was first published years later (1768) as an addition to a new and revised edition of the *Siècle de Louis XIV*, but at the beginning of 1760, Voltaire was already putting the finishing touch on the long chapters 24 and 25, both of which deal with Bonnie Prince Charlie's misadventures.[21] Their respective titles are fairly eloquent: "Entreprises, victoires, défaite, malheurs déplorables du prince Charles-Edouard Stuart—Débarquement du Prince Charles-Edouard dans une île d'Ecosse—Mœurs et lois des montagnards d'Ecosse—Ses premiers succès—Il prend Edimbourg—Il gagne un victoire complète à Preston Pans—Les Hollandais envoient servir en Angleterre des troupes qui avaient fait serment de ne point servir. . . ." (chap. 24), and "Suite des aventures du prince Charles-Edouard. Sa défaite, ses malheurs et ceux de son parti—Nouvelle victoire du prince Charles Edouard à Falkirk—Il livre un second combat le même jour—Bataille décisive de Culloden et victoire complète du duc de Cumberland—Des femmes combattaient pour le prince Edouard—Extrémité affreuse où le Prince Charles-Edouard est réduit—Le roi de France fait en vain intercéder en faveur du prince Edouard et de ses partisans—Lettre singulière de l'ambassadeur Van Hoey—Supplices sanglants. . . ."(chap. 25).

As a matter of fact, L'*Écossaise* was almost entirely inspired by the various episodes of the Jacobite rebellion and, were it not for the character of Frélon/Fréron (who only appears in a very limited number of scenes), one could easily detect a real political statement by Voltaire. The links between the "small" and the "great" history are numerous: in his *Siècle de Louis XV*, Voltaire describes the errand of the Prince in Lochaber, in *L'Écossaise* he makes it Lindane's birthplace. The Lord Murray of the play is none other than the double of John Murray, secretary to Prince Charles Stuart, who, according to Voltaire: "racheta sa vie en découvrant au gouvernement des secrets qui firent connaître au roi le danger qu'il avait couru," the secrets in question being in fact a list of Jacobite subscribers that included Lord Lovat. It is also to Montrose that Drummond went and publicized the famous manifesto translated into French by Voltaire under the title: "Manifeste du roi de France en faveur du Prince Charles-Edouard." This political aspect of *L'Écossaise*, with no halftones, may have escaped the French readers and spectators of the play, but it certainly did not escape its English translators and publishers.

To my knowledge, there never was any Scottish edition of *L'Écossaise*, although English translations were printed in London and Dublin as early as 1760, as well as at least one version in a translation of Voltaire's *Works* and an adaptation entitled *The English Merchant* and signed by George Coleman (1732–94) in 1767. With an epilogue by David Garrick, Coleman's play was performed at the Theatre Royal in Drury Lane; a second edition of it was published in London in 1767 and two Dublin reprints appeared in the same year. This adaptation was actually a form of consecration for Voltaire. On 14 November 1768, he wrote to Coleman: "vous avez furieusement embelli *l'Écossaise*, que vous avez donnée sous le nom de Freeport, qui est en effet le meilleur personnage de la pièce."

The first translation of *L'Écossaise* was published in 1760. It was anonymous and entitled *The Coffee House or Fair Fugitive, a comedy of five acts written by Mr. Voltaire*.[22] It appears in its turn as a perfect example of mystification since the least one can say is that it bears a very distant relation to the original. The process of fabrication starts with the title, which removes all allusions to Scotland. To make sure that no suspicious detail might uncover the political overtones of the play, the anonymous translator also decided to change the names of most characters. Only Lady Alton, Fabrice, and Freeport escape the censure. Lindane becomes Constantia, Lord Montrose is changed into Sir William Woodville, while a very English Belmont replaces Lord Murray; the rather insignificant Lucy is named Polly and, last but not least, Frélon is restyled as Scandal.

For all these changes, the translator offers a rather lame justification. Together with the rest of the preface, it contributes to convince the reader that, despite the illustrious authorial signature, nothing polemical will mar the enjoyment of the otherwise insipid sentimental story:

> As the scene is laid in England, and the names consequently English, I have taken the liberty to alter those of the original, and have given some of them at least an English termination. As to the rest, the translation is nearly literal; I have neither added to the author's wit, nor retrenched what he has thought proper to give. . . . As in his [Voltaire] late performance, called Socrates, he pretends to have translated it from the English language, so also, in his preface to this piece, he makes the same pretence; he attempts to imitate our freedom of thinking, and takes this method to palliate the freedom of his own. This piece, however, which we now present the reader, has nothing to shock the established modes of faith; Voltaire, in this, appears the amiable friend of man, without opposing any particular system.

Such an insistent denial of the controversial elements of the play shows quite convincingly that its political message did not pass unnoticed by the English censors. Even though the word "Scotland" was not totally excised from the text, the original critical remarks (especially the espionage charges expostulated by Frélon and Lady Alton) are strictly limited to the negative characters. For the other, positive characters, all allusions to Scotland are hushed. In act 4, scene 6, for instance, the crucial recognition scene between father and daughter is written as follows in the French version:

> Montrose: Vous êtes née dans le Lochaber! et témoin de tant d'horreurs! persécutée, errante, et si malheureuse avec des sentiments si nobles!

In English it becomes:

> Sir William: You were born, you say, in one of the northern provinces, and lost your father and your fortune by a civil war.

This is a perfect example of the art of euphemism and circumlocution. The determination to erase all the elements that could open up too recent scars sometimes extends to absurd details.

When Voltaire writes the passage where Lindane declares herself ready to follow her father even to the remotest countries, he has her say:

> Lindane: Je renoncerai à tout pour vous . . . je vous accompagnerai, s'il le faut, dans quelque île affreuse des Orcades.

In the translation, the line becomes:

> Constantia: If you fix your retreat, even among the desolate islands of the North, yet I will follow you.

Voltaire had merely voiced an opinion still widely held about the Highland landscape; the sublime had not yet reached the stern mountains, the desolate moors and the mighty cataracts of the North of Scotland, and these antipicturesque landscapes, far from suggesting enthusiasm, rather conveyed feelings of terror and disgust. It is quite clear that he intended not to raise a political quarrel, but at best an aesthetic debate.

The British readership had to wait for the second translation, by Reverend Francklin—presumably Thomas Francklin (1721–84)—published in 1763 in the seventh volume of Voltaire's dramatic works, to read a text that was, at last, relatively true to its original. As opposed to the 1760 translation, the title was not changed: *The Coffee-House, or the Scotch Woman*.[23] This new edition was so faithful as to offer a translation of the two dedicatory epistles, including the letter by Jérôme Carré, together with the translation of the prefatory note to the reader and Voltaire's own preface. But Franklin warns the reader that:

> This preface, with the two epistles dedicatory, contains nothing very intelligible or entertaining to an English reader; but as they are inserted in all the editions of the original, it was thought proper to translate them. One cannot indeed easily find out any reason why Mr de Voltaire chose to father this comedy on Mr Hume; or what end it could answer to tell so many long stories about a comedy, which, the reader will see, is, after all, but a very indifferent performance.

A harsh criticism indeed, but the text's integrity is preserved throughout. No characters' names are altered except Fabrice, who is anglicized into a Mr. Williams for the following reason:

Amongst the English and Scotch names, Mr Voltaire has inserted one that seems to have no relation to either, and called his coffee-house keeper Fabrice. I have taken the liberty to alter it to Williams.

Apart from this rather insignificant change, nothing has been cut from the text. In conformity with the original, Montrose tells Lindane (act 3, scene 6):

Montrose: Every word you utter pierces my soul: born in Lochaber! Persecuted, oppress'd and deserted!

Actually, only the passage concerning the Orkneys remains really distant from Voltaire's text:

Lindane: I am ready to follow you, I will accompany you, sir, to some far distant island, and there these hands shall labour to support you.

Such is, in brief, the odd itinerary of a multilevel French, Scottish, and English mystification; the complicated progress of a Scottish woman who had three fathers and was claimed by several causes. She took part in a French literary contest, though she thought she had enrolled in a Scottish rebellion, and was kidnapped by the English and camouflaged so as not to wake up the painful memories of too recent battles. If one adds to these adventures the ones told in the play itself, Voltaire's text offers a great variety of identities, aliases, and masks. In all these stories of betrayal, treason, travesty, and disguise, translation, as always, plays the leading part.

This play about Scotland and a Scottish woman, allegedly written by a Scotsman and partly inspired by one of the most famous philosophers in eighteenth-century Britain, began its intricate adventures in France and concluded them in England, without ever visiting Lochaber, the Orkneys, or even Edinburgh. The lie was complete and the mystification maintained to the end.

## NOTES

1. *Le Caffé ou L'Écossaise, comédie par Monsieur Hume, traduite en français,* Londres (in fact Geneva), by Cramer, 1760. This edition was rapidly followed

by another one, purporting to be from Avignon, printed by Louis Chambeau. Then, another one indicating Jérôme Carré as the translator appeared in London, still in 1760, followed by the first edition (also bearing London as the alleged printing place) to bear the name of Voltaire as the translator. A 1763 edition even bears the following farcical references: A. Avignon, Imprimeur-Libraire, près les Révérends Pères Jésuites.

2. The name of Jérôme Carré was used again in 1771 for an *Essais sur la poésie lyri-comique*, which was in fact attributed to Augustin Pierre Damiens de Gomicourt (1723–1790), the French translator of William Blackstone and author—among other things—of *Dorval, ou mémoires pour servir à l'histoire des mœurs du XVIIIe siècle* (1769).

3. *Requête adressée à M.M. les Parisiens, par Jérôme B. Carré, natif de Montauban, traducteur de la comédie intitulée: "Le Caffé ou l'Écossaise," pour servir de post-préface à la-dite comédie* (n.d., n.p.). It was printed under the form of a small volume of eight pages and contained an unsigned engraving showing Fréron standing near a table with a copy of *L'Écosseuse*. On the ground are a copy of *Les Calotins* and one of *L'Écossaise*. According to Bengesco *(Voltaire: Bibliographie de ses Œuvres* [Paris, Rouveyre & G. Blond, 1882],vol. 1), the first edition to include Carré's letter was printed in 1761 *(Seconde suite de mélanges de littérature, d'histoire et de philosophie)*. *L'Écossaise* is preceded by the "épître dédicatoire du traducteur à M. le comte de Lauragais," by Carré's "Requête," by the "Avertissement" and the preface to the first edition.

4. Frélon (a hornet in English) was quite a befitting nickname for Fréron, whom Voltaire considered so venomous that he wrote the following famous epigram:

> L'autre jour, au fond d'un vallon,
> Un serpent piqua Jean Fréron:
> Que croyez-vous qu'il arriva?
> Ce fut le serpent qui creva.

5. *L'Écossaise, ou le Café, comédie en cinq actes et en prose, de M. Hume, traduite par Monsieur de Voltaire, dernière édition, telle qu'elle est représentée pour la première fois par les comédiens français ordinaires du roi, le 26 juillet 1760*. This new edition is dated from Amsterdam, but was in fact issued by a Parisian printer. As to the alterations, see Voltaire, in his letter to d'Argental, on 6 July 1760, in *Voltaire, Complete Works, vols. 85 to 135: Correspondence and Related Documents*, ed. Theodore Besterman, 107 vols. (Geneva, Banbury, Oxford, 1968–1977), D9043 (hereafter cited as "Besterman").

6. For further details see Bengesco, *Voltaire*; also *Provisional Handlist of Separate Eighteenth Century Voltaire Editions in the Original Language* (Oxford, Voltaire Foundation, 1981), and Besterman, *Some Eighteenth Century Voltaire Editions Unknown to Bengesco* (4th ed. Oxford, Voltaire Foundation, 1973), *Studies on Voltaire and the Eighteeth Century*, vol. 111.

7. *L'Écossoise* (Paris, Duschesne, 1761).

8. *L'Écosseuse, parodie de l'Écossaise, opéra comique en un acte, par M.M. P\*\*\** [Panard] *et A\*\*\** [Anseaume], *représentée sur le théâtre de l'opéra comique le 4 septembre 1760* (Paris, Prault et Fils, 1760) and also (Paris, Cuissart, 1761). This

parody was also attributed to Poinsinat le jeune. *Les Nouveaux Calotins* (Paris, Cuissart, 1760).

9. Voltaire, who had not originally thought his play would ever be staged, was unable to prevent it from being used by the philosophers and presented as an answer to Palissot's play *Les Philosophes*, which they considered as a direct attack.

10. In his *Éloge de Richardson* (1762) Diderot expresses his admiration for Richardson's novels ". . . qui élèvent l'esprit, qui touchent l'âme, qui respirent partout du bien. . . ." *Oeuvres Esthétiques*, (Evreux, 1959), 29. Voltaire was less enthusiastic about Richardson than Diderot, writing to the Comte d'Argental in his letter of 16 May 1767: "Je n'aime assurément pas les longs et insupportables romans de *Paméla* et *Clarice*" (Besterman, D14179). Nevertheless, he recognized the appeal that the epistolary novel had for the public, and used *Pamela* as a source of inspiration for both his comedy *Nanine* and his short epistolary novel *Les Lettres d'Amabed*.

11. Colin Duckworth, "Voltaire's *L'Écossaise* and Palissot's *Les Philosophes*: A Stratagic Battle in a Major War," *Studies on Voltaire and the Eighteenth Century*, 87 (1972): 333–51. Colin Duckworth, "Madame Denis' Unpublished *Pamela*: A Link between Richardson, Goldoni and Voltaire," *Studies on Voltaire and the Eighteenth Century*, 51 (1967): 37–53.

12. Madame Denis, *Pamela*, act 3, scene 8. The original manuscript of the play is in the Houghton Library, Harvard. This quote is given by Duckworth in his article on Madame Denis's play.

13. Voltaire, *Le Café ou L'Écossaise*, in *Théâtre du XVIIIe siècle*, vol. 2, ed. Jacques Truchet (Paris, Gallimard, 1974), 205–6.

14. Ibid., 209.

15. Ibid.

16. Ibid.

17. See Alice Gipson, *John Home* (Caldwell, Idaho, 1916), 59–61.

18. Just like *L'Écossaise*, Voltaire's *Mérope* was inspired by the Italian tradition. In 1714, a *Mérope* by Maffei was staged in Modena; it was later translated into French, first by Freret (in 1728), then by du Bourg in 1743, the very same year of the Parisian premiere of Voltaire's *Mérope*, written between 1736 and 1737. The two plays are thematically very close, and both bring back into fashion this staple of the Greek theatrical tradition.

19. Jean Balcou, "L'Affaire de L'Écossaise," *L'Information littéraire* 3 (mai–juin 1969), 111–15.

20. George R. Havens and Norman L. Torrey, eds., "Voltaire's Catalogue of His Library at Ferney," *Studies on Voltaire and the Eighteenth Century* 9 (1959): 162, 170, 223. Voltaire also owned a copy of William Robertson's *History of Scotland during the Reigns of Queen Mary and King James VI* (1759), but it was the fourth London edition, which appeared a year after *L'Écossaise* in 1761.

21. Voltaire, *Siècle de Louis XIV, Nouvelle édition revue et augmentée, à laquelle on a ajouté un précis du siècle de Louis XV* (n. d., 1768), 4 vols.

22. *The Coffee House or the Fair Fugitive, a comedy of five acts written by Mr. de Voltaire* (Londres, J. Wilkie, 1760). And also, with identical title, printed by J. Potts, 1760.

23. "The Coffee-House or the Scotch-Woman, a comedy by Mr. Hume represented in Paris in 1760," *Dramatic Works of Mr. de Voltaire* (London, Newbery and Baldwin, 1761–1763), volume 7 (1763).

# Ossian and Belles Lettres:
# Scottish Influences on J.-B.-A. Suard
# and Late-Eighteenth-Century French
# Taste and Criticism

PIERRE CARBONI

JEAN-BAPTISTE-ANTOINE SUARD (1732–1817), THE INITIATOR OF THE VOGUE of Ossian in France, was by no means the greatest or the most original figure in the cultural life of late eighteenth-century France. An *habitué* of Madame Geoffrin's and, later on, of Julie de Lespinasse's salons, he was friendly with the philosophes, most of them twenty to thirty years his seniors, and died long after them under the second restoration of the monarchy. By that time France had gone successively through more than six different political regimes, but in cultural and literary terms it was not yet consciously or assertively romantic.

Because he was primarily a fashionable gazetteer who turned academician in 1774, Suard represents contemporary, and more precisely institutional, French taste and criticism in a more faithful way than his more distinguished and idiosyncratic colleagues. Though he never set foot on Scottish soil, Suard became William Robertson's friend and early translator,[1] as well as a major cultural mediator between Scotland and France. His pioneering enthusiasm for Ossian, rather than being prompted by a peculiar interest in Scottish Gaelic culture, was a response to the growing urge for updating French neoclassical dogmas. In a letter of April 1762, the baron de Grimm, Suard's cosmopolitan friend, expresses his generation's disregard for the conventional poetry of his age: "We are tired of a poetry that does not bear the mark of genius." Grimm notes by contrast that "the *poésies erses* that have been translated in several installments of the *Journal étranger* know a great success in Paris."[2] As a journalist and reviewer, Suard knew what his readership wanted: something new, something distant, something primitive, something sublime. Ossian seemed naturally to answer all those different, and often contradictory, demands. Moreover, Ossian was the essence of a newly defined Britishness: the Gaelic poems of a Scottish bard translated into fashionable English. British Ossian consecrated a new cultural domination that followed the *annus mirabilis* 1759 and the triumph of British war diplomacy. As co-editor, with his friend l'abbé Arnaud, of the *Journal étranger* (January 1760 to September 1762), a review of various articles translated from the international press, and later as editor of his own *Gazette littéraire de l'Europe* (March 1764 to February 1766),[3] Suard enabled the general reading public in France to enlarge its views, to accept foreign literatures and, with somewhat more reluctance, to accept foreign judgments on taste. In fact, the prevailing Anglomania of the French ruling class, whose models were becoming more and more bourgeois and cosmopolitan as the middling ranks were growing in number and power, was more a matter of fashion and inspiration than a proof of genuine regard for new cultural modes.

As a British import, the poetry of Ossian was bound to become fashionable, like tea-drinking and landscape gardening, but it also suited French tastes because it could be endorsed by the *Académie*. Whatever the democratic leanings of the French elite in the last decades of the Ancien Régime, the French Academy, founded by Cardinal de Richelieu in 1634, was still the formidable instrument of absolutism in matters of taste and culture and the institutional gateway to the temple of knowledge and the muses. Like so many second-rate French intellectuals, Suard was an aspiring academicien in his own right, though his first election to the Academy, in 1772, was immediately canceled on the king's order because he was too friendly with the dangerous philosophes. Yet Suard never ceased to support the absolutist and elitist dogmas of French neoclassicism. The so-called *Poems of Ossian*, the poetic cycle of the "Bard of Morven" that so many Romantics would acknowledge as a major influence, was in fact an academician in Scottish disguise. Prompted and vindicated in their spurious, but useful, authenticity by Hugh Blair and Henry Home, Lord Kames, both senior proponents of the Edinburgh belles-lettres school, James Macpherson's supposed "translations," because they respected most of the neoclassical precepts, allowed more tolerance to appear in French criticism in matters of mood, setting, and inspiration. As Fiona Stafford explains, "Macpherson opened a world of stormy mountain scenery, full of the grandeur and terror demanded by the new taste for the Sublime. At the same time, the appearance of antiquity gave a reassuring sense of permanence."[4] Stafford's analysis of Ossian's reception in Scotland is just as relevant in the French context.

The story of Ossian's revelation and lasting fame in France affords one of the most telling (though indirect) demonstrations of intellectual kinship between the Scottish Enlightenment and the French *lumières*. The triumphant French reception of Edinburgh and Glasgow literati is well known. Hume's most affectionate nickname, "le bon David," is but one example. And if we are to believe the novelist Marie-Jeanne Riccoboni's enthusiastic praise of Adam Smith in a letter written to David Garrick in French in 1765, the Scottish guests ("Oh ces Ecossois! ces chiens d'Ecossois!") often eclipsed their most famous French hosts: "I wish the devil would take away all our *gens de lettres*, all our *philosophes*, and bring me back Mr Smith."[5] Such excitement on the French side must not hide the fact that very few Scottish men of letters besides Hume and Smith ever came to France. As for the French, they were quite familiar with England but even fewer of them crossed the border into Scotland.

A more telling sign of Franco-Scottish (rather than Anglo-French) cross-fertilization can be found in the two nations' common cultural references, among which Ossian and Ossian criticism occupy a central position. Those who revealed Ossian to the French public were by no means marginal figures in eighteenth-century France. Turgot, who first translated anonymously for Suard's *Journal étranger* (16 September 1760) two short passages from the *Fragments of Ancient Poetry Collected in the Highlands of Scotland* (1760), which had been reprinted in the *London Chronicle* (21 June 1760), was a reforming economist, the king's intendant for the province of Limousin, and one of the earliest collaborators on the *Encyclopédie*. Later, in 1776, Turgot was elected to the *Académie des inscriptions et belles-lettres*, France's second academy, founded by Louis XIV's Minister Colbert in 1663, at the climax of royal absolutism in political and cultural terms. In Turgot's early translation, Suard found a powerful support for his defense of diversity and specificity rather than universalism and generality in taste and genres. Turgot himself believed that international reviews such as the *Journal étranger* would play a decisive role in the progressive elimination of national prejudices and narrow aesthetic dogmas: "I believe that the communications between the different nations of Europe will very likely persuade them that some genres may be accepted that they have not yet exercised."[6]

Following Turgot, Suard set himself the task of translating two more passages (January 1761), together with some critical reflections. Other passages appeared in December 1761. Another celebrated supporter of Suard's enterprise of cultural relativism was the editor of the *Encyclopédie*, Diderot himself. In a letter of 12 October 1761 to his friend Sophie Volland, Diderot promised that she also would have her "Scottish songs" and that he would translate for her the Ossianic episode of "Shilric and Vinvela." Diderot's translation, revised by Suard, was published in the *Journal étranger* in December 1761. To Sophie, Diderot recommends not only the singular beauty of those "songs of love and death," but more typically "the taste that prevails there together with incredible simplicity, strength and *pathétique*."[7] Right from the beginning, the dual nature of the supposed *Fragments*, singularity *and* taste, was clearly expressed by Diderot. It was exactly what the democratic philosophes and philanthropic aristocrats needed to open and expand the strict canons of the *Académie* without radically questioning the raison d'être of an institution in which they were gaining power. Likewise, in politics, those who championed reform, liberty, and the rights of man were seldom in favor of a total conversion to republicanism. Their political and cultural leanings were somewhat similar to those of the majority of Edinburgh literati, who were religious moderates and firm supporters of the British Revolution settlement, but also believed in conservative institutions and cultural hierarchies.[8]

Encouraged by the patronage of Turgot and Diderot, Suard carried on his translations as Macpherson's Ossianic works appeared, selecting passages that he put into elegant French for the readers of the *Journal étranger*, for example, "Lathmon" in January 1762, "Oïthona" in February 1762, and "Dar-Thula" in April 1762. He never tried to publish a complete translation of the *Poems of Ossian*. Le Tourneur's first complete French translation, *Poésies galliques d'Ossian*, came out as late as 1777. Following the negative opinion published in the influential *Journal encyclopédique* in January 1762 ("A French translation of that work would certainly be unbearable"), Suard focused on explaining Ossian's relevance in a cultural and critical perspective. In doing so, he promoted Scottish belles-lettres criticism of Ossian as much as the poems themselves. Suard's "Réflexions préliminaires sur l'histoire et le caractère de ces poèmes" (January 1761) was directly inspired by Hugh Blair's anonymous preface to the *Fragments* of 1760, and his "Nouvelles observations sur les poésies d'Ossian," which appeared in the *Gazette littéraire* on 1 July and 1 August 1765, derived from Blair's *Critical Dissertation on the Poems of Ossian* (1763), specifically the second edition that appeared in *The Works of Ossian, the Son of Fingal* in 1765. In a letter to Hume of 1 July 1765, Blair, who thought highly of himself, praised Suard for merely repeating his own opinion on the poems' authenticity and literary value: "Your Gazette Literaire, tho' not very profound, is executed however with much more Taste than any of our two stupid reviews. What excellent taste they show with respect to the Works of Ossian. . . ! I honour the author exceedingly."[9] France's Ossianism therefore echoed Blair's Ossianism, and thanks to the popularity of the poems, Blair gained a major reputation as a critic in France. Blair's fame as Ossian's earliest and most favorable critic indirectly popularized Scottish belles-lettres criticism in France at a time of extreme critical barrenness. Though clearly stating that his "Nouvelles observations sur les poésies d'Ossian" was a review of Blair's criticism, Suard boasted that his early enthusiasm for Ossian owed nothing to the Edinburgh professor's subsequent remarks: "We were flattered to find there several observations that we had made and printed ourselves in the Journal étranger."[10]

Voltaire, though himself an early anglomaniac, felt the danger of this Scottish intrusion on traditional French ground, not only because he feared for the cause of strict neoclassical orthodoxy but, more importantly, because he could not accept the demise of France's cultural imperialism in Europe. Reviewing Kames's *Elements of Criticism* (1762) in a letter to the editor of the *Gazette littéraire* (4 April 1764), the patriarch-turned-reactionary sarcastically derided Scotland's supposed ambition to rule European taste:

It is an astonishing consequence of the progress of human understanding that we now receive from Scotland several rules of taste in
the various arts, from epic poetry to gardening. The capacity of
human understanding increases daily, and we may soon expect to
receive poetics and rhetorics from the Orkney islands. But we would
rather like to see great artists in those countries than great reasoners
on the arts.[11]

Though he was himself the promoter of Scotland's newly acquired literary and critical fame, Suard could not refuse to print
Voltaire's letter in his own journal.

Suard, however, had the advantage of youth over Voltaire's
declining years. Suard's reviews and translations of Ossian, together with other contributions to the *Journal étranger* and the
*Gazette littéraire*, were published in Paris in 1768–69 in a four-
volume collection entitled *Variétés littéraires, ou recueil de pièces,
tant originales que traduites, concernant la philosophie, la littérature,
et les arts*. With that first collection, which went to a second edition in 1770, Suard's revelation of Ossian, which until then was
restricted to the mainly Parisian world of gazette readers, could
reach a much wider French book-reading public throughout the
country, and beyond its borders. In reducing, as we have seen,
the supposed works of Ossian into short episodes and enlightened poetry with criticism, Suard exercised a notable influence
on the nature of French Ossianism. He furnished France with
winter landscapes and heroic or sentimental scenes instead of
encouraging the public to read the poems as a full literary work.
In doing so, he promoted Ossian's status as an inspiration for
taste, not as an *opus magnum* that would, by its own coherence,
bring about an aesthetic revolution. Suard immediately perceived that Ossian and Ossian criticism could not be separated.
As Blair's biographer summarized it, "Macpherson's stuff was
meat for Blair's theories, and Blair's theories were . . . the food
on which Macpherson's poetical efforts throve and fattened."[12]
Thanks to Suard's *Variétés littéraires*, which remained popular
throughout the era of the French Revolution and Napoleon,
France's literary compositions and critical idiom at the turn of
the century were informed by Macpherson's Ossianic works and
Blair's literary theories.

The three decades of French history that separate the Revolution and the Restoration saw the climax of Ossianism and

belles-lettres criticism. In that period, Suard was the only surviving member of the circle of the *Encyclopédistes*. His role in the history of taste in France was to secure the Enlightenment's legacy amid the uncertainties of civic life. Most commentators, from the late nineteenth century to our day, have accused him of exercising a reactionary influence on France's cultural life and of delaying the advent of Romanticism in that country. Even if it is accepted that Romanticism represents progress in literary history, however, one cannot hold one man responsible for France's late conversion to literary Romanticism.

Several factors can help to explain why, in remaining faithful to Ossian and belles lettres, France, like Scotland, failed to become an early Romantic nation in the manner of Germany or England. Paradoxically, it is largely thanks to the momentous events of the French Revolution that Wordsworth and Coleridge formulated so clearly their aim to cut off English literature from its past. To the English Romantic poets at the end of the eighteenth century, Scotland was no longer the country where the primitive and natural poetry of the bards had been rediscovered a couple of decades earlier, as Ossian spuriously suggested. Rather, it was the nation where the most extreme brand of neoclassical criticism still subsisted. For instance, in the "Essay, Supplementary to the Preface" in his *Lyrical Ballads* (1798), Wordsworth stigmatizes Adam Smith as "the worst critic, David Hume excepted, that Scotland, a soil to which this sort of weed seems natural, has produced."[13] Later on, in *English Bards and Scottish Reviewers* (1809)—a poetic satire directed at Francis Jeffrey, the Scottish editor of the *Edinburgh Review* (1803–29) and successor of the likes of Smith and Blair—Byron showed that with the earlier development of Romanticism south of the border, the cultural roles traditionally assigned to Scotland and England were totally reversed. However, in the particular context of French literary history, the Scottish model, initially inspired by France's own belletristic tendencies at the end of the seventeenth century,[14] offered the advantage of change in continuity, precisely what France needed to compensate for its recent institutional tabula rasa.

Among France's earliest royal institutions to be restored by the Revolution, after having been abolished initially, are the *Académie française* and *Académie des inscriptions*. Both were dismantled by the radical *Convention montagnarde* in 1793, and both were revived only two years later by the more moderate *Constitution de l'An III* as the literary class of an *Institut de France*. As Suard had earlier tried to put it to Lebrun at the *Assemblée constituante* in August 1790, the academies, despite their aristocratic origin, had been instrumental in propagating the ideals of the Enlightenment that constituted the philosophical foundations of the Revolution. In regard to taste, the period that follows 1789 similarly acknowledges the Revolution's debt to the Enlightenment. France's total absence of originality in literature and criticism can be attributed to that powerful legacy. That France did not become as libertarian in taste as in politics may also be ascribed to the country's need for cultural stability during an age of political chaos. In that context, Suard's Ossian, the faithful transcription of Macpherson and Blair's Ossian, helped France to shape its new revolutionary culture under the protection of its old Enlightenment masters.

Much as Ossian had been sponsored earlier by the academic institutions of enlightened Scotland, Ossian's long-lasting fame in France was sponsored by the *Institut de France*, whose second, or literary, class was dominated by Suard, its *Secrétaire perpétuel* from February 1803. Suard's major reviews were published that year in his *Mélanges de littérature*, one year before a new edition of the *Variétés littéraires* appeared. Ossian's success was also promoted by Napoleon's personal taste, shaped largely by Cesarotti's Italian translation, *Poesie d'Ossian, figlio di Fingal, antico poeta celtico* (1763), which he carried with him on all his campaigns. In her *Mémoires*, Madame de Chastenay, an invaluable source concerning the era of the Directory (1795–99), recalls Bonaparte's "enthusiasm" for the poems when he visited her at Châtillon, in Burgundy, in spring 1797.[15] She also reports that a soirée at the Luxembourg in 1798, in the apartment of one of the powerful Directoires, featured songs "on beautiful verses imitated from Ossian" (267).

But the joint pressure of cultural and political power gives only one side of the answer to the question of the origins of France's late and somewhat anachronistic Ossianism. Three major features in contemporary French society found a positive echo in Ossian's poetry: patriotism, violence, and secularism. During the Revolutionary and Napoleonic wars, it was easy for France's nonmercenary, patriotic, and democratic army to identify itself with Fingal's warriors while it was fighting, like them, against the rest of Europe, and more precisely Saxon and Scandinavian Europe. But Ossian's violent episodes also appealed to those who rejected the Revolution. Macpherson's doomed warriors, and the inexorable decline of an ancient civilization, had a symbolic resonance for those who had narrowly escaped the bloody Reign of Terror. Ossian's "joy of grief," as defined by Blair,[16] was to be indulged in an atmosphere of "Celtic Twilight" by those who had witnessed the collapse of the Ancien Régime. As the exiled aristocrat Chateaubriand testified: "When in 1793 the Revolution hurled me into England, I was a great supporter of the Scottish bard: I would have used the spear to defend his existence against all odds, as that of old Homer."[17] While the Scottish literati of his day were emulating other European nations in terms of literary fame, as well as supporting the Scots militia cause,[18] Macpherson himself deliberately enhanced the ancient patriotic mood of *Fingal* (1762) by choosing a classical quotation from Virgil for its epigraph: "Fortia facta patrium." More than anything else, the poems, for all their renewed natural imagery, expressed an acute historical sense. This is not surprising. In David Hume's words, the eighteenth century was "the historical Age," and Scotland "the historical Nation."[19] Scotland, like France, was particularly distinguished for its historiography. More essentially, the eighteenth century was in both countries an age of dramatic historical events. With the Union of 1707 and the Jacobite risings, Scotland experienced tremendous social, political, and cultural changes that were only paralleled, though in a more brutal way and later in the century, by the French Revolution.

The last major characteristic of the poems of Ossian that appealed to the French at the close of the eighteenth century was their vague and secularized religion. As Hugh Honour puts it: "In [Ossian's] works, the supernatural element, so essential for primitive poetry, was represented by spirits who, like Shakespeare's ghosts, may be construed as memories, dream visions, and premonitions playing no decisive role in the lives of men."[20] In Macpherson's enlightened and vaguely deist Presbyterianism, France unconsciously found a model for her new abstract religion of heroic virtue, emancipated from the superstitions of the past. As Blair, the Edinburgh minister, explained in his *Critical Dissertation*, "Ossian's mythology is, to speak so, the mythology of human nature."[21] Whereas Robespierre's new abstract, patriotic worship failed in metaphorical language to celebrate the triumph of heroism and virtue, Ossian could remedy that defect.

Forsaking the traditional Catholic imagery or the conventional themes drawn from a god-ridden antiquity, Girodet's famous painting for the Malmaison, "The Apotheosis of Napoleon's Generals" (1802), illustrates Ossian's relevance to revolutionary France as a source of mystic inspiration. Although it does not represent an episode from the poems, the picture uses the Ossian myth to express the new French mystique of hero worship. The painting's full title is a masterpiece of revolutionary eloquence: "Les Ombres des héros français morts pour la patrie viennent habiter l'Elysée aérien où les ombres d'Ossian et de ses valeureux guerriers s'empressent de leur donner, dans ce séjour d'immortalité et de gloire, la fête de la Paix et de l'Amitié" [The Shadows of the French Heroes Who Died for the Fatherland Come to Dwell in the Heavenly Elyseum Where the Shadows of Ossian and His Brave Warriors Hasten to Celebrate, in That Seat of Glory and Immortality, the Festival of Peace and Friendship]. The allegory foreshadows Napoleon's aborted project to dedicate a Temple of Glory to the heroes of his *Grande Armée* on the site of *la Madeleine*'s church in Paris. The new temple was to be the military equivalent of the *Panthéon*, opened in 1791 in the vaults of the desecrated Parisian church of Sainte-Geneviève to receive Voltaire's ashes, and dedicated by the *Assemblée constituante* to the nation's great men.

An interesting, though somewhat anecdotal, hint was given in 1799 by Bonaparte's lieutenant, Marshal Bernadotte, who called his eldest son Oscar, after Ossian's offspring. The name now attached to Bernadotte's Franco-Swedish dynasty is more than a tribute to its instigator's literary tastes. In choosing a non-Christian name for his son, two years before France officially returned to Catholicism after Napoleon and Pope Pius VII signed their concordat in 1801, the Revolution's general consecrated the Convention's most extreme cultural ambition: to abolish the Catholic calendar of saints' feast days in an attempt to cancel all references to the old religion. In the words of the early French comparative critic Paul Van Tieghem, "Macpherson seems to have written for Europe,"[22] and one might add, for secular France. Macpherson's own "Dissertation concerning the

Æra of Ossian" had already proclaimed the independence of poetry from religion:

> It is no matter of wonder . . . that Fingal and his son Ossian disliked the Druids, who were the declared enemies to their succession in the supreme magistracy. It is a singular case, it must be allowed, that there are no traces of religion in the poems ascribed to Ossian, as the poetical compositions of nations are so closely connected with their mythology. But gods are not necessary, when the poet has genius.[23]

In 1762 Scotland was only beginning to discover the possibility of a secular culture that the literati (with several clergymen like Blair in their ranks) were trying to push forward in spite of the reluctant General Assembly of the Church of Scotland. Three decades later, secularism would become the pillar of French republican culture. It has remained so ever since.

But let us return to Suard's joint discovery of Ossian and belles lettres. Despite his former role in promoting the preeminence of the rules of taste over the rules of art, the old academician, confronted in the early nineteenth century with the stylistic *relâchement* of the postrevolutionary idiom, had set himself the task of reviving the traditional axioms of propriety, nobility, and purity in language. Though Ossian's triumph seemed to be complete in the various fields of culture, it was the triumph of base imitators. In France, at the beginning of the nineteenth century, "Ossianic" meant fashionable but poor quality official art. As Gurlitt, a citizen from Hamburg, noticed during his stay in Paris in 1802: "The Parisians want to have everything *à la Ossian* now that they know that Bonaparte is infatuated with him."[24] From June 1796, the *Théâtre de la République*—the new styling of the king's *Comédie-Française*—played Arnault's tragedy *Oscar, fils d'Ossian*. In the summer of 1804, the *Académie impériale de musique* started performing Jean-François Le Sueur's opera *Ossian ou les Bardes*. The minor genre of *opéra comique* also was affected by the wave of Ossianism, with Etienne Méhul's *Uthal* first performed in May 1806 by the composer of the revolutionary *Chant du départ* (1794).

In those new Ossianic works, nothing remained of Ossian's initial élan toward primitive simplicity and unspoiled virtue, and toward what Blair in his *Critical Dissertation* called "the

poetry of the heart."[25] Suard lavished praise on Ossian's contemporaries, "those wild men, whose soul is, so to say, totally
bare" / "toute au dehors" (Variétés, 1:183). To those who were
free from what Suard calls "the prejudices that prompted the superstitious admiration of Homer" (Variétés, 3:102), Ossian could
teach poetry and morality simultaneously. Since the artificiality
of eighteenth-century French poetry was only matched by the
current artificiality of manners, the only possible remedy lay in
a poetic and ethical example drawn from a primitive culture. As
Suard wrote in his "Réflexions préliminaires": "It is very likely
that poetry, which is only for us an artificial language, used to
be the simple and natural language of men at the time when
languages and societies were first constituted" (Variétés, 1:182).
But in Suard's mind, poetic instruction was not only a matter of
taste, it also dealt with morality:

> There is more to it: the advantage afforded by poetry is not limited
> to the expression of simple truth derived from speculation. Its main
> object is to interest, to move, to excite to the cause of virtue. . . .
> Example is the only moralist that can be useful, and nothing more
> powerfully excites the understanding or the heart than virtue when
> it[']s shown under its most attractive features. (Variétés, 3:104)

Here again Suard seems to echo Blair (who himself follows
Smith's definition from The Theory of Moral Sentiments), who
writes in his Critical Dissertation: "We behold no debasing passion among Fingal's warriors. . . . Ossian felt strongly himself;
and the heart, when uttering its native language, never fails, by
powerful sympathy, to affect the heart."[26]

The last living proof of Suard's influence on late-eighteenth-
century French taste was represented by Madame de Staël. Shel-
tered from the Empire's "bad taste" in her Swiss retreat at Coppet, Germaine Necker was as much an Ossian enthusiast as her
archenemy Napoleon, though in a different way. Having often
met Suard in the prerevolutionary Paris salon of her mother,
Madame Necker, around 1765,[27] she did not forget those childhood lessons, and continued to cultivate the original spirit of
enlightened Ossianism. After the Revolution, while exiled from
France at Bonaparte's request, she often wrote to Suard, asking
him to help her "purify [her] taste, or to use a better phrase,
[her] aesthetics," and she was convinced, along with her Hutch-

esonian masters, that there was "something higher in the decision of putting taste and morality under the same head" (letter
9, 4 November 1804). Madame de Staël's correspondence with
Suard covers some thirty years, until they both died, at some
months' interval, in 1817. Because he was some thirty years her
senior, and because he still lived in France, Suard was more wor-
ried than Madame de Staël about the general lowering of stan-
dards in his country. In a letter to her, alluding to the Empire's
censorship and the general lack of individual freedom, he compares contemporary Paris to Rome in the late Empire, and sees
only England [Britain] and printing as possible instruments of a
regeneration that could not have taken place in Rome (letter 4,
9 October 1802). Suard and Madame de Staël often asked their
mutual friend, Pierre Prévost, a professor of philosophy and
physicist from Geneva who, significantly, translated Blair's *Lectures on Rhetoric and Belles Lettres* into French in 1806, to carry
their mail through the Franco-Swiss border (letter 11, 3 May
1804).

Thanks to Suard's lessons, Ossian and belles lettres shaped
Madame de Staël's influential literary theory into the famous di-
chotomy between the *littérature du Nord* and the *littérature du
Midi* in *De la littérature considérée dans ses rapports avec les institutions sociales* (1800). Ossian's promotion to literary classic, in the
conclusion of Blair's *Critical Dissertation* ("We may boldly assign
him a place among those whose works are to last for ages"),[28] is
repeated one last time on the eve on the French Romantic period. Madame de Staël goes even further, interpreting Ossian as
the "origin" of northern literature, just as she defines Homer as
the "first source" of its southern equivalent.[29] However, in the
France of 1800, Ossian did not possess the freedom of the Romantics. As Suard, inspired by Blair, did in the 1760s, Madame
de Staël pictures him as a melancholy and virtuous Homer,
closer to the real author, Macpherson, than to the romantic per-
sonae of Byron or Shelley. In the same work, she praises Blair's
*Lectures* as "the best book [on eloquence] that can be found in
England [Britain]" (203).

Subsequently, in her novel *Corinne, ou l'Italie* (1807), Madame
de Staël imagines the perfect, though impossible, union of con-
traries between her Italianated English-born heroine, the neo-
classic poetess Corinne, and the young melancholy Scottish
peer Oswald, whose name suggests that of Oscar. What Madame

de Staël gathers from Ossian is expressed in Corinne's judgment on two paintings from her imaginary gallery, where "history and poetry make one with the landscape in a pleasing manner." One painting shows Cincinnatus leaving his plough in a rich southern setting, whereas the second painting shows the son of Cairbar sleeping for three days and three nights on his father's tomb, waiting for the bard to pay the last tributes to his father's memory. Madame de Staël describes the scene through Corinne's mouth: "The bard can be seen in the distance, walking down from the hill; the father's shadow is gliding over the clouds; the countryside is all frost; the trees, though stripped of their leaves, are moved by the wind, and their dead boughs and dry leaves follow the direction of the storm."[30] The painting draws tears in Oswald's sentimental Scottish eyes and prompts Corinne to sing Scottish romances to "the simple notes" of the harp, an instrument that is symbolically dual, both Apollonian and Celtic.

But Madame de Staël goes further in using a mixture of Ossianic and classical themes. One of the romances tells of "a warrior's farewell to his country and his mistress," but as Macpherson's pseudo-Gaelic epic, in eighteenth-century English, allowing the narrator to evoke Corinne's touching way of uttering the words "no more" that she calls "the most harmonious and the most sensitive in the English language" (189–90). As Madame de Staël shows, Ossian helped France to find new settings and inspirations, and to shape the nation's notion of sensibility under the reassuring form of a measured English prose. In Madame de Staël's systematic mind, as in that of Suard, the traditional distinction between genres still prevailed but, in keeping with Scottish belles-lettres criticism, it could no longer remain as clear-cut as in French classicism. As Blair wrote in his *Lectures*, "The truth is, verse and prose, on some occasions, run into one another, like light and shade."[31] The two novels that Chateaubriand published upon his return from emigration to England, *Atala, ou Les Amours de deux sauvages dans le désert* (1801) and *René, ou Les Effets des passions* (1802–5), illustrate Blair's point eloquently. They were not Ossianic in subject matter, as the failed productions of the Empire's official art. But they were full of poetic prose descriptions of the Scottish wilderness and abounded in melancholy feelings. French Romanticism was already at hand.

Thus, Suard's dual discovery of Ossian and Scottish belles lettres helped France to come to terms with its inner cultural contradictions between 1760 and the emergence of a self-styled
French Romanticism after 1820. It would be too easy, and totally wrong, to ascribe the resistance of neoclassicism in France
to Suard or even Madame de Staël's supposed aesthetic conservatism. Only in 1834 could Victor Hugo boast his bold and unprecedented transposition of the French Revolution's political
change in linguistic and literary terms, when he wrote: "I put a
red Liberty cap on the old dictionary."[32] As I have tried to show,
the short-term cultural consequences of the French Revolution
played a much more decisive part in the persistence of the pre-
revolutionary idiom, though in a somewhat debased form. To
those who blame late-eighteenth- or early-nineteenth-century
France for its blindness to possible Romantic interpretations of
Ossian, the study of Suard's influence can oppose one valid justification: France long remained faithful to early belletristic Ossianism because it received it from its original source, in the
Scottish Enlightenment.

## NOTES

1. Suard's translation of the first volume of Robertson's *History of the Reign of the Emperor Charles V* (1769), *L'Histoire de Charles-Quint*, appeared in 1771.

2. Friedrich-Melchior, baron de Grimm, *Correspondance littéraire, philosophique et critique*, 16 vols. (Paris, 1877–82), 5:67.

3. See Alfred C. Hunter, *J. B. A. Suard: Un introducteur de la littérature anglaise en France* (Paris, 1925).

4. Fiona J. Stafford, *The Sublime Savage: A Study of James Macpherson and the Poems of Ossian* (Edinburgh, 1988), 4.

5. Reproduced in John Rae, *Life of Adam Smith* (London, 1895), 211.

6. Anne-Robert-Jacques Turgot, baron de l'Aulne, *Œuvres de M. Turgot*, 9 vols. (Paris, 1808–11), 9:156.

7. Diderot, *Œuvres*, 20 vols. (Paris, 1875–77), 19:67.

8. Richard B. Sher, *Church and University in the Scottish Enlightenment: The Moderate Literati of Edinburgh* (Princeton and Edinburgh, 1985).

9. Quoted in David Raynor, "Ossian and Hume," in *Ossian Revisited*, ed. Howard Gaskill (Edinburgh, 1991), 157. The "two stupid reviews" to which Blair referred were the *Monthly Review*, a major opponent of the cause of Ossian, and the *Critical Review*, where Smollett had praised Ossian.

10. Jean-Baptiste-Antoine Suard, *Variétés littéraires,*_8 vols. (Paris, 1803 [An 12]), 1:198.

11. Voltaire, "Articles extraits de la *Gazette littéraire de l'Europe*," (mars–

novembre 1764), vol. 4 of *Mélanges*, in *Œuvres complètes*, 52 vols. (Paris, 1877–85), 25:161–62.

12. Robert Morell Schmitz, *Hugh Blair* (New York, 1948), 44.

13. *The Prose Works of William Wordsworth*, ed. W. J. B. Owen and Jane Worthington Smyser, 3 vols. (Oxford, 1974), 3:71n.

14. See Philippe Caron, "Aux Origines de la notion contemporaine de 'Littérature.' Le lexique et la configuration des grands secteurs du savoir profane en langue française de 1680 à 1760" (Ph.D. diss., University of Nancy II, 1987), 137.

15. Victorine de Chastenay, *Mémoires de Mme de Chastenay, 1771–1815* (Paris, 1987), 206.

16. Hugh Blair, "A Critical Dissertation on the Poems of Ossian" (1763), in *The Poems of Ossian, the Son of Fingal* (Edinburgh, 1812), 423.

17. François-René, vicomte de Chateaubriand, *Œuvres complètes de Chateaubriand*, 12 vols. (Paris, 1859–61), 3:135.

18. John Robertson, *The Scottish Enlightenment and the Militia Issue* (Edinburgh, 1985).

19. Hume to Wiliam Strahan, [August 1770], *The Letters of David Hume*, 2 vols., ed. J. Y. T. Greig (Oxford, 1932), 2:230.

20. Hugh Honour, *Neo-Classicism* (Harmondsworth, 1968), 65.

21. *Poems of Ossian*, 405.

22. Paul Van Tieghem, *Ossian en France* (Paris, 1917), 208.

23. *Poems of Ossian*, viii.

24. Quoted in Werner Hofmann, *Une Epoque en rupture, 1750–1830* (Paris, 1995), 322.

25. *Poems of Ossian*, 389.

26. Blair, *Critical Dissertation*, in *Poems of Ossian*, 443–44. Cf. Adam Smith, *The Theory of Moral Sentiments*, ed. D. D. Raphael and A. L. Macfie (Oxford, 1976), 10.

27. Robert de Luppé, introduction, *Madame de Staël et Suard: Correspondance inédite (1786–1817)* (Geneva, 1970), 8. The letters cited in the remainder of this paragraph are drawn from this collection.

28. *Poems of Ossian*, 448.

29. Germaine Necker, baronne de Staël-Holstein, *De la Littérature considérée dans ses rapports avec les institutions sociales* (1800 [An 9]; Paris, 1991), 216n.

30. Germaine Necker, Baronne de Staël-Holstein, *Corinne, ou l'Italie* (1807; Paris, 1841), 189.

31. Hugh Blair, *Lectures on Rhetoric and Belles Lettres*, 3 vols. (1783; Basil, 1801), 3:99.

32. Victor Hugo, "Réponse à un acte d'accusation," January 1834, *Les Contemplations* (1856).

# The French Taste for Scottish Literary Romanticism

## Andrew Hook

SCOTLAND'S PERFORMANCE IN THE AREA OF CULTURAL EXPORTS WENT ON improving throughout the eighteenth century; in the early decades of the nineteenth century, however, boom times arrived. In this period, the entire Western world became an eagerly receptive market for Scottish cultural goods. The nature of these goods was inevitably diverse, ranging from the ideas of the Scottish Enlightenment (Scottish commonsense philosophy above all) to the products of Scottish literary romanticism (especially Sir Walter Scott). Yet there was a certain uniformity in the reception of Scottish culture throughout Europe and America. Countries, as it were, bought into the whole package. Thus, it is not only in America that a taste for Thomas Reid and Dugald Stewart, Lord Kames and Hugh Blair and Adam Smith, coincided with an enthusiasm for *Ossian* and Scott; the pattern was the same in Germany, Italy, and France. Whether there is any kind of link between a taste for one group and a taste for the other is not my concern here, but I do wish to make it clear that Scottish literary romanticism represents only one strain in the Scottish contribution to French culture in this period.

Despite what I have just said about the Scottish cultural package being a kind of universal import, it would be foolish to argue that local conditions and circumstances had no bearing on individual countries' receptiveness to what Scotland had on offer. Thus, students of the Scottish contribution to eighteenth-century American culture make much of the facilitating factor represented by the close economic ties between the American colonies and the west of Scotland, as well as a range of other considerations that seem to produce a kind of sympathetic togetherness between Scottish and American society. These are circumstances likely to encourage American receptiveness to

Scotland's cultural exports. What, then, is the position in the case of Scotland's cultural relations with France?

In the first place, there is very little to suggest that the French case is in any way parallel to the American one. French society and Scottish society, that is, have almost nothing in the way of shared characteristics that might lead to French responsiveness to Scottish culture. On the other hand, circumstances did exist which made it probable that the French would at least recognize and identify Scottish culture without too much difficulty. The point is an important one because cultural historians assume much too readily that Scottish culture was everywhere recognized as Scottish even after the Union of 1707. In my view, that is a mistake. In the eighteenth century, and even more so in the nineteenth and twentieth centuries, the Scottishness of Scottish culture has always been problematical to the outside world. A modern English scholar, having devoted several paragraphs to citing evidence of nineteenth-century French enthusiasm for "the Scotch philosophy," concludes: "Obviously, so widespread an attention to this philosophy made for general Anglophilism."[1] In 1834 a Frenchman noted, in regard to the Sorbonne professor M. Villemain's thirty-seven lectures on the development of French literature in the latter half of the eighteenth century, that five were devoted to English writers: Samuel Richardson, David Hume, William Robertson, Edward Gibbon, and James Macpherson.[2] That's a margin of three to two in favor of the unrecognized Scots! Byron is no doubt a special case, at best only a marginal Scot. But it is worth noting that amid the general French enthusiasm for Byron—second only to that for Scott among British romantic writers—only Chateaubriand seems to have been aware of Byron's Scottish background, and then only because he saw a parallel between Byron's Scotland and his own Brittany.[3] For Europeans and Americans, the Scottishness of Scottish culture is not inevitably self-evident; and this is particularly so when the Scots in question are the North British literati.

My point, however, is that the general problem seems less applicable to the particular case of France and Scotland. This is because there are reasonable grounds for supposing that French consciousness of Scotland's existence, independent of England, survived into the eighteenth century. I hesitate to make too much of the so-called "Auld Alliance"—that medieval connection which linked Scotland and France in political terms through their shared opposition to the power of England. That alliance could have existed only as some sort of distant folk memory. But political connections had continued to bring France and Scotland together well into the modern period: from the time of the French Mary Queen of Scots and the Scottish civil wars, through to the Jacobite Pretender's Court at St. Germain in the eighteenth century. (That old link was to receive an unexpected but quite significant new life in the period 1796–1803, when members of the exiled Bourbon royal family took up residence in Holyrood Palace in Edinburgh.)

That this historic relationship between France and Scotland remained a meaningful one is best demonstrated by the French government's attitude toward Scotland in the years of the revolutionary war between France and Great Britain. France seems seriously to have believed in the 1790s that Scotland might be persuaded to join with France, overthrow English domination, and create a new Scottish republic. The existence of the Scottish Friends of the People and popular agitation for reform were seen as evidence of Scottish support for revolutionary principles; Thomas Muir, the Scottish reformer martyr, was welcomed as a hero on his arrival in France in 1797; and various publications asserted the Scottish right to freedom. One of the most famous was a letter to the people of Great Britain published in the *Moniteur*. Fascinating here is the way in which the case for Scottish freedom is made by an appeal to an heroic Scottish past: will the descendants of the immortal Ossian, those who successfully resisted the Romans, not be free? Did Wallace fight, Buchanan and Fletcher write, in vain? Discussing the same subject in 1799, Théophile Mandar, a leading revolutionary politician, appealed even more histrionically to the poet-warrior Ossian to inspire his Scots descendants with a love of liberty, ancient courage, and hatred of tyranny.[4]

Thus, politics helped to maintain a French consciousness of Scotland's separation from England. Of course, it is impossible not to notice how Scottish political reality is dissolved by an appeal to a wholly literary-based, romanticized past. The French reception of the Scottish literary tradition, which produced precisely this sense of Scottish history, is the main focus of my concern here.

Given the historical links that kept alive a French awareness of Scotland, France would seem to be an excellent market for the reception of Scottish cultural exports. In terms of the Scottish Enlightenment, this proved to be exactly the case. Eighteenth-century France was familiar with the work—and sometimes the persons—of most of the illustrious Scottish literati: Hume and Smith, Ferguson and Robertson, Reid and Stewart, Blair and Kames. The works of Tobias Smollett and James Thomson, Henry Mackenzie's *Man of Feeling* and James Macpherson's *Ossian*, were also familiar. And recent scholarship has confirmed that early nineteenth-century French philosophy was much influenced by the Scottish commonsense school: Destutt de Tracy, Royer-Collard, Victor Cousin, Théodore Jouffroy, and the group known as "les idéologues" all seem to have found Scottish philosophy in its post-Humean stage much to their taste.[5]

But the situation of Scottish literature in eighteenth- and early-nineteenth-century France was entirely different. In France, as in Italy and some other European countries, Scottish literature was facing trade barriers of a well-established and powerful kind. Established French culture was classical and neoclassical in its forms and themes. France was part of the essentially classical civilization of the Mediterranean world. France gloried in the achievements of its neoclassical writers, dramatists, architects, and painters. As far as official literary culture was concerned, French scholars and critics were convinced that their national traditions were all firmly in a classical mold. What the Scottish literary tradition had to offer—from an early eighteenth-century work like Allan Ramsay's *The Gentle Shepherd*, through John Home's *Douglas*, James Beattie's *The Minstrel*, and Macpherson's *Ossian*, to Burns and above all Scott—was something wholly different: not classicism but romanticism. The taste for Scottish literature went on increasing in Europe and America throughout the eighteenth century as literary sensibilities everywhere became more and more attuned to what would eventually become the music of romanticism. Scottish literature triumphed in the early decades of the nineteenth century because those were the years when romanticism finally established itself, for a period at least, as the dominant cultural force throughout the Western world. But the tradition of the new always meets resistance, and in the case of romanticism, this was nowhere more true than in those countries where the classical translation was most deeply rooted. Thus, in France a powerful and entrenched cultural establishment fought long and hard against acceptance of the new literature of romanticism, regularly denouncing it as a foreign import wholly out of character with the true traditions of French culture, and calling for resistance to all such "productions ossianiques, galliques, germaniques, helvétiques, shakespeariques and gothiques."[6] As the reference to *Ossian* here makes clear, Scottish literature was recognized as very much part of this wave of foreign writing; hence, rather than easy access to a receptive French readership, Scottish literature, and in particular its most popular manifestations in the form of Scottish literary romanticism, was from the beginning caught up in a central, ongoing, and bitterly contested debate about the very nature of French culture itself. This debate was at its height in the period around the fall of the Empire and the restoration of the monarchy, and thus inevitably had a political dimension. But in the end there was no simple division between conservatives and liberals. Pro- and antiromantic factions sprang up across the political spectrum. Different journals and magazines supported one or the other side; critics, publishers, and writers all became involved; the salons of Paris echoed with the debate. But when the contest was at its fiercest—roughly in the period from 1816 to 1830—Scotland, Scottish writings, and above all Walter Scott, became crucial contributors to the debate.

Scott did not become known in France until after 1815. The initial Scottish attack on French classicism had been led a full generation earlier by James Macpherson, whose alleged translations of the third-century Celtic bard Ossian played a key role in beginning to define the nature of the new romantic sensibility. For those who began to open up the debate over romanticism in France in the early years of the nineteenth century—A. W. von Schlegel, Simonde de Sismondi, Benjamin Constant, and other members of Madame de Staël's salon at Coppet in Switzerland—Ossian was a central player. In Madame de Staël's own books, *De La Littérature* (1800) and *De L'Allemagne* (1814), which were debated everywhere as providing a fully developed theory of romanticism, Ossian and the ossianique are foregrounded. Madame de Staël sees romanticism above all as a literature of the North, to be contrasted with the classical literature of the Mediterranean South. The Scottish Ossian is thus enormously important because he can be seen as the Northern Homer, the source of the literature of the North, to be set alongside his classical counterpart.

*Ossian* had been available to French readers since 1776–77 in the translation by Le Tourneur. But as elsewhere in Europe, it took some time for the *Ossian* vogue to get underway in France. Chateaubriand became an *Ossian* enthusiast during his trip to America in the 1790s; in London in 1793 he was translating John Smith's *Gaelic Antiquities* (1780), a kind of alternative *Ossian* that became widely known in France and was frequently published alongside Le Tourneur's version of Macpherson. Chateaubriand's own *Génie du Christianisme* (1802) contains numerous Ossianic allusions, and the anguished hero, René, tries to work out his sorrows in the barren mountains of Scotland. Amédée Pichot, later to become a minor writer and translator and a kind of entrepreneur in the Franco-Scottish literary exchange, read *Ossian* as a young man about 1810. By then Pierre Baour-Lormian had published new versions of Le Tourneur's Macpherson in his *Poésies Galliques*.

According to Pichot's biographer, "Ossian made a deep and lasting impression on [Pichot's] imagination, and began the romantic interest in the far north of Scotland which was to be fostered and developed by his subsequent reading and travels."[7] It appears that Baour-Lormian's *Ossian* first dazzled Lamartine. In *Les Confidences* (1849) he tells us how he was overwhelmed by the world of *Ossian* when he was sixteen: he plunged into "this sea of shadows, of blood, of tears, of ghosts, of foam, of snow, of mists, of wintry cold."[8] The Alpine landscape and mountains around him became versions of the archetypal Ossianic settings of the poems. But Madame de Staël, Chateaubriand, Pichot, and Lamartine are no more than examples of a French taste for *Ossian* that had been fast developing since the closing years of the eighteenth century. Looking back from the perspective of 1821, a writer in *Le Miroir* had no doubt about the significance of *Ossian* in the development of the French taste for romanticism:

Having emerged from the forests of Germany, the romantic style was launched on the Ossianic shores of Scotland, from where it was hurled upon France. Welcomed with enthusiasm by a people in love with novelty, it had to struggle only against some partisans of ancient literary doctrines whose voices were smothered by the sounds of the harps of the North.[9]

The most famous of all the French enthusiasts for *Ossian* was the Emperor Napoleon himself. Throughout all his military campaigns, the poems of Ossian remained his favorite reading. In 1816, in conversation with Lady Malcolm in St. Helena, he boasted that his influence was responsible for bringing the poems into such vogue throughout Europe: "It was I—I made them the fashion."[10] Clearly there is an element of megalomania here, but Napoleon's enthusiastic patronage of the poems was unquestionably important, particularly in the context of *Ossian*'s influence not just on literature but on the arts in general. In early nineteenth-century France, the vogue for *Ossian* is apparent not just in the debate over literary romanticism but in painting, music, and the theater. Paul Duqueylar produced the first French Ossianic painting in 1801: *Ossian Singing the Funeral Hymn of a Maiden*. Napoleon's patronage was crucial: both Gérard's *Ossian Evoking the Spirits with the Sound of his Harp on the Banks of the Lora* and Girodet's *Ossian and His Warriors Welcoming the Heroes of France to Elysium* were commissioned for Malmaison, the Empress Josephine's Parisian residence, while Ingres's *The Dream of Ossian* was commissioned in 1812 for the imperial apartments in the Quirinal in Rome. The Barbus group of young artists in David's atelier in Paris were all *Ossian* enthusiasts, and numerous other French Ossianic paintings were subsequently produced.

Ingres probably saw Le Sueur's opera *Ossian ou les bardes* —with words by Baour-Lormian—produced in Paris in 1804 as another result of Napoleon's patronage: Le Sueur had been working on the opera since the 1790s. A second opera on an Ossianic theme, *Uthal*, with music by Étienne-Nicolas Méhul and words by Bins de Saint-Victor, was produced in 1806. And earlier, in 1798, A. V. Arnault had written a tragedy on an Ossianic theme called *Oscar, son of Ossian*.

Given this degree of French enthusiasm for *Ossian*, it is perhaps surprising that little evidence has emerged of French interest in John Home's play, *Douglas*. *Douglas* held the stage in Britain and America for almost a hundred years as an outstanding example of modern tragedy: Young Norval and Lady Randolph were parts played by all the leading performers of the period. First performed in 1756, *Douglas* predated Macpherson's *Ossian* by several years, but there is little doubt that the play's enduring success owed much to the way it could be "ossi-

anized," or made assimilable to the ancient Scottish elegiac Ossianic world. Voltaire, however, mistakenly believed that John
Home was David Hume's brother, and no French translation of
*Douglas* seems to have been made until that by Amédée Pichot
in 1822. The French Baron Baert-Duholant who, like Madame
de Staël's friend, Benjamin Constant, studied at the University
of Edinburgh in the 1780s, subsequently published an account
of his stay in Great Britain in which he mentions *Douglas*'s con-
tinuing popularity, but there is little to suggest that the play
ever quite caught on in France.

France's relative lack of interest in Home's *Douglas* warns us
not to assume that the French excitement over *Ossian* necessarily led to an interest in Scottish literary romanticism in general.
Chateaubriand's enthusiasm for *Ossian* does seem to have led
him to Beattie's *The Minstrel* (1771–74) and in due course to
Byron; Pichot, as we have seen, went on from Macpherson to a
general admiration for, and interest in, Scottish writing. But
there is no evidence that the French reading public, or even the
literary world, followed a similar pattern. During and after the
Revolution, and under the Empire, there is no sign of any particular interest in recent Scottish writing. However, for the various
political reasons alluded to earlier, Scotland never entirely faded
out of French consciousness, and there is some evidence that
this awareness was given new life after Napoleon's final defeat
at Waterloo. Occupied Paris seems to have been fascinated by
the Scots regiments in the Allied army; their kilts and tartans
and bagpipes—echoes perhaps of that familiar Ossianic
world?—were specially noteworthy. And at the Paris opera a
new ballet, *L'Heureux Retour*, was performed with special additions, including a party of Scottish Highlanders dancing traditional reels.

Perhaps these circumstances help to explain French interest
in at least one contemporary Scottish work that played a crucial
part in the romanticizing of an heroic Scottish past: Jane Porter's 1810 novel, *The Scottish Chiefs,* which did more than any
other single work to popularize Wallace, Bruce, and the struggle
for Scottish independence throughout Europe and America. A
French translation appeared soon after the novel's original appearance, and it was reprinted in 1814 and 1820. A melodrama
based on the text was written by the immensely productive,
popular dramatist Guilbert de Pixérécourt in 1815, but perform-

ances were banned, allegedly because the work expressed hatred
for the English! However, in 1819 *Les Chefs Écossais* was given
forty-six performances in Paris at Porte-Saint-Martin, and thirteen performances in the provinces. Jane Porter's novel and its
great success have traditionally been seen as creating at least one
of the factors which encouraged Walter Scott to look again at
the early chapters of *Waverley*, and then decide to go on to complete and publish the first of the Waverley Novels in 1814. The
Parisian boulevard performances of *The Scottish Chiefs* may well
have done something similar, by encouraging French interest in
the subject matter of the early Waverley Novels. By 1819 Scott's
name was beginning to be known in France, but it was only in
the 1820s that Scott would achieve his astonishing success,
bringing to an extraordinary consummation the French taste
for Scottish literary romanticism that had begun with Macpherson's *Ossian*.

There can be no doubt that in the decade 1820–30 Scotland
and France were linked culturally in an embrace stronger than
anything the politics of the "Auld Alliance" had ever achieved.
The debate in politics and literature between the old and the
new was at its fiercest in these years, but the ordinary reading
public, and ordinary theatergoers in Paris, were already, as it
were, voting with their feet. The new melodramas presented in
the boulevard theaters in the city were increasingly popular,
whatever the views of traditional critics on their artistic merit.
Similarly, the new gothic and historical prose romances, with
their frequently lurid and sensational subjects and themes, were
very much to the popular taste, whatever the views of national-
ist and conservative critics. But even as early as 1820, all this
excitement and debate and cultural upheaval was beginning to
take on a strongly Scottish dimension. Soon Scotland itself was
a topic of debate among writers and artists, critics and journalists, intellectuals and the leaders of fashionable society.

Was this renewed interest in Scotland a consequence of the
French success of the Waverley Novels? Or were Scott and his
fiction so immensely popular in France because they were
caught up in, and helped to give identity to, an existing French
inclination that was waiting to be exploited? I am not able to
give a clear answer to these questions. I have no doubt at all that
in France, as elsewhere, the existing recognition of Scotland, in
almost mythopoetic terms, as a northern land of vaguely Ossia-

nic splendor and gloom, did much to facilitate Scott's enormous success. The Scotland that Scott wrote about in the early Waverley Novels was in no way identical to that created by Macpherson's *Ossian*. Scott's Scottish past was the past of history, and relatively recent history at that—not of some remote and legendary bygone age. Unlike Macpherson, Scott evoked recognizable Scottish scenes and landscapes: identifiable mountains, lochs, rivers, castles, towns. Nonetheless, readers, particularly perhaps foreign readers, might well have seen in Scott a kind of confirmation—now given all the authenticity of specific people, events, settings, landscapes—of what they had already imagined Scotland to be.

My own view, then, is that Scott was a success waiting to happen; he was the right person in the right place at the right time. Yet there is still no disputing that Scott had an immense impact in France simply as a writer in his own right. When his work began to be read in France, Byron was easily the most popular foreign writer, appealing to the growing French taste for the new romanticism. But in terms of popular readership, and as a model for French writers, Byron in the 1820s would be quickly overtaken by his Scottish compatriot. Scott soon had no rival in the range and depth of his impact on French culture as a whole during the Restoration period.

Scott's novels began to appear in French translations from 1816, when a version of *Guy Mannering* was published. By the end of 1820, nine of the Waverley Novels had been translated. French knowledge of Scott's fiction largely preceded knowledge of Scott's poetry; no extensive translation of the poems appeared before that of Amédée Pichot in 1821. But French awareness of Scott was growing even before his works were becoming generally available. The end of hostilities between France and Britain after 1815 inevitably meant a rapid increase in direct contacts between the two countries. The British flocked to Paris, while French travelers visited Britain, often to report back to the French administration on the state of the British economy and on British society in general. Several of these French visitors published accounts of their travels, but the first to appear in 1815 was a record of a visit to Britain several years earlier: Louis Simond's *Journal of a Tour and Residence in Great Britain during the years 1810, 1811,* published in Edinburgh in 1815, and in Paris in 1816 and 1817. Having lived in the United States for twenty

years, Simond visited Britain with his wife and niece, Charlotte
Wilkes of New York, and was already well aware of contemporary developments in British literature. In America Simond had
become a reader of the *Edinburgh Review,* and in Edinburgh he
met Francis Jeffrey, who would subsequently travel to New York
to marry his niece. A close friend of Stendhal, Simond would
become a key figure in promoting romanticism in France.

Since Simond's 1815 travel book reveals him as a Scott enthusiast, it cannot be doubted that he had much to say of this excit-
ing new Scottish author in the Parisian salons and artistic circles
in which he moved. Again, as early as November 1817, the
writer Charles Nodier, another future visitor to Scotland from
France, was reviewing *Old Mortality* in the *Journal des Débats.*
Thus, in the period 1815–20, French interest in Scott was already stirring. In the 1820s, however, it would cease to be an
interest and become a vogue, a fashion, one might even say a
mania. Looking back from 1852, Charles de Boigne, author of a
short account of his stay in the Scottish Highlands, wrote of
Scott: "after having invented Scotland, he made it fashionable."[11] As far as masses of ordinary French readers were concerned, Boigne was almost certainly right. An advertisement of
1840 suggested that by then at least two million copies of the
Waverley Novels had been published in France, and for the vast
majority of their readers Scott and Scotland must have been
well-nigh interchangeable. In 1832 Stendhal suggested that
Scott had already had some two hundred imitators in France;[12] a
modern scholar's version is that in the period 1823–26, "Walter
Scott and his novels generated a virtual *Waverley* craze. Scores of
French adolescents, taking *Quentin Durward* and other stories as
their models, composed a flood of historical fiction."[13]

The critics and commentators of the day make it clear that it
is almost impossible to exaggerate the French Scott craze. Here
is the critic of *L'Abeille* in 1821, writing on *Kenilworth:*

> Here for your Walter Scott! Here for your Walter Scott! Hurry up gen-
> tlemen, and you especially, ladies; it is marvellous, it is new; hurry;
> the first edition is exhausted; the second is reserved in advance; the
> third will disappear as soon as it appears from the press. Run, buy;
> good or bad, what does it matter! Sir Walter has put his name to it,
> that is enough.[14]

All this was obviously heavily ironic, but the point of Scott's amazing popularity is merely underlined. (This particular comment ends with the exclamation: "Long live England and the English!" Is this another irony, or simply an example of the identity problem that I regard as Scotland's perennial difficulty?) Again in 1821, a writer in *Le Miroir* confirmed that the Scott vogue was already well underway: "Thanks to the library Ladvocat, the name of Sir Walter Scott is in every mouth and his works in every salon."[15]

The early 1820s saw a rush of articles in the French periodicals and newspapers on Scott, Scotland, Scottish literature, and Scottish themes. Nodier, Pichot, and other French travelers to Scotland were responsible for many of these articles. Philarète Chasles, for example, another key figure in the Franco-Scottish cultural exchange, wrote frequently for both the *Revue Encyclopédique* and the *Revue Britannique*. Chasles had been a refugee in Britain for a number of years and had become an enthusiast for English and Scottish romantic writers, including both Scott and Burns. The Scott vogue undoubtedly stimulated French interest in Scottish writers in general. Chasles and others, including Pichot, and other French travelers in Scotland, helped to make Burns known at least in French literary circles. Chasles even undertook translations of Burns, and some of them appeared in the French periodicals. What has to be recognized, however, is that the French interest in Burns or Jane Porter or Hogg—or even in Macpherson's *Ossian* —is not even remotely on the scale of the commitment to Scott.

In the late 1820s Scott was a major force in almost every aspect of French culture—literature, the theater, opera, music, songs, and paintings. Even street and household culture was affected. Pontmartin, whose *Mémoires* appeared in 1885–86, insisted that in 1827 the Scott craze was to be found in "costumes, fashions, furniture, shop-signs and theater-hoardings."[16] This is the period of cravats and bonnets "à la Walter Scott," and of the duchess of Berry's masked balls, where all the guests dressed as characters out of the Waverley Novels. Pixérécourt and other popular dramatists plundered the novels to fill Paris's boulevard theaters with a whole series of Scott melodramas. As many as four different productions were sometimes available on the same night in 1827. The story was much the same with opera: *La Dame Blanche,* with music by Boieldieu and libretto by Scribe, was first performed in 1825, and it would receive one thousand performances before the end of the century. The French were major contributors to the century's one hundred or so Scott-inspired operas, and Berlioz, Bizet, and Boieldieu are only among the most famous French composers who found inspiration in Scott. In French painting, too, the Scott theme is much in evidence. At the Paris Salon exhibition in 1831, over thirty canvases were directly inspired by the Waverley Novels, and their painters included Delacroix, Delaroche, and Alfred and Tony Johannot. (Delacroix, indeed, seems to have had a special interest in things Scottish: in 1831 he wrote to a friend telling the story of "Tam O'Shanter," which he claimed to have read in the original, and there is at least one "Tam O'Shanter" drawing of Tam's gray mare.)

Given that the Scott vogue seems to have invaded almost every aspect of French cultural life, one can understand all too readily Stendhal's suggestion that the French nation had gone mad over Walter Scott. But there remains the issue of how far Scott was identified with Scotland, how far an enthusiasm for the Waverley Novels spilled over into at least an interest in all things Scottish. What is reasonably clear is that Scott's own appeal eventually transcended even the major division which characterized French literary culture in the 1820s. At the opening of the decade, the classical critics were dismissive of all prose fiction: serious literature meant only poetry and drama. But Scott's historical fiction gained at least a measure of respectability for the novel form. Similarly, although Scott was originally taken up by French romanticists, for whom Byron and Scott became easily the most significant foreign authors, the political divisions between the royalist and liberal romantic camps did not in any way interfere with the general appreciation of Scott. So perhaps it is best to see Scott as unique, a special case, independent of any Scottish context.

For many ordinary French readers of Scott, this could easily have been the case. But for some, at least, Scott could not have emerged as just another foreign, or even English author. I have already argued that Scott gave a new and decisive definition to vague French images of Scotland deriving from the Ossianic tradition. But particularly for those who moved in the influential circles of French intellectual discussion in the salons of Paris, Scott's link with Scotland must have been self-evident. Louis Simond, mentioned above, a Scott enthusiast whose account of his travels in Scotland was published just when the first translations of the Waverley Novels were beginning to appear in Paris, illustrates the point very well. Simond frequented the salon Stapfer. Philip Albert Stapfer was a Protestant clergyman of cosmopolitan interests whose salon inherited the liberal tradition of the Coppet group and was attended by bourgeois liberals, writers, journalists, professors and travelers. The same group also attended the biweekly receptions of the art critic Etienne Delécluze. British ideas, and British writers such as Byron and Scott, were welcomed in these groups, and there can be no doubt that Simond had discussed Scott, Jeffrey, and the *Edinburgh Review,* and shared his knowledge of Scottish culture with Stendhal, Benjamin Constant, Prosper Mérimée, Victor Cousin, and many other artists and intellectuals. Throughout the 1820s Simond remained a key figure in Franco-British cultural relations, close to the editorial staff of the *Globe* newspaper, a major force in the French debate over romanticism, run by Stendhal, Delécluze, J.-J. Ampère, and others.

The significant point is that Simond, with his detailed knowledge of Scott and Scotland, is in no way a unique figure in Parisian cultural circles. It should already be clear that the period 1815–30 saw a steady procession of French visitors to England and Scotland, a substantial proportion of whom went on to publish accounts of their travels, and quite a number of them were figures well known in the Paris salons. In the years immediately after 1815, most of these visitors were, as we have seen, savants mainly interested in the state of British society, its industry, science, and commerce. In a sense, their interest in Scotland was still an interest, broadly speaking, in the Scottish Enlightenment and its social and economic consequences. Thus, the economist J. B. Say came to study the Scottish universities; Charles Dupin was interested in the Scottish seaports and business centers; J. B. Biot investigated scientific research; and in 1822 M.-A. Jullien visited New Lanark to study Robert Owen's famous industrial and social experiment. Around 1821, however, a new kind of French visitor began to appear in Scotland, attracted less by the intellectual achievements of the Enlightenment than by the successes of Scottish literary romanticism. For these French visitors, the trip to Scotland was above all a literary pilgrimage; what they went to see were the places and land-

scapes, scenes and settings, made famous by Scotland's romantic writers. The French, that is, simply joined the Germans,
Americans, Italians, and the rest on the familiar tour of Scotland's classic ground: Edinburgh and the Borders, Loch Katrine
and the Trossachs, the Ossian country, the Scott country, even
the Burns country. In the 1820s alone, some half-dozen accounts of such tours appeared in France, and some at least were
written by figures of major influence in Parisian artistic and cultural life.

Charles Nodier, for example, whose *Promenade from Dieppe to
the Mountains of Scotland* appeared in 1822, was a major voice
in the French debate over romanticism. A Catholic royalist in
politics, he was a regular visitor at the salon of the Deschamps
in rue Saint-Florentin, alongside other royalists such as Victor
Hugo and Alfred de Vigny as well as liberals and even Bonapart-
ists. Freshly returned from Scotland, he must have talked to all
of them about his experiences, emphasizing perhaps what
emerges from his travel book: an extraordinary emotional reaction to Holyrood and Mary Queen of Scots, and a remarkable
veneration for Sir William Wallace. In 1824 Nodier's position in
Parisian circles became even more significant when he was appointed custodian of the Arsenal Library. The influential friends
who nominated him had both accompanied him on his Scottish tour. The spacious Arsenal salon soon became, for royalists
in particular, a successor to that of the Deschamps, and Nodier's
audience expanded to include Hugo, Saint-Beuve, Dumas, de
Vigny, Lamartine, and the philosopher Jouffroy. To the Arsenal
also came the leading romantic painters, including Delacroix,
Alfred Johannot, and Boulanger.

The salon of Mary Clarke became yet another center for the
Scottish theme in Paris. British in background, with a Scots
grandmother, Clarke had settled in France but toured Scotland
in 1822, writing a series of letters to friends in France describing
her experiences. What emerges once again is an enthusiasm for
Scotland's romantic literature and romantic scenery: Melrose
and Edinburgh, Burns and Scott, Scottish ballads and folklore.
These were among the topics of her Paris evenings, when the
guests included Victor Cousin, Thiers of the *Globe*, Stendhal
(with whom she fell out), Ampère, Mérimée, and Claude Fauriel,
an original scholar who would initiate the study of folklore in
France.

Yet another French traveler in Scotland in 1822 was the Marquis de Custine. His book, *Mémoires et Voyages*, did not appear in Paris until 1830, but after 1822 he was also very much part of Paris's literary world, counting among his friends Hugo, Balzac, Lamartine, and Philarète Chasles. A brilliant talker, Custine was thus an important figure in royalist romantic circles, articulating the most intense, personal response to *Ossian* and Ossianic scenes (though less enthusiastic about Scott), and expressing an aristocratic disdain for the growing numbers of ordinary tourists in the Trossachs.

There is good evidence, then, that the Scottish theme had become an important part of French intellectual and artistic life in the 1820s. Each new article in a periodical such as the *Revue Britannique* or *La Quotidienne* or the *Revue Encyclopédique*, each new Scott translation, and each new published account of a visit to Scotland, must have served to keep alive the topic of Scott and Scotland. Of course, Scott himself remains the crucial figure; it was the Waverley Novels that made Scotland familiar territory for an enormous French audience. But it is equally clear that in French literary, artistic, and intellectual circles, Scott was not an isolated figure emerging from a "great unknown." The achievements of the Scottish Enlightenment had long been recognized in France, and from the late eighteenth century the French taste for Scottish literary romanticism had been growing. In the 1820s, with Scott's amazing success, this French interest in things Scottish simply reached new heights. But it must be reiterated that the French experience was not unique, since elsewhere in Europe, in the same period, the Scottish theme was emerging with similar vividness.

I argued earlier that Madame de Staël played a key role in developing the French taste for Scottish literary romanticism. Let me conclude by referring to a comment made by her cousin's son, Louis-Albert Necker de Saussure, a student for two years at the University of Edinburgh from 1806–8, and subsequently professor of geology at Geneva. His Scottish experience seems to have converted Necker de Saussure into a kind of Franco-Scot, and he chose to spend the last twenty years of his life living in Portree on the Hebridean isle of Skye. However, his book describing his Scottish experience in the period 1806–8 was not published until 1821. It appeared, in other words, just at the point when boom times in Franco-Scottish cultural relations were about to begin. The book's characteristics are all suggested by its full title: *Travels in Scotland; Descriptive of the State of Manners, Literature, and Science.* The author, that is, writes more as an intellectual and social observer than as an ardent romanticist of the 1820s kind. He also writes from a profoundly pro-Scottish perspective, much concerned to defend the Scots from English prejudices, insisting on Scotland's significant continental connections with Holland, France, and Switzerland. He is ready even to question whether "the astonishing progress which the Scots have made in the course of the last century" was really a consequence of the Treaty of Union with England. And in his introduction he pays eloquent tribute to Scotland's economic and cultural achievements:

> The Scottish Lowlands show to foreigners their flourishing and popular cities, their seaports animated by the most active commerce, their luxuriant fields, their manufactures carried to the highest point of perfection, and their celebrated Universities, which produced those literary and scientific characters, those profound geniuses, and eloquent legislators, who have given to Scotland that literary renown which it this day enjoys in the estimation of all Europe.[17]

Necker de Saussure clearly has the successes of the Scottish Enlightenment most in mind. At the moment when his book was appearing, however, it was, significantly, Scottish literary romanticism, represented above all by the novels of Sir Walter Scott, that was pushing Scotland's "literary renown" to unprecedented heights in France and all of Europe.

## NOTES

1. Eric Partridge, *The French Romantics' Knowledge of English Literature* (Paris, 1924), 302.
2. Ibid., 310–11.
3. F. Chateaubriand, *Essai sur la littérature Anglaise* (Paris, 1840), 300.
4. For details of the *Moniteur* letter and Mandar, see Margaret I. Bain, *Les Voyageurs Français en Écosse 1770–1830* (Paris, 1931), 104–6.
5. See Victor Cousin, *Les Idéologues et les Écossais* (Paris, 1985).
6. Quoted in Paul T. Comeau, *Diehards and Innovators: The French Romantic Struggle, 1800–1830* (New York, Bern, Frankfurt, Paris, 1988), 52.
7. L. A. Bisson, *Amédée Pichot, A Romantic Prometheus* (Oxford, 1943), 180.

8. Alphonse de Lamartine, *Les Confidences* (Paris, 1900), 118.

9. Quoted in Comeau, *Diehards and Innovators*, 105.

10. Sir Pulteney Malcolm, *A Diary of Saint Helena* (London, 1929), 25.

11. Quoted in Bain, *Les Voyageurs Français en Écosse*, 125.

12. Partridge, *French Romantics' Knowledge of English Literature*, 259.

13. Comeau, *Diehards and Innovators*, 143.

14. Quoted in Comeau, *Diehards and Innovators*, 109.

15. Ibid.

16. Quoted in Partridge, *French Romantics' Knowledge of English Literature*, 121.

17. L.-A. Necker de Saussure, *Travels in Scotland* (London, 1821), iv–v.

# *"Peine forte et dure"*: Scott and France

In 1826, AS IMPENDING FINANCIAL CRISIS SHADOWED HIS HORIZON, Walter Scott recorded a convivial evening spent with friends:

> I could not help thinking in the midst of the glee what late gloom was over the minds of three of the company, Cadell, John Ballantyne, and the Journalist's. What a strange scene if the surge of conversation could suddenly ebb like the tide and [shew] us the state of people's real minds. . . . Life could not be endured were it seen in reality.[1]

An equable man, Scott was also perfectly aware that not only the interests of a good social evening but his interest as a writer lay in preserving the veneer of sociability and steering clear of violent controversy: "God knows I would fight in honourable contest with word or blow for my political opinions but I cannot permit that strife to 'mix its waters with my daily meal,' those waters of bitterness which poison all mutual love and confidence betwixt the well disposed on each side" (*Journal*, 63–64). Reason exerts a powerful check on impulse. Knowing the strength of his passions, he avoided their arousal and regretted occasions when he had been "hurried off [his] feet" into "more forward and more violent" reactions than were compatible with prudence (*Journal*, 93).

Just at this point, however, and against the advice of his publisher and friends, Scott penned the splenetic and provocative "Letters from Malachi Malagrowther on the Proposed Change of Currency." The issue—of limiting the power of the Scottish banks to issue banknotes—came at a moment when Scott was personally sensitive, even to rawness, on matters of financial control. He was the first, ruefully, to recognize the irony of his intervention: "It is ridiculous enough for me in a state of insolvency for the present to be battling about gold and paper currency—it is something like the humorous touch in Hogarth's 'Distressd Poet' where the poor Starveling of the muses is engaged when [in] the abyss of poverty in writing an Essay on payment of the National Debt and his wall is adorn[d] with a plan of the mines of Peru" (*Journal*, 103).[2]

In entering the lists against the government and "this violent experiment on our circulation" (*Journal*, 120), and on the side of the uncontrolled system of credit which was indirectly but certainly proximately responsible for the collapse of his own financial affairs, Scott might be seen as engaged in a kind of self-destructive battle against his own interests, and certainly against prudential politics. In a further twist of irony, as his journal entry notes, the Bank of Scotland, whose ancient rights he saw himself defending, was the very institution which, as the representative of his creditors, was currently threatening to put him under the *"peine forte et dure"* of sequestration.[3] The compounded and conflicting impulses at work in the episode suggest that the exigencies of extreme financial duress exposed some extraordinarily complex tensions in Scott, tensions which we might expect to find reflected elsewhere in his writing. Discussing the "Malachi Letters," Lockhart does not doubt "that the splendida bilis which, as the Diary shows, his own misfortunes had engendered, demanded some escape-valve."[4] But to see it merely as redirected spleen on Scott's part is to miss the extent to which the literal breakup of his fortunes precipitated a crystallization of violent and contradictory passions into the texture of his imaginative writing. In this sense, the "Malachi Letters" (and, I shall go on to suggest, his subsequent writings on France) are less an escape valve than a discovery of new regions of creative energy. My reading of Scott's late "French" works complicates the picture we have inherited of the stoical Tory Sir Walter in his last days of physical dissolution, holding out sadly and a touch pathetically against the inevitable march of Reform. We should also, I believe, be aware of an energetic and angry writer harnessing in the very tasks to which his bankruptcy condemned him a violent fury against the constraints of illness and sequestration. These narratives generate some powerful images of that "unendurable" private reality beneath the convivial surface and open up new areas of narrative to fiction and to historiography.

The Malachi episode reveals more clearly than anything hitherto in Scott's writing that the moderate Hanoverian who feared insurrection above all things knew himself, perhaps inevitably, also secretly drawn to it:

> I do believe Scotsmen will shew themselves unanimous at least where their cash is concerned. They shall not want backing. I incline to cry with Biron in *Love's Labour's Lost*
> > More Ates More Ates—stir them on.
> I suppose all imaginative people feel more or less of excitation from a scene of insurrection or tumult or of general expression of national feeling. When I was a lad poor Davie Douglas used to accuse me of being *cupidus novarum rerum* and say that I loved the stimulus of a Broil. It might be so then and even still
> > Even in our ashes glow their wonted fires. (*Journal*, 97–98)

At this time Scott was overseeing the move out of his Edinburgh home and arranging its sale for the benefit of his creditors. Suppressed and displaced anger at the humiliation of his own financial collapse directly fuels "Malachi's" animus. Images of rage and violence compound powerfully with metaphors of law and control in journal entries that begin to define a position of defiant, almost Faustian, isolation:

> I never have yet found nor do I expect it on this occasion that ill will dies in debt or what is called gratitude distresses herself by frequent payments. The one is like a ward-holding and pays its Reddendo in hard blows—the other a blanch tenure and is discharged for payment of a red-nose or a pepper-corn. He that takes the forlorn hope in an attack is often deserted by those that should support him and who generally throw the blame of their own cowardice upon his rashness. We will see this will end in the same way. But I foresaw it from the beginning. The Bankers will be persuaded that it is a squib which may burn their own fingers and will curse the poor pyrotechnist that compounded it—if they do—they be d——d. (*Journal*, 102)

The passage's rhetorical richness is matched only by its sense of personal desolation. Hostility spills out of the political pamphlet and onto the page of his private thoughts. Scott courted and positively welcomed the animosity in which the Malagrowther letters involved him; they were a proud warning to the world that it took pity on him in his predicament at its own peril: "On the whole I am glad of the bruilzie as far as I am concerned; people will not dare talk of me as an object of pity—no more 'poor manning'" (*Journal*, 103).

Scott's dreams on the night of this entry cast a powerful light on the internal face of this open defiance: "Slept indifferently and dreamd of Napoleon's last moments and last illness. . . . Horrible death—a cancer on the pylorus—I would have given something to have lain still this morning and made up for lost time. But *Desidiae valedixi*. If you once turn on your side after the hour at which you ought to rise it is all over" (*Journal*, 102). At the moment when his sleeping imagination looks right into the abyss, the waking self pulls back from the brink. Stoicism and duty win out—but only just.

In addition to *Woodstock* and the "Malachi Letters," Scott was deep in the composition of his *Life of Napoleon*. Begun in prosperity when he was himself the "Napoleon of Letters" and Constable (as Scott affectionately dubbed him) the "Napoleon of Publishing," the work continued in very different circumstances after the financial crash. It immediately took on a new purpose as a major money-earner for Scott's creditors, and rapidly expanded under his hands from its originally projected three volumes to an eventual nine, of which the first two were a synoptic history of the French Revolution. The dream recorded at this crisis of his own fortunes suggests that he had begun to make a close identification between his own fate and that of the mighty protagonist to whose ambitions his politics were so strongly opposed. Napoleon's triumphant career closed in disgrace, captivity and unendurable physical pain. Scott already knew ruin and isolation; pain and disease inexorably followed, as the journal charts with poignant stoicism.

The point, however, of this essay is not to detail the obvious parallels between Napoleon's fate and that of Scott, but to suggest that Scott's writings on French subjects were energized by the same potent combination of politics and personal emotion that propelled the "Malachi Letters"; that evoking a France which could be an acceptable location for disorderly emotions of rage, anarchy, and violence, he found new creative areas at a low point in his personal fortunes, when he was forced to work under duress and the constant threat of sequestration.[5]

When Scott began the *Life of Napoleon* in 1825, the France of the Revolution was a readily available site for a moralized story of violence in which political purpose is overtaken and swamped by anarchic rage:

> Violence succeeded to violence, and remonstrance to remonstrance. The Parliament of Paris, and all the provincial bodies of the same description, being suspended from their functions, and the course of regular justice of course interrupted, the spirit of revolt became general through the realm, and broke out in riots and insurrections of a formidable description. . . . the arm of power was paralysed, and the bonds of authority which had so long fettered the French people were falling asunder of themselves.[6]

Through the retrospective filter of the Terror, the events of the French Revolution epitomized for Scott, as for all conservative writers, the animal instincts inherent in humanity, and the terrifying ever-present possibility of their release into ordinary life. The excesses of the Revolution, like the career of Napoleon, allowed for a kind of sanctioned vengefulness even in writers devoted to moderation and the rule of law.[7] Under such extreme circumstances, men lose imaginative independence and become beasts in very reality: the French people under the reign of Terror are as cows being driven toward the shambles:

> As the victims approach the slaughter-house, and smell the blood of those which have suffered the fate to which they are destined, they may be often observed to hesitate, start, roar, and bellow, and intimate their dread of the fatal spot, and instinctive desire to escape from it; but the cudgels of their drivers, and the fangs of the mastiffs, seldom fail to compel them forward, slavering, and snorting, and trembling, to the destiny which awaits them. (*Life of Napoleon*, 2:1937)

Terror, however, releases also "an extraordinary energy," which with the threat of death "awakens the strongest efforts in those whom they menace" (*Life of Napoleon*, 2:190). As the *Life of Napoleon* progresses, its emphasis shifts away from the consequences of public disorder toward an interest in the figure of the angry overreacher who had capitalized on the anarchic potential liberated by the Revolution to further his own ambitions. Summing up Napoleon's character in the final pages of the work, Scott shows understanding if not sympathy for the erstwhile Emperor's violent torment, "racked . . . almost to a frenzy" by the constraints that bound him in defeat:

> he was a man tried in the two extremities, of the most exalted power and the most ineffable calamity, and if he occasionally appeared presumptuous when supported by the armed force of half a world, or unreasonably querulous when imprisoned within the narrow limits of St. Helena, it is scarce within the capacity of those whose steps have never led them beyond the middle path of life, to estimate either the strengths of the temptations to which he yielded, or the force of mind which he opposed to those which he was able to resist. (*Life of Napoleon*, 9:342)

Scott's French writings explore the possibility that in the balance of extremities, moderation and prudence may cease to be available as viable moral stances. Enlightenment requires the free operation of imagination.

In an *Encyclopaedia Britannica* article as early as 1818, Scott described the shortcomings of the system of chivalry as the paradoxical product of its own values: "Extremes of every kind border on each other . . . we are ourselves variable and inconsistent animals, and perhaps, the surest mode of introducing and encouraging any particular vice, is to rank the corresponding virtue at a pitch unnatural in itself, and beyond the ordinary attainment of humanity" (*Prose Works*, 6:39, 43). After the financial crash of 1826, he determined quixotically to write himself free of his creditors, in a spirit which he specifically likened to that of chivalry:

> I will involve no friend either rich or poor—My own right hand shall do it—. . . I might save my library etc. by assistance of friends and bid my creditors defiance. But for this I would in a court of Honour deserve to lose my spurs for—No, if they permit me, I will be their vassal for life and dig in the mine of my imagina[tion] to find diamonds (or what may sell for such) to make good my engagements, not to enrich myself. (*Journal*, 65, 68)

As Scott subjected himself in the name of an ideal of honor to unnatural and excessive self-discipline, both his journal and his fictional and historical writings became increasingly fascinated with, and preoccupied by, anarchy, disorder, and very unheroic emotions, located at the historical point of the breakup of chivalry. Digging under duress in the mine of his imagination, Scott uncovered in his subsequent writings the muddy underside of the extreme and perverse determination to free himself from debt unaided. Within heroic purpose and noble self-sacrifice, torture, pain, and anger lay concealed; and, to a fascinating and I think significant extent, he found a fictional home for them in France.[8] The life which could not be endured in reality might be imaged in narrative. It has often been noted that Scott's largest subject is the forging of a new order from the decaying ruins of the old; the "French" works seem remarkable in the license they give him to explore the less palatable aspects of this desperate transitional upheaval. Throughout them, chivalry is character-ized by extremes which, in seeking to exalt human nature un-naturally, destabilize it and expose the brutality which in Scott's writing lurks always within excessive idealism.

The *Life of Napoleon* was not, however, the first of Scott's writ-ings to take on a French subject. *Paul's Letters to his Kinsfolk* (1819), the journalistic product of Scott's visit to the battlefield of Waterloo, and *Quentin Durward* (1823), the first "non-En-glish" Waverley novel, come before the *Life of Napoleon* (1827), *Anne of Geierstein* (1829), and the "fifth series" of *Tales of a Grandfather*, concerning French history, which Scott was writing in 1831 as he revised *Quentin Durward* for the "Magnum Edi-tion" of his works.

In 1822, as he was beginning to think about the novel that would become *Quentin Durward*, Scott knew less about France and French history than about any of the locales and epochs of his previous novels. He wrote to his friend John Morritt of "hav-ing an admirable little corner of history fresh in my head" (*Let-ters*, 7:308); France was a terrain on which his imagination could freely play. The introductory chapter of *Quentin Durward* draws a direct line of historical connection backward from the disrup-tive consequences of the French Revolution to the breakup of chivalry under the reign of Louis XI in the second half of the fifteenth century. The book's narrator (a gentleman whose for-tunes have failed in the economic depression that followed the Napoleonic Wars) "expectorates his bile" against the French na-tion as a whole, then seeks semiexile with a French aristocrat who has been similarly dispossessed by the Revolution, and who turns out to be the descendant of Quentin Durward and the custodian of his story.[9] The narrative that follows is at once a political fable with harshly realistic implications and a fairy tale that plays on the irrational violence and arbitrary resolutions of the genre. King Louis's château of Plessis-les-Tours is a fortress surrounded with vicious "snares and traps, armed with scythe-blades, which shred off the unwary passenger's limb as sheerly as a hedge-bill lops a hawthorn-sprig, and calthrops that would pierce your foot through, and pit-falls deep enough to bury you in them for ever; for you are now within the precincts of the royal demesne" (57).

Violent and unheroic death, such as characterized both the French Revolution and Louis's France, organizes this book. Three hangings structure the plot, and two climactic beheadings punctuate its action: that of the saintly Bishop of Liège and then—in poetic revenge—of his murderer the Wild Boar, by Quentin's uncle and representative, Le Balafré, "scar-face." Quentin is associated with all three hangings, and indeed the same inglorious fate threatens to overtake him throughout the novel. Codes of justice do not pertain here: it is a grotesque world in which dead bodies hang "like grapes on every tree" (108). Its chamber of horrors is Loches, home to the cages where men are penned like dangerous beasts (222), and to whose compounded image of torture and incarceration Scott would later return in horrified fascination.

The novel's two central historical figures, Charles, duke of Burgundy and King Louis XI, are equally degenerate products of the system of chivalry: mirror images, each embodies the opposite of the extreme which characterizes the other: "As Louis never sacrificed his interest to his passion, so Charles . . . never sacrificed his passion, or even his humour, to any other consideration" (44). The one thing they share is a delight in inflicting pain: an uneasy conference of war is resolved in harmony when they set dogs on a man as though he were a beast of prey (455). Mutual hatred informs their relationship, however, and their struggle for power over France is the historical backdrop to the story of the personal adventures of Quentin Durward. Undoubtedly the cautious and politic Louis has the upper hand over Charles, whose emotional intemperance constantly tends to work against his political and personal interests. He, too, in the pervasive imagery of the book, becomes beastlike in his encounters with the king, a "large and surly mastiff," who "growls internally, erects his bristles, shows his teeth, yet is ashamed to fly upon the intruder, . . . and therefore . . . endures advances which are far from pacifying him, watching at the same time the slightest opportunity which may justify him . . . seizing his friend by the throat" (407). Images of bestiality and wanton cruelty pervade the novel; Louis "caresses his victim like the cat, which can fawn when about to deal the most bitter wound"; he lives among his lawless companions as "a keeper among wild beasts" (5, 42). His intimates are a pair of hangmen and torturers, Trois-Eschelles and Petit-André, the visible physical agents of the infliction of pain, associated with his royal and arbitrary power, but dissociated from his person. In them, he keeps his own wild beasts. Associating Louis's practice of torture with the breakup of chivalry, Scott identifies the systematic infliction of physical pain with the moment of cultural uncertainty, and anticipates modern analyses of terrorist regimes.[10]

Charles has an outlawed and even more brutal counterpart in William De la Marck, an embodiment of almost archetypal violence and lawlessness, the terror of a recognized but disowned beastly part of the psyche which Scott's prose evokes with extraordinary vividness:

> an unusual thickness and projection of the mouth and upper jaw, which, with the huge projecting side-teeth, gave that resemblance to the bestial creation . . . joined to the delight that De la Marck had in haunting the forest so called, originally procured for him the name of the Boar of Ardennes. The beard, broad, grisly, and uncombed, neither concealed the natural horrors of the countenance, nor dignified its brutal expression. . . . flinging himself back in his seat, he grinded his teeth till the foam flew from his lips. (301, 307)

In different ways, Charles, the Wild Boar, and Louis all exhibit the kind of brutality which unmakes civilization. Scott's location of the struggle of policy, anger, and violence for power over the body politic in French history was necessarily colored and directed by his view of the events of the French Revolution which also, in the Terror, cast back into people's bodies the trauma of a society in upheaval. More specifically, the revisions and additions Scott made to the novel in 1831 suggest that returning to the French ground he located there some crucial— and probably unacceptable—aspects of his own experience in the intervening years, and (because my point is finally more critical than biographical) that this pressure of circumstances on the writing invigorates a new kind of penetrative language into narrative.

In particular, Scott expanded the characterization of Louis, to create a more complex psychological study than in the novel's first edition of 1823.[11] In the light of his work on the *Life of Napoleon* and the defiant self-image constructed in the *Journal*, Scott reconceived the fifteenth-century French king as a Mephistophelian "Fallen Spirit," imprisoned in the consequences of his own prudential policies. The most significant revisions, however, concern the increased prominence and emphasis Scott gives right at the outset to Louis's end: discredited, living out a sequestered existence in self-imposed isolation, he is a man in torment. Inflicting torture on others, he also suffers it in his own person:

> So great were the well-merited tortures of this tyrant's deathbed, that Philip de Comines enters into a regular comparison between them and the numerous cruelties inflicted on others by his order; and, considering both, comes to express an opinion, that the worldly pangs and agony suffered by Louis were such as might compensate the crimes he had committed. (9)

The Magnum introduction cites too Fénélon's graphic account of the King's last days of suspicion and fear:

> Il ne connoît ni les doux plaisirs, ni l'amitié encore plus douce. Si on lui parle de chercher la joie, il sent qu'elle fuit loin de lui, et qu'elle refuse d'entrer dans son coeur. Ses yeux creux sont pleins d'un feu âpre et farouche; ils sont sans cesse errans de tous cotés; il prête l'oreille au moindre bruit, et se sent tout ému; il est pâle, défait, et les noirs soucis tirent de son coeur de profonds gémissemens, il ne peut cacher les remords qui déchirent ses entrailles. Les mets les plus exquis le dégoûtent. Ses enfants, loin d'être son espérance, sont le sujet de sa terreur; il en a fait ses plus dangereux ennemis. Il n'a eu toute sa vie aucun moment d'assuré. (9–10)

It's a terrifying picture. Though Scott's own last dark days were outwardly very different, surrounded as he was by family, friends, and well-wishers, it is hard not to be moved by the thought of what it must have meant to him to transcribe such a passage in 1831, a few months before the death that he knew could not be far from him either.

*Quentin Durward* is also, though, a novel "governed," as Jana Davis has put it, "by the positive discourse of the moral imagination."[12] Quentin is both an imaginative hero and a man who is unafraid to initiate violent action. The novel's ugly opening scenes implicate him in the world of Louis; unlike Scott's earlier heroes, in extremity he does not temporize: "as if he sought for that death from which all others were flying, [he] endeavoured to force his way into the scene of tumult and horror, under apprehensions still more horrible to his imagination, than the realities around were to his sight and senses" (289). The narrator's description of the "scene" is, under the influence of this quickening imagination, raised from sheer brutality to a demonic fable akin to Tam O'Shanter's vision in Kirk Alloway or Wandering Willie's visit to hell in *Redgauntlet*:

> As they approached the hall, the yells of acclamation, and bursts of wild laughter, which proceeded from it, seemed rather to announce the revel of festive demons, rejoicing after some accomplished triumph over the human race, than of mortal beings, who had succeeded in some bold design. . . . there was now such a scene of wild and roaring debauchery, as Satan himself, had he taken the chair as founder of the feast, could scarcely have improved. (299–300).

The imaginative heightening of the narrative vision generates a space for Quentin's decisive intervention in the scene of meaningless violence to make sense of its chaos. "Destroy this faculty [of imagination]," as Dugald Stewart had written, "and the condition of man will become as stationary as that of the brutes."[13] More than once Scott records in his journal the fear of losing this humanizing, motive freedom under the *"peine forte et dure"* of forced labor (*Journal*, 91). This is the space that the pressure of extremes meeting threatens to crush.

*Anne of Geierstein*, written less than two years after the completion of the *Life of Napoleon*, which Scott was then revising for a new edition, tells again the story of the epoch of *Quentin Durward*, this time from the Burgundian side. Uniquely in Scott's oeuvre, it returns to the same ground and the same historical characters as a previous novel. Despite his sense of its potential interest, Scott seems to have entertained toward *Anne* a violent antipathy, such as he never expressed in relation to other writing tasks, even in this straitened period. It is a "confounded novel," its catastrophe "vilely huddled up"; in frustration he decides "by heave[n] I will finish Anne this day . . . I don't know why nor wherefore but I hate Anne" (*Journal*, 526, 524, 553). The entry hastily adds that he refers to Anne of the novel, not the two real Annes who tended him in his querulous sickness and toil (his daughter and young niece). Subliminally, perhaps, they too have become his "keepers."

*Anne of Geierstein* is a book poised literally and figuratively on the brink of an abyss. In its opening chapter, the young protagonist is seen paralyzed with fear in a precipitous landscape imaged as the product of some violent and bloody battle: "The gaunt precipice which remained behind, like the skeleton of some huge monster divested of its flesh, formed the wall of a fearful abyss."[14] To escape from being torn to pieces by vultures, he must take a step "[a]cross a dark abyss, at the bottom of which a torrent surged and boiled with incredible fury" (29). Quentin's imagination spurred him to intervene actively in the scene of violence at Schonwaldt; Arthur, on the contrary, "sensitive to a powerful extent to all those exaggerations which, in a situation of helpless uncertainty, fancy lends to distract the soul" (196), is incapacitated by his fearful imaginings, both now and later in the book when he finds himself "on the brink of the subterranean abyss" in a dungeon.[15] On both occasions, he has to be rescued from his paralysis by Anne of Geierstein, the mysterious "Maiden of the Mist" whose imagination does not terrorize her actions. As Scott noted in relation to his own circumstances, the real terror of torture lies in the imagination of the event: its actuality may paradoxically prove a liberation of sorts, if only from fear of the unknown. A journal entry for 3 February 1826 suggestively associates his bankruptcy with torture, and with France:

> John Gibson came to tell me in the evening that a Meeting to-day had approved of the proposed trust. I know not why but the news gave me little concern. I hear it as a party indifferent. I remember hearing that Mandrin testified some horror when he found himself bound alive on the wheel and saw an executioner approach with a bar of iron to break his limbs. After the second and third blow he fell a laughing and being askd the reason by his confessor said he

laughd at his own folly which had anticipated increased agony at
every blow when it was obvious the *first* must have jarrd and confounded the system of the nerves so much as to render the succeed-
ing blows of little consequence. I suppose it is so with the moral
feeling. (*Journal*, 76)[16]

Pain cannot be imagined, it can only be feared; we fear what we
cannot imagine. Imagining the unimaginable, however, may
finally be equivalent to enduring the unendurable. Taking up
this issue, *Anne of Geierstein* shows how imagination can be recu-
perated from moral paralysis and fear to inform action.

If the imaginative focus of the revised 1831 *Quentin Durward*
is the torturing, mentally tormented politic King Louis, that of
*Anne of Geierstein* is the intemperate Charles. To an even greater
extent than in the earlier novel, fury and its consequences structure the action of *Anne*. Unbalanced by the presence of Louis
XI (who remains in the background of this novel), the excessive
anger of Charles takes on new emphasis. Scott constructs an un-
historical meeting between the duke and the estates of Burgundy at Dijon, where Charles rages at the commoners'
obduracy against his threats, calling them "beasts of burden,"
like the bewildered herds of the French Revolution: "must thou
and thy herd come hither, privileged, forsooth, to bellow at a
prince's footstool? Know, brute as thou art, that steers are never
introduced into temples but to be sacrificed, or butchers and
mechanics brought before their sovereign, save that they may
have the honour to supply the public wants from their own
swelling hoards!" (386) Unlike the nominal heroes Quentin and
Anne, Scott presents both Louis and Charles as in different ways
paralyzed by the need to inflict on others the terror which
floods their own existences. Torture may be the product of the
imagination, but it also kills it. As Elaine Scarry puts it, "physical
pain is able to obliterate psychological pain because it obliter-
ates all psychological content, painful, pleasurable, and neu-
tral."[17] Repeatedly the journal records Scott "putting away"
painful reflection by forcing himself back to his daily *poena*.

The faculty of imaginative sympathy with the sufferings of
others, which is the spur to heroic action through the Waverley
series, is in these "French" writings threatened at its source by a
mesmerizing and debilitating preoccupation with violence and
pain. Scott's ability (for which there is ample evidence in the

journal) at this crisis of his own fortunes to identify and understand the undercurrent of anger in his heroic self-sacrifice to duty, and (following the "Malachi Letters") to cast it into the powerful portraits of Louis and Charles, is the source of the particular challenge in the imaginative blend of these late French writings.

Archibald de Hagenbuch, whose "fury blinds even his avarice" (165), is the novel's counterpart of William de la Marck. Arranging to meet the English heroes surrounded by the "instruments of torture, which the cruel and rapacious governor was in the habit of applying to such prisoners from whom he was desirous of extorting either booty or information" (182), he is accompanied by his executioner Francis Steinenherz. Like Petit-André and Trois-Eschelles, with whom he explicitly compares himself (183), Steinenherz is the agent of legitimatized vengeance, the projected violence of authority whose very presence is an act of intimidation. Hagenbuch's menace plays on the imaginations of his victims at their most vulnerable point: "Perchance the rack may make you both find your tongues; and we will try it on the young fellow first . . . since thou knowest we have seen men shrink from beholding the wretched joints of their children, that would have committed their own old sinews to the stretching with much endurance" (190). "Inarticulate . . . rage" follows the failure of his threat. Rendered impotent, in a fitting coup of poetic justice Hagenbuch is executed by his own executioner. The murderous and the suicidal impulses come violently together.

The "fifth" and final series of *Tales of a Grandfather*, which Scott first conceived (for his own profit rather than that of his creditors) as he was finishing the *Life of Napoleon* in 1827, and on which he worked during 1831 as he revised *Quentin Durward*, presents a vision of public history constantly cut into by human suffering and the capacity for disorder. This work, part of Scott's educational project for his young grandson, is the final epitome and apogee of the earlier observation in the *Life of Napoleon* that "it is not useless that men should see how far human nature can be carried, in contradiction to every feeling the most sacred, to every pleading whether of justice or humanity" (*Life of Napoleon*, 2:92). As in the poignant late journal entries, confusions, elisions, and omissions in the manuscript of *Tales of a Grandfather* seem to embody in the text the anarchy Scott feared in his person and in a nation facing the unknown consequences of parliamentary reform. But there is no failing of imaginative vision; indeed, it seems as though in these late writings Scott perhaps comes close in a new way to finding an idiom for that "unendurable reality" which so much of his own life and writing had been devoted to keeping at bay.[18] Whereas Scott's fictions of France provided him with a way of looking glancingly into the indefinite, fearful world of impulse and passion, while retaining his hold on the realities of the everyday world, the late *Tales of a Grandfather* draw their reader inescapably into the landscape of horror. The animal ferocity of the insurgents of Liège stirred up by Louis has this time around a shocking bodily physicality: "As these tumultuary soldiers returned from Tongres to Liège they indulged their innate cruelty by tearing to pieces some of the bishop's confidential servants and throwing the gobbets of their flesh at each others' heads in derision."[19] Louis himself is now directly implicated in the general climate of barbarous inhumanity, and takes delight "in hearing with his own ears the exclamations and cries of those who were subjected to torture" (307).

What kind of impulse led Scott to create such sadistically murderous scenes for the edification of his beloved and sickly nine-year-old grandson? Elaine Scarry's description of how "physical pain wipes out psychological content" may help.[20] Both Scott and his grandson suffered intensifying physical disability by this point; indeed, both—as he knew—were dying.[21] The descriptions of grotesque brutality in the late *Tales of a Grandfather* seem to operate in two ways: the apparently gratuitous description of cruelty serves at once to wipe out emotional horror, and to reengage the imagination at a moment when pain threatens to swamp the mind with the "single, overwhelming discrepancy between an increasingly palpable body and an increasingly substanceless world."[22] Through these late French writings, prudent moderation of an enlightened kind comes to seem an increasingly inadequate reaction at the furthest reaches of human experience.

Seeing all around him the unendurable realities of life in dissolution, Scott seems to have been tempted more than once by despair, as when he learned of the suicide of his niece's husband Colonel Huxley. If the fear of death was an abyss, death itself might offer the welcome prospect of closure. After his wife

Charlotte died, he fought to maintain his stoicism but recorded the ferocity of the struggle: "I do not know what other folks feel, but with me the hysterical passion that compels tears is a terrible violence—a sort of throttling sensation" (*Journal*, 152). His body became the graphic battleground of warring emotions; kidney stones and bloody urine caused his chamber pot to resemble (as he put it ruefully) "a field of battle" (quoted in Johnson, *Sir Walter Scott*, 2:1008), just as he was describing Napoleon's bloody campaigns in Russia.

Near the end of the manuscript of the last *Tales of a Grandfather*, in a passage which is one of his final visions of France, Scott returns to that metaphor of Louis's torture cages, so powerful in both *Quentin Durward* and *Anne of Geierstein*, with an arresting account of how the king carried these images of his torment with him wherever he went, like pent extrusions of his own animal nature: "It is remarkable that when the king travelled these cages with their unfortunate inhabitants were always dragged in his train as if they had containd wild beasts instead of human creatures, and as if the owner had been jealous of his menagerie and would not part with them out of their sight" (*Tales of a Grandfather*, 164). In some way these instruments of torture seem to confirm not only his power, but his reality. They make pain visible, the unpalatable palpable. Finally, the account of Louis's monstrosity reaches mythic and fairy-tale proportions in a surpassingly grotesque image of life's atrocity which unites the dying old man and the death of young children: "A bath was prepared for this royal patient composed of the warm blood of infants, the effect of which was to refresh the blood of the old decayed man, soften its crudities, and restore its circulation. But we dare not believe this of man born of a woman, even if that man be Louis XI" (*Tales of a Grandfather*, 165). It is Scott's most horrifying image of the violence done to children by their parents' pain. This image and that of the flesh-throwing soldiers of Liège would alone serve to qualify the point first made by James Hogg in his own defense, and later by Hogg's critics, that Scott's writing has no idiom for the horrors and atrocity of human behavior in warfare. It needs to be reflected back into our reading of the Waverley novels as a whole.

Scott's France is no land of Enlightenment. It is, rather, the battleground of the passions: anger and self-control, authority and freedom, policy and impulse, and—perhaps most fundamentally—pain and imagination. "In all subjects of deep and lasting interest," as Coleridge first put it, "you will detect a struggle between two opposites, two polar forces, both of which are alike necessary to our human well-being, and necessary each to the continued existence of the other."[23] I have suggested that the interaction of Scott's personal experience at the end of his life with his articulation of French subjects generated a peculiarly charged, dark and violent aspect of this perennial and archetypal struggle, which took it out of the realm of the contest between the "loyalists and their opponents" of which Coleridge speaks and, in contradiction to the way we usually read Scott, out of the realm of "social humanity" and prudential moderation altogether.

The journal strikes out angrily at the effect of bodily and mental constraint on the freedom which imagination both requires and creates: "A man cannot write in the House of correction and this species of *peine forte et dure* which is threatend would render it impossible for one to help himself or others" (*Journal*, 91). The "House of correction" is also the house of pain; the etymological connection of *poena* and punishment comes clear in Scott's use of the French word *"peine."* The pain/punishment was for Scott, as perhaps for everyone, at once the product of events (national, economic, genetic) beyond his control, and self-invoked. Punishment, as Bruce Beiderwell (following Foucault) notes, is both pain *and* control.[24] These "French" works repeatedly encounter the unpalatable reality that because we get what we have not deserved as well as what we have, pain always includes—and evokes—revenge, *poena*, as well as justice. If the imagination is paralyzed by the violence and anarchy which it projects and inflicts, the same qualities may also be brought back into the mind's sphere of creative activity. We may see Scott in these final years like Arthur Philipson bracing himself to cross the abyss:

> He laid a powerful restraint on his imagination, which in general was sufficiently active, and refused to listen, even for an instant, to any of the horrible insinuations by which fancy augments actual danger. . . . "If I move with decision, step firmly, and hold fast, what signifies how near I am to the mouth of an abyss?" (*Anne of Geierstein*, 18)

The power of these French writings is that they both do and do not listen to the insinuations of the imagination at the point of extremity.

## NOTES

1. *The Journal of Sir Walter Scott*, ed. W. E. K. Anderson (Oxford, 1972), 44–45. Subsequent references are given by page number in the text.

2. As J. G. Lockhart and others since have noted, Scott's bankruptcy, brought on as it was by the crash of the London money market after a period of feverish speculation, was itself a consequence of the circumstances which led the government to impose measures of restraint on the issue and exchange of small banknotes in both Scotland and England. See P. H. Scott, "The Malachi Episode," preface to *The Letters of Malachi Malagrowther* (1826; reprint, Edinburgh, 1981), xi.

3. In a letter to the Duke of Wellington, John Wilson Croker put a different construction on the association of Malachi with Scottish banking interests, seeing it as an act little short of sycophancy: "Walter Scott, who, poor fellow, was ruined by dealings with his booksellers, and who had received courtesy and indulgence from the Scotch bankers, thought himself bound in gratitude to take the field for them, which he did in a series of clever, but violent and mischevious letters." Quoted in Scott, "Malachi Episode," xx.

4. J. G. Lockhart, *The Life of Sir Walter Scott*, 7 vols. (Edinburgh and London, 1837–38), vi, 225.

5. Other scholars have noted these similarities, though I would not wish to take them as far as the schematic bill of equivalences drawn up by Edgar Johnson: "The creation of Abbotsford had been his imperial ambition, the financial crash of 1826 his Moscow, his wife and children and James Ballantyne the victims who had gone down with him in his defeat, and his sedentary lodgings in St. David's Street and Walker Street his St. Helena." *Sir Walter Scott: The Great Unknown*, 2 vols. (London, 1970), 2:1068. Donald Horward, on the other hand, sees Scott as uncompromisingly critical of Napoleon's ambition, citing the *Life*'s assertion that his "ambition, equally insatiable and incurable, justified Europe in securing his person, as if it had been that of a lunatic, whose misguided rage was not directed against an individual, but against the civilised world" (3:365). See Horward, "Napoleon, His Legend, and Sir Walter Scott," *Southern Humanities Review* 16 (1982): 10. These views, as I suggest in this essay, may be inconsistent but were not incompatible, given the powerful and contradictory forces in play throughout Scott's "French" works. The other novel in which many of the same issues surface equally uncomfortably, though in slightly different ways, is *The Fair Maid of Perth* (1828).

6. *Life of Napoleon Buonaparte*, vols. 8–16 in *The Prose Works of Sir Walter Scott*, 28 vols. (Edinburgh, 1834–36), 1:100–101. Subsequent references to this edition are in the text.

7. See, for example, *The Letters of Sir Walter Scott*, ed. H. J. C. Grierson, 12 vols. (London, 1932–37), 3:440: "although I rather grudge him even the

mouthful of air which he may draw in the Isle of Elba yet I question whether the moral lesson would have been completed either by his perishing in battle or being torn to pieces (which I should have greatly preferred)."

8. Journal entries show that French topics engaged him freshly at this stressful time: on 19 February he notes taking comfort from the "Chronicle of the Good Knight Messire Jacques de Lalain" (94), and on 8 March 1826, "Being jaded and sleepy I took up *Le Duc de Guise en Naples*. I think this, with the old *Mémoires [relatifs à l'Histoire de France]* on the same subject which I have at Abbotsford, would enable me to make a pretty good essay" (107). The essay was indeed written and appeared in the *Foreign Quarterly Review*, 4:355.

9. *Quentin Durward*, ed. S. L. Manning (Oxford, 1992), 18. Subsequent quotations are to this edition and are identified by page number in the text.

10. As Elaine Scarry puts it, "at particular moments when there is within society a crisis of belief—that is, when some central idea or ideology or cultural construct has ceased to elicit a population's belief either because it is manifestly fictitious or because it has for some reason been divested of ordinary forms of substantiation—the sheer material factualness of the human body will be borrowed to lend that cultural construct the aura of 'realness' or 'certainty.' " *The Body in Pain: The Making and Unmaking of the World* (New York and Oxford, 1985) 14.

11. For further information on the nature of these revisions, see note on the text, *Quentin Durward*, xxix–xxxv.

12. Jana Davis, "Sir Walter Scott and Enlightenment Theories of the Imagination: *Waverley* and *Quentin Durward*," *Nineteenth-Century Literature* 43 (1989): 437–64, quoting 444.

13. Dugald Stewart, *Collected Works*, ed. Sir William Hamilton, 11 vols. (Edinburgh, 1852), 2:467. Quoted in Davis, "Sir Walter Scott and Enlightenment Theories of the Imagination," 459.

14. *Anne of Geierstein* (1829; Oxford, 1912), 14. Subsequent references are identified by page number in the text.

15. In *Quentin Durward*, the "subterranean abyss" is, explicitly, the "abode of terror," the "apartment for torture" (26).

16. Scott owned *The Authentic Memoirs of the Remarkable Life and surprising Exploits of Mandrin, Captain-General of the French Smugglers, who for the space of nine months resolutely stood in defiance of the whole Army of France, etc.* (1755).

17. Scarry, *Body in Pain*, 34.

18. A perfectly deliberate aim on his part, as the "Introductory Epistle" to *The Fortunes of Nigel* (Oxford, 1912) makes eloquently plain: "grant . . . that I should write with sense and spirit a few scenes, unlaboured and loosely put together, but which had sufficient interest in them to amuse in one corner the pain of body; in another, to relieve anxiety of mind; in a third place, to unwrinkle a brow bent with the furrows of daily toil; in another to fill the place of bad thoughts, or to suggest better; in yet another, to induce an idler to study the history of his country; . . . might not the author of such a work, however inartificially executed, plead for his errors and negligences the excuse of the slave, who, about to be punished for having spread the false report of a victory, saved himself by exclaiming—'Am I to blame, O Athenians, who have given you one happy day?' " (xx–xxi).

19. *Tales of a Grandfather: The History of France,* 2nd ser., ed. William Baker and J. H. Alexander (De Kalb, Ill., 1996), 117. I am grateful to the editors for supplying a photocopy of their prepared version of the manuscript deposited in the Walpole Collection of the King's School, Canterbury, from which they allowed me to quote while the volume was awaiting publication.

20. Scarry, *Body in Pain*, 34.

21. The connection becomes inescapable when Scott, in 1831, comes to describe Louis's decline: "The health of Louis had for some years been failing, and he had sustained at least one shock of an apoplectic nature. As early as 1481 the king had sustained two shocks of this disorder, supposed to be brought on by too much thought and application to business" (*Tales of a Grandfather*, 310). Scott himself, of course, met ill health and apoplexy with stubborn overwork in the months following the financial crash.

22. Scarry, *Body in Pain*, 30. Sophia conveyed to her father the boy's enthusiastic reaction to the bloodthirsty events of the earlier series of *Tales of a Grandfather*; Johnny Lockhart, she wrote in a letter of 27 February 1828, was now "mad about knights and bravery and war" (quoted by Anderson in *Journal*, 436).

23. Coleridge to Thomas Allsop, 8 April 1820, in *Collected Letters of S. T. Coleridge*, 6 vols., ed. Earl Leslie Griggs (Oxford, 1956–71), 5:33.

24. Bruce Beiderwell, *Power and Punishment in Scott's Novels* (Athens and London, 1992), vii.

# French Art and the Scottish Enlightenment

## Duncan Macmillan

The status of scottish thought in france during the enlightenment has long been accepted. What is less familiar is the considerable impact of Scottish ideas on the development of French
art. These were transmitted both through Scottish literary and
philosophical texts and through the direct influence of Scottish
painting.

By extension, therefore, art may be viewed as a branch of Enlightenment thought in Scotland.[1] One eloquent witness to
such an idea is Allan Ramsay's portrait of Jean-Jacques Rousseau
(1766). Commissioned by David Hume, it is a key document in
the intellectual exchange between Scotland and France. But
while such a painting can stand for the richness of that exchange and the place of art within it in the 1750s and 1760s,
only with the emergence in the 1780s of Jacques-Louis David as
the champion of a new kind of painting in France would it come
to be clearly reflected in French art. The art of Gavin Hamilton,
a Scot based in Rome, a conduit for Enlightenment ideas, played
an important role in this development. This new kind of painting continued to evolve with accelerating radicalism in the
years after the fall of Napoleon. As it did so, I will argue, Scottish
links of this kind grew even more important. Throughout the
period, they helped to shift progressive art in France toward a
psychological, subjective point of view that by the late 1820s is
recognizable as the one that has shaped modern art.

This article will first explore the reflection of Scottish art and
ideas in certain key paintings by David. It will then look at
French art in the years just after the fall of Napoleon, when the
philosophy of Thomas Reid had a major impact. This was at first
indirect, through the study of expression developed from Reid's
philosophy by Sir Charles Bell and set by him in relation to the
novel idea of the physiology of mind. Here my discussion will

128

focus on Géricault and his circle between roughly 1815 and 1824. But this part of the argument is also extended by evidence of the parallel impact of Reid's philosophy on Delacroix through the teaching of Victor Cousin. Finally, in the late 1820s these new ideas were extended by the impact on French painting of Sir Walter Scott's novels and their interpreters among the Scottish painters.

I

David's style changed radically when he went to Rome for the first time in 1775. Gavin Hamilton was then the doyen of the painters there. A contemporary wrote of him: "being the most renowned of all the history painters of this age [he] is highly respected at Rome."[2] Hamilton had an open studio where he often kept works on an easel for years on end. In them he pioneered a dramatic new form of epic history painting. The key works were a series of six pictures from Homer's *Iliad*, undertaken between 1759 and the early 1770s, but he also painted a small number of pictures with Roman subjects. He made a point of having his work engraved so that it would be well known beyond his circle in Rome.

David's relationship to Hamilton is reflected in the pictures that he painted with Homeric subjects in Rome and back in France in the years following this first journey. His *Andromache Mourning Hector*, for instance, is a simplified version of Hamilton's treatment of the same subject. David's painting of the *Body of Hector* is similarly a single figure taken directly from Hamilton's composition *Achilles Vents his Rage on Hector*. When David returned to Rome in 1784 to paint his first masterpiece, *The Oath of the Horatii*, it is not surprising that Hamilton should still have been his model. The compositional debt of his picture to Hamilton's *Death of Lucretia*, or as it is usually incorrectly called, *The Oath of Brutus*, has been often observed, but its implications for the meaning of David's picture have never been explored.[3]

Hamilton's picture was commissioned in 1763. It was completed in 1767 and engraved by Cunego.[4] But in 1779 Hamilton also completed a second, virtually identical version, which had been on his easel most of the time that David was in Rome be-

**Jacques-Louis David (1748–1825).** *Andromache Mourning Hector,*
**1783. Louvre, Paris, France. Copyright Giraudon/Art Resource, NY.**

**Gavin Hamilton (1723–1798).** *The Oath of Brutus,* **1766 (engraving by Cunego).**

tween 1775 and 1780 and was certainly seen by him then. *The Oath of Brutus* is a modern title. Hamilton's title was *The Death of Lucretia*, for the picture tells the story of how Lucretia, after her brutal rape by Sextus Tarquinius, kills herself, not from shame, but as a challenge to the men, to compel them to act.[5] Inspired by her, Brutus swears revenge. The Tarquins are overthrown and the republic is founded.

Hamilton was drawing attention to the fact that these consequences had been brought about by the actions of a woman. In case anyone missed this point, he reiterated it in two other, related pictures in which women take heroic stands against tyranny and violence: *Agrippina Landing at Brundisium with the Ashes of Germanicus* and *Volumnia's Appeal to Coriolanus*. The first of these pictures treats the story of Agrippina, the granddaughter of Augustus and the wife of Germanicus. When Germanicus dies suddenly and mysteriously, the emperor Tiberius is suspected of arranging his murder in order to eliminate a popular rival. In a gesture of mute but public accusation of the emperor, Agrippina carries her husband's ashes to Rome. With Tarquin, tyranny was driven out of Rome; with Tiberius, it returned. *The Death of Lucretia* and *Agrippina Landing at Brundisium* stand at either end of the history of the republic. In both, women confront tyranny and brutality to champion the natural virtues of sympathy, loyalty, and affection. Similarly, in Hamilton's third picture, *Volumnia's Appeal to Coriolanus*, it is women—the wife and mother of Coriolanus—who save Rome from his wrath by their appeal to natural feeling. What Hamilton proposes in these three paintings, therefore, is that it is not the "masculine" principle of action which promotes civilization and the amelioration of the human condition, but the "feminine" principle of feeling.

As early as 1775, Jean Antoine Julien followed Hamilton's example by painting in Rome *Caracalla Assassinating his Brother Geta in the Arms of his Mother.* In this portrayal of an unusual subject, fratricide, en route to tyranny, is compounded with the violation of the natural feelings of a woman by the outrage of maternal love. David's *Oath of the Horatii* is equally brutal. The sister of the Horatii, Camilla, loves one of the Curatii, and her love is reciprocated. Hers is the crime of Juliet: loving outside the clan. In the painting, her brothers, the Horatii, swear an oath to avenge this insult. Subsequently, when they have killed her lover and his brothers, they kill Camilla herself. This murder was the scene that David first considered in a drawing for the composition,[6] which makes it clear that his true subject is the outrage of natural feeling by the primitive brutality of the heroic code. A contemporary critic, conscious of this theme, commented on the cruelty of David's subject.[7]

This cruelty is usually overlooked, and the picture is seen as a celebration of the manly virtues, the stern code of duty that would be called for by the French Revolution. But if, instead, David is following the inspiration of Hamilton beyond simple compositional dependence, to echo in addition the meaning of the *Lucretia*, then the *Oath of the Horatii* has a point very different from the one that is conventionally attributed to it. Instead of celebrating manly virtue, what it actually proposes is that the brutal, anachronistic social code of the Horatii is obsolete and rebarbative. In this sense, the subject of the picture is much more progressive than is usually thought.

In his six pictures from the *Iliad*, Hamilton grafts a similar meaning onto Homer. He departs from Homer's story to draw a specific contrast between Achilles's rage and brutal thirst for vengeance—heroic, but primitive and antisocial passions—and the tragic consequences for the gentle, natural affections of Hector and Andromache, which are representative of the feelings on which society is built. David's painting of Hector and Andromache reflects this aspect of Hamilton's approach directly. Showing Hector's wife and child alone with his corpse, David simplifies Hamilton's composition to stress that it was they who most felt Hector's tragic death: that it was natural affection that was violated by the brutality of the code of vengeance by which he was killed. So, too, in the *Horatii*, David points to the disparity between the violence and brutality of the masculine code of honor and the gentle, social feelings personified by the female actors in the drama, though shortly to be violated in Camilla's murder.

Later, in his painting of *Brutus and the Lictors*, David would rejoin the story of Brutus, taking up the narrative a few years after the death of Lucretia. Brutus's sons betrayed the new Republic. As first magistrate he found himself in the terrible position of having to judge and condemn them. His sacrifice mirrors Lucretia's. She gave herself for the greater good, and he gave what was even more dear, his own sons. Thus David's subject maintains the link with Hamilton's. That link goes further too. This was a commission from the crown and originally instead of Brutus and the Lictors David had proposed another subject that Hamilton also painted, Coriolanus and Volumnia. This fact clearly suggests that his train of thought was indeed parallel to Hamilton's and later, in *The Intervention of the Sabine Women*, he took up unambiguously the underlying theme of Hamilton's pictures of heroic femininity. The subject is the mirror image of the *The Oath of the Horatii*, for the Sabine women, who had been carried off by the Romans in the celebrated rape, triumph precisely where Camilla had so tragically failed. In David's picture the Sabines are attacking the Romans to recover their womenfolk, but the Sabine women intervene. Plutarch tells the story of how the women came between the Romans, now their husbands, and the Sabine men who were their fathers and brothers, and how their leader, Hersilia, now wife of Romulus, appealed

**Jacques-Louis David (1748–1825).** ***The Intervention of the Sabine Women*, 1799. Louvre, Paris, France. Copyright Alinari/Art Resource, NY.**

successfully to sympathy and natural affection over the atavistic claims of pride and honor.

What we see here is not only a kind of protofeminism, but the presentation of the evolution of society as dependent on feeling represented by the sentiments and actions of these heroic women. But if it is dependent on feeling, society becomes a psychological construct, and this perhaps gives us a clue as to where these ideas are coming from, confirmed by Hamilton's own place in the Scottish Enlightenment community. His first paintings on these themes, *Agrippina* and *Lucretia*, were conceived in or near 1759.[8] His painting of *Andromache Mourning Hector* can also be seen as a reflection of these ideas. It too was conceived in 1759 and that was the year that Adam Smith's *Theory of Moral Sentiment* was published. Smith and Hamilton were born in the same year and had been students at Glasgow University at the same time. Both were pupils of Francis Hutcheson and remained loyal to his teaching and his central idea of moral sense, or, as Smith put it in the title of his book, moral senti-

ment. Smith's *Theory of Moral Sentiment* set in a clear social context the view of imagination that he shared with Hume, as well
as with Adam Ferguson and Hugh Blair. Society depends on
sympathy, he argues, and sympathy on imagination. But in his
paintings, Hamilton seems to go further even than Smith to
identify this view of sympathy directly with the feminine role
in society. He argues in effect that the evolution of society from
barbarism depends on the ascendancy of the feminine principle. Smith's own reputation was high in France. Indeed, it is
striking that in 1798, the year before David completed his painting of the *Sabine Women*, Sophie de Grouchy, marquise de Condorcet, published the third translation of his book into French,
with an additional commentary of her own on the theme of
sympathy, *Lettres à Cabanis sur la sympathie*.[9]

But there is also a contradiction here. In the same circle as
Smith, Adam Ferguson and Hugh Blair were promoting the argument that primitive feeling is superior in its expression, and
provides a model for art. Blair was of course a champion of
Ossian, and in 1767 Ferguson wrote: "The artless song of the
savage, the heroic legend of the bard, have sometimes a magnificent beauty which no change of language can improve and
no refinement of the critic reform."[10] Hamilton certainly sub-
scribed to this view. Thomas Blackwell's *An Inquiry into the Life
and Writings of Homer* was a primary inspiration for his Homeric
pictures,[11] and Blackwell was one of the earliest champions of
this brand of primitivism. He saw Homer as preclassical and
wrote specifically of the freedom of expression of feeling that he
saw as the distinctive quality of such an era: "For so unaffected
and simple were the manners of those times that the folds and
windings of the human breast lay open to the eye."[12]

The younger painters in Hamilton's circle like Alexander Runciman and David Allan were also among the pioneers of the
primitive in art. Runciman's *Hall of Ossian*, painted in 1772, was
the first and the grandest painted interpretation of Ossian. It is
notable, therefore, that it was in David's circle that these ideas
first emerged in France, and that Duqueylar's huge painting of
*Ossian Singing* is the best evidence of this and of the ideology
of the shadowy group among David's followers known as Les
Primitifs. As for David, it seems that even at his most austere he
never adopted such radical ideas. But in his art he nevertheless
presents a view of history shaped by feeling, by this psychologi-

cal view of society pioneered in Scotland by Smith and his contemporaries. This turn of philosophy toward psychology, and of
art toward the expression of feeling, pioneered by the Scots,
would continue to shape progressive French painting in the
next generation.

## 2

If sympathy binds society psychologically, expression,
equally psychological, is its medium of exchange.[13] But in a context shaped by the philosophy of moral sense, if feeling has a
moral quality, then so does expression, the means by which we
externalize it. This is why the quality of expression associated
with primitive art was to be valued. It was evidence of the working of the imagination and the free play of feeling on which morality depends. Following this logic, in Scotland painters turned
to the study of expression. Following the same logic and at just
the same moment, their colleagues in medicine also developed
a parallel interest in expression. In France, a contemporary comment on the link between sympathy and expression was provided by Cabanis in *Rapports du Physique et du Moral*, a series of
Mémoires to l'Institut in years IV and V (1796–97), published in
1802. At one point, referring directly to Adam Smith and the
Scottish philosophy of moral sense, Cabanis comments on the
social role of expression and its function of communicating
sympathy: "Par la seule puissance de leurs signes, les impressions peuvent se communiquer d'un être sensible à d'autres
êtres qui, pour les partager, semblent alors s'identifier avec
lui."[14]

Cabanis is also credited with the first serious attempt to describe psychological phenomena on a physiological basis. In
this he influenced Phillipe Pinel, celebrated for freeing the luna-
tics of their chains and pioneer of the humane treatment of in-
sanity. But this more direct study of human psychology was also
a major area of Franco-Scottish exchange. Pinel himself had
close links with the Edinburgh medical school. He translated
works by William Cullen, who was, following Hoffman, among
the pioneers of belief in the importance of the nervous system,
and thus through it, of the eventual convergence of philosophy

and physiology. Another Edinburgh physician, Andrew Duncan, was a parallel figure to Pinel.

Cabanis's proposal of the physiological nature of the mind itself is also perhaps dependent on the account of sensation in Thomas Reid's *An Inquiry into the Human Mind, on the Principles of Common Sense* (1764), which had been anonymously translated into French as early as 1768. Indeed, Reid explicitly proposes that through sensation, all perception must have a physical basis.[15] Cabanis echoes Reid directly when he describes how sensation works directly on the mind, how it depends upon "les operations directes de la sensibilité."[16] Reid proposes that sensation is the medium by which the external world impinges on the mind. By means of an intuitive process, it provides the signs, "the natural language" that is the basis of perception. But Reid also argues that expression is a complementary function in the reverse direction. There, the mind's own activity is manifested physically in the body and so, in turn, as Cabanis observed, following Reid exactly, makes itself apparent as "a natural language" of signs to those around us. If perception depends on intuition, expression, too, is a manifestation that is nonrational and can even be completely involuntary. Reid argues that both must depend on a physiological chain of connection, and that both are the special study of art. In addition, with expression, art becomes even more closely involved, because if it is the mind's external manifestation, the study of expression can perhaps provide a gateway to the mind's inner working. Thus, art becomes a partner in the fledgling science of psychiatry.

Reid's challenge to science to explore the physiological basis of perception and expression was the starting point for Charles (later Sir Charles) Bell. Bell was a student of the Edinburgh physicians and surgeons but also of the philosopher Dugald Stewart, Reid's principal pupil, and of the painter David Allan. Charles and his elder brother John learned to draw and indeed paint because of the importance of visual analysis for surgery. In 1794 John published at Edinburgh the first volume of *Engravings, Explaining the Anatomy of the Bones, Muscles, and Joints*. Charles assisted with later volumes. The brothers made the drawings and prints for this work themselves, for reasons set out by John in the preface:

As I proceeded in writing a book of anatomy, I felt more and more, at every step, the necessity of giving plates to it; for a book of anatomy without these seemed to me no better than a book of geography without its maps . . . making an abstract subject of one belonging to the senses chiefly, and attempting to obtain by words, those ideas which must come to him through the eye.

When he comes to the aesthetics of his approach, Bell is even more interesting:

No painter in natural history, in botany, in mechanics, nor in anything that relates to science, would dare to draw without his subject immediately before him: but anatomists, who most of all need this clearness and truth, have been most of all arbitrary and loose in their methods; not representing what they saw, but what they themselves imagined, or what others chose to report to them.

To correct this defect, John Bell made his own prints from his own drawings of his own dissections, never generalizing, but drawing in any one case from one individual only. Charles Bell followed his brother's lead directly, first in his published drawings in *The Anatomy of the Brain; Explained in a Series of Engravings* (1802), then in his *Essays on the Anatomy of Expression in Painting* (1806), which drew the painter and the anatomist together. He then went on to make his major contribution to science, *Idea of a New Anatomy of the Brain*, published first in 1811 and more fully in 1821 in *Philosophical Transactions*, and soon after translated into French in the *Revue Britannique*. In these publications, Bell demonstrates that Reid was right and that sensation and expression are the result of a direct, physiological system of communication provided by two distinct sets of nerves, sensory and motor. His French biographer, Amedée Pichot, a leading Anglophile who was a doctor himself and after 1825 the editor of the *Revue Britannique*, wrote: "What these experiments have especially established is the distinct endowments and functions of each nerve; and the general arrangement of the whole system into two portions,—the one applicable to motion, the other to sensibility."[17]

This identification of the two categories of nerves and of their specific functions is seen as one of the fundamental discoveries of modern science (although Bell's claim to the discovery was not uncontested). But if his methods were anatomical, the premises of this great medical discovery were still ultimately philosophical, just as the methods were also artistic. *Essays on the Anatomy of Expression in Painting* was not a digression from Bell's main work but an important stage in a discussion in which art, as a partner, had a practical role. Art in this context was therefore a link between the philosophical originality of Reid and the beginnings of modern neurology, and with it, of psychiatry. This was recognized at the time, and in his biography of Bell, Pichot remarks that *Essays on the Anatomy of Expression* "already contained the elements of his [Bell's] great discovery."[18] Bell's work on the physiology of the brain and nervous system was recognized immediately in France, where parallel studies were being pursued. But his reputation there had been established independently of his medical research. After the battle of Waterloo, shocked to find that twenty thousand wounded French soldiers had no medical assistance, he worked among them for three straight days and nights.

In *Essays on the Anatomy of Expression*, Bell's declared purpose is to explore how the mind is made apparent in the body. If painters are to represent the workings of intellect and emotion, this has to be done through the study of expression—the signs by which we understand what is going on in the minds of those around us. Art too must operate in a psychological environment. Bell's approach was radical. In his introduction he fiercely attacks the academic and neoclassical traditions (though he modified his views in later editions). In his criticism of academic figure drawing, he explicitly anticipates Degas: "The display of muscular action in the human figure is but momentary. . . . The artist must catch, as it were intuitively, what is natural."[19]

*Essays on the Anatomy of Expression* was not translated into French, but Géricault certainly knew it. In 1819 and 1820 he visited England with *The Raft of the Medusa*. At the studio of David Wilkie, he saw and admired his *Chelsea Pensioners*. Wilkie had been a champion of Bell's approach since their days together in Edinburgh, and it was for his command of expression that Géricault admired this picture:

I shall mention to you only the one figure that seemed the most perfect to me, and whose pose and expression bring tears to the eye however one might resist. It is the wife of a soldier who, thinking only of her husband, scans the list of the dead with an unquiet, hag-

**Théodore Géricault (1791–1824).** *The Raft of the Medusa,* **1819. Louvre, Paris, France. Copyright Alinari/Art Resource, NY.**

gard eye . . . Your imagination will tell you what her distraught face expresses.[20]

Expression interested him, and one reason was perhaps that Bell's *Essays on the Anatomy of Expression* had already played a role in the evolution of *The Raft of the Medusa.* In its conception, the picture, with its grisly subject, exactly meets Bell's challenge:

> It is only when the enthusiasm of an artist is strong enough to counteract his repugnance to scenes in themselves harsh and unpleasant, when he is careful to seek all occasions of storing his mind with images of human passion and suffering . . . that he can truly deserve the name of a painter. I should otherwise be inclined to class him with those physicians who, being educated to a profession the most interesting, turn aside to grasp emoluments by gaudy accomplishments rather than by the severe and unpleasant prosecution of science. (Bell, *Essays,* 156)

Then Bell writes, again almost setting a prescription for Géricault: "The mingling of despair and rage and bodily pain is a very difficult study for the painter. But he must be able to express these mingled emotions; or else how shall he represent the varieties of death which the historical painter must exhibit?" (118).

Delacroix's *The Barque of Dante* and *The Massacre at Scio* and Ary Scheffer's *Femmes Souliots* are all similar "terrific" themes to *The Raft of the Medusa*. All represent people in extreme circumstances and in a state of terrified despair. But as direct testimony to the link of Géricault's picture to Bell, at least two of Bell's illustrations from *Essays on the Anatomy of Expression* are reflected directly in the finished painting. The head of a man at the center, seen from a low angle and with his eyes cast upward, closely resembles one illustration from Bell. A dead man lying on his back to the extreme left of the composition, with a sharp profile and head thrown back, echoes an illustration of death in Bell's book that seems to have been particularly popular in Géricault's circle. It inspired a study of a severed head in Chicago, ascribed to Géricault's associate, Champmartin. It also appears in Delacroix's *Barque of Dante* (rotated through ninety degrees in one of the figures clinging to the side of the boat). Even in the painting by Scheffer of Géricault laid out on his deathbed, this image from Bell seems to underlie the portrait of the dead artist.

In both *The Barque of Dante* and *The Massacre at Scio*, Delacroix also explores the use of extreme expression. A large part of *The Massacre at Scio* could be a textbook illustration of a phrase from Bell: "The relaxation of the muscles in languor, faintness and sorrow—of bodily pain and anguish and of death." And among the various images of death in the picture, the head of the dead woman with a child at her breast, if it is also turned through ninety degrees, is again close to the illustration of death in *Essays on the Anatomy of Expression*.

But this same detail also reveals by a different route Delacroix's interest in expression. Just such a scene painted by Aristides of a baby at the breast of its dead mother was celebrated by Pliny as representing the highest command of expression in the art of ancient Greece. This example was cited in Count Algarotti's *Essay on Painting*, where a discussion of expression is remarkable for its advocacy of a naturalistic approach. (It is testimony to the rapidity of the exchange of ideas across Europe upon which this whole argument depends that on its publication Alg-

**Eugéne Delacroix (1798–1863).** *Scenes from the Massacre at Scio,*
**1824. Louvre, Paris, France. Copyright Giraudon/Art Resource, NY.**

arotti sent a copy of his book to David Hume for his comments.)
Algarotti's essay does seem to have interested Delacroix too, for
Algarotti goes on to discuss the *Medea* of Timomachus as an example of expression balanced by decorum in classical art. *Medea*
is a subject that Delacroix turned to a decade later in an important picture which suggests that he too was now seeking to rec-

oncile the demands of expression with his own sense of classical decorum.[21]

In Bell's phrase, Géricault's "severe and unpleasant prosecution of science" in his preparation for *The Raft of the Medusa* is also legendary. But it seems that here too he was being faithful to Bell and to his recommendation that the artist (like the anatomist) must study the real thing, however grim. This is how Bell puts it in *Essays on the Anatomy of Expression* : "It appears to me too often that a painter is too apt to take his ideas of death from the stage. But it is scarcely possible that from such a source he can derive the materials of a natural, simple or terrific representation" (123). He must study death itself, and few came as close to the spirit of this morbid injunction as Géricault, in his painting of the severed heads of a man and a woman. But here there is another link, for Géricault seems to have turned for inspiration not to the guillotine, as one might suppose with such an image, but to the studies of anatomy published by Charles Bell's brother, John. Exactly the same composition of two severed heads laid out on a cloth appears as an illustration to the first volume of *Engravings, Explaining the Anatomy of the Bones, Muscles, and Joints*. Throughout, the illustrations in this book reflect the same grim, unflinching realism. Given the importance of the publication and the reputation of Scottish medicine in France, there is no reason why it should not have been known to Géricault.

This argument takes us still further into the early history of psychiatry, however. In 1817 the first systematic course in the study of mental disease was launched in Paris by Jean E.-D. Esquirol, a pupil of Pinel who employed the study of physiognomy as an aid in the classification of mental diseases. With this end, Esquirol commissioned and collected portraits of the insane. In 1825 Alexander (later Sir Alexander) Morison, Esquirol's principal Scottish disciple, published *Outlines of Lectures on Mental Diseases*, his Edinburgh lectures of 1823, the first ever given on the subject in Britain. He included thirteen illustrations from Esquirol's collection, the first to be published. In 1840 Morison published his complete work on this topic, *The Physiognomy of Mental Diseases*.

This kind of study is also accepted as the motive behind Géricault's studies of the insane. These portraits originally belonged to E. J. Georget, Esquirol's favorite pupil. Esquirol's own approach was closer to the fashionable ideas of the phrenologists than to Bell, but Georget, writing about the appearance of the insane, closely reflects Bell's view of the mobility of expression: "Il est difficile à decrire la physionomie des alienés: il faut l'observer pour en conserver l'image . . . Les physionomies sont presque aussi différents que les individus."[22]

It is surely this approach that is seen in Géricault's astonishing studies. Astonishing, but not unprecedented, for in Edinburgh at the turn of the century, when Bell was forming his thesis, Henry Raeburn and David Wilkie were painting very similar pictures. Raeburn's *Baillie William Galloway* (1798) and Wilkie's *Chalmers-Bethune Family* (1804), for instance, though they were not linked to any psychiatric study, are penetrating studies of expression, something that is unusual in the history of portraiture. Bell and Wilkie were close, but both these pictures clearly reflect the wider currency of this turn-of-the-century debate in Edinburgh, where expression was a topic that united philosophical, artistic, literary, and physiological interests. Wilkie went on to develop a kind of painting that was social because it was psychological, and was psychological because it was based on the study of expression. From his remarks about Wilkie, Géricault clearly understood this, as later did both Bonington and Delacroix, who learned from Wilkie and Walter Scott together this psychological approach to narrative.[23] Within the framework of early psychiatry, Géricault and Georget parallel the exchange between Bell and Wilkie, but it was adumbrated before that by Reid himself: "There are certain modifications of the human face, which are natural signs of the dispositions of the mind. . . . an excellent painter or statuary can tell, not only what are the proportions of a good face, but what changes every passion makes in it" (*Inquiry*, 1:163).

3

In the light of the close relationship between painting and philosophy that underlay this partnership between painting and medical science, it is suggestive to find that at just this moment Delacroix was attending Victor Cousin's lectures on Scottish philosophy, which focused on Reid's theory of perception. Many years later Delacroix wrote: "When I left College, I too

**Sir David Wilkie (1785–1841).** *Willian Chalmers-Bethune, His Wife Isabella Morison and Their Daughter Isabella,* 1804. **National Galleries of Scotland.**

wanted to know everything; I thought I was becoming a philosopher with Cousin."[24] But he also recorded his enthusiasm at the time, writing to a friend in 1818: "I should be very glad too if we could once again attend the opening of Cousin's course."[25] In his journal in May 1823, he noted: "I decided to paint scenes from the Massacre at Scio. I go to see Cousin tomorrow."[26] Here *The Massacre at Scio*, the picture that is widely viewed as a turning point in the history of French art because in it Delacroix is thought to have approached "scientific" realism for the first time, is associated directly with Cousin's teaching. It is Delacroix's treatment of aerial perspective that is seen as the distinctive feature of *The Massacre at Scio*, and Constable, whose work Delacroix noted at this time, was also an important example here. Nevertheless, given his interest in philosophy, just how specific Reid is in making these links between painting and perception, and just how suggestive his arguments might have been to Delacroix (as they almost certainly had been to Wilkie's close friend Constable), can be illustrated by Reid's discussion of this phenomenon:

> However certain our judgment may be that the colour (of an object) is the same, it is as certain that it hath not the same appearance at different distances. There is a certain degradation of the colour, and a certain confusion and indistinctness of the minute parts which is the natural consequence of the removal of an object to a greater distance. Those that are not painters or critics of painting, overlook this and cannot easily be persuaded that the colour of the same object hath a different appearance at the distance of one foot and of ten, in the shade and in the light. But the masters in painting know how, by the degradation of colour and the fusion of the minute parts, figures which are upon the same canvass, and at the same distance from the eye, may be made to represent objects which are at the most unequal distances. They know how to make objects appear to be of the same colour by making their appearance really of different colours. (Reid, *Inquiry*, 1:136)

Though Reid's philosophy was known in eighteenth-century France, a fresh study of it was begun in lectures given at the Ecole Normale by P. P. Royer-Collard in 1811–14. Later Royer-Collard concentrated on the central matter of Reid's philosophy: "Le problème de la perception des objets extérieurs."[27] The last year of his course was interrupted when Royer-Collard was called away by the Restoration, but Cousin succeeded him and carried on directly where his teacher had begun, extending his syllabus to cover the whole of Scottish philosophy in a series of lectures later published as *La Philosophie Écossaise*. Theodore Jouffroy, translator of Reid and pupil of Cousin, says simply that what Royer-Collard began, Cousin completed: the reconstruction of French thought on Scottish "common-sense" principles.[28]

Space does not permit an exploration of Reid's theory of perception here, but one key passage is worth considering in regard to its relationship to painting:

> I cannot therefore entertain the hope of being intelligible to readers who have not by . . . practice acquired the habit of distinguishing the appearance of objects to the eye from the judgment that we form of their colour, distance, magnitude and figure. The only profession in life wherein it is necessary to make that distinction is painting. The painter hath occasion for an abstraction with regard to visible objects somewhat similar to that which we here require; and this indeed is the most difficult part of his art. For it is evident if he could fix the visible appearance of objects without confounding it with the thing signified by that appearance, it would be as easy for him to paint from the life . . . as it is to paint from a copy. (Reid, *Inquiry*, 1:135–37; see also 190–91, 362–64)

This passage contains two principal points. The first is that here, as in the earlier example, Reid refers directly to painting to illustrate his radical theory that perception depends on the intuitive—physiological—response of the mind to physical sensation. But secondly, following this, Reid argues that the painter's task is to put down these sensations, unedited, as they strike the retina. The painter must separate the sign from the signified. This is a difficult, specialized task, he says. The rest of us need not be conscious of these signs, but the painter must make the effort to separate them from the meaning we perceive in them. He must forget prior knowledge in order to describe the sensation that precedes perception. The spectator then reads the record the painter puts down as though these were the original retinal impressions.

The painter must be naive. As Reid famously disposed of the role of ideas in perception, it seems he had also inadvertently disposed of them in painting. But ever since Bellori's essay, *The*

*Idea*, published in 1640, it had been a central tenet of the academic theory of art that it is as a vehicle for the ideal—the whole Platonic structure of ideas—that art has meaning. Now it seemed that art, like everything else, had no coherence except that which it was given by the subjective experience of the spectator. So painting became autonomous.

The radical implications of this conclusion are already reflected in the painting of Raeburn.[29] Delacroix and Bonington understood them, too. Delacroix later became more conservative and sought to stem the tide of change, but his efforts were in vain and later in the century this idea of the autonomy of painting became central to progressive French art. First Courbet embraced naïveté; then the Impressionists pursued more single-mindedly than anyone else ever did Reid's idea that the painter should record the unedited impressions of the retina. When this happened, however, it had not lost its direct link with Reid, for in 1842 Cousin, reforming the baccalaureat, made Reid's works one of a tiny number of set books for the compulsory syllabus in philosophy (Adam Ferguson was also among the chosen authors). With the appearance in 1844 of a new translation of Reid's *Inquiry* in a duodecimo student edition, Reid's ideas became universally familiar.

The wider implications of all this reach far beyond the Enlightenment, but they do illustrate the broader point. Each example given above reflects the fact that the central originality of Scottish thought was its recognition that all knowledge is conditioned by human psychology. It is colored by feeling. Art must take account of this by becoming relative and psychological. It can no longer be ideal. This, in the very broadest terms, was the change that French painting underwent in the three opening decades of the nineteenth century.

4

In the French academic tradition, history, through history painting, was the great model of the ideal, but in the Waverley Novels, Walter Scott presented history itself as relative and psychological—not a great reservoir of general, objective truth, but only contingent, the sum of the infinity of individual, subjective experiences. Scott's reputation in France was enormous and from an early date it impinged on art.

In 1820 Pichot had published prose translations of his poems, which included the first French biography of the author. Pichot's three-volume *Voyage Historique et Littéraire en Angleterre at en Écosse* (1825 and also published in English, German, and Dutch)[30] includes a remarkable account of English and Scottish literature and painting. He distinguishes between them, but his chief objective and the goal of his voyage was to record his meeting with Scott in Edinburgh. In fact he met Scott twice, and every detail of these encounters was recorded verbatim.

Pichot's next book, *Vues Pittoresques de l'Écosse* (1826), was intended as a pictorial guidebook to the sites in Scott's novels. Bonington featured prominently among the artists employed. Although he had never been to Scotland, he contributed eleven topographical views and two narrative illustrations, one to *Rob Roy* and the other to *The Legend of Montrose*. Meanwhile in 1824, Ary Scheffer and Horace Vernet both exhibited pictures inspired by Scott. Vernet's painting was *Allan MacAulay*, also from *The Legend of Montrose*. It is a small picture, but the dramatic, tartan-clad figure standing against a wild Highland landscape instantly recalls Raeburn's full-length Highland portraits. Raeburn, whose work was much engraved, was not unknown in France. Pichot mentions him several times and, in turning to him, Vernet was adapting the only available iconography that could match the heroic grandeur perceived in Scott.

Ary Scheffer also approached Scott through Scottish painting. His picture in 1824 was *L'Enterrement du jeune pêcheur* from *The Antiquary*. The picture is now in the Hermitage. The scene is one where Scott himself invokes Wilkie as the model. There are detailed resemblances between Scheffer's composition and Wilkie's *Distraining for Rent*, where Wilkie depicts the tragic insecurity of the lives of working people. Scheffer likewise uses the genre idiom to describe a scene of tragedy among ordinary people. The principal figures are closely analogous in the two paintings. In both of them, the main character stares distractedly, beyond the reach of any small comfort that is offered. In both, too, the mother, or in Scheffer's picture perhaps it is a sister, is collapsed with grief. The children are concerned, but barely comprehending spectators, and one of them looks inward. In both pictures, one character sits apart to the right, separated from the main action by preoccupation with a task. In Wilkie's picture it is the bailiff's clerk; in Scheffer's it is the grandmother, striving to keep her grief at bay by concentrating fiercely on carding wool. In both pictures, one standing figure dominates the composition, though their dramatic roles are very different, for the bailiff is the source of distress in *Distraining for Rent*, while in Scheffer's picture the same figure attempts to offer comfort. Finally, not only is the general spacial structure similar, but in both compositions still-life objects sit on the ground between the viewer and the action.

There are, of course, other echoes in Scheffer's picture, of Greuze perhaps and of Hogarth, even of Poussin. The last scene of the *Harlot's Progress* seems to be invoked in several details, for example in the woman standing, looking down into the coffin. Hogarth had also been an important part of Wilkie's inspiration in *Distraining for Rent*. If Scheffer was looking at him too, it suggests that the discussion about Hogarth which Charles Lamb had opened in England in 1811 was finding an echo in France.[31] Lamb argued for the fundamental seriousness of Hogarth and compared him to Poussin, to Poussin's disadvantage. In his picture, Wilkie was certainly responding to the encouragement implicit in such arguments for his belief in the seriousness of his own art, but if such views were also finding a response in France, it was an important stage in the collapse of the academic hierarchy of the genres.

Scheffer's choice of model was a bold one, for *Distraining for Rent* was not popular with the authorities. It was so radical that, after its exhibition, it was almost suppressed: "The objection was to the subject; as too sadly real, in one point of consideration, and as being liable to a political interpretation in others. Some persons, it is said, spoke of it as a factitious subject."[32] In spite of this, the relationship between Scheffer's painting and Wilkie's seems to be beyond doubt, but it does also present a puzzle. Wilkie's picture was not engraved until 1828. After its exhibition and purchase by the British Institution in 1816, it was not shown, though it may have preserved its notoriety. Its radical reputation might also explain why, when Abraham Raimbach applied for permission to engrave it, it was refused. The British Institution would not want their ownership to be made so public. However, he then offered to buy it, and he did so over a period of four years. Then in his memoirs he records that in 1824: "On completion of the etching of this plate [*Distraining for Rent*] I made an excursion for a few weeks to Paris. . . . Of the flattering reception I met with from my brother artists, the French engravers, I find it difficult to speak without unbecoming egotism."[33]

Unfortunately for the argument being made here, this visit took place in the late summer or autumn of 1824, during his son's "autumn recess" from Westminster school. It is not clear, therefore, how Scheffer could have known the picture in time to have made use of its inspiration in his Salon picture earlier in the year. Perhaps Raimbach's purchase made it news. His own comment on his reception in France makes it clear that what he was doing was of interest to the artistic community there. He had also completed the etched outline of the picture, so it must have been in his studio for a while and so have been available to any visiting French friends.

What was radical in Wilkie's picture was the way it proposed that great moral examples in art do not necessarily need to illustrate great deeds. For Scott, too, history was no longer the grand design. It was the sum of the infinitely complex web of individual experiences, great and small. For artists, the example of Scott and Wilkie subverted the ideals of traditional history painting, puncturing its grandeur by proposing it should be constructed from the detailed observation of human behavior, hitherto the humble province of genre painting. Following this, the signal success of Wilkie's *The Chelsea Pensioners* was that in it he presented history in this way, the historic moment of the news of Waterloo, seen not as the triumph of grand ideas or heroic deeds, but as the shared experience of ordinary people with all their diversity of response and in the common light of day, for aerial perspective was a key concern of Wilkie's in this picture. Thus history became the present. Genre and history could no longer be distinguished and history painting would never be the same again.

Pichot saw this picture when it was first exhibited and described this diversity of individual responses: "Wilkie n'a négligé aucun détail de la physionomie de chaque personnage; tous sont francs et naturels."[34] Pichot visited Wilkie's studio in 1822, but he seems not to have seen Wilkie's first essay in actual, past history in the manner of Scott's psychological drama, the picture of *Knox Preaching* that Wilkie had recently undertaken. Not

**Sir David Wilkie (1785–1841).** *Chelsea Pensioners Reading the Waterloo Despatch,* **1822. The Board of Trustees of the Victoria and Albert Museum.**

knowing this picture, Pichot comments instead on William Allan as the only painter of actual history: "Le rival de Wilkie, Écossais comme lui, est Allan."[35] But though it was not finished until 1832, Wilkie's *John Knox* quickly became well known. Delacroix saw it in 1825. *The Murder of the Bishop of Liège,* a subject from *Quentin Durward* that was begun two years later, is unusual in Delacroix's work, and it owes a clear debt to Wilkie's painting. But like Wilkie's picture, Delacroix's is also notably Rembrandtesque. It seems that Wilkie led Delacroix to Rembrandt. Most unexpectedly, this is apparent in *The Execution of Doge Marino Faliero,* a picture that Delacroix valued especially highly. It is clearly reminiscent of the latest state of Rembrandt's etching, *Christ Presented to the People.*

There is also a link in the subject of this latter painting to Wilkie's *John Knox,* however. Delacroix was certainly aware that in Byron's story, in the name of democracy, Marino Faliero challenged authority exactly as Knox did, but with a very different result. Where Knox triumphed, Faliero was executed as a traitor. But though the outcome differed, both pictures represented even the great moments of history as contingent, the product of individual feelings and actions.

**Eugéne Delacroix (1798–1863).** *The Murder of the Bishop of Liège,*
**1829. Louvre, Paris, France. Copyright Lauros-Giraudon/Art
Resource, NY.**

In this way, argued Charles Nodier, Scott reflected "le côté réel
de l'humanité."[36] By his evocation of reality through individual
experience, he provided the modern alternative to the epic. Following Wilkie, Delacroix recognized that Rembrandt's approach
to narrative through psychological naturalism directly paralleled this quality in Scott. We see the same train of thought in
Bonington, too. He saw Wilkie's work and admired it, and he
produced a series of paintings linked to Wilkie that demonstrate
his interest in expression. The hunched, staring figure of Bonington's *The Antiquary*, for instance, clearly echoes Wilkie's figure
of John Knox, but it echoes equally the strange portrait that
Wilkie painted of the Earl of Kellie, which was also in his studio
when Bonington visited London in 1825.

Bonington's most ambitious painting is *Quentin Durward at
Liège*. In it he confronts directly the implications of the novel
approach to history that by this time Wilkie shared with Scott.

**Richard Parkes Bonington (1802–1828).** *Quentin Durward at Liège,* **1825–26. Nottingham City Museums and Galleries; The Castle Museum and Art Gallery.**

*Quentin Durward* is Scott's homage to Cervantes. The young, naive hero inadvertently gets entangled in great events, actually subverting history as he does so. At the moment of the action in Bonington's picture, he has wandered aimlessly into the nearby city from the castle of the bishop of Liège. There, to his surprise and bafflement, he has become the object of the excited attentions of the populace. As it turns out, because he is wearing the headgear of the royal bodyguard of Scottish archers, he has been taken for the King's representative. But not only had he strayed perfectly idly into Liège, Durward had actually forgotten what hat he was wearing. It was completely by accident that it was the helmet of the Scots guards.

Bonington's most ambitious history painting depends on a case of mistaken identity. Durward is not an antihero so much as a nonhero. Bonington paints him as a knight in shining armor, but he does so ironically. He knows that history and history painting have ceased to be concerned with tales of heroes. History itself is as shifting and aimless as the constantly changing kaleidoscope of human behavior that he describes so vividly in the anarchic crowd of people who surround Durward in his picture.

Bonington's central motif, showing Quentin Durward between two large burghers of Liège, clearly indicates the direction of his thought. It is a motif that Wilkie had used in his painting *The Village Festival*. He did so deliberately to invoke the choice of Hercules, the subject proposed by the earl of Shaftesbury as the ideal of history painting, satirized by Hogarth in *The March of the Guards to Finchley* and in the first scene of his Election series, and rendered by Reynolds as *Garrick between Tragedy and Comedy*, the choice that Wilkie himself felt at just this moment he had to make between comic painting and serious history. According to Delacroix, Bonington faced the same dilemma. Significantly, neither chose the classic road of high art.

Pichot summarized the impact of all this in France in 1825. In the introduction to *Voyage Historique et Litteraire en Angleterre et en Écosse*, he formulates explicitly the opposition between a natural art, based on experience, that he identifies with Wilkie and the Scots, and an artificial one imposed from above. Writing about literature, he extends his remarks to include art also:

Comment la littérature sera-t-il l'expression de la societé si vous lui défendez les allusions qui se présentent le plus naturellement? Il ne faut pas s'étonner de voir le ministère favoriser de ses grandes phrases les systèmes prétendus classiques, et qu'il faudrait appeler ministériel, système qui tend à nous priver d'une littérature populaire en condamnant les auteurs à invoquer sans cesse les dieux et les grands hommes de Rome et d'Athènes, ou à défigurer les sujets nationaux sous les formes consacrées par l'antiquité. . . . Ces dans l'opposition que figure l'élite de nos grands talens.[37]

That was prophetic. Courbet spent his life in opposition, doing battle with "l'art ministériel." The future of modern art lay in this "art naturel," and it was in part at least rooted in Scots empiricism.

## NOTES

1. See Duncan Macmillan, *Painting in Scotland: The Golden Age* (Oxford, 1986).

2. John Aikman of the Ross to John Forbes, 29 August 1767. Aikman Papers, the Ross, Lanarkshire.

3. I have dealt with this topic more fully in "Woman as Hero: Gavin Hamilton's Radical Alternative," in *Femininity and Masculinity in Eighteenth-Century Art and Culture*, ed. Gill Perry and Michael Rossington (Manchester, 1994), 78–98. I have also further extended the discussion in "The Iconography of Moral Sense: Gavin Hamilton's Sentimental Heroines," *British Art Journal* I, no 1 (autumn 1999), 46–55.

4. Ibid., 79.

5. As she stabs herself, Lucretia says: "Death will be my witness. Give me your solemn promise that the adulterer shall be punished—he is Sextus Tarquinius. He it is who last night came as my enemy disguised as my guest, and took his pleasure of me. That pleasure will be my death and his too if you are men." Livy, *The Early History of Rome*, trans. Aubrey de Selincourt (London, 1971), 98.

6. This subject was also close to the painting *The Death of Virginia* by Nathaniel Dance, a young associate of Hamilton. Dance's picture was engraved in 1760.

7. *Memorie per le Belle Arti* (Rome, 1785), 36.

8. See Macmillan, "Woman as Hero," 80, 84, and 96 n. 11.

9. Sophie de Grouchy herself was both a philosopher and an amateur painter. Her husband, the philosopher Condorcet, indirectly a victim of the Terror, had also been one of the first champions of women's rights. As a member of the Convention's committee on education, he was instrumental in the commission of a study of women's education from Mary Wollstonecraft, a friend of de Grouchy. David had belonged to the same social circle as she did until 1792. For an analysis of de Grouchy's commentary of Smith's *Theory of Moral Sentiments*, see Deidre Dawson's essay in the current volume.

10. Adam Ferguson, *An Essay on the History of Civil Society* (Edinburgh, 1978), 173.

11. See Macmillan, *Painting in Scotland*, 40.

12. Thomas Blackwell, *An Inquiry into the Life and Writings of Homer* (London, 1735), 35.

13. For a wider discussion of this topic, see Duncan Macmillan, "Géricault et Charles Bell," in *Géricault*, 2 vols., ed. Régis Michel, Louvre, Conférences et Colloques (Paris, 1996), 1:449.

14. P.-J.-G. Cabanis, *Rapports du Physique et du Moral*, 2 vols. (Paris, 1802), 1:114:

La sympathie morale offre encore des effets bien dignes de remarque. Par la seule puissance de leurs signes, les impressions peuvent se communiquer d'un être sensible, ou considéré comme tel, à d'autres êtres qui, pour les partager, semblent alors s'identifier avec lui. On voit les individus s'attirer ou se repousser: leurs idées et leurs sentiments, tantôt se répondent par un langage secret, aussi rapide que les impressions elles mêmes, et se mettent dans une parfaite harmonie; tantôt ce langage est le souffle de la discorde: et toutes les passions hostiles, la terreur, la colère, l'indignation, la vengeance peuvent, à la voix et meme en simple aspect d'un seule homme, enflammer tout à coup une grande multitude; soit qu'il les inspire contre lui-même, par le point de vue sous lequel il s'offre à tous les regards. Ces effets et beaucoup d'autres qui s'y rapportent, ont été l'objet d'une analyse très fine: la philosophie écossaise les considère comme le principe de toutes les relations morales.

15. Reid, *Inquiry into the Human Mind, on the Principles of Common Sense*, in *Works*, 2 vols., ed. Sir William Hamilton (Edinburgh, 1846), 1:187.

16. Cabanis, *Rapports du Physique et du Moral*, 1:23.

17. Amedée Pichot, *Sir Charles Bell, Histoire de sa Vie et de ses Travaux* (Paris, 1858; English trans., London, 1860), 96.

18. Ibid., 49.

19. Charles Bell, *Essays on the Anatomy of Expression in Painting* (London, 1806), 1.

20. Quoted in Lorenz A. Eitner, *Géricault: His Life and Work* (London, 1983), 218. For the dating of this letter to May 1820, see Géricault, *Catalogue of the Exhibition at the Grand Palais* (Paris, 1991), 292.

21. Count Francesco Algarotti, *On Painting* (Bologna, 1755; English trans., Glasgow, 1764), 117.

22. E. J. Georget, *De la Folie* (Paris, 1820), 132–33.

23. Duncan Macmillan, "Sources of French Narrative Painting," *Apollo* (1993): 297.

24. Eugene Delacroix, *Journal*, 4 October 1855, ed. and trans. Walter Pach (New York, 1948), 51, 362.

25. 6 November 1818 to J.-B. Pierret, in *Eugene Delacroix: Selected Letters, 1813–63*, ed. and trans. Jean Stewart (New York, 1971), 48. See also letter to Francois Buloz, 25 November 1853: "He [Planche] wrote a good article on Cousin for you" (in *Revue des Deux Mondes*, 15 November 1853).

26. Delacroix, *Journal*, May 1823, 51.

27. Thomas Reid, *Oeuvres*, trans. Theodore Jouffroy, 5 vols. (Paris, 1828), 3:299.

28. Ibid.

29. See Macmillan, *Painting in Scotland*, 79–80.

30. Pichot's book and the wider relationships it reflects are the subject of an article by the present author "A Journey through England and Scotland: Wilkie and Other Influences on French Art of the 1820s," *British Art Journal* II, no. 3 (spring, summer 2001), 28–35.

31. Charles Lamb, "On the Original Genius of Hogarth; with some Remarks on a Passage in the Writings of the late Mr. James Barry," in *The Works of Charles Lamb*, 5 vols. (New York, 1884), 4:138–64.

32. *Memoirs and Recollections of the Late Abraham Raimbach*, ed. M. T. S. Raimbach (London, 1843), 163.

33. Ibid., 124.

34. Amedée Pichot, *Voyage Historique et Littéraire en Angleterre et en Écosse*, 3 vols. (Paris, 1825), 1:162.

35. The full title was *The Broken Fiddle: A Scene at a Fishing Town in the Neighbourhood of Edinburgh*.

36. "Et maintenant qu'un homme dispose des annales de l'humanité comme Homère de celui du peuple Grec, . . . qu'il rapproche les êtres réels à travers les siècles, dans la voie merveilleuse de l'infini . . . Sa mission est de dégager des voiles mystiques de la Comédie Divine, du Paradis Perdu . . . le côté réel de l'humanité, comme l'*Iliade* a extrait la figure grecque du système des epopées symboliques des Achéenes et des Pelasges." Charles Nodier, *Quotidienne*, 17 December 1821, "Oeuvres Complètes de Scott," quoted in Raymond Setbon, *Libertés d'une écriture critique: Charles Nodier* (Geneva, 1979), 200.

37. Pichot, *Voyage Historique*, Avant Propos, xi.

# Part II
## Encylopaedias and Natural History

# The Tortoise and the Hare: A Comparison of the Longevity of the *Encyclopaedia Britannica* with the *Encyclopédie*

FRANK A. KAFKER

IN THE ANONYMOUS PREFACE TO THE FIRST EDITION OF THE *ENCYCLOPAE-dia* Britannica, published in 1771 in Edinburgh, its publishers, the engraver Andrew Bell and the printer Colin Macfarquhar, and its editor, William Smellie, make the following claim: "Instead of dismembering the Sciences, by attempting to treat them intelligibly under a multitude of technical terms, they [the compilers of this encyclopedia] have digested the principles of every science in the form of systems or distinct treatises, and explained the terms as they occur in the order of the alphabet (1: v)." According to the preface, this stress on long syntheses rather than on many short dictionary definitions, organized alphabetically, made the *Britannica* superior to all previous encyclopedias, including the best-known encyclopedia of the eighteenth century, the first edition of the *Encyclopédie*, also known as the Paris *Encyclopédie*, edited by Denis Diderot and Jean Le Rond d'Alembert.

Such a claim of superiority was advertisement, not fact. The *Encyclopédie* also had long synthetic articles and much more. As a book of knowledge, the first edition of the *Britannica* compares very unfavorably to the *Encyclopédie* in depth, breadth, and accuracy of coverage, in the choice of up-to-date and authoritative secondary sources, and in originality of thought. After all, how could a three-volume quarto set compiled largely by one man, Smellie, with 160 copperplates compiled by Bell, rival the *Encyclopédie*'s seventeen folio volumes of articles compiled by more than 140 contributors and eleven folio volumes of engravings containing some 2,500 copperplates, designed, engraved, and explained by more than 60 contributors?[1] The Paris *Encyclopédie* was one of the great encyclopedias of all time, not only as a work of social criticism but also as a book of knowledge, whereas Smellie's encyclopedia was pedestrian compared not only to the *Encyclopédie* but also to many French, German, and Italian encyclopedias of the eighteenth century. The first edition of the *Britannica* was not even much of an improvement over the last edition of Ephraim Chambers's *Cyclopaedia*, published twenty years earlier, in 1751–52.[2]

Yet in one important respect the publication of the *Britannica* was superior to that of the *Encyclopédie*: it outlasted the *Encyclopédie*, in the sense that it went into revised editions and supplements from 1771 to 1810 and beyond, whereas the *Encyclopédie*'s editions and supplements began in 1751 and ended in 1782 (see appendixes A and B at the end of this chapter). This is a paradox that needs investigation.

One possible explanation why the *Britannica* outlasted the *Encyclopédie* is that the editors of the *Encyclopédie* after Diderot and d'Alembert were a lackluster group, and their editions failed to attract an audience. But in fact every one of the later editions of the *Encyclopédie* had press runs of more than 1,000 sets, and the *Supplément*, the quarto, and the octavo editions each had press runs that amounted to more than the first edition's press run of some 4,225 sets. The quarto and octavo, cheap reprints, were much less expensive to purchase than the first edition.[3] In addition, at least one of the later editors, Fortuné-Barthélemy de Félice, the publisher as well as the editor of the Yverdon *Encyclopédie*, was certainly the equal of the editors of the early editions of the *Britannica*, that is, Smellie, James Tytler, Macfarquhar, George Gleig, and James Millar. None of these men produced an edition comparable in size to the fifty-eight-volume quarto Yverdon *Encyclopédie*, and none of them recruited as many as the forty or more collaborators whom Félice recruited. These included such eminent scholars as Leonhard Euler, Joseph-Jérome Le François de Lalande, and Albrecht von Haller, as well as contributors from Berlin, Amsterdam, The Hague, Pavia, Valence, Reims, Grenoble, and especially Paris and various cities in Switzerland. Also, although the Yverdon *Encyclopédie* borrowed much from the first edition of the *Encyclopédie* and was less original or daring, it contains fewer typographical errors, and its coverage of biography, geography, and astronomy was superior.[4] Félice died in 1789, but another talented editor of a later edition of the *Encyclopédie*, Jean-Baptiste Robinet, lived to 1820. He edited the five-volume folio *Supplément*. Recruiting some fifty collaborators, including Lalande, Haller, Michel Adanson, and Jean-François Marmontel, Robinet filled in gaps left by the *Encyclopédie*'s treatment of geography, history, literature, and other branches of learning. He then went on to edit other multivolume reference works.[5] Thus, comparing the relative competence of the various editors of the *Encyclopédie* with the editors of the early editions of the *Britannica* does not provide the key to the *Britannica*'s greater longevity.

A second possible explanation is that the publishers of the various editions of the *Encyclopédie* were less enterprising than Bell and Macfarquhar. Bell and Macfarquhar were certainly outstanding publishers. They recognized that none of the British universal reference works of the arts and sciences appearing from 1752 to 1771 was published outside London, that none was longer than three folio volumes, and that none had captured the market. These included, among others, the first and second edition of William Owen and others' *New and Complete Dictionary of Arts and Sciences* (1754–55, 1763, 1763–64), the second edition of John Barrow's *New and Universal Dictionary of Arts and Sciences* (1756), the second edition of Barrow's *Dictionarium polygraphicum* (1758), and several editions of Temple Crocker and others' *Complete Dictionary of Arts and Sciences* (1764–68). Thus, a way remained open for a Scottish venture of a similar sort. Bell and Macfarquhar increased their profits by publishing in installments as well as by publishing complete sets. They held down costs by keeping the number of paid contributors small, copying from other sources rather than spending for new material, having Macfarquhar's printing shop produce much of the work, and giving the responsibility for the engravings to Bell himself. They knew how to find a niche and call attention to their venture, for they chose a good title and a good format. The *Britannica* was the first Scottish universal reference work of the arts and sciences to be organized alphabetically; it was the first eighteenth-century British universal reference work of the arts and sciences to call itself an encyclopedia, a commercially valuable name thanks to the success of the *Encyclopédie*; it was the first British eighteenth-century encyclopedia to be published in quarto; and it was one of the earliest, although not the first, British encyclopedias to stress long syntheses rather than short dictionary definitions.[6] Also, as we shall see, Bell and Macfarquhar knew how to get along with those in power in Scotland and England.

Still, compared to Charles-Joseph Panckoucke, the publisher of three of the later editions of the *Encyclopédie*, Bell and Macfarquhar were small-fry publishers. Panckoucke, whom Robert Darnton has called "the greatest impresario of the Enlightenment,"[7] joined the corporation of Parisian booksellers in 1762 at age twenty-six and quickly became a publishing magnate.[8] In 1768 he entered the encyclopedia business with gusto. For 200,000 livres he bought the reprint rights and the engravings of the Paris *Encyclopédie* from André-François Le Breton and the other publishers. Over the course of the next thirteen years, Panckoucke formed partnerships to complete a reprint of the *Encyclopédie*, a supplement, a cheap edition, and an index (see Appendix A).[9] A publisher of imagination and enormous energy, he employed many more workers and owned more presses than Bell and Macfarquhar. He certainly had the capacity to produce one revised, superior edition of the *Encyclopédie* after another until his death in 1798 if he had wished to do that; so also could his son-in-law Henri Agasse, who took over Panckoucke's business from 1794 until his death in 1813, and Pauline Panckoucke Agasse, Henri's widow, who took over from 1813 until her death in 1832.[10]

Instead of concentrating on improving the *Encyclopédie*, however, Panckoucke paid more attention to reprints, supplements, and cheap editions of the work; and then from 1782 until 1832, he, his son-in-law, and his daughter worked on other projects, including their largest publishing venture, the *Encyclopédie méthodique*, about 157 volumes of text plus 53 volumes of plates. Rather than being a general encyclopedia of the arts and sciences, the *Méthodique*, a rival of the *Encyclopédie*, consists of separate volumes on individual branches of knowledge. Panckoucke was not only its publisher but also its general editor.[11] Panckoucke, therefore, harmed the long-term prospects of the *Encyclopédie* by his work on various other encyclopedias.

In contrast, Bell and Macfarquhar enhanced the long-term prospects of the *Britannica* by concentrating their energy and capital on it, their largest publishing venture, and by seeking to expand and improve each edition. For example, the first edition was three quarto volumes, the second ten quarto volumes, the third eighteen quarto volumes, and the fourth twenty quarto volumes. With the much expanded third edition, they succeeded in fending off serious competition from Abraham Rees's *Cyclopaedia*, which had appeared in installments from 1778 to about 1785 and in five folio volumes from the late 1770s to the 1780s. A revision of Chambers's *Cyclopaedia*, with impressive engravings, Rees's work quickly went into several reprintings.[12] Moreover, whereas the first and second editions of the *Britannica* were largely one-man shows by Smellie and Tytler, respectively, Bell and Macfarquhar started recruiting and paying individual contributors for articles in the third and fourth editions. The press runs of the *Britannica* were impressive, reportedly from about 3,000 to 3,500 sets for the first edition, 3,000 to 4,500 for the second edition, 13,000 for the third edition, and 3,500 to 4,000 for the fourth edition.[13] Bell and Macfarquhar became very rich.

The business acumen of Bell and Macfarquhar is not the only reason for the greater longevity of the *Britannica*. Panckoucke was astute too. At first he sought to produce a thoroughly revised edition and continue the legacy of Diderot and d'Alembert. In 1768 he invited Diderot and Voltaire to comment on the improvements they would recommend for a future edition, and the next year he spread the word to various journals that he was planning a new edition. For example, the author of an article in the *Journal encyclopédique* of 15 February 1769 took Panckoucke's information and wrote of the forthcoming "entièrement neuf" edition: "Chaque partie de l'Encyclopédie sera reprise en entier, refondue, étendue, rectifiée. Les erreurs, les redites, les contradictions, qui ont été inévitables dans la Ire édition, seront corrigées. . . . On nous assure . . . que les hommes les plus distingués dans les sciences, les arts & la littérature, sont actuellement occupés à ce travail."[14]

But this new edition never came to pass. Panckoucke claimed in 1789 that the chancellor of France, Maupeou, had in 1769 threatened him if he tried to publish such an edition. Instead, Maupeou permitted him to publish only a literal reprint. But when Panckoucke began to print such a reprint, the copies of the first three volumes were seized in 1770 and placed in the Bastille. Panckoucke moved the publication to Geneva with two Swiss publishers, Gabriel Cramer and Samuel de Tournes, and others as partners. The Venerable Company of Genevan Pastors, the French government, and the Archbishop of Paris, Christophe de Beaumont, all tried to prevent this edition from being published in Geneva, but Panckoucke overcame the difficulty; and the Geneva folio reprint was published from 1771 to 1776, with the first three confiscated volumes released from the Bastille only in 1776.

Panckoucke's troubles suggest other reasons why the *Britannica* outlasted the *Encyclopédie*: the contrast between the political and business climate and the nature of the audience on the Continent, especially in France, with that of Great Britain. Before the French Revolution, the French government exercised prepublication censorship and placed other serious obstacles in the way of publishing a new, thoroughly revised, luxury edition of a work that it regarded as a battering ram against Christianity and an advocate of political reform.[15] Even if a French publisher risked embarking on such an expensive edition, it faced stiff competition from the various French, Italian, and Swiss editions of the *Encyclopédie* and from the *Encyclopédie méthodique*.[16] Furthermore, with the coming of the French Revolution, the newspaper and the pamphlet proved to be better able to capture the fast-moving events of the time in France and perhaps on the Continent in general, and thus had greater appeal to the public taste than any multivolume general encyclopedia. Also, with the massive increase of printed matter, the cost of publishing multivolume works in France became much greater at a time when the audience for them had shrunk.[17] Under very trying circumstances, Panckoucke and then his heirs were able to continue publishing the *Encyclopédie méthodique*,[18] but no new large-scale general French-language encyclopedia was published from 1789 until the 1820s.[19] In any event, Napoleon would have prevented a new edition of the *Encyclopédie* in the lands he ruled because of its freethinking and politically reformist views. Consider, for example, the experience of the atheist Jacques-André Naigeon in 1765 and in 1802. His article "Unitaires" in the first edition of the *Encyclopédie* claimed simply to describe and decry the main tenets of Unitarianism, but if one read between the lines, the article actually sought to undermine the belief in God, the divinity of Christ, the sacraments, predestination, and the ecclesiastical organization of the Catholic Church.[20] Some thirty-seven years later, in 1802, seeking to spread his passionate atheism once more, he edited an edition of Montaigne's *Essais* and prefaced it with an irreligious fore-word. Napoleon, attempting to win the support of Catholics, had it expurgated.[21]

The British political, business, and literary scene was differ-ent. During most of the eighteenth century, there were fewer restrictions on freedom of expression. For one thing, prepubli-cation censorship had been illegal in England since 1695, and censorship had relaxed in Scotland with the abolition of the Scottish Privy Council in 1708.[22] We know of no instance where the government impeded the publication of the *Britannica* and only one possible instance where they may have censored it. When the article and plates of "Midwifery" appeared in the first edition, some readers were supposedly offended by the explicit account of normal and abnormal childbirth and protested to the civil authorities, who reportedly told the purchasers to rip out the offending pages and ordered the publishers to destroy the plates.[23]

It is true that in Britain severe restrictions were placed on free-dom of expression during the French Revolution and Napole-onic era because of the fear of sedition,[24] and that James Tytler, the editor of the second edition and perhaps the beginning of the third edition of the *Britannica*, ran into trouble sometime after he ended his tenure as editor. During 1791–92, in articles and pamphlets, he expressed sympathy for the French Revolu-tion, called for the redistribution of seats in the House of Com-mons, urged citizens not to pay taxes until their demands for change were satisfied, and castigated public officials. Then, in the midst of much agitation for reform in Scotland, his pam-phlet *To The People and Their Friends*, which appeared in late 1792, led to his indictment in the first of a series of sedition tri-als in Scotland. Tytler fled to Ireland rather than stand trial, and he was outlawed *in absentia* by the Scottish Court of the Justici-ary on 7 January 1793. He remained in Ireland until 1795, plot-ting the overthrow of the British government, and then lived in Massachusetts until his death in 1804.[25]

Bell and Macfarquhar held conservative political views and disapproved of Tytler's politics during the French Revolution. In 1793, when Tytler's mistress approached Macfarquhar for some help in supporting herself and her twin daughters in Tytler's ab-sence, he rejected her request brusquely and denounced Tytler.[26] Four years later, the preface to the third edition, while acknowledging some of Tytler's articles, gave him only a back-handed compliment: "A man who, though his conduct has been marked by almost perpetual imprudence, possesses no common share of science and genius" (1:xv). The editions of the *Britannica* from 1771 to 1810 contained no radical message; instead, they supported the existing powers and lauded the Hanoverian monarchy.[27] In fact, the *Supplement* to the third edition edited by Gleig and published by Bell's son-in-law, Thomson Bonar, promoted a zealous anti-French, anti-Jacobin viewpoint, and Gleig states in its dedication to George III: "*The French* Encyclopédie *has been accused, and justly accused, of having disseminated, far and wide, the seeds of Anarchy and Atheism. If the* ENCYCLOPAEDIA BRITANNICA *shall, in any degree, counteract the tendency of that pestiferous Work, even these two Volumes will not be unworthy of your* MAJESTY'S *patronage. . . ."*

Also, the period of the French Revolution and Napoleonic rule did not shrink the market for English-language multivolume general encyclopedias, as it did the market for French-language ones. For the British reader, unlike the French, the vogue for newspapers, novels, and other popular literature did not result in a neglect of comprehensive works of learning. More than ten of these were published in Britain. They included William Henry Hall and Thomas Augustus Lloyd, the *New [Royal] Encyclopaedia* (3 vols.; 1789– [1791]; 3 vols.; [1797?]); Edward Augustus Kendall, *A Pocket Encyclopedia* (6 vols.; 1802; 4 vols.; 1811), *The English Encyclopaedia* (10 vols.; 1802); Newton Bosworth, John Mason Good, and Olinthus Gregory, *Pantologia* (12 vols.; 1802–13); George Selby Howard, *The New Royal Encyclopaedia Londonensis* (3 vols.; [1802]), Alexander Aitchison, *The Encyclopaedia Perthensis* (23 vols.; 1806); [Jeremiah Joyce, not George Gregory?], *A Dictionary of Arts and Sciences* (2 vols.; 1806–7); [Jeremiah Joyce, not William Nicholson?], *The British Encyclopedia* (6 vols.; 1809); David Brewster, *The Edinburgh Encyclopaedia* (18 vols.; 1830 [1808–30]); William Enfield, *The New Encyclopaedia* (10 vols.; 1809); G. Jones, J. Jones, and John Wilkes, The *Encyclopaedia Londinensis* (24 vols.; 1810–29); Thomas Exley and William Moore Johnson, *The Imperial Encyclopaedia* (4 vols.; 1812); and Abraham Rees, *The Cyclopaedia* (45 vols.; 1819–20 [1802–20]), as well as the third and fourth editions of the *Encyclopaedia Britannica*.[28] Thus, after 1815, the *Britannica* faced formidable competition, but to meet it was no longer the responsibility of Macfarquhar, who died in 1793 before the completion of the third edition, or Bell, who died in 1809 before the completion of the fourth edition.[29] Instead, the burden rested with Archibald Constable, the chief publisher of the fifth and six editions plus a *Supplement to the 4th*, 5th, and 6th Editions. He proved equal to the task, but that is another story.[30]

In conclusion, the publishing history of the early editions of the *Britannica* differs strikingly from that of the *Encyclopédie*, and the *Britannica* was more successful in at least one important respect: its many editions extended over a longer period of time. This is but one reason why these early editions deserve to be brought out of the shadow of the *Encyclopédie*. Their publishers and editors also merit attention. We have noted the business acumen of Bell and Macfarquhar. Besides their work on the *Britannica*, the editors Smellie, Tytler, and Gleig distinguished themselves: Smellie as a printer and natural scientist, Tytler as a pioneering balloonist and political radical in his later years, and Gleig as a Scottish Episcopal prelate and theologian.[31] In addition, the *Britannica*'s contents should be studied as a way to understand the Scottish Enlightenment, just as the *Encyclopédie* has been studied as a way to understand the French Enlightenment. Perhaps most important, the *Britannica*, by means of one improved edition after another published in Scotland, promoted a common British identity and became the leading eighteenth-century British encyclopedia, providing the foundation of the oldest continuously published encyclopedia still in existence.

## APPENDIX A. THE EDITIONS OF THE *ENCYCLOPÉDIE* FROM 1751 TO 1782

This list of editions is derived from Robert Darnton, *The Business of Enlightenment: A Publishing History of the "Encyclopédie"* (Cambridge, Mass., 1979), esp. 33–37; John Lough, *Essays on the "Encyclopédie" of Diderot and D'Alembert* (London, 1968), 1–110; Frank A. Kafker, ed., *Notable Encyclopedias of the Late Eighteenth Century: Eleven Successors of the "Encyclopédie," Studies on Voltaire and the Eighteenth Century* 315 (1994): 51–142.

1. Paris Edition, 1751–1772. 28 vols. in folio (text: 17 vols., 1751–1765; plates: 11 vols., 1762–1772). Edited by Denis Diderot and Jean Le Rond d'Alembert. Paris: André Le Breton and others.
2. Lucca Edition, 1758–1776. 28 vols. in folio (text: 17 vols., 1758–1771; plates: 11 vols., 1765–1776). Edited by Ottaviano Diodati. Lucca: Vincent Giuntini.
3. Leghorn or Livorno Edition, 1770–1779. 33 vols. in folio (text: 17 vols., 1770–1775; plates: 11 vols., 1771–1778; *Supplément*: 5 vols.; 1778–1779). Edited by Giuseppe Aubert. Leghorn (Livorno): Aubert.
4. Yverdon Edition, 1770–1780. 58 vols. in quarto (text: 42 vols., 1770–1775; *Supplément*: 6 vols., 1775–1776; plates: 10 vols., 1775–1780.) Edited by Fortuné-Barthélemy de Félice. Yverdon: Félice.
5. Geneva Reprint of Paris Edition, 1751–1772 [1771–1776]. 28 vols. in folio (text: 17 vols., 1751–1765 [1771–1774]; plates: 11 vols., 1762–1772 [1771–1776].) Geneva: Charles-Joseph Panckoucke and others.
6. *Supplément* of Paris Edition, 1776–1777. 5 vols. in folio (text: 4 vols., 1776–1777; plates: 1 vol., 1777). Edited by Jean-Baptiste Robinet. Paris and Amsterdam: Panckoucke and others.
7. Quarto Edition, 1771–1781. 45 vols. in quarto (text: 36 vols., 1777–1779; plates: 3 vols., 1778–1779; *Table*: 6 vols., 1780–1781). Edited by Jean-Antoine de Laserre. Geneva [Lyon and Neuchâtel]: Panckoucke and others.
8. Octavo Edition, 1778–1781. 39 vols. in octavo (text: 36 vols., 1778–1781; plates: 3 vols., 1779–1781). Lausanne and Berne: Sociétés typographiques of Lausanne and Berne.
9. *Table*, 1780. 2 vols. in folio. Compiled by Perre Mouchon. Paris, Amsterdam, and Lyon: Panckoucke and Marc-Michel Rey.

N.B. There are also mixed sets of various editions of the *Encyclopédie* with different dates of publication.

## Appendix B. The Editions of the *Encyclopaedia Britannica* from 1771 to 1810

*This list of editions is derived from Kafker, ed., *Notable Encyclopedias of the Late Eighteenth Century,* esp. 181; Frank A. Kafker, forthcoming articles on Andrew Bell and Colin Macfarquhar in the *New Dictionary of National Biography*; Thomas Constable, *Archibald Constable and His Literary Correspondents*, 3 vols. (Edinburgh, 1873), 2: 311–15.

1. First Edition, 1771. 3 vols. in quarto. Edited by William Smellie. Edinburgh: Andrew Bell and Colin Macfarquhar.
2. Reprint, 1773. 3 vols. in quarto. London: Edward Dilly and Charles Dilly.
3. Reprint, 1775. 3 vols. in quarto. London: John Donaldson.
4. Second Edition, 1778–1783 [1784]. 10 vols. in quarto. Edited by James Tytler. Edinburgh: Bell, Macfarquhar, and others.
5. Third Edition, 1797. 18 vols. in quarto. Edited by George Gleig, Macfarquhar, and perhaps Tytler. Edinburgh: Bell and Macfarquhar.
6. *Supplement* to Third Edition, 1801. 2 vols. in quarto. Edited by Gleig. Edinburgh: Thomson Bonar.
7. *Supplement* to Third Edition, 1803. 2 vols. in quarto. Edited by Gleig. Edinburgh: Bonar.
8. Dublin Edition, 1790–1797. 18 vols. in folio. Edited by James Moore. Dublin: Moore.
9. *Supplement* to Dublin Edition, 1801. 2 vols. in quarto. Edited by James Moore. Dublin: Moore.
10. American Edition, 1790–1798. 18 vols. in quarto. Edited by Thomas Dobson. Philadelphia: Thomas Dobson.
11. *Supplement* to American Edition, 1803. 3 vols. in quarto. Edited by Dobson. Philadelphia: Dobson.
12. Fourth Edition, 1810. 20 vols. in quarto. Edited by James Millar. Edinburgh: Bell.

## NOTES

1. On the first edition of the *Encyclopaedia Britannica*, see Frank A. Kafker, "William Smellie's Edition of the *Encyclopaedia Britannica*," in Frank A. Kafker, ed., *Notable Encyclopedias of the Late Eighteenth Century: Eleven Successors of the "Encyclopédie," Studies on Voltaire and the Eighteenth Century* 315 (1994): 145–82; on the first edition of the *Encyclopédie*, see John Lough, *The "Encyclopédie"* (London, 1971); Jacques Proust, *Diderot et l'Encyclopédie*, new ed. (Paris, 1995); Arthur M. Wilson, *Diderot* (New York, 1972); Frank A. Kafker, *The Encyclopedists as a Group: A Collective Biography of the Authors of the "Encyclopédie," Studies on Voltaire and the Eighteenth Century* 345 (1996); Frank A. Kafker and Madeleine Pinault Sørensen, "Notices sur les collaborateurs du Recueil de

planches de *l'Encyclopédie*," *Recherches sur Diderot et sur l'Encyclopédie* 18–19 (1995): 201–29.

2. For articles on various eighteenth-century encyclopedias, see Frank A. Kafker, ed., *Notable Encyclopedias of the Seventeenth and Eighteenth Centuries: Nine Predecessors of the "Encyclopédie," Studies on Voltaire and the Eighteenth Century* 194 (1981); Kafker, ed., *Notable Encyclopedias of the Late Eighteenth Century*.

3. On the press runs of the various editions of the *Encyclopédie*, see Robert Darnton, *The Business of Enlightenment: A Publishing History of the "Encyclopédie"* (Cambridge, Mass., 1979), 33–37; Mario Rosa, "*Encyclopédie*, 'Lumières' et tradition au 18e siècle en Italie," *Dix-huitième siècle* 4 (1972): 127; Kathleen Hardesty [Doig], *The "Supplément" to the "Encyclopédie"* (The Hague, 1977), 17; Kathleen Hardesty Doig, "The Yverdon *Encyclopédie*," in Kafker, ed., *Notable Encyclopedias of the Late Eighteenth Century*, 90–91.

4. Doig, "Yverdon *Encyclopédie*," 85–116.

5. "Avertissement," *Supplément à l'Encyclopédie*, 5 vols. (Amsterdam, 1776–77), 1:i–iv; Hardesty [Doig], *"Supplément"*; Kathleen Hardesty Doig, "Notices sur les auteurs des quatre volumes de 'Discours' du *Supplément à l'Encyclopédie*," *Recherches sur Diderot et sur l'Encyclopédie* 9 (1990): 157–70; John Lough, "The Contributors to the *Encyclopédie*," *Studies on Voltaire and the Eighteenth Century* 223 (1984): 518–28, 556–64; Raymond F. Birn, *Pierre Rousseau and the Philosophes of Bouillon, Studies on Voltaire and the Eighteenth Century* 29 (1964):136–40; Terence Murphy, "Jean Baptiste René Robinet: The Career of a Man of Letters," *Studies on Voltaire and the Eighteenth Century* 150 (1976): esp. 187–88, 201–31; Alain Nabarra, "Robinet, Jean-Baptiste (1735–1820)," in *Dictionnaire des journalistes (1600–1789)*, ed. Jean Sgard (Grenoble, 1976), 316–18.

6. Frank A. Kafker, forthcoming articles on Andrew Bell and Colin Macfarquhar in the *New Dictionary of National Biography*. Denis de Coetlogon, *Universal History of the Arts and Sciences* (1745) had already adopted a treatise system.

7. Darnton, *Business of Enlightenment*, 394.

8. On Panckoucke's early years, see Suzanne Tucco-Chala, *Charles-Joseph Panckoucke & la librairie française* (Pau, 1977), 47–125.

9. Darnton, *Business of Enlightenment*.

10. On the huge size of Panckoucke's publishing business during the French Revolution, see Carla Hesse, *Publishing and Cultural Politics in Revolutionary Paris, 1789–1810* (Berkeley, Cal., 1991), 72, 171, 188–89. Regarding the business operated by Panckoucke's son-in-law and daughter, see ibid., 188–89, and Christabel P. Braunrot and Kathleen Hardesty Doig, "The *Encyclopédie méthodique*: An Introduction," *Studies on Voltaire and the Eighteenth Century* 327 (1995): esp. 5, 14–15.

11. Darnton, *Business of Enlightenment*; Braunrot and Doig, "*Encyclopédie méthodique*," 1–151.

12. Stephen Werner, "Abraham Rees's Eighteenth-Century *Cyclopaedia*," in Kafker, ed., *Notable Encyclopedias of the Late Eighteenth Century*, 183–99.

13. On many of the contributors to the third edition, see "preface," 1:xv–xvi; for the fourth edition, see "preface," 1:xv–xvi. On the press runs of the various editions, see Archibald Constable to Richard Phillips, 22 December 1812, Columbia University Rare Books and Manuscripts Library, X032EN1, Agreement, Minutes, and Letters Relating to the *Encyclopaedia Britannica*,

1812–1822, fol. 138, and Archibald Constable to Joseph Robinson, autumn 1821, in Thomas Constable, *Archibald Constable and His Literary Correspondents*, 3 vols. (Edinburgh, 1873), 2:311–14.

14. Quoted in John Lough, "The Panckoucke-Cramer Edition," in *Essays on the "Encyclopédie" of Diderot and D'Alembert* (London, 1968), 53–54. The information in this paragraph and the one that follows is drawn from this article, 52–110.

15. For restrictions placed on publishing in the Old Regime, see, among others, Robert Darnton and Daniel Roche, eds., *Revolution in Print: The Press in France, 1775–1800* (Berkeley, Cal., 1989); William Hanley, "The Policing of Thought: Censorship in Eighteenth-Century France," *Studies on Voltaire and the Eighteenth Century* 183 (1980): 265–95; Hesse, *Publishing and Cultural Politics*, 1–20; Nicole Hermann-Mascard, *La Censure de livres à Paris à la fin de l'ancien régime* (Paris, 1968).

16. In 1776 Panckoucke again decided to produce a thorough revision of the Paris *Encyclopédie* with his brother-in-law, Jean-Baptiste-Antoine Suard, as editor. But he gave up this project by 1778 because it conflicted with some of his other plans for editions of the *Encyclopédie*. See Darnton, *Business of Enlightenment*, 44–89, 395–97, 401–2, 421–22, 555–56; Lough, "Panckoucke-Cramer Edition," 109–10.

17. Hesse, *Publishing and Cultural Politics*; Jeremy D. Popkin, *Revolutionary News: The Press in France, 1789–1799* (Durham, N.C., 1990); Dale K. Van Kley, "New Wine in Old Wineskins: Continuity and Rupture in the Pamphlet Debate of the French Pre-Revolution," *French Historical Studies* 77 (1991–92): 447–65; Darnton, *Business of Enlightenment*, 484–86.

18. Darnton, *Business of Enlightenment*, 481–96; Braunrot and Doig, "*Encyclopédie méthodique*," 13–16.

19. Gert A. Zischka, *Index lexicorum: Bibliographie der lexikalischen Nachschlagewerke* (Vienna, 1959), 7; "Les encyclopédies," *La Grande Encyclopédie* 15 (n.d.): 1013.

20. "Unitaires," *Encyclopédie* 17 (1765): 387–401.

21. Jean-Philibert Damiron, "Naigeon et accessoirement Sylvain Maréchal et Delalande," in *Mémoires pour servir à l'histoire de la philosophie au XVIIIe siècle*, 3 vols. (Paris, 1858–64), 2:436–39.

22. Frederick Seaton Siebert, *Freedom of the Press in England, 1476–1776: The Rise and Decline of Government Control* (Urbana, Ill., 1965), 260–392; William James Couper, *The Edinburgh Periodical Press*, 2 vols. (Stirling, 1908), 1:77–112.

23. This act of censorship is reported in Paul Kruse, "The Story of the *Encyclopaedia Britannica*, 1763–1943" (Ph.D. diss., University of Chicago, 1958), 51–52, but no source is cited. The account in Clifton Fadiman, Bruce L. Felknor, and Robert McHenry, eds., *The Treasury of the Encyclopaedia Britannica* (New York, 1992), 7, differs somewhat: "There is a tradition that either the monarch George III or his court chamberlain was so incensed by the detailed illustrations of the birth process that he ordered all loyal subjects to rip out and destroy the offending plates."

24. See, for example, Philip Anthony Brown, *The French Revolution in English History* (1918; reprint, New York, 1965); Henry W. Meikle, *Scotland and the French Revolution* (Glasgow, 1912); Arthur Aspinall, *Politics and the Press, c.*

*1780–1850* (1949; reprint, Brighton, 1973), esp. 33–42; Clive Emsley, *British Society and the French Wars, 1793–1815* (London, 1979); H. T. Dickenson, ed., *Britain and the French Revolution, 1789–1815* (New York, 1989); E. W. McFarland, *Ireland and Scotland in the Age of Revolution: Planting the Green Bough* (Edinburgh, 1994).

25. James Fergusson, *Balloon Tytler* (London, 1972), 114–54; Meikle, *Scotland and the French Revolution*, 112, 115 n. 3, 132; McFarland, *Ireland and Scotland*, 72, 96–97, 123 n. 18, 123 n. 19, 136–38.

26. Fergusson, *Balloon Tytler*, 134; [Robert Meek], *A Biographical Sketch of the Life of James Tytler* (Edinburgh, 1805), 19–21.

27. For example, see Kafker, "William Smellie's Edition of the *Encyclopaedia Britannica*," in Kafker, ed., *Notable Encyclopedias of the Late Eighteenth Century*, 170–74, and the dedication to George III in the third and fourth editions.

28. "Dictionaries of Arts and Sciences," *Eclectic Review* 5 (1809): 541–53; Robert Collison, *Encyclopaedias: Their History Throughout the Ages*, 2nd ed. (New York, 1966), 109–10, 174–78; Richard Yeo, *Encyclopaedic Visions: Scientific Dictionaries and Enlightenment Culture* (Cambridge, U.K., 2001), esp. 291, 292; some of these encyclopedias were also published in installments. For further information on them, see their entries in the *British Library General Catalogue of Printed Books to 1975* and the *National Union Catalog Pre–1956 Imprints*.

29. The third edition appeared in installments from 1788 to 1797 and as eighteen quarto volumes dated 1797; and the fourth edition appeared in installments from about 1801 to 1810 and as twenty quarto volumes dated 1810. See Kafker, forthcoming articles on Bell and Macfarquhar in the *New Dictionary of National Biography*.

30. Kruse, "Story of the *Encyclopaedia Britannica*," 102–45; Yeo, *Encyclopaedic Visions*, 251–76.

31. Stephen W. Brown, "Smellie, William," in the *Dictionary of Eighteenth-Century British Philosophers*, ed. John W. Yolton, John Valdimir Price, and John Stephens, 2 vols. (Bristol, 1999), 2:804–8; Fergusson, *Balloon Tytler*; William Walker, *Life of the Right Reverend George Gleig* (Edinburgh, 1878).

# The *Encyclopaedia Britannica* and the French Revolution

### KATHLEEN HARDESTY DOIG

IN THE 1820S, WHEN THE WHIG JUDGE HENRY COCKBURN LOOKED BACK on Scotland at the turn of the nineteenth century, he placed the French Revolution at the center of Scottish experience: "Everything rung, and was connected with the Revolution in France; which, for above 20 years, was, or was made, the all in all. Everything, not this or that thing, but literally everything, was soaked in this one event."[1] Cockburn's assessment of the influence of the Revolution on Scottish life is often quoted, but the sentence following it is not, even though it adds a crucial element to the picture: "Yet we had wonderfully few proper Jacobins; that is, persons who seriously wished to introduce a republic into this country, on the French precedent."

This qualification about the state of affairs in Scotland could apply equally well to the rest of Britain, where the cataclysm across the English Channel was interpreted along existing lines of political and class affiliation. The French experiment did reinvigorate the small minority of organized artisans and shopkeepers, whose attempts at burgh reform had begun to flag.[2] Among the masses, however, the deep native conservatism was strengthened, as demonstrated by the hundreds of loyalist clubs that mushroomed throughout the British Isles.[3] The Pitt government, at one with the propertied and professional classes, launched a full attack against the "innovators," and there was widespread fear that the modest calls for a more representational Parliament would escalate into a massive French-style overthrow of civil and religious order. The "flag-waving French-hating Church and King Tory" of the 1790s also fully supported the draconian repressions instituted by the government,[4] culminating in the suspension of habeas corpus in 1794 and the Two Acts against treason and sedition in 1795. The earlier treason trials of 1793–1794 had resulted in many convictions. Although Thomas Hardy, John Horne Tooke, and others were acquitted in the most famous of these trials in late 1794, the government was the ultimate winner, in that radical activity was effectively squelched for a long period. In Scotland, tests of anti-Jacobin orthodoxy were applied to prospective advocates (barristers) for many years, and there were no antigovernment meetings in Edinburgh after the trials until 1816.[5]

The threat seemed greater, in fact, in the northern part of the kingdom than elsewhere in Britain. Widespread literacy meant that "seditious" writings, such as Thomas Paine's *Rights of Man*, had a larger audience among the working class.[6] James Macintosh's *Vindiciae Gallicae* (1791), a reply to Edmund Burke's *Reflections on the French Revolution*, had a strong impact on educated reformers.[7] By 1792, political clubs, most notably the Society of Friends of the People, were active. The conservative majority of the ruling and professional classes, the press, and the Church of Scotland rose in opposition to these potentially destructive forces.[8]

They were soon joined by a work in a genre that had not so far delved deeply into politics, at least in Britain. British encyclopedism had not followed the great Paris *Encyclopédie* in this respect. No English-language encyclopedias were noted for reformist stances, particularly not the *Encyclopaedia Britannica*, which was growing in prestige and popularity as it went into new editions relatively quickly. After a successful three-volume first edition (1768–1771), the *Britannica* had expanded to ten volumes in the second edition (1777–1783 [1784]), edited by a brilliant but improvident chemist and man of letters, James Tytler. By the early 1790s, the eighteen-volume third edition (1788–1797) was well underway. Although Tytler probably played some part in it,[9] his direct participation ceased when he garnered the distinction of being among the first Britons charged in the sedition clampdowns in 1793. Tytler fled rather than face trial, and eventually died an expatriate in the United States. His post-*Britannica* career as an outspoken reformer remains one of the more arresting facts in the history of encyclopedism, since the edition for which he was responsible was inoffensive enough to attract numerous subscriptions, in all likelihood mainly from the Scottish gentry and the professional classes.

The third edition of the *Britannica* was also a commercial success, with between 5,000 and 13,000 copies printed.[10] The chief editor at the beginning seems to have been one of the publishers, Colin Macfarquhar, who had also played a role in editing the earlier editions. He was assisted by a roster of local collaborators, including George Gleig, an Episcopal Church of Scotland minister. Although his career had been stymied by squabbles with his prelate, Gleig would finally be consecrated head of the Brechin diocese in 1808 and would become primus of the small contingent of Scottish Episcopalians in 1816. When Macfarquhar died in 1793, Gleig took over the editorship of volumes 13 through 18. He then wrote and compiled most of a two-volume *Supplement* (1801), which is imbued with his own interests and concerns, and which would remain his most important work.[11] This third edition and the *Supplement* would become organs of propaganda in the campaign against Jacobinism in Great Britain. The political content was thus to some extent accidental, since Gleig happened to assume charge just as the situation in France was deteriorating and becoming more threatening to Britain. In addition, it is worth noting that Scottish Episcopalians had finally achieved conditional toleration in 1792; Gleig's trumpeting of anti-Jacobinism was perhaps in part inspired by a desire for more rapid assimilation.

As H. T. Dickinson notes, events of the 1790s stimulated a "more organized and more sophisticated popular conservatism" that was based in fact on long-standing opinions,[12] which can be traced through all the early editions of the *Britannica*. One such attitude that becomes prominent in the third edition is condescension toward the French and their civilization. In business, for example, the English annuity system is presented as superior to the French method.[13] This attitude was subsequently reinforced in many articles in the *Supplement*, as the Revolution intensified this prejudice. There are general warnings, for example, about "French principles" and "innovations" in a range of *Supplement* articles, including biographical articles such as "Chaumette" and entries on topics of general interest such as "Passigraphy" (a form of universal writing ridiculed as an example of the French love of novelty).

The denigration of French values also derived in part from a general conviction pervasive in British culture, and adopted without question in the *Britannica,* that British institutions were superior to all others. The notion is especially prevalent in the numerous entries touching, directly or tangentially, on the British social structure. Contributors assume the existence of a "natural aristocracy of the country" ("Army," 2:343). They pontificate about forms of consumption and clothing appropriate to individuals' social status ("Luxury") and about the danger of elevating someone too quickly above his or her original level ("Burns" [Robert], *Supplement*). A social structure based on ranks, in short, is thought to be "essentially necessary to the existence of civil order" ("Chivalry," 4:696). Since "Chivalry" appears in an early volume, the observation is probably not a comment on contemporary French attempts to promote equality. But "Nobility," in volume 13 (the first volume edited completely by Gleig), very likely *is* referring to the new régime in France when it asserts that "it is safer to remain as we are," with a structure whose faults are known, rather than risk a change that might "destroy many of the pleasures, of social life" (13:88). William Blackstone (a primary source for entries on legal terms throughout the early editions) and the *Gentlemen's Magazine*, both bastions of the conservative mentality, are quoted for further support of this principle. A stable class structure, viewed as founded on natural principles, implies the corollary of an unchanging form of government, a connection the *Britannica* endorses. The French are paraded as a counterexample in such later articles as "Prejudice," where a major argument for maintaining the existing form of government is the natural inability of the populace to implement political change in a rational manner.

The *Britannica* justifies the British system as flowing from and safeguarding the liberty of citizens, but where despotism holds sway, the *Britannica* is willing to consider change. Only in this case, and only in the measure necessary to restore what it defines as freedom, does the encyclopedia endorse the concept of revolution. Following this guideline, the third edition praises the people's revolt against the aristocratic party in Geneva in early 1789 as a means of restoring liberties ("Geneva") and condones the original revolution in France because the Third Estate was oppressed by a despotic monarchy ("Peasant," "Prejudice," "Revolution"). The *Britannica* sees no trace of such oppression in Britain, however. The British nobility has supposedly been under control since Tudor days, and the commons have been raised in status ("Revolution," 16:151). Allusions to resulting modern-day liberties are inserted in dozens of articles. The message to readers is clear: their own social order, ancient and perfected, should not be altered. The claims of modern-day reformers are given no hearing, and are rarely even mentioned. When their inconvenient criticisms of such inequities as skewed representation in Parliament must mar the rosy scene, the reformers—including men like Richard Price, who is otherwise well regarded—are deemed guilty of an "extravagant attachment" to an unsuitable form of government ("Price" [Richard], *Supplement*, 2:504).

When individuals go beyond the initial step of eliminating despotism in order to restore liberties, anarchy and violence ensue. Such is the thesis of the series of articles that chronicle the French Revolution. The notion is not developed chronologically in the *Britannica*; production dates of the third edition meant that early entries, such as "Bastile" [*sic*], could make no mention of the events of 1789. "France," in volume 7, might have broached the subject in its updating of the second-edition essay, but the account stops short at 1789. The author explains that he chose not to continue with a potentially "imperfect or dubious narration." He could not predict at that point, probably the very early 1790s, whether the republicans would prevail, or whether it would eventually be necessary to "recount a new train of events tending to shake the novel fabric, and to restore the puissance and splendor of *royalty*, though the sceptre of *despotism* should be swayed no more" (7:445). The author refers forward to "Revolution," hoping that a dénouement might be known by the time of that article's appearance.

It was not. The fifty-page article "Revolution" covers events only through 1795, when the war between Britain and France was still not decided and the threat of a similar revolution in England, although diminished because of the harsh repressions, still haunted the nation. The *Britannica*'s history of these crucial years is a product of this atmosphere. It is true that most of the facts in the account conform with modern histories. The list of causes of the Revolution is fairly evenhanded, and Gleig and the lawyer and miscellaneous writer Robert Forsyth (the authors are identified in the preface) claim to have consulted works "not unfriendly to democracy" ("Revolution," 16:199), although none of them are ever identified.[14] But the essay is not dispassionate. The tone is that of Burke, although little is borrowed directly from him. An exception is the memorable passage on the defilement of Marie Antoinette's bedroom by revolutionaries and the forced departure of the royal family from Versailles on 6 October 1789, transcribed with only slight changes of wording ("Revolution," 16:163–64). Every section of the article bears a cautionary tale for the British reader. This is what happens, the authors imply, when religion is undermined, when an old, privileged nobility is overthrown, when false notions of liberty are allowed to run rampant, and when a populace without the ties of property or the decorum instilled by education is able to gain control. The final sentence of the narrative passes from oblique language to a direct statement of Tory themes. As in much British anti-Jacobin writing, the tone is apocalyptic, and the cadences suggest the pulpit that Gleig occupied: "If the horrible deeds of darkness which have been acted on the theatre of France cannot make us contented with the government under which we live, and which has been brought to its present state of perfection, not by the metaphysical speculations of recluse philosophers, but by observation and the practical experience of ages, we shall be considered by posterity as a people incapable of instruction, and ripe for the greatest miseries in which we may be involved" (16:199–200).[15]

The same tone pervades the last important statements on the Revolution in the third edition. They appear incongruously in a digression in the article "River," by the natural philosopher John Robison. While defining the word "nature," Robison launches into a diatribe against the current French meaning of the term, "that indescribable idol . . . being held forth by her zealous high-priests to the refined vanity of man as a sort of mirror" (16:302). The passage is a harbinger of the tract on the conspiracy theory that Robison was probably already writing, and which we shall see cited in the *Supplement*. Like that essay, "River" notes the significance of masonic affiliations, in this case regarding a certain Brigonzi, grand master of the lodge "Des Mousses," whom Robison had seen in St. Petersburg as *machiniste de l'opéra*, now scornfully described as reappearing as one of the "most active priests" in the ceremony at Notre Dame celebrating nature (16:302). Other common themes include the importance of Voltaire, the bloody effects of this "philosophy," and the danger to Britain. The text helps to explain the intense interest of this scientist in fighting the philosophic spirit. For him, nature does not produce "chance fragments of a fatal chaos"; it is, rather, "that admirable system of general laws" by which God connects and regulates the various parts of the structure (16:303).

Gleig's *Supplement* continues the chronicle of Revolutionary events and develops the anti-Jacobin message, which is all the more intense for being concentrated in only two volumes. For the chronicle, the author of the article "Revolution," who was very likely Gleig himself,[16] picks up the narrative at the exact spot where the third edition had left off and provides another fifty-page essay that reaches the year 1800. The slant is the same, with a good supply of derogatory expressions describing the Jacobins and the foibles of the various governments. Much of the article concerns the early Napoleonic military campaigns; the general himself is depicted as a usurper but not yet a tyrant. Again, few sources are mentioned. This chronology is followed by ten additional pages where the writer purports to correct errors in the third-edition article. Without exception, they place the Ancien Régime in a better light and the republicans in a worse one. Many of the comments are misleading, others incorrect. The reader of the *Supplement* is told, for example, that the clergy and nobility enjoyed only trifling tax exemptions, that the third edition had exaggerated the miseries of French peasants relative to their Scottish counterparts,[17] that Necker was to blame for everything that followed, and that *lettres de cachet* were less abused of, and pensions less generous, than claimed. Gleig quotes at several points a new work published in 1800, the *Annals of the French Revolution* by the émigré ex-minister Antoine-François Bertrand de Moleville. A long section bemoans the different moments when the evolution toward Jacobinism might have been checked if only various figures or groups had been firmer—a clear justification of the fierce measures that had so far kept Jacobinism at bay in Great Britain. The resulting sense of victory inspires a confident conclusion that would turn out to be less than astute political forecasting: Napoleon will not last long, he writes, because both Jacobins and royalists hate the new government.

Near the end of this second and last volume of the *Supplement*, there is an update in the work's final word on the subject. It appears in a note to the biographical entry on Count Aleksandr

Suvarov, precisely dated 4 September 1800 (*Supplement*, "Suworow"). Stung by Napoleon's recent victories, a subdued Gleig admits that he had thought that "the progress of the French revolution . . . would, by this time, have taken a very different turn" (*Supplement*, 2:635n.). Predictably, there is a scapegoat: the faulty allied military command in the Italian campaign. But there is no further conjecture about cheerful future outcomes. The Napoleonic adventure was beginning to appear as worrisome as the republicanism of the previous decade.

Supporting this chronicle of events is another group of entries in the *Supplement*. Once again, there are few direct references to Burke, beyond the praise for his early perspicuity in his biographical entry: when the French set up a government based on the rights of man, "he predicted that torrent of anarchy and irreligion which they have since attempted to pour over all Europe" ("Burke," *Supplement*, 1:137). Instead, the *Supplement* emphasizes a more recent argument, which had been developed most comprehensively by the abbé Augustin Barruel in his *Mémoires pour servir à l'histoire du jacobinisme* (1797–1798, and translated into English during the same years). Barruel held that various sects of materialists and republicans had schemed to overthrow the Ancien Régime and had planned similar attempts throughout Europe.[18] Supporting this view, but supposedly written without knowledge of Barruel's history, was the Scottish work referred to above, John Robison's only nonscientific publication, *Proofs of a Conspiracy against All the Religions and Governments of Europe, Carried on in the Secret Meetings of Free Masons, Illuminati, and Reading Societies* (1797), which went through four editions in Edinburgh, Dublin, London, and New York within a year. The conspiracy theory had never been popular with the English right-wing press,[19] but Gleig clung to it. Even after the publication of Jean-Joseph Mounier's *De l'Influence attribuée aux philosophes, aux francs-maçons et aux illuminés, sur la révolution de France* began to discredit it in 1801, Gleig is said to have preached in favor of the conspiracy theory at Stirling in 1803.[20] Both Barruel and Robison are major sources for the *Supplement*, as is the *Anti-Jacobin Review*, to which Gleig and Robison contributed a number of articles. As an active preacher, Gleig fully grasped the value of repeating his message. He hammers at it in biographical entries as well as under other headings as disparate as "Institute" and "Guillotine."

According to the conspiracy scheme, freemasons played a major role in planning the Revolution. Gleig fully accepts this explanation, bringing back the term "Masonry" in the *Supplement* in spite of the "copious detail" in the third edition, "to warn our countrymen against the pernicious superstructures which have been raised by the French and Germans on the simple system of British masonry" (Free "Masonry," *Supplement*, 1:176). Quoting both Robison and Barruel,[21] the three-page article recounts details about a corrupted, continental form of the initiation ceremony, culminating in the decapitation of a mannequin, all of which is calculated to chill a British soul. Lest an obtuse reader miss the point, Gleig ends with a blunt query expressing church-and-king concerns. "Have there been no symptoms of sedition and irreligion among us," he asks, "that we should be so confident that the quality and liberty of our lodges will never degenerate into the equality and liberty of the French Jacobins?" (*Supplement*, 1:179). He holds that Masonry is not as harmless as its younger adepts would have it, since it demands an oath, in violation of religion, and goes against British liberty in its demand for unlimited obedience to a human being. Gleig's solution to the menace is a milder version of the official repressions of sedition: let the lodges close down, voluntarily, for the moment.

The *Supplement* wages a more extensive and vitriolic attack against a second and related branch of alleged conspirators, the Illuminati. A biographical entry sets the tone by describing the effects of "this philosophic culture" on the morals of Carl Bahrdt, a member of an offshoot of the sect ("Bahrdt," 1:58). Bahrdt's sexual immorality and dishonesty are described with verve, in passages drawn from Robison. The latter is also cited in the major article on the subject, "Illuminati," but Barruel is the chief source for this fourteen-page essay. It explains in detail the organization of the sect and the different degrees of membership in it. Like "Masonry," the article is informational only to the degree necessary for rousing the reader to action; the genre is exhortative, not factual writing. To conservatives, the intensity of feeling was commensurate with the danger represented by the Illuminati: "the real object of this order was, by clandestine arts, to overturn every government and every religion; to bring the sciences of civil life into contempt; and to reduce mankind to that imaginary state of Nature when they lived independent of each other on the spontaneous productions of the earth" (*Supplement*, 1:769). As in "Bahrdt," the moral failings of individuals are interpolated in the argument; the escapades of the founder, Adam Weishaupt, are told in phrases dripping with irony. The organization as a whole is said to be corrupt, even in seemingly wholesome undertakings. For example, local branches of the Illuminati were given the laudable charge of establishing libraries, but were told to steal any necessary books. This moral degradation is symptomatic of the political danger. In language attributed to Illuminati texts, the sect is depicted as subscribing to *"the rights of man"* and the goal that "PRINCES AND NATIONS SHALL DISAPPEAR FROM THE FACE OF THE EARTH" (*Supplement*, 1:776).[22] The change of typeface here and in other passages, which is also favored by Barruel and Robison in their conspiracy works, betrays a frenzy at odds with the reasoned demonstration that the *Supplement* is purporting to convey. Elsewhere in the *Supplement*, as in the satirical italicizing of certain quotes in the article "Brissot" (*Supplement*, 1:116), typography is used with the same rhetorical intent.

Following Barruel and Robison, Gleig expands the conspiracy to include a third group, which is at once the most diffuse and the most guilty. The French philosophes are accused of setting the stage for what later occurred during the Revolution.[23] There is no major inclusive article of the extent of "Illuminati," although a short one, "Jacobins," sets out the program . It offers a Barruelian take on the plan to overthrow altar, throne, and civil society. The mischief is traced to Voltaire, who is blamed for founding the group and recruiting into it men like Diderot and d'Alembert. This interpretation is developed in various biographical entries, included in the *Supplement* because the subject had died recently or because Gleig wished to make a point. Such is the case of Diderot, who had not merited inclusion in the third edition (as Voltaire and D'Alembert had), but is allotted almost three pages in the *Supplement*. Gleig points to the *Encyclopédie* as an integral part of the conspiratorial plan and variously describes its editor as the possessor of "a great fund of moral sentiments and philosophical ideas," an atheist, and a "wretch" (*Supplement*, 1:490–91). In regard to personal morality—always indicative in Gleig's mind of the soundness of a moral system—Diderot is said to have cheated his benefactress, Catherine the Great, by selling her a nonexistent library. Along with an account of how Voltaire tricked his publishers, this characteristically inaccurate story was a favorite, also appearing in "River" and, in the *Supplement*, "Condorcet."

In discussing actual Revolutionary figures, the *Britannica* abandons its usual circumlocutions about character flaws. In "Condorcet," for example, harsh accusations are made about personal disloyalty and the espousal of a vicious morality. Mirabeau is one of many whose life is summarized in a pitiless epithet: he is described as a "monster of wickedness" who fully deserved the *lettres de cachet* showered on him by his family ("Mirabeau," *Supplement*, 2:262). Ridicule is a favorite technique used to diminish a person, as in the patrician scorn for Fabre d'Eglantine's political qualifications: "he was thought to have sufficient merit to be removed from the office of fabricating comedies to that of fabricating constitutions" ("Eglantine," *Supplement*, 1:558).

Two of the small number of philosophical articles in the *Supplement* exist chiefly to educate readers about the materialism that Gleig sees at the heart of the conspiracy. The first is a little over a page under the title "Action," which the editor brings back in order to stress, in a fairly murky explanation, that an agency of mind does exist in the universe. He is responding in part to natural philosophers content with purely material agents, but his main onus is against "that pretended philosophy which excludes the agency of mind from the universe" and which has led to "dreadful consequences . . . in another country" (*Supplement*, 1:3). More important is "Critical Philosophy" (entered under "Philosophy"). The biographical entry on Kant had promised that a well-known Frenchman would provide the essay; he is identified in "Critical Philosophy" only as "an exile from his wretched country" (*Supplement*, 2:353). The article consists of three pages quoted from the French writer and annotated by Gleig, summarizing Kantian philosophy under nineteen marginal tags. This is followed by an equally long evaluation by Gleig, who lambastes Kant's obfuscating language and imperfect logic. The real mischief of this philosophy is analyzed in the last two columns of the essay: "detestable doctrines . . . have been dragged from its bottom" and lead easily to atheism (*Supplement*, 2:359).

The *Supplement* does not detail the effects of this philosophy on society in any systematic way. For the most part, there are sweeping references to persecution and upheaval. A few entries, however, do elaborate on various aspects of the new culture prevailing in post-Revolutionary France. A deistic sect is described and mocked in "Theophilanthropists." "Institute" is more favorable toward changes in education and the academy system, acknowledging that "the proceedings of the national institute have hitherto been abundantly interesting" (*Supplement*, 2:10). The following subentry, "National Instruction," changes to sharp criticism. Based on an unidentified French miscellany, the extract provides an overview of the new system of public education and state-supported research. Gleig then editorializes in the last column, qualifying his approval of certain reforms by throwing doubt on the ability of the French to maintain them, and ranting at the godlessness of the primary schooling now in place. He closes with a quotation from Cicero's *De natura deorum* about how public officials must uphold religion. There is no word of emulating that part of the French plans which aimed at making elementary education more available across social classes. A clue to the Tory's probable ambivalence on this subject can be found in "Oeconomists," which quotes Barruel's accusation that the Physiocrats used free schools to manipulate mass opinion.

Paramount in the *Supplement*'s depiction of post-Revolutionary France is the rhetoric used to decry the arbitrariness and violence in the administration of justice. The appeal to a sense of moral outrage is evident in the language of many statements, such as this one from "Lavoisier": "he suffered on the scaffold, merely because he was rich! . . . [he] provoked the jealousy of a crew of homicides, who made a sport of sacrificing the lives of the best of men to a sanguinary idol" (*Supplement*, 2:72).[24] The worst horror, in Gleig's eyes, lies in the violation of law by legislators themselves. In their most notorious act, the execution of the king, they "coolly departed, not only from every principle of justice, but also from the very letter of that law which conferred authority on themselves" ("Damiens," *Supplement*, 1:481). Louis XVI is described here as "their innocent, their amiable sovereign." Gleig has little room for gray areas in his resonant sentences.

The mode of administering justice is evoked in the article "Guillotine," which is complemented by a plate depicting two scenes: a close-up of an execution whose victim resembles Louis XVI, and another, longer view with an entire guillotine and piles of severed heads representing various groups that have suffered in the Revolution. The article itself does not directly explain the operation of this instrument, as a purely informational encyclopedia would have done. The author is more interested in his political message, which covers language ("the sentimental slang of philanthropy"), the mental cruelty of such a form of execution, and the malleability of the populace. In regard to the last of these themes, he quotes the report of a commissioner who took the guillotine on a tour of the provinces: "the multitude, the stupid worshippers of *Notre Dame* look at our lady the guillotine; are silent, become serious, and their doubts vanish.—they are converted . . . *in hoc signo vinces*" (*Supplement*, 1:723). The conjoining of stupidity and sacrilege, in a

**Plate 29, 1801 *Supplement* to the *Encyclopaedia Britannica*. The French source has not been identified.**

scene that opens the imagination as it closes an article, shows Gleig at his most skillful as a compiler.

Clearly, in the third edition of the *Encyclopaedia Britannica*, and especially in the *Supplement*, Gleig accepted Diderot's principle that a repository of knowledge could also be a *machine de guerre* in political controversies and attempts to reform society, but the Scottish editor did not acknowledge this debt of inspiration. The third edition is silent on the subject, and when Gleig takes the opportunity in the *Supplement* to express his own views about the political function of an encyclopedic work, he is careful to differentiate his goals from those of the *Encyclopédie*. In the dedication to George III, no mention is made of the scientific or literary value of these volumes. The main worth of his labor consists, rather, in combating the *Encyclopédie*, "that pestiferous Work . . . [which has] disseminated, far and wide, the seeds of Anarchy and Atheism" (*Supplement*, 1:iv). Gleig's insistence on the *Britannica* as a corrective to the *Encyclopédie* on political matters suggests an awareness of the genealogy of the British work, as well as the desire to redefine encyclopedic propaganda by displacing the French predecessor.

The vociferous rhetoric Gleig adopted was completely uncharacteristic of British encyclopedism, as were many of the texts he compiled. They occupy a niche midway between the pamphlets of a Hannah More and philosophical studies aiming at impartial analysis: the entries related to the Revolution are impassioned and short on empirical evidence, but they have a certain internal logic. It derives from the ambient system of moral and religious beliefs and from scientific reasoning, which for Gleig, Robison, and many of their peers were closely related. The distance is not far from Robison's notion of nature as a system of general laws instituted by God and regulating all operations, to the conspiracy theory, where perplexing events can be explained in terms of a central force. In the natural world, and in the solid scientific articles filling the rest of the third edition and the *Supplement*, events happen in processes that can be understood and often replicated. In the human, political world of the Revolution, the *Britannica* sought, and believed it had found, the same understanding. By tracing the causes and sequence of such a happening, the encyclopedia could allow readers to reproduce it in imagination. In so doing, they might spare their country the rigors of a laboratory experiment.

# NOTES

I would like to thank Frank A. Kafker and Richard B. Sher for helpful comments.

1. Henry Cockburn, *Memorials of His Time* (1856; reprint, New York, 1973), 70.

2. H. T. Dickinson, *British Radicalism and the French Revolution, 1789–1815* (London, 1985), 7–9.

3. H. T. Dickinson, "Popular Conservatism and Militant Loyalism, 1789–1815," in *Britain and the French Revolution, 1789–1815*, ed. H. T. Dickinson (Basingstoke, 1989), 103–25; Robert R. Dozier, *For King, Constitution, and Country: The English Loyalists and the French Revolution* (Lexington, Ky., 1983), chap. 3, "The Loyal Association Movement," 55–75.

4. The quoted expression is from Frank O'Gorman's *British Conservatism: Conservative Thought from Burke to Thatcher* (London, 1986), 20.

5. Cockburn, *Memorials*, 80–81; Philip Anthony Brown, *The French Revolution in English History* (London, 1918), 169.

6. Brown, *French Revolution in English History*, 160–61. See also William Ferguson, *Scotland: 1689 to the Present* (New York, 1968), 198–203, for a brief overview of elementary schooling in the eighteenth century.

7. Henry W. Meikle, *Scotland and the French Revolution* (1912; reprint, New York, 1969), 56–60.

8. On the press, James J. Sack, *From Jacobite to Conservative: Reaction and Orthodoxy in Britain, c. 1760–1832* (Cambridge, 1993), 12–14, shows the political connections of various right-wing journals. The Church of Scotland had become, as Burke is reputed to have said in a parliamentary debate, "culpably obsequious to every measure of Government" (quoted in Meikle, *Scotland and the French Revolution*, 201).

9. Frank A. Kafker, "The Achievement of Andrew Bell and Colin Macfarquhar as the First Publishers of the *Encyclopaedia Britannica*," *British Journal for Eighteenth-Century Studies* 18 (1995): 144, summarizes what is known of Tytler's involvement. For information on the content of the early *Britannica*, see this article and the forthcoming work on the first three editions by Kafker, Doig, Loveland, and others.

10. *Encyclopaedia Britannica*, 11th ed., "Encyclopaedia," 378.

11. See Emily Lorraine de Montluzin, *The Anti-Jacobins, 1798–1800: The Early Contributors to the Anti-Jacobin Review* (Basingstoke, 1988), 97–98, and the biography of Gleig in the *Dictionary of National Biography*, 7:1302–3.

12. Dickinson, *Britain and the French Revolution*, 10.

13. *Encyclopaedia Britannica, or a Dictionary of Arts, Sciences, and Miscellaneous Literature*, 3rd ed., 18 vols., "Annuities" (Edinburgh, 1797). Future references to this edition, and to the *Supplement to the Third Edition of the Encyclopaedia Britannica, or a Dictionary of Arts, Sciences, and Miscellaneous Literature*, ed. George Gleig, 2 vols. (Edinburgh, 1801), will be given in the text. Individual volumes do not bear the actual date of publication. References to biographical entries include the given name in brackets where there is more than one entry under the surname.

14. Pierangelo Castagneto, "Uomo, natura et società nelle edizioni settec-entesche dell'*Encyclopaedia Britannica*," *Studi settecenteschi* 16 (1996): 468, points to the Annual Register as a major source for the compilers of this article.

15. In "The Responses of Scottish Churchmen to the French Revolution, 1789–1802," *Scottish Historical Review* 73 (1994): 196, Emma Vincent demon-strates that this was a major argument in the group of sermons she studied. Recurring themes in these sermons (see esp. 195–202) echo those in the *Britan-nica*.

16. In the "Advertisement" to the *Supplement*, Gleig refers to his use of "dif-ferent and opposite works on the French revolution, and what are emphati-cally called *French principles*" (1:v). While he may be referring to additional articles about the Revolution, the phrase suggests that he is the principal au-thor of "Revolution." Castagneto, "Uomo, natura e società," 470, and n. 91, n. 92, discusses Gleig's major sources: Robison; William Playfair's *History of Jacobinism, Its Crimes, Cruelties and Perfidies . . . Robespierre* (Edinburgh, 1795); and Antoine-François Bertrand de Moleville, *Mémoires secrets, pour servir à l'his-toire de la fin du règne de Louis XVI* (Paris, 1797).

17. The author asserts that Scottish peasants still had to perform *corvées*, suggesting a justification of the system based merely on its presence in two different countries.

18. Seamus Deane, *The French Revolution and Enlightenment in England, 1789–1832* (Cambridge, Mass. and London, 1988), 5–11, traces the various el-ements of the conspiracy theory already present in Burke's *Reflections*, and the personal contacts between Burke and the chief proponents of the theory.

19. Sack, *From Jacobite to Conservative*, 32–33. By means of a chart of the causes of the Revolution as stated in 1,931 conservative pamphlets, Gayle T. Pendelton, "English Conservative Propaganda during the French Revolution, 1789–1802" (Ph.D. diss., Emory University, 1976), 320, shows that 177 blamed the philosophy of the Enlightenment, 58 blamed the abuses of the Ancien Régime, and so forth; the conspiracy theory, mentioned in 24 pam-phlets, was the least popular explanation.

20. Deane, *French Revolution and Enlightenment*, 32. Mounier's book was fa-vorably reviewed by Francis Jeffrey in the first article of the first issue of the *Edinburgh Review* in 1802 (ibid., 11).

21. Gleig seems to use his sources accurately. In "Freemasonry," for exam-ple, the sections from *Proofs of a Conspiracy* can be found on 20–22 in the 3rd ed. (Philadelphia, 1798). The sections from Barruel are taken from his *Memoirs, Illustrating the History of Jacobinism* (Hartford, 1799), vol. 2: "The Antimonar-chical Conspiracy."

22. The third edition includes an analysis of the concept in "Right." It holds that coupling "rights" and "man" in the same phrase is odd. Men are bound by duties; they do not have rights, which imply immunity from cen-sure if the right thing is not done.

23. Margaret C. Jacob, *Living the Enlightenment: Freemasonry and Politics in Eighteenth-Century Europe* (New York and Oxford, 1991), 10, points out that Barruel was the first to claim that "the Enlightenment had also, in some sense, caused the French Revolution."

24. Gleig's political bias is perhaps also responsible for the niggardly praise of the achievements of the other discoverer of oxygen, Joseph Priestley, who was also one of the most notorious reformers in Britain. He is described as an "indefatigable experimenter . . . but facts the most brilliant remained frequently unproductive in his hands" (*Supplement*, 1:70).

# French Thought in William Smellie's Natural History: A Scottish Reception of Buffon and Condillac

JEFF LOVELAND

WHETHER OR NOT THERE WAS, AT SOME LEVEL, "ONLY ONE ENLIGHTEN-ment," as Peter Gay insisted, recent studies have emphasized the movement's diversity and its ties with varying cultural conditions, a choice in accord with the increasing popularity of sociocultural history.[1] One valuable tool in the effort to identify national and social sub-Enlightenments has been the study of how different groups read (or did not read) the Enlightenments of others. The French reception of Locke and Newton, for example, has long been commented on as a sign of differences between the British and French Enlightenments, and studies of the diffusion of the *Encyclopédie* and other eighteenth-century French texts have uncovered affinities with, and resistances to, the French Enlightenment in other parts of the world. Likewise, the study of individual reactions to eighteenth-century texts, whether from home or abroad, has done much to add concreteness to generalizations about different national, regional, and socioeconomic Enlightenments. For although such reactions cannot be projected onto social classes and nations without careful attention to the possibilities and probabilities of personal idiosyncrasy, larger claims about Enlightenments and their receptions must always draw on particular claims about members of groups.

This essay examines one Scottish reaction to two important figures of the French Enlightenment, the naturalist-philosopher Georges-Louis Leclerc de Buffon (1707–88) and the philosopher Etienne Bonnot de Condillac (1714–80). William Smellie (1740?–95), the Scot in question, was well acquainted with Continental and French natural history and philosophy, and this

192

makes him an ideal vehicle for exploring differences between the French and Scottish Enlightenments. Smellie's reading of Buffon and Condillac can obviously not be imputed to Scotland directly or in its entirety, but it does cast light on Franco-Scottish relations in the Enlightenment. At the same time, this study points to Smellie's distinctiveness in the Scottish Enlightenment and adds depth to our knowledge of this fascinating printer-naturalist. Indeed, my choice of Buffon and Condillac reflects neither their similarity (they were extraordinarily different in most respects) nor their ability to represent the French Enlightenment, but rather their usefulness in pointing to several of Smellie's more interesting intellectual characteristics and tensions.

## WILLIAM SMELLIE, SCIENCE, AND HIS FRENCH INTERTEXTS

Smellie, now known chiefly as the editor of the first edition of the *Encyclopaedia Britannica* (1768–71), has been called with some justice the "most learned printer of his day."[2] He was born in the outskirts of Edinburgh to a builder and stonemason. A master printer in Edinburgh from 1765 onward, he was at the same time a prolific man of letters. Among other activities, he edited or helped to edit the *Scots Magazine* from 1759 to 1765 and the *Edinburgh Magazine and Review* from 1773 to 1776, translated a substantial portion of Buffon's *Histoire naturelle* (as the *Natural History*, 1780–85), wrote an original *Philosophy of Natural History* (1790–99), and produced a large number of pamphlets, essays, and short biographies, some of which were published in his posthumous *Literary and Characteristical Lives* (1800). Responsible for a large family, lacking commercial astuteness, and exhibiting sporadic, rebellious behavior with important patrons, Smellie remained poor and marginal despite his hard work and intelligence.[3]

An interest in medicine and the sciences, especially natural history, animated much of his intellectual existence. Early support for his scientific avocation came from the printing firm of Hamilton, Balfour, and Neill, to which he was apprenticed in 1752. Realizing that education could only heighten his value in what was at the time Edinburgh's leading scholarly publishing house, his employers allowed him to pursue his education at the

University of Edinburgh. Along with Greek, Hebrew, traditional humanities, and mathematics, his academic experience would ultimately include courses on botany with Charles Alston and John Hope, lectures on chemistry by William Cullen, and lectures on anatomy by Alexander Monro, *primus*. Besides his former professors, he soon made the acquaintance of other local luminaries such as Joseph Black and James Hutton. Around 1760 he considered becoming a physician but, having married in 1763, he contented himself with strengthening the treatment of medicine in the *Scots Magazine*.[4]

Throughout the 1760s, Smellie wrote essays on such subjects as spontaneous generation, final causes, and the history of the earth (Kerr, 2:213–16), and his correspondence from the period abounds with scientific musings and speculations (Kerr, 1:129–32, 137–40, 177–86, 194–96, 250–51). Many of his early writings achieved an audience of sorts, if only as letters or public addresses to the Newtonian Society—which he helped to organize, along with other antiestablishment clubs[5]—and many more would reappear in his later works. At the end of the 1760s, he was able to combine his scientific and medical interests with his lifelong commitment to popularization by editing William Buchan's *Domestic Medicine* (1769) and the first edition of the *Encyclopaedia Britannica*.[6] His role in both works has been overstated. Little suggests that he did more than compress and massively edit the former,[7] while in the latter case he merely chose and compiled extant texts except in a small number of original sections, notably the article "Aether" and the third part of "Botany."[8] Still, his involvement with these projects testifies to a considerable competence in medicine and the sciences.

Thanks to his training, contacts, and essays, Smellie's status as a natural historian earned him consideration for the Regius chair of natural history at the University of Edinburgh when the incumbent, Robert Ramsay, was taken ill in the 1770s.[9] Rejected in favor of John Walker, in part because of his failure to secure the right patrons, Smellie attempted to establish himself as a lecturer on the "Philosophy and General Economy of Nature" at the Society of Antiquaries, but this venture too was crushed by Walker and his supporters, who preferred to maintain the university's monopoly on scientific education. The remains of his canceled lectures, augmented with *juvenalia* and other materials, were eventually published in his two-volume *Philosophy of*

*Natural History*.[10] The book was translated into Danish and German and went through more than thirty-five editions between 1790 and 1874, nearly all of them North American, thanks to its adoption and adaptation for use as a textbook at Harvard University by physician John Ware.[11] As the culminating statement of Smellie's scientific and philosophical views, the *Philosophy of Natural History* will constitute the focus of my remarks here, but a few of Smellie's early essays and his translation of Buffon's *Histoire naturelle* will also receive attention.

Long before undertaking his translation of the *Histoire naturelle* in the 1780s, Smellie had familiarized himself with several of the important figures in contemporary French natural history. As a young man, he read Noël-Antoine Pluche's *Spectacle de la nature* (1732–50), available in English from 1733 onward (Kerr, 1:129–30). Compiling the *Encyclopaedia Britannica* around 1770, he borrowed material liberally from the mostly untranslated *Histoire naturelle* and summarized research by the eminent French naturalists René-Antoine Ferchault de Réaumur and Joseph Pitton de Tournefort. The time Smellie spent translating Buffon's *Histoire naturelle* was probably important in orienting his thinking toward France and the Continent, but his knowledge of Francophone science grew in other directions as well. In the *Philosophy of Natural History*, he regularly cites the Genevan Charles Bonnet and devotes a whole section to Condillac's *Traité des sensations* (1754). Relations between Scottish and French intellectuals were generally close in the eighteenth century, thanks to the cosmopolitan character of the elite Republic of Letters,[12] but Smellie was more conversant with the French than most of his fellows.

Smellie remained a Scot and a Briton in many ways, even as he concerned himself with French natural history. In his article "Aether" in the *Encyclopaedia Britannica*—cited by Larry Laudan as emblematic of Scotland's exceptionally harsh stand against hypotheses—he proudly endorses the empirical methodology of Bacon, Locke, and Newton.[13] Soon after its publication, he defended Thomas Reid's *Inquiry into the Human Mind* (1764) against its detractors (Kerr, 1:304–16; Wood, introduction, ix–x), and in 1785 he ascribed much of animal and human behavior to innate instinct in a lecture to the Royal Society of Edinburgh, later expanded and published in the *Philosophy of Natural History* (1:144–59). He saw final causes all through nature and shied away from the heterodox, to say nothing of the atheistic. These traits suggest a conflict with Smellie's French sources, or at least the more radical among them. Pluche, a Jansenist who urged humility in the study of nature, may have seemed at home in Presbyterian Scotland, while Réaumur's stance against speculative thinking may have endeared him to British Baconians, but what about Condillac and Buffon? Did Condillac's reduction of thought to sensation not contradict Reid, not to mention the notion of innate instinct? And was Buffon not associated with systematizing, moral license, and atheism?

## BUFFON

Exactly when Smellie came into contact with Buffon's *Histoire naturelle* is not clear. In the late 1740s, Hope, his professor, studied botany in Buffon's stronghold, the Parisian Jardin du Roi, and he may have mentioned the *Histoire naturelle* in his courses. Smellie's published correspondence makes no mention of Buffon before the time of the *Encyclopaedia Britannica*. The bibliographical reference to Buffon in the opening pages of the *Britannica* comically misstates his name as "Bouffon." The article "Canis," containing a first textual reference to Buffon (*EB*, 2:22), perpetuates the error, but by the time of "Generation" (*EB*, 2:671) the spelling had been rectified and would remain consistent to the end of the series. Were the *Britannica* not replete with orthographic inconsistencies and simple typographical errors,[14] one might infer that Smellie became well acquainted with Buffon only in the course of his work on the *Britannica*. In any case, uncredited borrowings from Buffon begin in the first volume of the series, with the article "Bos."

All in all, the *Britannica* borrows material on some dozen animals from the *Histoire naturelle*, mostly without specifically naming its source, and generally mixing passages from Buffon with material from elsewhere. Articles indebted to Buffon include "Bos," "Canis," "Capra," "Elephas," "Equus," "Felis," "Hystrix," and "Lepus." Since Buffon's *Histoire naturelle* had not yet been extensively translated into English in 1768,[15] Smellie was almost certainly transcribing and translating from the French original. In at least a few cases, he ended up using his translations for the *Britannica* as a starting point for his official translation of the *Histoire naturelle* some ten years later, but most of the material taken from Buffon in the *Britannica* was too freely translated and too mixed with other sources to be of much help in Smellie's more careful rendering of the whole *Histoire naturelle*. Indeed, the article on the horse in the *Natural History*, one of the few that obviously depends on a prior translation in the *Britannica*, is one of the least faithful translations in the series.[16]

Most of the articles on animals in the *Encyclopaedia Britannica* owe nothing to Buffon, and one may wonder why Smellie chose the limited collection of borrowings from Buffon that he did. Like other abridgers of the *Histoire naturelle*, Smellie drew primarily on Buffon's famous poetic descriptions of everyday and symbolic animals, among them his description of the lion (the "king of the animals"), the "noble" horse, the malicious cat, the stupid sheep, and the "peaceable" elephant. This suggests a certain admiration for Buffon's style, a point to which we will have occasion to return. But the articles inspired by Buffon are not limited to poetry or facile generalizations. Not only do they add a rare touch of ethology to a work oriented toward listlike, Linnaean systematics; they also touch on some of Buffon's principal theories. In "Canis," for example, Smellie reproduces Buffon's genealogical tree of the various breeds of dogs, which shows how they derive by climatic "degeneration" and crossbreeding from a single root, the "shepherd's dog." One can fault the presentation for scrimping on background and exaggerating the quickness of degeneration, which Buffon had spread out over generations,[17] but the article nonetheless offers much beyond poetry.

Smellie's interest in Buffon as a theorist is confirmed by the prominent role accorded to him in several of the *Britannica*'s short articles on physiology. "Generation" reviews three major hypotheses regarding sexual reproduction—Harvey's ovism, Leeuwenhoek's vermism, and Buffon's epigenesis—and seems favorable to the latter despite a concluding protest of nescience.[18] In "Nutrition," Buffon's theory of organic molecules is presented alone, as a plausible hypothesis to explain digestion and growth. The similarity of "Generation" to passages in the *Philosophy of Natural History* (2:129–32) suggests that Smellie may have written it himself. In any case, as editor of the *Britan-*

*nica*, he was clearly enthusiastic enough about Buffon's ideas to allow their inclusion alongside other materials.

Smellie's was neither the first nor the last eighteenth-century translation of Buffon's *Histoire naturelle*, but it was the most readable, and arguably the best.[19] Unlike extracts of the series published from 1751 onward, and unlike Oliver Goldsmith's *History of the Earth and Animated Nature* (1774), which has sometimes been considered a translation of the *Histoire naturelle*, Smellie's translation is comprehensive, containing nearly everything Buffon wrote for the first fifteen volumes of the series as well as a considerable portion of volumes 3 and 5 of the *Supplément*.[20] The only major omissions from the first fifteen volumes are Buffon's opening methodological discourse, which Smellie judged redundant and defamatory toward Linnaeus, and Louis-Jean-Marie Daubenton's descriptions of animal anatomy, which Smellie found "dry and uninteresting" (*NH*, 1:xviii–xix). Unlike William Kenrick's six-volume *Natural History of Animals, Vegetables, and Minerals* (1775), Smellie's translation does not attempt to follow Buffon word by word—a characteristic that makes it more readable and sometimes more accurate, since Kenrick was prone to deforming Buffon's larger points in his haste to translate words, and since he sometimes translated words to misleading cognates. Still, Smellie's work on the *Natural History* belies Kerr's romantic claim that he translated freehand after digesting six to eight pages of text in his head (Kerr, 2:118), for the great majority of sentences in Smellie's translation can be readily identified with similarly structured sentences in Buffon's original. Like Kenrick, Smellie reordered many of the articles. He also added occasional corrective footnotes as well as regular footnotes situating animals in a Linnaean-style taxonomy. As Aaron Garrett has noted, Smellie often condensed Buffon's prose, and he occasionally changed, abridged, and added to sections of text (Garrett, introduction, vi). Nevertheless, the work remains a generally faithful and accurate representation of the opening subseries of the *Histoire naturelle*, and one still in use by Anglophone historians.

A contemporary review of the translation in the *Critical Review* made the odd suggestion that Smellie had improved on the original French version by deflating Buffon's notorious literary eloquence, so that his sometimes fanciful hypotheses could be seen for what they were, in plain English (Kerr, 2:126–27).

Smellie himself, who never pretended to have disarmed Buffon's silver tongue, would later stress the dangers to truth inherent in the latter's "irresistible" style (*PNH*, 2:59). A second commentator for the *Critical Review* brought the issue to a more concrete level, noting Smellie's treatment of Buffon's second, newly published history of the earth, the "Epoques de la Nature" (1778). Instead of translating the "Epoques" directly, Smellie chose to pare down and restructure it so as to downplay the "theory" and emphasize "facts," since only these would be likely to interest the "cool and deliberate Briton" (*NH*, 9:258–59). Delighted to find the "charms" of Buffon's eloquence neutralized with no concomitant damage to his "facts" (Kerr, 2:127–28), the *Critical Review* thanked Smellie heartily, confirming his judgment about British character.

This supposed annulment of eloquence through large-scale abridgement and reconstruction was a singular instance, and claims about Smellie's treatment of Buffon's eloquence need to be examined primarily in light of his usual practices. Here we find ample proof that Smellie preferred clear, sometimes overly clear prose to elegant turns of phrase. Translating Buffon's famous sentence "tout cela posé, raisonnons" (*HN*, 1:77), for example, Smellie managed to come up with "having enumerated these facts, let us try what conclusions can be drawn from them" (*NH*, 1:13). Moreover, despite his promise in his translator's preface to attempt to follow Buffon's stylistic ebbs and flows as closely as possible (*NH*, 1:xix–xx), Smellie seems to have been reluctant to follow Buffon into the higher, more "noble" registers of language. When Buffon made use of such periphrases as "l'astre du jour" or "l'astre de lumière" for the sun, for example, Smellie most often wrote simply "sun." A particularly striking example of his imperviousness to Buffon's poetry is his description of a comet coming "to receive the influence of solar heat" (*NH*, 6:252) rather than of a comet coming to "se parer de nouveaux feux" (*HN*, 12:vi). Furthermore, as mentioned earlier, Smellie was not averse to cutting whole phrases here and there when he judged Buffon redundant, as in the latter's overwrought description of "uncultivated nature" (*HN*, 12:xi–xiii; *NH*, 6:257–60). Still, Smellie's insistence on clarity and everyday vocabulary should not be exaggerated, for he follows Buffon closely in many stylish passages. Moreover, short of pointedly neglecting Buffon's hypotheses, as he did in the "Epoques de la

Nature," it is not clear how much Smellie could have been expected to disarm them through depoeticizing. Buffon's critics often equated his style and his systematizing. Thanks to its literary denotations and epistemological connotations, the expression *roman de physique* and its derivatives provided an ideal nucleus for such an equation. Beyond propaganda, however, the equivalence appears shaky, particularly since the expression *roman de physique* acquired currency as an aspersion on the much less obviously stylistic Descartes.[21] In any case, we shall see that Smellie was less adamantly opposed to hypotheses than he sometimes pretended.

Smellie's interest in, and dependence on, Buffon continued to the end of his life. At a most superficial level, a huge section of the *Philosophy of Natural History* (2:157–240) is lifted more or less verbatim from Smellie's translation of Buffon's anthropological essay, "Variétés de l'espèce humaine" (Wood, introduction, xix). More importantly, Buffon's positions are brought to bear on a great many of the subjects discussed. Often he is reprimanded for going too far, as in his condemnation of taxonomy and in his hypothesizing, but the sheer amount of attention lavished on his ideas suggests that Smellie never quite extricated himself from dependence on Buffon.

Having sketched out Smellie's contact with Buffon's work, let us examine the tensions evoked above as likely to characterize relations between a freethinking French philosophe and a Scottish reader. Religion constitutes an obvious starting point. Smellie was aware of the charges aimed at the *Histoire naturelle* and its author on this score. His friend David Dalrymple, Lord Hailes tried to dissuade him from translating a series of which parts were "atheistical" (Kerr, 2:160–61; Wood, introduction, xix–xx). Like many of his contemporaries, Smellie may never have been convinced that Buffon was an atheist, if indeed he was,[22] but he did specifically and repeatedly reject two of Buffon's potentially antireligious ideas, namely his critique of final causes and his neo-Cartesian view of animals as machines.[23] In neither case, however, was the divide as unambiguous as it might at first appear. For with regard to final causes, Smellie conceded their perfect irrelevance as physical principles (*NH*, 2:70–71), and with regard to animal mechanism, Buffon was hardly dogmatic or even consistent.[24]

As for Buffon's licentiousness, which had titillated the French for some years already, Smellie appears to have found it unproblematic, despite his denunciation of Linnaeus's "obscene" ascription of sexuality to plants in the *Encyclopaedia Britannica* and elsewhere (*EB*, 1:653; *PNH*, 1:248). He translated Buffon's vivid descriptions of animal sexuality faithfully and without euphemism, and even added a footnote explaining Buffon's oblique reference to a legendary French court for trying the impotent (*NH*, 4:428). Propriety may have been a virtue for Smellie, as he declares in the *Philosophy of Natural History* (2:78), but it was not a virtue that he interpreted with any great narrowness. The puritanical trappings of his attacks on the sexual system are probably best seen as reflecting a more general outrage, for Smellie, who was described by Robert Burns as a "veteran in genius, wit, and b[aw]dry," was not averse to using sexual metaphors in his personal correspondence, even before the *Encyclopaedia Britannica*.[25]

Smellie's view of Buffon's hypothesizing is more difficult to gauge. In the *Encyclopaedia Britannica*, we have seen, he endorses the empirical method and warns of the danger of framing hypotheses. Even in the *Philosophy of Natural History*, where hypotheses are granted a heuristic role (2:150), he professes a tranquil nescience, reminiscent of Pluche's, in the face of nature's inner structure (1:276). Not only do we not know how nature works, we never will know, he asserts several times (1:52, 208, 215, 335, 2:128–29). As Paul Wood has noted, these attitudes align him with his more methodologically conservative intellectual peers, notably Reid.[26] Despite his principles, however, Smellie himself was fond of hypothesizing, a fact recognized by his friends and admirers (Kerr, 1:132, 187, 194). In 1764, for example, he read a theory of dreams before the Newtonian Society, explaining their existence on psychological, moral, and physical grounds.[27] This would be reprinted in the *Philosophy of Natural History,* a text overflowing with original and unoriginal scientific conjectures. Volume 2 in particular contains "a vast alloy of superfluous, frivolous, and fanciful speculations," in the words of the *Monthly Review*.[28] All are limited in scale, compared with the world-building systems of Descartes or Buffon, but the prevalence of theoretical matter in the *Philosophy of Natural History* belies Smellie's earlier affirmations of Baconian empiricism. Many of Smellie's summaries of other philosophers' hypotheses conclude with the caveat that none can be verified because nature is unknowable. This attitude reflected his conviction that nurturing skepticism in readers was a fundamental duty of the scientific popularizer.[29] But his skepticism neither quelled his penchant for theoretical natural history nor prevented him from expressing favor for certain hypotheses over others.

In the end, despite his occasional habit of regressing into nescience after presenting a theory of nature, Smellie had a life-long interest in scientific hypotheses, and he accorded them at the very least a relative truth. Indeed, as Charles Withers has argued, the comparatively theoretical nature of Smellie's scientific interests may have contributed to his exclusion from the Regius chair of natural history.[30] This is not to say that his natural history lacked a factual, practical side. In the early 1760s he worked closely with Hope, even winning a prize for his collection of dried local plants in 1764. Had he pursued this relationship and the various "useful" forms of natural history in which Hope was active,[31] Smellie might have stood a better chance of obtaining the Regius chair, but his involvement in collecting and taxonomy diminished after the mid-1760s.[32] Similarly, his 1765 essay attacking the Linnaean system of plant sexuality privileged miscellaneous facts over a generally accepted theory.[33] But skeptically or not, Smellie was dealing in theories, here as elsewhere, rather than with collecting, taxonomical description, or projects for agricultural improvement or reforestation. Walker, in contrast, may have been susceptible to philosophical and theological speculation, but his thirty years of fieldwork for utilitarian purposes defined him as a practical improver of the sort favored by the Edinburgh establishment.[34] Smellie may not have been a philosopher-naturalist in the French sense, but by the late 1760s he was perhaps more akin to Buffon than he dared to admit.[35]

In his *Philosophy of Natural History* in particular, Smellie adopts several postures analogous to Buffon's in the *Histoire naturelle*. To justify their relatively theoretical perspective, both authors define themselves against the dominant approach to natural history in the second half of the eighteenth century, Linnaean taxonomy. Both note the wordiness, the obscurity, and the arbitrary character of Linnaean natural history (*PNH*, 1:523, 2:7–8; *HN*, 1:9, 18–20, 37–41), and both propose to write broad science for a broad group of readers (*PNH*, 1:viii, 44, 53,

134; *HN*, 1:3, 12:i). Thematic, Aristotelian natural history is an inspiration to both (*PNH*, 2:10–18; *HN*, 1:45–48). Neither rejects taxonomy completely, but both pronounce it empty unless integrated into something more theoretical (*PNH*, 1:523, 2:1, 8; *HN*, 1:9, 21–24, 50–51). As Phillip Sloan has observed, Buffon ended up endorsing and even focusing on taxonomy to the extent that it was supposed to reflect genealogical relations, whereas Smellie merely considered it a convenient, if minimally interesting, formalism.[36] Both nonetheless questioned the reality of taxonomy, conjuring up a vision of nature as continuous, almost infinite, and thus little susceptible to definitions and classification (*PNH*, 1:3, 17, 512, 520–26, 2:3; *HN*, 1:3–5, 11–12, 20, 25). In all these gestures, Smellie is as measured as Buffon is brash and hyperbolic, but despite Smellie's criticism of Buffon's extremism (*PNH*, 2:59–66), he ends up defending popular, philosophical natural history in similar ways. Simple parroting on Smellie's part might be alleged, since his *Philosophy of Natural History* borrows liberally from the *Histoire naturelle* on many particulars, but Smellie also rejects a great many of Buffon's views. In any case, the theoretical, democratic aspirations that these strategies serve to justify were longstanding features of Smellie's natural history.

All in all, then, Smellie strays a good deal from the empirical methodology he proposes in "Aether," both in his early writings and his *Philosophy of Natural History*. As Withers has noted, Smellie's approach to natural history, like Buffon's in a small way, was more deductive and broadly philosophical than Baconian,[37] despite his protests of nescience. He may have lacked Buffon's extremism and the greater part of his confidence in overarching systems, but what interested him above all in natural history was its theoretical framework, not some Baconian setting forth of instances.

## CONDILLAC

In his views of human and animal psychology, Smellie matched his praise for Reid with consistent adherence to the notion that innate instincts frequently underlie thought and behavior. In the *Philosophy of Natural History* he upbraids Buffon for his failure to realize that animals' behavior is often inborn and not simply the consequence of mechanical learning. Specifically, Smellie ridicules Buffon's assertion that bees merely learn their social behaviors from the necessity of living together in close proximity (*PNH*, 1:422–25), although in his translation ten years earlier he had let the same assertion slip by with no adverse comment (*NH*, 3:284–88). On a more constructive note, he is quick to postulate innate "principles" and "instincts" to explain behavior such as suckling, sociability, and migration (*PNH*, 1:145, 425, 473–503), just as Reid had done to explain human thinking.

Given Smellie's repudiation of Buffon's antinativistic model of psychological functioning, one would expect him to have only contempt for Condillac. For despite Buffon's eagerness to cleanse the animal mind of instinct and foresight, Buffon, like Locke, never made a concerted effort to reduce higher mental faculties such as judgment and memory to products of experience. Condillac, on the contrary, was dissatisfied with the vestiges of nativism he perceived in Locke's autonomous mental "powers," and in his *Traité des sensations* he conducts a mental experiment with a statue to prove that the traditional mental faculties are no more than sensations combined. The statue, organized like a human on the inside, begins the treatise with no ideas.[38] Condillac then successively unveils its various senses, first alone and then in combinations, to show how they contribute to the formation of knowledge. A dualist in principle, Condillac ends up slipping into a form of psychological monism or materialism.[39]

Amazingly, Smellie's *Philosophy of Natural History* pronounces Condillac's *Traité des sensations* "a most ingenious performance" and devotes nine pages to an admiring summary of its contents (Wood, introductory, xxii; *FNH*, 1:187–95). Unfortunately, Smellie's discussion goes little beyond exposition, and one can only conjecture what he saw in Condillac's "performance." Was he moved by Condillac's arguments against autonomous mental faculties—this after having registered no discomfort with traditional psychological language before this time? Did he perceive no contradiction between Condillac's hypersensationism and his own longstanding allegiance to a form of nativism? How, in general, are we to reconcile Smellie's praise for the *Traité* with his enthusiasm for Reid and his insistence, regarding Buffon, that learning and experience are inadequate bases for explaining how people and animals function?

Smellie had been exposed to a similar narration of psychic "awakening" in his translation of Buffon's *Histoire naturelle*. In volume 3, Buffon concludes a discussion of the senses with a poetic, first-person account of a fully developed man in his first moments of existence after being created. True to sensationist doctrine, Buffon's "Adam" is at first unable to discern much more than disorganized light, but he soon manages to understand enough of the world to walk, pick fruit, and eat. Condillac's statue, benefiting from its author's more methodical approach, is much slower to learn and yield its insights and, as Jean Piveteau has noted, Frédéric-Melchior de Grimm's suggestion that the *Traité* was a plagiarism of Buffon's brief morceau de style is undiscerning.[40] Still, beyond their foundation in sensationist psychology, the two accounts share a critical insistence on their subjects' initial inability to distinguish themselves and their mental faculties from their sensations and the world around them. Buffon's first man appears to have judgment and other mental faculties from the beginning: "Je crus d'abord que tous ces objets étaient en moi" (*HN*, 3:364). At the same time, like Condillac's statue, Buffon's first man presents himself at least periodically as being no more than sensation, as in his reaction to ambient sounds: "Je me persuadai bientôt que cette harmonie était moi" (*HN*, 3:365).

Smellie's translation of this imagined, purely phenomenological monism suggests that he was uneasy with, or impervious to, the idea of a mind consisting of sensation alone. Not all the first man's effusions about his immanence in sensation are mistranslated, but a surprising number are, and in a subtle but consistent way. All through the narration, Smellie's first man takes small but crucial steps away from the expressed monism of his French double. In the following, theoretically equivalent passages, notice how Smellie's man distances himself from the impinging aural sensation that overwhelms his French fellow:

Je me persuadai bientôt que cette harmonie était moi. (*HN*, 3:365)
[(I) was convinced that these harmonious sounds existed within me.] (*NH*, 3:50)

Even more suggestive is the following translation, where Smellie replaces two partial equations of mental existence and the senses with a reference to hierarchical psychological "powers" and "faculties":

> Je ne savais si je n'avais pas laissé dans le sommeil quelque partie de mon être, j'essayai mes sens, je cherchai à me reconnaître. (*HN*, 3:369–70)
> [I suspected that sleep had robbed me of some part of my powers: I tried my different senses, and endeavored to recognize all my former faculties.] (*NH*, 3:56)

Buffon's dabbling in phenomenological monism in these and other passages undoubtedly testifies more to simple curiosity about inner experience than to a will to theorize the mind as a pure product of sensation. As mentioned above, faculties such as judgment and memory arrive in the narration early and without explanation, and the first man's provocative declarations about his psychic constitution are all tagged as momentary impressions, not final truths. At the same time, Buffon's evident striving for poetic effect all through the account probably contributes to the first man's apparent monism. As the above passages indicate, talk of being and identity is inherently more dramatic and more forcefully poetic than talk of powers and faculties. Here, as elsewhere in the *Histoire naturelle*, Buffon was happy to capitalize on the stylistic potential of his ideas. The amplifying metonymy to which monism lends itself in these descriptions cannot be dismissed as wholly ornamental, but the obviously stylized character of the account points to a mutual reinforcement of substance and form.

It seems doubtful that Smellie deliberately downplayed the monism in Buffon's narrative in order to square it with his own views, since he correctly translated many of Buffon's more explicitly heterodox opinions, before refuting them in footnotes! More likely, Smellie read Buffon's phenomenological monism as little more than dramatic, imprecise metonymy, and sought to express it in plainer language. All through his translation of this exceptionally turgid section, Smellie suppressed apostrophe, metaphor, and redundant verbiage, and it is easy to imagine that he "clarified" Buffon's pseudomonism in exactly this spirit.

With this possibility in mind, let us return to Smellie's reception of Condillac's *Traité*. Histories of philosophy that mention

Condillac tend to make his reduction of Lockean powers to sensation the central point of the *Traité* and even of Condillac, and it may well have been the primary interest of the *Traité* in his own view.[41] Paradoxically, however, it is a point easily forgotten in large parts of the text. As Bernard Baertschi has pointed out, the structures of natural language, often based on the premise of mental faculties or psychic homunculi, make it difficult for Condillac to express his novel reduction of psychic faculties to sensation.[42] Often he lapses into language implying independent mental faculties, as when he states in the *Traité* that certain sensations give rise to hope or fear (39), rather than specifying, in accordance with his theory, that they are hope or fear. Compensating for such lapses is Condillac's insistence, here and there in the *Traité*, that the various faculties are no more than sensation. Exemplary, in this sense, are the opening pages of the *Traité*, where Condillac derives the most basic faculties of attention and memory from the simple juxtaposition of felt sensations (17, 19). Toward the end of the *Traité*, on the other hand, Condillac tends to take previously derived faculties for granted rather than waste time and space repeating deconstructions.

In other words, Smellie could easily have overlooked or chosen to marginalize Condillac's reduction of psychic faculties to sensation. Little indicates, in any case, that he felt any more enthusiasm for Condillac's wholehearted project of reducing the faculties to sensation than for Buffon's halfhearted one. Specifically, in Smellie's summary of the *Traité*, there is not much suggestion that the most basic faculties are equivalent to, or even produced by, sensation. In Smellie's paraphrase, Condillac's statue no doubt gets its knowledge from sensation, but it seems to rely on Lockean powers to process them. Memory, in particular, is never deconstructed into anything more basic. Smellie's first reference to it, wholly different from Condillac's, postulates its existence with no attempt at analysis: "By means of agreeable and disagreeable smells frequently repeated, these sensations would remain in his memory and produce desire and aversion" (*PNH*, 1:187).

It is worth noting that Smellie's fantastical 1760 account of a fetus awakening to existence in its mother's womb, in an essay on the "Origin of Selfishness" that was part of a longer dissertation on public spirit, assumes the same nativism of basic psychological faculties.[43] The goal of the essay is to prove that a certain kind of selfishness, a benign form of self-interest common in the British Enlightenment's sciences of man, is well established in the human fetus even before birth. Toward this end, Smellie's fetus learns and acquires ideas and concepts while inside the womb, among them a desire for "self-preservation" (*LCL*, 320). Motoring its development, significantly, are powers that are left largely unanalyzed. Regarding memory, for example, Smellie suggests that the fetus has a "power" or at least a "natural tendency" to remember its past (*LCL*, 321–22). This faith in the faculties as inborn powers would persist through the time of his reading of Condillac.

If Smellie managed to overlook or ignore Condillac's dissolution of the faculties because of its unobtrusiveness, what of Condillac's sensationism in general, manifest throughout the *Traité*, and a seeming affront to a nativist such as Smellie? As mentioned above, the *Philosophy of Natural History* bemoans Buffon's sometime view of animals as learning machines without elaborate inborn characteristics and ascribes many human and animal behaviors to innate instinct. Ironically, the chapter immediately preceding Smellie's glowing review of the *Traité* is devoted to instinct and claims to demonstrate that "the reasoning faculty itself is a necessary result of instinct" 1:145). Yet despite this provocative prefatorial claim, none of Smellie's examples of reasoning reduced to instinct involve abstract and sensory reasoning, the primary objects of Condillac's *Traité*. In the chapter in question, Smellie rises well beyond suckling to such instincts as fear, morality, and superstition (1:152–54), but judgment, comparison, and sensory reasoning are never mentioned. The sheer lack of overlap between the two chapters makes it difficult to speak of contradiction. Moreover, Smellie's discussion of the senses in the pages immediately preceding his appraisal of the *Traité* reveals him to be by and large a sensationist in the critical matter of sensory psychology. Reid is credited at one point with dismantling the pseudoproblem of children's upside-down vision, a supposed consequence of their inverted retinal images among proponents of the "ideal system" (1:182) but, in agreement with sensationists, Smellie insists that the sensation of visual distance must be learned, and learned via touch (1:177, 184–87). Whatever he may have believed when he defended Reid's *Inquiry* in 1765, Smellie, by this time, had clearly distanced himself from Reid's nativistic view of the senses in favor of a more classically sensationistic one.

Finally, Smellie's innate instincts were designed in such a way as to be compatible with learning. As Norman Daniels has observed, Reid himself was ambiguous on the genesis of his innate instincts, suggesting at times that they were mere dispositions, subject to developmental triggering, and at other times that they were "preprogrammed" necessities, present from birth.[44] Smellie spelled his views out somewhat more clearly. In his chapter on instinct in the *Philosophy of Natural History*, he distinguishes three degrees of innateness among instincts (1:144). First come "pure instincts," fully formed at birth, and last come instincts "improvable by experience and observation." Distinctively human instincts such as love and morality all fall into this latter category; they are more dispositions than innate necessities. Similarly, Smellie's early account of the fetus attaining awareness suggests that with regard to mental instinct, he interpreted innateness in a very weak way, making it little more than a natural potential. The very openness of his nativism may have allowed him to read the *Traité* as a developmental account of innate capacities, and thus as a variation on his own early essay in that direction.

For all Smellie's allegiance to dualism and nativism, then, neither the monism nor the sensationism of the *Traité* need have repelled him. There remains, however, the question of why he so enjoyed the *Traité*, a question made interesting by his seeming imperviousness to the monism that is often considered the work's central point. Perhaps Smellie read and appreciated the *Traité* primarily as a refutation to Berkeley's idealism. The *Traité* does show how the external world is phenomenologically imposed on human beings via the sense of touch, and its value as an antidote to Berkeley's idealism was well known among Condillac's readers. In his eagerness to quash Berkeley with any arms available, Smellie may well have forgotten his youthful declaration that common sense alone can prove the existence of external objects (Kerr, 1:306–7). On the other hand, Berkeley is mentioned neither in the *Traité* nor, more importantly, in Smellie's account of it.

More likely, Smellie appreciated the *Traité* as a detailed account of mental development, not as a univocal system of any sort. His essay on the fetus shows him curious about mental be-

ginnings by 1760. His enthusiasm for Reid's *Inquiry* is also revealing, for the Inquiry resembles Condillac's *Traité* in its
organization and focus if not in its tenets. Unknowingly conjuring up Condillac, Reid muses at one point: "If the original perceptions and notions of the mind were to make their
appearance single and unmixed, as we first received them from
the hand of nature, one accustomed to reflection would have
less difficulty in tracing them."[45] Flexible in his nativism, less
opposed to hypotheses, and largely sensationistic in the matter
of sensory reasoning, Smellie was free to find in the *Traité* what
Reid had only dreamed of.

## CONCLUSION

If Smellie did interpret Condillac's statue as traditionally dualistic and compatible with his own tempered nativism, it could
be said to be a case of poetic justice. If Locke's *Essay* could be
stripped of its providentialism and skeptical overtones in the
passage to France, why should Condillac's *Traité des sensations*
not have arrived in Scotland shorn of its monism and praised
by an admirer of Reid? Condillac meant many things to many
people, as Isabel Knight has observed,[46] but this must be
counted one of the odder examples. Condillac's theoretical affinities with fellow sensationist David Hume have long been re-
marked on, but his apparent compatibility with Reid in
Smellie's philosophy is surprising and noteworthy.

Condillac's impact on eighteenth-century Scotland, as on England and Ireland, was undoubtedly slight. His reception there,
if in fact there was one to an appreciable extent, has never been
studied, and Smellie's reading of the *Traité* may not have been
typical. Of all Condillac's writings, only the *Essai sur l'origine des
connaissances humaines* (1746) was translated into English during the eighteenth century. Thomas Nugent, the translator, an
Irishman living in London with an honorary degree from Aberdeen, used his preface to summarize Condillac's *Traité des sensations*, which had already been published by the time of the
translation in 1756. His description of the *Traité* reflects Condillac's intentions more clearly than does Smellie's brief account
of it, though Nugent magnifies Condillac's concern with providence and the famous problem of Molyneux.[47] In any case,

Smellie's reading of Condillac suggests a possible reconciliation between schools of philosophy not ordinarily considered as being related. Willful interpretation and theoretical flexibility counted for a good deal in Smellie's ability to wed Condillac and Reid, but so too did his concern for the smaller questions of psychology lurking in the interstices of their philosophical systems. Smellie's interest in Condillac and Reid was no doubt theoretical to a certain extent. The very presence of psychology, and more specifically of the supremely counterfactual *Traité des sensations* in the *Philosophy of Natural History*, could only heighten the contrast between Smellie's natural history and that of Walker, his more practical rival in natural history. On the other hand, Smellie's interest in psychology, theoretical though it was, was neither as systematic nor as rigid as Reid's or Condillac's.

Unlike the *Traité*, Buffon's *Histoire naturelle* was well known and widely read in eighteenth-century Scotland, and the reactions of contemporaries suggest that Smellie's perspective was both typical and unusual regarding Buffon. Paul Wood has documented Buffon's reception in Scotland, paying particular attention to Reid, and the attitudes he chronicles are similar to Smellie's, if sometimes more negative. Many Scots, while grateful for the factual content of the *Histoire naturelle*, registered dismay at its theological implications, its critique of taxonomy, and its systematizing.[48] The reviews of Smellie's translation mentioned above suggest that Scottish impressions of Buffon's style were lukewarm as well, a reaction perhaps inevitable beyond France's eminently literary elite culture. Smellie, for his part, was as appreciative as his fellows of Buffon's many facts, and perhaps as unhappy with his heterodoxy and overdone style. Like other Scots as well, he expressed discomfort with Buffon's systems and harangues against Linnaeus. On the other hand, he was more theoretical than most Scottish naturalists and thereby more inclined to tolerate Buffon's systematizing within certain bounds. As Wood notes, Reid himself was hypocritical in condemning Buffon's systems, since he ended up developing—though not publishing—his own theory of generation after pronouncing the whole venture a "folly."[49] How widespread this double standard may have been is unclear. In any case, Smellie's writings testify to a passion for theoretical natural history, to the neglect of taxonomy, collecting, and simple description, and his protests of skepticism regarding hypotheses do not fully square with his patient attention to Buffon's and others' theories of digestion and reproduction. Likewise, his relative lack of interest in taxonomy and his related acceptance of the continuity of nature ally him with Buffon and separate him from a number of Scottish thinkers more deeply committed to the taxonomical tradition. Wood has argued plausibly that Scotland's spirited defense of Linnaean taxonomy derived in part from the Scottish Enlightenment's attachment to universities, and specifically from the necessity in which professors found themselves to organize the natural world for presentation to students.[50] Smellie, only peripherally involved with the university and excluded by fiat from its virtual monopoly on useful natural history, had little reason to feel invested in the Linnaean endeavor.

Smellie, all in all, was profoundly immersed in the Scottish and British Enlightenments. He believed in God and final causes, followed Locke and Reid on many philosophical issues and, theoretical though he was, stopped short of embracing the large-scale systems of his French peers. In his journalism he has been credited with creating an influential, confrontational style of criticism,[51] and this polemical posture marked several of his scientific texts, notably his critique of plant sexuality and the article "Aether" in the *Encyclopaedia Britannica*. Elsewhere in his scientific writings, though, Smellie epitomizes the generally nonoppositional character of the British Enlightenment—writing as an Addison rather than as a Swift, in Stephen Brown's terms.[52] Where French philosophes such as Buffon typically presented their intellectual universe as an apocalyptic struggle between light and dark, good and bad, description and taxonomy, Smellie exhibited a willingness to find merit in most of what he read (*PNH*, 2:17) as well as a dislike for exaggeration and overstatement. It was no doubt thanks to this pragmatic, open attitude that he was able to find so much of value in two French philosophers who were not obviously suitable for quick transposition into Scotland.

## NOTES

I would like to express my thanks to John McEvoy, Richard Sher, and Frank A. Kafker for their comments on this article, and to the Charles Phelps Taft Memorial Fund for financial support.

1. See Peter Gay, *The Enlightenment: An Interpretation: The Rise of Modern Paganism* (New York, 1966), 3. The trend toward recognizing national Enlightenments is sometimes traced to Adrienne Koch, ed., *The American Enlightenment: The Shaping of the American Experiment and a Free Society* (New York, 1965), 36–41. A broad survey can be found in *The Enlightenment in National Context*, ed. Roy Porter and Mikulá Teich (Cambridge, 1981). Other studies have fragmented even these national Enlightenments into regional and sociocultural sub-Enlightenments. Representing this tendency with regard to France and Scotland are such works as Alan Charles Kors, *D'Holbach's Coterie: An Enlightenment in Paris* (Princeton, 1976); Robert Darnton, *The Literary Underground of the Old Regime* (Cambridge, Mass., 1982); Daniel Roche, *Le Siècle des lumières en province* (Paris, 1978); *The Glasgow Enlightenment*, ed. Andrew Hook and Richard B. Sher (East Linton, U.K., 1995); *Aberdeen and the Enlightenment*, ed. Jennifer J. Carter and Joan H. Pittock (Aberdeen, 1987).

2. Robert Kerr, *Memoirs of the Life, Writings, and Correspondence of William Smellie*, 2 vols. (1811; reprint, Bristol, 1996), 1:1 (cited hereafter as "Kerr"). Beyond this account, biographical material can be found in the following studies by Stephen W. Brown: "Smellie, William (1740–95)," in *Dictionary of Eighteenth-Century British Philosophers*, ed. John W. Yolton et al., 2 vols. (Bristol, 1999), 2:804–8; "William Smellie and the Printer's Role in the Eighteenth-Century Edinburgh Booktrade," in *The Human Face of the Book Trade: Print Culture and its Creators*, ed. Peter Isaac and Barry McKay (Winchester, U.K., and New Castle, Del., 1999), 29–43; "William Smellie and the Culture of the Edinburgh Book Trade, 1752–1795," in *The Culture of the Book in the Scottish Enlightenment*, ed. Paul Wood (Toronto, 2000), 61–86; and the introduction to William Smellie in *Literary and Characteristical Lives* (1800; reprint, Bristol, 1997), v–xxi; and in Richard B. Sher, introduction to Kerr, 1:v–xviii; Frank A. Kafker, introduction to the *Encyclopaedia Britannica, or a Dictionary of Arts and Sciences* (cited hereafter as *EB*), 3 vols. (1768–71; reprint, Bristol, 1997), 1:vi–vii, xi–xii.

3. Paul Wood, introduction to William Smellie, *The Philosophy of Natural History* (cited hereafter as *PNH*), 2 vols. (1790–99; reprint, Bristol, 2001), 1:vi; Brown, introduction, vii–viii; Brown, "Smellie and the Printer's Role," 37–42; Brown, "Smellie and the Book Trade," 74–83.

4. Brown, "Smellie and the Book Trade," 65–67.

5. See Roger L. Emerson, "The Scottish Enlightenment and the End of the Philosophical Society of Edinburgh," *British Journal for the History of Science* 21 (1988): 35–36, 38; Brown introduction, xv–xvi.

6. On his devotion to popularization and the quarrels it occasioned with his more elite-minded publishers, see Brown, "Smellie and the Book Trade," 68–73; Brown, "Smellie and the Printer's Role," 33; Brown, introduction, ix–x.

7. C. J. Lawrence, "William Buchan: Medicine Laid Open," *Medical History* 19 (1975): 21–22; Richard B. Sher, "William Buchan's *Domestic Medicine*: Laying Book History Open," in Isaac and McKay, eds., *Human Face of the Book Trade*, 46n. For evidence to the contrary, see Kerr, 1:221–26; Brown, "Smellie and the Book Trade," 74n.

8. Jeff Loveland and Frank A. Kafker, "William Smellie's Edition," in a forthcoming study of the early editions of the *Britannica*, ed. Kafker; Kerr,

1:365, 2:335–36. On the first edition of the *Britannica* in general, see Kafaker, introduction, v–xiii; Brown, "Smellie and the Book Trade," 69–73; Frank A. Kafker, "William Smellie's Edition of the *Encyclopaedia Britannica*," in *Notable Encyclopedias of the Late Eighteenth Century*, ed. Kafker, *Studies on Voltaire and the Eighteenth Century* 315 (1994): 145–82.

9. For accounts of his failure, see Charles W. J. Withers, "Natural Knowledge as Cultural Property: Disputes over the 'Ownership' of Natural History in Late Eighteenth-Century Edinburgh," *Archives of Natural History* 19 (1992): 289–303; Steven Shapin, "Property, Patronage, and the Politics of Science: The Founding of the Royal Society of Edinburgh," *British Journal for the History of Science* 7 (1974): 1–41; Brown, "Smellie and the Book Trade," 80; Emerson, "Scottish Enlightenment," 33–66; Kerr, 1:332–33, 2:88–98; Brown, introduction, viin, xiv; Brown, "Smellie," 805.

10. On the contents and origins of the *Philosophy of Natural History*, see Wood, introduction and *PNH* 1:245–46; Kerr, 2:99, 224–25, 264–87.

11. Ware's edition of the *Philosophy of Natural History*, published from 1824 to 1874, abandoned the second volume and substantially altered the first. Ware rewrote many passages, added an eighty-seven-page taxonomical introduction "principally derived from Cuvier," and omitted seven of the original twenty-two chapters as well as Smellie's most controversial arguments, namely the ones about plant sexuality and reason as instinct. See William Smellie, *The Philosophy of Natural History*, ed. John Ware (Boston, 1824), 16n, 111–13. On the text's use at Harvard, see Kafker, introduction, xii; Aaron V. Garrett, introduction to *Natural History, General and Particular by the Count de Buffon* (cited hereafter as *NH*), trans. William Smellie, 9 vols. (1780–85; reprint, Bristol, 2000), 1:viiin. On translations of the *Philosophy of Natural History*, see Kafker, introduction, xii; Wood, introduction, xv. Kerr alludes to a French translation (2:298), but I have not been able to find it.

12. See J. H. Brumfitt, "Scotland and the French Enlightenment," in *The Age of Enlightenment*, ed. W. H. Barber et al. (Edinburgh, 1967), 318–29; Emerson, "Scottish Enlightenment," 53–55; Daniel Gordon, *Citizens without Sovereignty: Equality and Sociability in French Thought, 1670–1789* (Princeton, 1994), 135–36.

13. *EB*, 1:31–32; Larry Laudan, *Science and Hypothesis: Historical Essays on Scientific Methodology* (Dordrecht, 1981), 124–25.

14. Kafker, "William Smellie's Edition," 150–53.

15. On early translations, see Garrett, introduction, v; Stephen F. Milliken, "Buffon and the British" (Ph.D. diss., Columbia University, 1965), 407–9; Jeff Loveland, *Rhetoric and Natural History: Buffon in Polemical and Literary Context*, *Studies on Voltaire and the Eighteenth Century* 3 (2001): 177–78 Jeff Loveland, "The *Histoire naturelle* in English, 1775–1815," forthcoming.

16. Cf. *EB*, 2:506–9; Georges-Louis Leclerc de Buffon, *Histoire naturelle, générale et particulière* (cited hereafter as *HN*), 15 vols. (Paris, 1749–67), 4:174–257; *NH*, 3:306–84. The widely available third and fourth editions of Smellie's translation differ little from the first edition except in their reordering of certain sections.

17. Typically, Smellie writes: "The great Danish dog, when carried to Ireland, the Ukraine, Tartary, etc. is changed into the Irish dog, which is the

largest of all dogs" (*EB*, 2:22). This presentation of degeneration as quasi-immediate would be only partially rectified in Smellie's later translation for the *Natural History*. Cf. *HN*, 5:225–29; *NH*, 4:38–42.

18. Milliken, "Buffon and the British," 343.

19. Ibid., 407–9; Garrett, introduction v–vi.

20. Here I am referring to volumes in the original quarto edition. Smellie could have worked from a subsequent edition in which volume 3 of the *Supplément*, containing addenda on animals, would have already been merged with the main text, but he apparently did not. See Paul-Marie Grinevald, "Les Editions de L'*Histoire naturelle*," in *Buffon 88: Actes du colloque international*, ed. Jean Gayon et al. (Paris, 1992), 631–37; Kerr, 2:129–43.

21. Loveland, *Rhetoric and Natural History*, 43–44, 50–51.

22. See Jacques Roger, *Buffon: Un philosophe au Jardin du roi* (Paris, 1989), 567; Gurdon Wattles, "Buffon, d'Alembert and Materialist Atheism," *Studies on Voltaire and the Eighteenth Century* 266 (1989): 285–317.

23. See for example *PNH*, 1:144–59, 397–98, 2:401; *NH*, 3: 467n, 509n. See also Garrett, introduction, xx. The first edition of Smellie's translation of Buffon's *Natural History* contains a lengthy defense of final causes in its preface. Exceptionally, the passage does not appear in the usually identical second, third, or fourth editions. See Paul Wood, ed., *Thomas Reid on the Animate Creation: Papers Relating to the Life Sciences* (Edinburgh, 1995), 59, and "Buffon's Reception in Scotland: The Aberdeen Connection," *Annals of Science* 44 (1987): 178n; Smellie's preface to the first edition of his translation of Buffon's *Natural History* (Edinburgh, 1780–85), 1:xii–xiiin. Cf. Wood, *Thomas Reid*, 7–8.

24. Roger, *Buffon*, 370–71; Loveland, *Rhetoric and Natural History*, 62–63.

25. See Kerr,1:xvi, 138. Stephen Brown has suggested to me that Smellie's opposition to plant sexuality was based on his unwillingness to see "love" broken off from reason or instinct. See also Brown, "Smellie," 807; François Delaporte, *Nature's Second Kingdom: Explorations of Vegetality in the Eighteenth Century*, trans. Arthur Goldhammer (Cambridge, Mass., 1982), 141–45.

26. Wood, introduction, x–xi, xxi. On Reid and hypothesis, see Laudan, *Science and Hypothesis*, 86–110; Wood, *Thomas Reid*, 24–25.

27. *PNH*, 2:361–403. On the origin and meaning of his theory, see Kerr, 1:179–85; Wood, introduction viii, xxi–xxii; Brown, "Smellie and the Book Trade," 67–68; Brown, "Smellie," 807–8. For a reaction to Smellie's theory, see the *Monthly Review*, 2nd ser., 37 (April 1802): 419–20.

28. *Monthly Review*, 2nd ser., 37 (April 1802): 422. While more positive regarding volume 1, the *Monthly* chides Smellie for presuming "to decide on the intentions of Providence." See *Monthly Review*, 2nd ser., 5 (June 1791): 183–84. Wood discusses the theological aspect of Smellie's ideas in his introduction, viii–ix, xvii–xviii.

29. Brown, "Smellie and the Printer's Role," 34–36; Brown, introduction, xi. See also the analysis of Reid's skepticism in Wood, *Thomas Reid*, 12, 19.

30. Withers, "Natural Knowledge," 289–303.

31. On Hope's natural history, see A. G. Morton, *John Hope, 1725–1786, Scottish Botanist* (Edinburgh, 1986); Emerson, "Scottish Enlightenment," 61; Roger L. Emerson, "The Edinburgh Society for the Importation of Foreign Seeds and Plants, 1764–1773," *Eighteenth-Century Life* 7 (1982): 73–95. Notice

Hope's relations with Walker in Emerson, "Edinburgh Society," 82, 87; Morton, *John Hope*, 18; Charles W. J. Withers, "The Rev. Dr. John Walker and the Practice of Natural History in Late Eighteenth-Century Scotland," *Archives of Natural History* 18 (1991): 201.

32. According to Brown, Smellie continued to work on his collection for twenty years after presenting it to Hope, but he ended up with the same number of specimens in 1782 as in 1764. See Brown, "Smellie and the Book Trade," 65, 68; Kerr, 1:92–93. On Smellie's proposal to stock the museum of the Society of Antiquaries, see Kerr, 2:67–68.

33. Wood, introduction, vii–viii, xx–xxi. On Hope's encouragement, see Morton, *John Hope*, 23–24. On the context of Smellie's argument, see Delaporte, *Nature's Second Kingdom*, 91–148; A. G. Morton, *History of Botanical Science: An Account of the Development of Botany from Ancient Times to the Present Day* (London, 1981), 238–41; James L. Larson, *Interpreting Nature: The Science of Living Form from Linnaeus to Kant* (Baltimore, 1994), 69; *Monthly Review*, 2nd ser., 5 (June 1791): 182.

34. Withers, "Rev. Dr. John Walker," 202, and "Natural Knowledge," 289–303; Charles W. J. Withers, "Improvement and Enlightenment: Agriculture and Natural History in the Work of the Rev. Dr. John Walker (1731–1803)," in *Philosophy and Science in the Scottish Enlightenment*, ed. Peter Jones (Edinburgh, 1988), 102–16; Emerson, "Scottish Enlightenment," 61.

35. On the breadth of natural history in Scotland and France, see Frans A. Stafleu, *Linnaeus and the Linnaeans* (Utrecht, 1971), 211; Emerson, "Scottish Enlightenment," 57–63.

36. Phillip Sloan, "The Buffon-Linnaeus Controversy," *Isis* 67 (1976): 356–75; Roger, Buffon, 405–41.

37. Withers, "Natural Knowledge," 294.

38. Etienne Bonnot de Condillac, *Traité des sensations; Traité des animaux* (cited hereafter as *Traité*) (1754; Paris, 1984), 11.

39. Sylvain Auroux, "Condillac, inventeur d'un nouveau matérialisme," *Dix-huitième siècle* 24 (1992): 153–63; John C. O'Neal, *The Authority of Experience: Sensationist Theory in the French Enlightenment* (University Park, Pa., 1996), 19–22.

40. Jean Piveteau, introduction to *Oeuvres philosophiques de Buffon* (Paris, 1954), xxv–xxvi. See also Laurence L. Bongie, "A New Condillac Letter and the Genesis of the *Traité des Sensations*," *Journal of the History of Philosophy* 16 (1978): 85–87; Isabel F. Knight, *The Geometric Spirit: The Abbé de Condillac and the French Enlightenment* (New Haven, Conn., 1968), 83.

41. Bongie, "A New Condillac Letter," 88.

42. Bernard Baertschi, "La Statue de Condillac, image du réel ou fiction logique?" *La Revue philosophique de Louvain* 82 (1984): 336, 338–39.

43. William Smellie, *Literary and Characteristical Lives* (cited hereafter as *LCL*; 1800; reprint, Bristol, 1997), 313–26. See also Kerr, 2:422–25; Brown, "Smellie and the Book Trade," 67–68. Cf. John Locke, *An Essay concerning Human Understanding*, ed. Alexander Campbell Fraser, 2 vols. (New York, 1959), 1:92 (bk. 1, chap. 3, no. 2).

44. Norman Daniels, *Thomas Reid's Inquiry* (New York, 1974), 102.

45. Thomas Reid, *An Inquiry into the Human Mind*, in Reid, *Philosophical Works*, 2 vols. (1764; Hildesheim: 1967), 1:99.

46. Knight, *Geometric Spirit*, 2–3.

47. On Condillac's influence outside France, see Robert G. Weyant, introduction to Condillac, *An Essay on the Origin of Human Knowledge* (Gainesville, Fla., 1971), xiv–xv, xix–xx; Ellen McNiven Hine, *A Critical Study of Condillac's Traité des systèmes* (The Hague, 1979), 1, 7–8; H. Wildon Carr, introduction to *Condillac's Treatise on the Sensations*, trans. Geraldine Carr (Los Angeles, 1930), xv–xvi. The summary of the *Traité* by Thomas Nugent is in his introduction to Condillac's *An Essay on the Origin of Human Knowledge* (1756; Gainesville, Fla., 1971), xiii–liii.

48. Wood, "Buffon's Reception," 169–90; Wood, *Thomas Reid*, 4–9. At least one Scot, however, found Buffon refreshingly "empirical." See Wood, "Buffon's Reception," 186.

49. Wood, "Buffon's Reception," 178–79, and *Thomas Reid*, 9.

50. Wood, "Buffon's Reception," 188.

51. Brown, "Smellie and the Printer's Role," 40–41.

52. Brown, introduction, x–xi.

# III
## Philosophy and Political Thought

# The Souls of Beasts:
# Hume and French Philosophy

A.E. Pitson

On the relation between animal and human nature, the views of Descartes and Montaigne represent two extremes, and David Hume may be seen as attempting to steer a middle way between them.[1] Although Hume does not refer to Descartes by name in this context, it is evident that some of his remarks about nonhuman animals are made with Descartes in mind. The extent of Hume's acquaintance with the writings of Montaigne is less clear, though there are references to Montaigne in both the second *Enquiry* (*EPM*, 8.9) and the *Essays* ("The Sceptic," 179 n. 12). In the light of the broad exposure that Hume had to France and French thought,[2] however, it seems beyond question that he would at least have been aware of Montaigne's philosophical views, both directly and from the writings of others, including Descartes himself, who refers explicitly to Montaigne's views about nonhuman animals. While Hume's observations about the differences between people and animals provide a contrast with the degree of parity allowed by Montaigne, Hume's emphasis upon the similarities marks a sharp disagreement with Descartes.

Descartes's views on animal and human nature set the stage for the philosophical debates with which this essay is concerned.[3] These reflect his dualistic conception of a human being as a combination of mind and body, considered as distinct kinds of substance. While the body is evidently something spatially extended, the mind, on Descartes's account, lacks the attributes associated with spatial extension, its essence being located in thought. The body itself is considered by Descartes to be a kind of machine, unlike the mind where our ability to exercise freedom of will originally belongs. What, then, of the case of animals? In brief, they are, according to Descartes, no more than machines or automata, for unlike human beings they are not possessed of minds or souls—or, at least, not as we are. In the case of perception, for example, Descartes declares that animals see only as we do when our mind is elsewhere. In these circumstances, our visual impressions involve events in the optic nerves which may cause our limbs to make various movements in a quite mechanical way. Thus, when animals see things, and react accordingly, they are simply behaving like automata (*Letters*, 36). Insofar as animals experience sensation or passion, they do so, according to Descartes, in a way that is quite independent of thought, and so once more they differ crucially from human beings (*Letters*, 206). If animals may be said to have souls at all, this is so only in the sense that there are blood-based fluids which move the machine of the body as they flow through arteries from the brain into the nerves and muscles (*Letters*, 36, 146). While the soul of an animal thus lies in the blood, the rational souls of human beings cannot in the same way be drawn out of the potentiality of matter (*Letters*, 36).

Descartes's contention that animals are a kind of *natural automata* (*Letters*, 244) is obviously a highly controversial claim, associated with an important seventeenth- and eighteenth-century debate about the mentality of animals. Descartes argues for his claim on the basis that a distinguishing mark of rationality, as an essential feature of mind, is the use of *language*, and that animals, unlike men, have no language (*Philosophical Writings*, 140; *Letters*, 206–7; 244–45). It might be objected that some animals, at least, do display a capacity for communication, and even what might well appear to be a kind of language (as in the case of the dance of the bees and the vocalizations of dolphins). But Descartes would regard these systems of communication as being far too limited to bear serious comparison with any human language. We are able, for example, to arrange our speech in different ways, in order to reply appropriately to whatever is said to us (*Philosophical Writings*, 140). Animals, on the other hand, emit sounds or perform movements that are limited to the expression of passions like hope and fear (*Letters*, 207). If animals *did* have a language, they would be able to communicate their thoughts to us. Human language is infinitely productive and not limited to the particular kinds of stimulus that appear to be associated with communicatory behavior in animals. Thus, there is a basis for denying that animals genuinely use signs as we do, to enable others to understand our thoughts (*Letters*, 247; *Philosophical Writings*, 140).

Another point that Descartes makes in this context is that the apparent absence of anything like a spoken language in animals, which would enable them to communicate with us as well as among members of their own species, is not a result of their lacking the relevant kind of physiology. He mentions the case of a magpie, for example, which may be trained to imitate some of the sounds of human speech. On the other side of the coin, there is the case of human beings born deaf and dumb, who are able to communicate by means of a sign language in spite of their inability to employ the organs of speech. Descartes regards these circumstances as evidence that the failure of animals to communicate by means of language results from the absence of thought or reason. If he is right, then it is a mere prejudice to suppose that dumb animals think (*Letters*, 243). Nature acts on animals simply according to the disposition of their organs, and any appearance of rationality in their behavior may be accounted for in this way.

According to Descartes, there are in fact two means by which we are able to distinguish human beings from both animals and machines. Apart from the criterion provided by language, there is also the possibility of appealing to the distinctive features of human *action*. The latter bears on the point that machines, for example, not only perform various functions (as in the case of watches and clocks) but also in many instances perform them rather better than we are able to do. But this, according to Descartes, does not mean that the machines are acting from knowledge; rather, it is a matter of essentially mechanical relationships among their parts. The point is that machines are adapted only to perform certain specific functions; reason, however, is a "universal instrument," which allows its possessor to adapt behavior to any contingencies that may arise (*Philosophical Writings*, 140). Animals and machines are incapable of the diversity that would enable them to act in all the different circumstances of life as we are able to do. Thus, while they may in some instances perform in ways that would for us depend on the use of thought or reason, these performances must be ascribed to the influence of nature, in accordance with the "disposition of their organs," rather than to thought or knowledge (*Philosophical Writings*, 141; *Letters*, 207).

There were two very different kinds of responses to Descartes within French philosophy. The first is represented by Pierre Bayle, whose writings were well known to Hume.[4] Bayle embraces the Cartesian view of beasts as automata on the basis of its theological advantages. He has in mind two particular points. One has to do with the belief that we are immortal by virtue of possessing a soul distinct from the body. So long as beasts are automata, we are spared the embarrassment of ascribing to them souls that would make them immortal. On the other hand, if we were prepared to ascribe to beasts material and mortal souls, we would be forced to arrive at a similar view of ourselves. So it is preferable to suppose that beasts are entirely without souls, material or spiritual (*Dictionary*, 216–17, 225). (Descartes's reply would be that the tests of language and action show that human beings are not just machines, while at the same time they distinguish them in this respect from nonhuman animals.)

Bayle's second point relates to the Augustinian principle that since God is just, suffering is a necessary proof of sin. In other words, if we allow that beasts undergo painful sensations, we either have to reject Augustine's principle or suppose them capable of moral agency. Descartes's view of animals spares us the difficulties that appear to arise here (*Dictionary*, 220–21). Bayle also responds directly to the scholastic view that while beasts do not possess rational souls, we may suppose them to have sensitive souls. He rejects this argument on the ground that if beasts do possess a soul which is capable of sensation, then they must also be capable of reasoning, that is, the souls of beasts would be of the same species as those of man *(Dictionary*, 233). In any case, a sensitive soul would not, by itself, provide a system that would account for the range of activities in which animals engage. This might explain why some philosophers have been prepared to grant rational souls to beasts (Bayle refers here to Celsus, in *Dictionary*, 239). Bayle, however, continues to prefer the automaton hypothesis, and in doing so concludes his discussion by rejecting the alternative provided by Leibniz's theory of preestablished harmony *(Dictionary*, 247–54).[5]

A quite different kind of response to Descartes occurs in the writings of the French Enlightenment philosopher La Mettrie.[6] As the title *L'homme machine* indicates, La Mettrie applies the Cartesian view of animals as machines to human beings. Thus, for La Mettrie the resemblances between ourselves and animals—for example, in respect to the anatomy of the brain (*Machine Man*, 9)—indicates that Descartes's view of animals as machines should also be extended to man. The resemblances to which La Mettrie refers evidently have an important bearing on the capacity of animals for learning. It may even be possible, he suggests, for animals such as the great apes to be taught a language as deaf-mutes have been (*Machine Man*, 11–12)—a suggestion that anticipates by two centuries an important area of research. The similarity of the apes' structure and functions to our own prevents us from ruling out this possibility. Contrary to the supposed "primal distinction" between humans and animals, "external signs" reveal the possession by animals of thought and feeling, including such feelings as remorse, even if they are incapable of recognizing the difference between right and wrong (*Machine Man*, 19–20; cf. *Treatise on the Soul*, 50, on the signs of feelings in animals). In a striking image, La Mettrie writes that nature has used the same dough for both man and animals, merely changing the yeast. While Descartes sees the brain and its organization as providing a causal basis for the activities of the soul, La Mettrie argues that the soul should be identified with the brain. What philosophers call the soul is nothing more than a principle of thought and action located in the brain (*Machine Man*, 28). If we compare the body to a clock, then the soul considered as part of the brain is a mainspring of the whole machine (*Machine Man*, 31; *Treatise on the Soul*, 56, 65).[7] There is only one substance in the universe, and what distinguishes man from animal is the sheer complexity of his organization (*Machine Man*, 33–34). We do not need to posit a soul as something distinct from the body in order to account for thought, since there is nothing to rule out a priori the possibility that thought might be a property of organized matter (*Machine Man*, 35). Even if Descartes were right, then, about the machinelike nature of animals, it would not follow from this that animals are incapable of thought and feeling—any more than our mechanistic character prevents us from being sentient or intelligent.

To return to Descartes, it is important to note a crucial point arising from his argument: the fact that an animal or machine is capable of doing something which in a human being would require thought and intelligence is not in itself a reason for ascribing such capacities to the animal or machine. This point has a direct bearing on the debate about animal mentality initiated by Descartes's predecessor, Montaigne.[8] Montaigne argues that animals behaving in a way which, in human beings, would demand skill and intelligence should be credited with the same sort of mentality. Among the many examples of animal lore to which he appeals are those of swallows returning in the spring to their nesting places and fish that appear to respond to astronomical events like the solstice and the equinox. He suggests that "from similar effects we should conclude that there are similar faculties" (*Apology*, 25); that is, animals employ the same method of reasoning as us when we do anything. But this is precisely what Descartes denies. Since we are not entitled to ascribe to animals reason as a "universal instrument," the kinds of performance that Montaigne mentions are attributable to the way in which nature acts on these animals, as the mechanism of the clock explains how it is able to measure time more accurately than we are able to do in spite of our rationality (*Letters*, 207; *Philosophical Writings*, 117).

Montaigne's claims about the relation between animal and human nature reflect the idea that we have an unduly exalted view of our own nature in comparison with that of beasts. This, in turn, might be seen as an expression of Montaigne's version of Pyrrhonism, with its emphasis on human ignorance and the limitations of reason in arriving at truth. Our predicament is summarized in the following aphorism: "There is a plague on man: his opinion that he knows something" (*Apology*, 53). Intellectual pride leads us to suppose that we possess distinctive powers of reason that elevate us above beasts. Although knowledge can come only through the senses, their fallibility effectively prevents there from being any such thing as knowledge (*Apology*, 170–75). In these respects, as in others, Montaigne's epistemology is in striking contrast to that of Descartes, for whom truth and certainty are, with the use of the right kind of method, attainable goals. It is, in any case, scarcely surprising that Montaigne should see evidence of the same capacities for ratiocination in animal behavior as in our own actions. Nor is it surprising that he is prepared to allow that animals are able to communicate with each other by the use of meaningful sounds, as well as gesture, facial expression, and so on, considered as a kind of sign language (*Apology*, 17–19). Descartes appears to have just these kinds of claims in mind when he refers explicitly to Montaigne as one of those who is prepared to ascribe understanding or thought to animals (*Letters*, 206). One of the crucial points Descartes has to make in response to such claims is that they depend on the external resemblance, in certain respects, between our own behavior and that of animals, and that this external resemblance, in itself, is not enough to establish that there is any resemblance in the corresponding internal activities (*Letters*, 54).

It seems true, in fact, that Montaigne is unduly prone to accept at face value animal performances which might be seen as the product of thought and reasoning, without considering possible alternative explanations. One thinks here, for example, of the well-known case of the horse Clever Hans, whose apparent ability to count was revealed as a response to subtle behavioral cues.[9] Descartes's own suggestion that in many of these cases, at least, the animal's behavior may be compared to that of a mechanism, like a watch, appears to receive further support from studies in ethology, which have shown how kinds of animal behavior that appear to exhibit intelligence may in fact be inflexible, "wired in" routines resulting from natural selection. There is good reason, therefore, to think that Montaigne is just wrong to claim that the beatings of birds' wings cannot be attributed entirely to "some ordinance of nature," as opposed to thought or understanding (*Apology*, 34). In these respects, Descartes might be considered to have the better of Montaigne in the debate about animal mentality, though we should note that this is by no means to vindicate Descartes's own view that animals are no more than automata. While it may be true that Montaigne exaggerates the degree of similarity, in respect of the capacities for thought or intelligence, between animal and human nature, it may also be true that there are points of resemblance for which Descartes fails to allow. This, indeed, seems a reasonable conclusion to be drawn from this phase of the debate about animal mentality, and it is one for which Hume's arguments provide strong support.

On Hume's account, there are many important aspects of our nature as human beings that we share in common with animals, and to this extent Hume is in clear disagreement with Descartes. But Hume also recognizes a number of crucial differences between human and animal nature, and these place him at some distance from Montaigne. Hence, he arrives at a kind of *via media* between these two philosophical positions.

## THE SIMILARITIES BETWEEN HUMANS AND ANIMALS

Just as there are obvious physiological similarities between men and animals, so also, according to Hume, is there a close resemblance in the "anatomy" of human and animal minds (*Treatise*, 2.1.12.2). In sum, "animals undoubtedly feel, think, love, hate, will, and even reason" as we do, albeit in a "more imperfect manner" (*Essays*, 592). Many of Hume's references to animals are intended precisely to illustrate this point. In effect, the kinds of resemblance he has in mind fall into two categories. First, there are the epistemological ones. Both men and animals are equipped not only to acquire beliefs from experience, but also by means of both prudence and intelligence to act directly on the natural world (*Essays*, 582). There seems to be a distinction within animal behavior between those actions that reflect the conditioning effects of experience, such as avoidance of fire, and those that involve more complex patterns of behavior. But actions of the former kind, according to Hume, rest upon a process of association that is characteristically at work also in the causal beliefs of human beings. In a word, it is *habit* that is typically responsible for our own expectations, as it is for the conditioned responses of animals. Thus, rather than *oppose* reason in human beings to what might be dismissed as instinctive behavior in animals, we should recognize that reason itself characteristically functions as a kind of instinct arising from past observation and experience (*Treatise*, 1.3.16.9). We may protest that our behavior is distinguished from mere instinct by a certain flexibility, but Hume suggests that there are instances of animal behavior that exhibit a degree of sagacity—as in the case of nest-building, an example also found in Montaigne (*Apology*, 19). We now know that for some species, at least, such activity is largely instinctive. But there are other cases in which animal behavior exhibits a kind of experimental activity that appears to contrast with behavior of a merely "vulgar" nature.

One of the crucial points Hume wants to make in relation to such observations is that if philosophers have been led to ignore these resemblances between animal and human behavior, it is because they ascribe a kind of "refinement of thought" to human beings that would exceed not only the capacity of animals but also, for that matter, the capacity of many human beings. When we see what ordinarily passes as reasoning in men for what it is—the conditioned propensity to form expectations on the basis of past experience—then we also see that there is no obstacle to acknowledging the evident resemblance between ourselves and animals, at the "internal" level of belief as well as regarding the external actions we share in common. The latter point is illustrated also by the case of noninferential beliefs, such as those concerning the objects of the senses (*EHU*, 12.7). We therefore have good reason to reject the Cartesian conception of the nature of human thought or reason in favor of the alternative supplied by Hume in his epistemology.

The other point of resemblance with which Hume is concerned belongs to the area of the passions. "The chief spring or actuating principle of the human mind," Hume tells us, "is pleasure or pain" (*Treatise*, 3.3.1.2). There is no reason to suppose that animals differ in this respect—indeed, Hume indicates that, like us, animals are motivated to obtain pleasure and avoid pain (*Treatise*, 1.3.16.2). They will accordingly also be liable to experience the same sorts of passion or emotion—both "indirect," as in the case of pride and humility (*Treatise*, 2.1.12) and love and hatred (*Treatise*, 2.2.12), and "direct," as in the case of fear and grief (*Treatise*, 2.2.12.6). Similarly, volition, as the immediate effect of pleasure and pain, is something we share in common with animals (*Treatise*, 2.3.9.32). The fact that animals experience the same kinds of passion as us indicates that they will also be susceptible to the same mechanism for the communication of passions, namely, sympathy, as Hume in fact confirms (*Treatise*, 2.2.12.6). It is interesting to note that Montaigne also stresses the importance of sympathy in the lives of both humans and animals (*Apology*, 36), though his understanding of this notion may differ somewhat from Hume's.

The parallels that Hume finds between human and animal minds have a more than merely epistemological or psychological significance. Descartes claims that we are not only superior to animals in reasoning power but also that we differ from them in possessing an immortal mind or soul. It is scarcely surprising that Hume finds himself obliged to reject any such claim. If we accept that the minds of animals are mortal, then the analogies between their mental capacities and ours should lead us to reach a similar conclusion about human minds *(Essays, 597)*. We are reminded here of Bayle's discussion, referred to above.

## THE DIFFERENCES BETWEEN HUMAN AND ANIMAL NATURE

We have seen that Hume is prepared to acknowledge differences in degree between the mental capacities of men and animals. He mentions other, comparatively trivial, differences, both anatomical and temperamental *(Treatise, 2.1.12.2)*, but indicates that these pale beside the many striking continuities to be observed at the level of both body and mind. There are, however, two points of difference that do appear to be of special importance. The first is our superiority in knowledge and understanding *(Treatise, 2.1.12.5)*. If it is true that one person may obviously surpass another in the ability to reason, it appears also to be true that people collectively surpass animals in this respect *(EHU, 9.5 n, 20)*.[10] Hume thus reminds us of our ability to carry our thoughts beyond our immediate situation to remote places and times, and to theorize about our experience *(Essays, 82)*. By comparison, animals appear to be without curiosity or insight and to be confined in their thoughts to the things around them. Hume is anxious to stress, however, that we should not think of ourselves as having been especially favored by virtue of our superior reason; for we find that our reason is proportionate both to our wants and to our period of existence *(Essays, 593)*. The suggestion that we are able to find a natural explanation for the difference in reasoning powers between ourselves and animals—that nature provides us with the intelligence required to meet our needs *(Essays, 147)*—makes Hume's position fully consistent with an evolutionary account of the development of such powers.

The other especially important difference between humans and animals lies in the area of the passions—in particular, in the fact that, compared with us, animals are "but little susceptible either of the pleasures or pains of the imagination" *(Treatise, 2.2.12.3)*. This difference is in fact directly related to the first one: since the judgments of animals concern the things around them, their feelings will not transcend the immediate effects upon them of these things. In more general terms, animals will be less likely to experience those passions that require some effort of thought or imagination (*Treatise*, 2.2.12.8).

These two respects in which we differ from animals explain why there are kinds of belief that we do not share with them. A case in point is belief in God or, more generally, the beliefs associated with religious practices and institutions. Hume does seem to regard this as a way in which we differ from animals— and, if so, there is once more a contrast with Montaigne, for whom the behavior of some animals provides evidence of their possession of religious notions (*Apology*, 33). Although religious belief may not be universal, it is certainly widely diffused throughout human societies (*NHR*, 98). This view requires Hume to identify those features of human nature that would explain the prevalence of religious belief, and also account for its absence among animals. His view, in brief, is that early religion was polytheistic: humans had little understanding of the natural events governing their lives and were inclined therefore to ascribe them to a variety of deities. In doing so, they exhibited what Hume describes as a kind of "trembling curiosity" which, combined with ignorance of natural causes, led to an anthropomorphic conception of invisible powers that must then be appeased (*NHR*, 39–43; cf. 54). Monotheism was originally a development from these "vulgar" beliefs, one of the "limited deities" finally being conceived of as supreme (*NHR*, 57). The forces of human nature at work here are a curiosity about the causes of natural events together with an "active imagination" (*NHR*, 62), which leads us to clothe these deities in human form; but these features of our nature are precisely the ones which, for Hume, distinguish us from animals.

Hume himself evidently sees the differences to which I have referred as having a direct bearing on what is, perhaps, the crucial point of contrast between ourselves and animals, that is, the absence in animals of a moral sense (*Treatise*, 2.1.12.5). The function of the moral sense is to enable us to discern the qualities of character which, on Hume's account, render actions virtuous or vicious. In order for the moral sense to operate in this way, it must—like the bodily senses—be subject to a process of correction. This reflects the essentially partial nature of sympathy as the source of our approval of those qualities of character with beneficial tendencies. Sympathy operates more strongly in regard to people who are acquaintances of ours, than to those people, like strangers and foreigners, whose actions are unable directly to affect us (*Treatise*, 3.3.1.14; cf. *EPM*, 5.42). But there is, in spite of this, a constancy in our approbation of moral qualities, as there is in our perception of such characteristics as the size of an object. We arrive at stable moral judgments by fixing on some *steady* and *general* points of view—ones which abstract from features peculiar to our present situation (*Treatise*, 3.3.1.15; *EPM*, 9.6). As we should expect, Hume makes a similar suggestion about our aesthetic judgments (*Essays*, 237–41). It is only by adopting the general or common view, in fact, that we discern those qualities of mind or character which make a person virtuous or vicious, or those forms or qualities of objects which make them beautiful or ugly (*Treatise*, 3.1.2.4; *Essays*, 232–33).

Now, our ability to take the common or general view reflects just those respects in which we differ crucially from animals. There are, for example, rules for judging the merits of works of art, but in order for our responses to conform to these rules, a certain "delicacy of imagination" is required (*Essays*, 231, 234). We have to develop the ability to view the objects that provide the focus for our judgments of beauty or ugliness with a degree of detachment, while also attending to their features of form or style *(Essays*, 237–38). When Hume remarks on the comparative imperfections of feeling in animals, and their lack of susceptibility to the pleasures and pains of the imagination, he is surely implying the absence of that delicacy of imagination on which our aesthetic sensibilities depend. This delicacy of imagination itself depends on a "sound understanding," which enables us to discern the end or purpose of a work of art, and the degree to which it is achieved *(Essays*, 240–41). This is just the kind of case in which, for Hume, we display a knowledge and understanding superior to those of animals. It is perhaps unusual enough to find persons who are endowed with the kind of good sense and delicate imagination associated with the arbiter of aesthetic merit. But the capacity appears to be one that belongs only to persons and not, given their inferiority in thought and feeling, to animals.

It is reasonably clear that these observations apply equally to what Hume has to say about the operation of the moral sense, which also requires a kind of imaginative ability to abstract from our personal relation to the agent whose mind or character is the object of our appraisal. And in doing so we obviously exercise our capacities for rational reflection. As Hume puts it, "reason pave[s] the way" for sentiments of praise and blame: in order for our moral judgments to achieve the objectivity associated with the general view, distinctions need to be made, conclusions drawn, comparisons formed, relations examined, and facts ascertained (*EPM,* 1.9). It is just this kind of exercise of understanding of which animals appear to be incapable; and it is also, therefore, this deficiency that would explain their lack of a moral sense.

These points about the moral sense may also help to explain why Hume would be reluctant to classify animals as moral agents.[11] The nature of this connection is problematic, but for Hume the actions of animals cannot be considered as virtuous or vicious. This becomes clear when Hume attempts to explain why vice, for example, cannot consist in relations discerned by the understanding. In short, the reason is that the same relations may have different characters or causes, as illustrated by the fact that while "incest in the human species is criminal, . . . the very same action, and the same relations in animals have not the smallest moral turpitude or deformity" (*Treatise,* 3.1.1.25). Where, then, does the criminality of human incest lie, and why is it not a feature of the same relations in animals? For Hume, the criminality of an action resides in the state of mind of the agent: specifically, his passions or principles (*Treatise,* 2.3.2.7; cf. 3.3.1.4). Animals, it appears, are incapable of the relevant sorts of passions or principles of mind. In the case of incest, the vice of such relations in humans essentially consists in their threat to the family, and hence the "superior turpitude and moral deformity" of incest (*EPM,* 4.8). Given that society originates in family life (*Treatise,* 3.2.2.4), we may therefore condemn someone who knowingly engages in an incestuous act for willfully violating a rule on which society, and thus the subsistence of the species, depends. This enables us to see why Hume would consider animals incapable of committing incest as a criminal act, for to do so would require them to possess some sort of conception or awareness of the rule being violated.[12] And such an awareness is scarcely compatible with their inability to engage in the kind of imaginative abstraction from immediate and individual circumstances that is required for the operation of the moral sense.

As for the motivating principles or passions that are relevant to performing incest as a criminal act, they are ones which exhibit a lack of self-command, or of strength of mind (*EPM*, 6.15). When we act in accordance with the rules that prohibit sexual intercourse with certain kinds of kindred, we exhibit the influence of the calm passions, as Hume classifies them, over the immediate temptations we may encounter. These passions reflect "a general prospect of their objects" on which we form rules of conduct that enable us to achieve long-term profit or enjoyment. The association of the calm passions with a "general prospect" suggests that they belong exclusively to human beings in virtue of their superior understanding. This is relevant also to the nature of the *violent* passion associated with incest as a criminal act. In those cases where an object excites contrary passions, "we naturally desire what is forbid, and take a pleasure in performing actions, merely because they are unlawful" (*Treatise*, 2.3.4.5). In this respect, the state of mind of the person guilty of incest as a criminal act differs crucially from that of an animal involved in the same kind of relation. Strictly speaking, an animal cannot be *tempted* to perform incest: the violent passion by which it is excited does not reflect the appeal of the forbidden or unlawful that provides the source of temptation for a human agent in the grip of contrary passions.

Two further points have a bearing on Hume's view of the comparison between humans and animals. We have seen that Hume is prepared to ascribe the indirect passions of pride and humility to animals. Yet these passions play a crucial role in the operation of the moral sense: the sentiment of approbation, for example, is associated with the agreeable passion of love or pride. How is this view to be reconciled with the denial that animals are moral agents? The problem seems to be exacerbated by the fact that the object of these passions, according to Hume, is the self (*Treatise*, 2.1.2.2). I am proud of something, for example, only if there is an *association* in my mind between the idea of that thing and that of myself. But if pride involves an idea of the self, its occurrence in animals would seem to suggest that they must have a similar status to us. I believe, however, that the idea of self which Hume ascribes to animals is relevantly different from the one involved in the case of human pride or humility. Thus, he indicates that the pertinent idea of self in humans comprises both mental and bodily qualities (*Treatise*,

2.1.9.1), while pride in animals is concerned solely with qualities of the latter kind (*Treatise*, 2.1.12.5). In other words, the animal's idea of its body is linked associatively with that in which
it takes pride. The occurrence in animals of the indirect passions
is therefore consistent with the view that they differ from us in
lacking a moral sense, or the capacity for moral agency.

There is a related issue arising from Hume's account of the
mechanism of sympathy. Hume certainly thinks that animals
are susceptible to this mechanism for the communication of
passions. But if it is also true that "sympathy is the chief source
of moral distinctions" (*Treatise*, 3.3.6.1), how is this truth to be
reconciled with the denial that animals are moral agents? Once
more, the crucial issue is the part played here by the idea of self.
Sympathy, like the indirect passions, is supposed to involve the
idea of the self, in this case because it so enlivens the idea we
form of other beings' mental states that we come to share those
states with them (*Treatise*, 2.1.11.7). We should, however, consider just how *self*-conscious this process has to be. When Hume
talks about "the easy communication of sentiments from one
thinking being to another" (*Treatise*, 2.2.5.15), he seems to be
referring to a process that may be relatively unreflective, and
that, as he says in the same place, enables us to "observe the
force of sympathy thro' the whole animal creation." According
to Hume, there is a kind of emotional contagion that enables
the passions to pass "with the greatest facility" from one person
to another (*Treatise*, 3.3.3.5). Similarly, in regard to animals, "affections" such as fear and anger may be communicated from
one to another, quite independently of any knowledge of their
original causes (*Treatise*, 2.2.12.6). But if sympathy may thus operate quite unreflectively, then the fact that animals also partici-
pate in this process would not, as such, imply a consciousness
of self that would put them on a par with us. It may be true that,
in virtue of the passions they experience, and their susceptibility to sympathy, animals share some of the features that make
us moral agents,[13] but Hume is justified, I think, in seeing relevant differences which deprive animals of that status.

The various points referred to above bear directly on another
crucial point of difference, on Hume's account, between humans and animals. This has to do with our status as *social*
beings. Our essentially social nature is reflected in such institu-

tions as property and the associated social virtues and vices. Animals, on the other hand, are incapable of such relations as those of right and property (*Treatise*, 2.1.12.5). Hume's explanation for this difference in the status of humans and animals is that, whereas wants and means are balanced in animals (so that their appetites are proportioned to their means of satisfying them), in humans there is an "unnatural conjunction of infirmity, and of necessity" (*Treatise*, 3.2.2.2). Humans must labor to produce the food they require as well as their clothing and shelter. This is possible only within society, which enables them to combine forces to achieve collectively what they would be incapable of doing individually, to divide labor so as to give scope to individual abilities, and to provide mutual security. The "original principle of human society" is the "natural appetite betwixt the sexes, which unites them together"; a concern for their offspring then "becomes also a principle of union betwixt the parents and offspring, and forms a more numerous society" (*Treatise*, 3.2.2.4). Children themselves thus become aware of the advantages of society, while their life within the family prepares them for it. By contrast, the "uniting principle" in animals is provided entirely by instinct, as opposed to reason and forethought (*EPM*, Appendix 3.9 n). Once more, it is the difference in degree of knowledge and understanding that accounts for the distinctive features of human existence.

There is a further aspect of man's social nature that provides a crucial contrast with the situation of animals, and this has to do with the possession of a language. The purpose of language is of course to enable individuals to communicate with each other, and in this way make possible an "intercourse of sentiments" (*EPM*, 5.42). Language arises through a sense of common interest in the existence of such an institution, and is comparable in this respect to systems of exchange in which gold and silver become established as common measures (*EPM*, Appendix 3.8; *Treatise*, 3.2.2.10). The important point to recognize here is that in order for language to be invented as the means for expressing universal sentiments (*EPM*, 9.8), its users must themselves be capable of adopting the general view that makes the existence of such sentiments possible, insofar as they arise from the general interest (*EPM*, 5.42). Indeed, unless we take this general view, we will be unable to appreciate the common interest which is served by the institution of language itself and requires that, in order to communicate at all, we should be prepared to adopt a disinterested perspective. Now we know that animals are, for Hume, incapable of the general view associated with the operation of the moral sense. They will also therefore fail to possess a language that provides the vehicle for judgments of approval and disapproval.

So far Hume might appear to endorse the argument that Descartes tried to use to establish that animals lack minds or souls, namely, that they have no language. But, in fact, what is established by the above observations is only that animals do not have a language like ours. It remains possible that some animals may nevertheless at least communicate their individual sentiments to each other by means of the sounds they utter; and this possibility is recognized by Hume's observation that animals have a kind of "natural speech" that is intelligible to their own species (*Dialogues*, 127). In this respect, Hume's position is more in sympathy with that of Montaigne (e.g., for example, 19, 23). Unlike Montaigne, however, Hume is in a position to distinguish the kinds of communication that occur in animals from language as used by human beings.

We should notice an important implication of the distinctively social nature of human beings as compared with animals. This is that our relations with animals cannot themselves be social ones, for that would presuppose a degree of equality which, as we have seen above, does not exist. Thus, if we have any obligations to animals, they cannot be of the kind associated with justice, whose rules precisely reflect our human condition. But even if we do find ourselves masters of animal creation (*Dialogues*, 168), this does not mean that we may simply treat animals as we please. For their combination of a degree of rationality with inferior mental and bodily powers binds us "by the laws of humanity to give gentle usage to these creatures" (*EPM*, 3.18). They are appropriate objects of our compassion and kindness even if they are strictly unable to make any claims upon us. Thus, even if animals are not to be classified as moral agents, they are—unlike, presumably, machines—objects of moral concern. In this respect, Hume's position provides an enlightened alternative to that of Descartes, while avoiding the extravagant view of animal mentality to be found in Montaigne.

# NOTES

1. The writings of Hume to which I will be referring are these: *A Treatise of Human Nature* (hereafter, *Treatise* with references by book, part, section and paragraph number), ed. David F. Norton and Mary J. Norton (Oxford: Oxford University Press, 2000); *An Enquiry Concerning Human Understanding* (hereafter, *EHU* with references by section and paragraph number), ed. Tom L. Beauchamp (Oxford: Oxford University Press, 1999), and *An Enquiry Concerning the Principles of Morals* (hereafter, *EPM* with references by section and paragraph number), ed. Tom L. Beauchamp (Oxford: Oxford University Press, 1998); *Essays, Moral, Political, and Literary* (hereafter *Essays*), ed. Eugene F. Miller (Indianapolis, 1987); and *The Natural History of Religion* (hereafter *NHR*) and *Dialogues Concerning Natural Religion* (hereafter *Dialogues*), from *Hume on Religion*, ed. Richard Wollheim (London, 1963).

2. In a letter of March or April 1734, Hume claimed to have read "most of the celebrated Books in Latin, French & English" between the ages of eighteen and twenty (*The Letters of David Hume*, ed. J. Y. T. Greig, 2 vols. [Oxford, 1932], 1:16). He also spent two lengthy periods in France, during which he became acquainted with many French intellectuals, and subsequently corresponded with some of them about their writings. For extensive documentation of the many works in French with which Hume is likely to have been familiar, see especially David Fate Norton and Mary J. Norton, *The David Hume Library* (Edinburgh, 1996), 27–33.

3. See the first volume of *The Discourse on the Method* in *The Philosophical Writings of Descartes*, trans. John Cottingham, Robert Stoothoff, and Dugald Murdoch (Cambridge, 1985; hereafter *Philosophical Writings*); and *Descartes: Philosophical Letters* (hereafter *Letters*), trans. Anthony Kenny (Oxford, 1970).

4. I shall be referring, in particular, to Pierre Bayle, *Historical and Critical Dictionary: Selections*, trans. Richard H. Popkin (Indianapolis, 1991), hereafter *Dictionary*. The *Dictionary* was published originally in 1697, but various enlarged editions subsequently appeared. The remarks of Bayle to which I will be referring form part of an extended discussion that occurs in the entry on Rorarius. Hume refers to a book by Bayle in a letter of March 1732 (see Greig, *Letters of David Hume*, 1:12), and there is a reference in the *Treatise* (1.4.5.22n) to the entry on Spinoza in Bayle's *Dictionary*.

5. Bayle nevertheless appears to have real difficulties with Descartes's view of animals as automata insofar as it might lead to a similar view of other men—something he judges to be the weakest part of Cartesianism (*Dictionary*, 231).

6. The works of La Mettrie with which I am especially concerned are *L'homme machine*, originally published anonymously in 1747, and *Histoire naturelle de l'âme*, originally published under a pseudonym in 1745. These works achieved considerable notoriety, and it seems reasonable to suppose that Hume would have become acquainted with the views they contain. These two works of La Mettrie, together with other writings, have recently been republished in *Machine Man and Other Writings*, trans. Ann Thomson (Cambridge, 1996). My references will be to this edition, under the headings of *Machine*

*Man* (an amended version of *L'homme machine*) and *Treatise on the Soul* (a revised version of the original *Natural History*).

7. This image of the clockwork man resonates throughout a debate about the possibility of thinking matter that occurred in both Britain and France in the eighteenth century. The debate reflects various themes that may be traced back to Descartes—the possibility of providing mechanistic explanations of various types of animal behavior, for example, and the notion that properties like thought and volition can belong only to something that is immaterial. Hence, a focus for this debate was provided by Locke's suggestion in the *Essay Concerning Human Understanding* that God might have made it possible for matter to think. In fact, it is Locke who links the debate about thinking matter in eighteenth-century British philosophy with La Mettrie's development of the idea of man as a machine. Hume's own comments on the materialist/immaterialist debate occur in *Treatise*, 1.4.5. For a valuable overview of this important phase of philosophical discussion about men, machines, and animals, see John W. Yolton, *Thinking Matter: Materialism in Eighteenth-Century Britain* (Oxford, 1984).

8. Montaigne's views are to be found in *An Apology for Raymond Sebond* (London, 1987), hereafter *Apology*.

9. For an account of this case, see Peter Carruthers, *The Animals Issue: Moral Theory in Practice* (Cambridge, 1992), 122–23. It is worth comparing this case with Montaigne's own example of the counting oxen (*Apology*, 29).

10. Cf. *Apology*, 31, where Montaigne suggests that, in regard to intelligence, there is a greater difference between one man and another than between some men and some beasts.

11. Substantial and difficult issues of interpretation involving this topic are discussed in greater detail in A. E. Pitson, "The Nature of Humean Animals," *Hume Studies* 39 (1993): 301–16.

12. See, in this connection, Hume's remarks about murder as the violation of a maxim arrived at through common interest and utility (*EPM*, 4.20). Since animals, given their comparative inferiority of reason, are incapable of taking the general point of view on which recognition of rules and their utility depends, they cannot willfully violate the maxim involved.

13. Thus, according to Hume, we may conceive of a virtuous horse, just as we may also think of a golden mountain, by joining together ideas which are consistent with each other (*EHU*, 2.5). This is not to suppose that anything corresponds to such complex ideas of imagination.

# The Representation of Adam Smith and David Hume in the *Année Littéraire* and the *Journal Encyclopédique*

HARVEY CHISICK

TODAY DAVID HUME AND ADAM SMITH ARE REGARDED AS THE TWO MOST important representatives of the Scottish Enlightenment. In this essay I will attempt to determine how they were perceived by their contemporaries across the channel. To this end, I will examine the place that Hume and Smith are accorded in two of the most important literary periodicals of the second half of the eighteenth century, the *Année Littéraire* and the *Journal Encyclopédique*.[1] I will first consider the number and extent of reviews devoted to each author. This will yield profiles of Hume and Smith that are not quite in accord with our perceptions of these authors today. Then, having seen which works are given the most space in the two periodicals, I will examine how they were evaluated.

Before turning to these Scottish authors, it is advisable to consider their Francophone reviewers. The *Année Littéraire* and the *Journal Encyclopédique* have been chosen for two reasons. First, their duration is extensive enough to allow us to follow responses to these authors from the mid-1750s to the French Revolution, and secondly, both were successful ventures with, for the time, considerable readerships.[2] The *Année Littéraire* was founded in 1754 by Elie Catherine Fréron, one of the outstanding literary figures of the second half of the eighteenth century, and one who is regarded as having a claim to having established modern literary criticism.[3] Fréron died in 1776, but his journal continued to appear under the management of his widow until 1790, when she abandoned it to work on a royalist daily.[4] The *Année Littéraire* has often been regarded as supporting absolutism and the Catholic Church, but recent work on Fréron and his journal has recognized in it a progressiveness and openness to Enlightenment values.[5] The *Journal Encyclopédique* was founded by Pierre Rousseau of Toulouse in 1756, and continued to appear until 1793. It was published outside the borders of France, first in Liège, and then in Bouillon. As its name suggests, it saw itself as progressive, and an organ for advanced Enlightenment views.[6] The way the two periodicals treat Hume and Smith will provide points of reference that should allow us to appreciate how their works were received by the contemporary Francophone public.

The fact that the French enjoyed cultural hegemony during the eighteenth century might be expected to lessen the interest of journalists working in the dominant language of the time in the productions of less established national literatures. Van Tieghem's monograph on the *Année Littéraire* has shown that this was far from being the case for Fréron's journal. During more than two decades under the editorship of Fréron, the *Année Littéraire* devoted between fifteen and twenty percent of its space to reviews of foreign works. This figure fell to between twelve and thirteen percent under his successors.[7] Impressed by the number of works of foreign origin reviewed in Fréron's periodical, Van Tieghem believed that the *Année Littéraire* was unrivaled in this respect.[8] While research has not so far been done to allow us to verify this hypothesis, the openness of the *Journal Encyclopédique* to foreign works seems as great as that of Fréron's journal. Moreover, at least in the cases of Smith and Hume, the *Journal Encyclopédique* reviewed the original English editions of the works of these authors, whereas the *Année Littéraire* normally awaited translations before addressing them.

A final point needs to be made about the two periodicals. Both were, of course, literary journals, and this meant, in the context of this period, that the overwhelming preponderance of their copy consisted in book reviews that normally ranged between ten and twenty pages. The literary public wanted reviews of new (or reprinted) works, and that is what it got. The *Année Littéraire* was strict in its adherence to this formula, so that announcements, anecdotes, articles, and letters to the editor account for only a small amount of space in the journal—up to about ten percent while Fréron was editor.[9] The *Journal Encyclopédique,* on the other hand, was conceived in a somewhat broader manner. During the 1770s and 1780s its reviews tended to be shorter than those of the *Année Littéraire,* and it included more anecdotes, news, and incidental matter. It also included a separate section for political news, though that part of the journal is not under consideration here. Because of the slightly different self-definition of the two periodicals, one would expect the *Année Littéraire* to restrict its treatment of Hume and Smith largely to reviews of their works, and the *Journal Encyclopédique* to adopt a more varied approach.

How, then, were Hume and Smith represented in these two periodicals? I will begin with Smith's case, which is simpler from the point of view of publication history. Smith published the *Theory of Moral Sentiments* in 1759 and *An Inquiry into the Nature and Causes of the Wealth of Nations* in 1776. The first work had two translations into French and three editions before the Revolution. The first translation, by Eidous, was published anonymously as *Métaphysique de l'âme* in 1764. The second, translated by the abbé Blavet simply as *Théorie des sentimens moraux,* appeared in 1774–75 with one publisher, and again in 1782 with another. All three of these editions appeared with a Paris imprint. An anonymous translation of the *Wealth of Nations* in four volumes was published in 1778–79 in the Hague. In 1781 a six-volume translation, apparently again by Blavet, appeared.[10] A two-volume edition with the dual imprints London and Paris appeared in 1788, while a translation by Roucher in four volumes, which promised a volume of notes by Condorcet, was published in Paris in 1790–91.[11]

The profiles of Smith in these two periodicals show some striking differences. While the *Année Littéraire* devotes only two reviews to Smith's works, both to the *Theory of Moral Sentiments,* the *Journal Encyclopédique* has a total of seven, two on this work, and five on the *Wealth of Nations.* The *Journal Encyclopédique* reviewed the English edition of the *Theory of Moral Sentiments,* immediately upon its appearance in 1759 (*JE,* 1759, 7–ii: 3–18) and then reviewed the sixth English edition in 1791 (*JE,* 1791, 7: 12–21), but there devoted less space to the book than to its author, who had recently died.[12] The *Année Littéraire,* on the other hand, reviewed the *Theory of Moral Sentiments* only when it appeared in French translation. It devoted an extensive review to the Eidous edition of 1764 (*AL,* 1764, 6: 145–68), and an even longer one to the Blavet translation in 1774 (*AL,* 1774, 7: 23–48). Thus, while the *Année Littéraire* and the *Journal Encyclopédique* each reviewed Smith's work on moral theory twice, the more conservative journal devoted twice the number of pages to the *Theory of Moral Sentiments* than the reputedly more progressive one.

If the *Année Littéraire* and the *Journal Encyclopédique* held substantially different views of the Enlightenment, this is hardly reflected in their treatment of Smith's treatise on ethics. The journalists of both periodicals express concern about the implications of self-interest and cultural relativism in ethical theory. Both praise Smith for rooting his ethics in human nature,[13] and for retaining the connection between religion and morality. In his summary of the *Theory of Moral Sentiments,* written in 1759, the *Journal Encyclopédique* reviewer asserts:

> And this is sufficient about this work, which has appeared so admirable to us by the force and beauty of its style and the nobility of its sentiments, by the correctness and originality [*nouveauté*] of its thought, by the imposing tone of its reasoning. But what renders it even more precious is that everything in it is inspired by the purest virtue, that Religion is respected throughout. It is indeed sad that the looseness [*libertinage*] of our century renders such praise necessary. (*JE*, 1759, 2–viii: 28)

Similarly, five years later, after observing that the theories of La Rochefoucauld, Mandeville, and Hobbes allow no sound bases for distinguishing vice from virtue, the journalist of the *Année Littéraire* called the *Theory of Moral Sentiments* "this excellent work," and praised the clarity and precision of its style. He then continued:

> Further, he [Smith] inspires the taste for virtue. M. *Smith* seems filled with it, and his theory of the sentiments does as much credit to his heart as it does to his mind. If all our philosophers were like him, Religion, Morality, even Literature, that is to say, all that is most elevated, most holy, most lovable would be equally safe, and the fatherland would not have to take alarm at the sacrilegious outrages of all our false sages who, under the pretext of instructing and enlightening, imperceptibly sap the most solid foundations, unrelentingly attacking by their impious and dangerous system the respectable principles from which derives the peace of Empires. (*AL*, 1764, 6: 166–68)

If Fréron's rhetoric is more intense than that of the *Journal Encyclopédique,* the evaluations of Smith's treatise on ethics are substantially the same in both journals.[14]

Smith's epoch-making *Wealth of Nations* was reviewed five times by the *Journal Encyclopédique,* twice when the work first appeared in 1776 (*JE,* 1776, 7: 3–15 and 252–63), once when a new French edition was published in 1788 (*JE,* 2: 396–408), and twice more when the Roucher translation was published (*JE,* 1790, 7: 391–402 and 1791, 2: 429–44). Together, these reviews take up sixty pages of text in the journal.[15] As it had done in the case of the *Theory of Moral Sentiments,* the *Journal Encyclopédique* did not wait for a translation into French, but reviewed the first English edition of Smith's work.

In its reviews of the *Wealth of Nations,* the *Journal Encyclopédique* was fair, and generally favorable. The reviewer of the first edition in 1776 accepts both the labor theory of value and the doctrine of free trade. He argues, however, that *ad hoc* monopolies are often useful, and questions both Smith's claim that merchants make the best improvers of land, and the accuracy of his account of the origin of feudal rights (*JE,* 1776, 7: 261, 11, 14).[16] This review lacks the enthusiasm that one might have expected a major Enlightenment periodical to show for one of the great classics of the movement. The reviewer concludes with this observation:

> The last chapter of this work, in which we find new ideas joined with fairly commonplace ones, has for its subject national debts. Without doubt the most important aspect of this question is finding the means to pay them off, and this M. S[mith] fails to do. Unfortunately it is not enough to have a ball of string to find one's way out of this labyrinth. (*JE,* 1776, 7: 263–64)

In 1788 the bulk of the *Journal Encyclopédique's* review of a translation of Smith's work is largely positive, and again consists of an analytical summary. And again the approval is tempered by reservations. Though Smith is said sometimes to adopt the prejudices of his own country, this has not prevented him from "receiving and deserving great praise from those who busy themselves with political subjects. There are verbose passages in his work; but there is also order, clarity, and profundity" (*JE,* 1788, 2: 408).

The 1790 review of the *Wealth of Nations* was written, exceptionally, by a reader of the *Journal Encyclopédique,* and not by one of the editors. This anonymous contributor was an enthusiastic partisan of economic liberalism, and a great admirer of Smith. The English, he asserted, had the most advanced economic theory, and of British economic theoreticians Smith was preeminent, "by the profundity of his researches, by the exactness of his method, the precision of his observations, the clarity and the extent of his arguments" (*JE*, 1790, 7: 393). In the last and more extensive part of this review, however, the writer sought to demonstrate that not only did the new translation of Roucher not do justice to Smith's "immortal production," but also that it was worse than the earlier, also imperfect, translation (*JE*, 1790, 7: 395, 394–402).[17] The review of the third volume of the new Roucher translation in 1791 reverts back to the normal style of the *Journal Encyclopédique* and consists largely of citations. It is enlivened, however, by a spirited denunciation of colonial slavery and the forcefully expressed wish that blacks finally be allowed to share the advantages of the new French constitution (*JE*, 1791, 2: 439).

The obituary of Smith that the *Journal Encyclopédique* published belatedly in 1793 reflects the ambiguity of its reviews. It describes Smith in his youth at Oxford as completely given to work, naturally melancholic and having a "stupid and gauche appearance" (*JE*, 1793, 2: 547). In his choice of a profession, Smith is said to have been by temperament incapable of business and by conviction inappropriate for the church, "for he had very early adopted Voltaire's principles on religion" (547–48). He is further said to have been much influenced by the encyclopedists and by Hume. It is also alleged that, although called to Glasgow as professor of logic and moral philosophy, Smith shifted the emphasis of his lectures to commerce and industry in order to ingratiate himself with the influential merchants of the town (548). There are, to be sure, favorable elements in this sketch of Smith's character, as, for example, his returning the entire tuition fees for a course part of which he was unable to complete. Yet the overall impression is far from favorable, and one wonders if the negative tone of this article was influenced by the hostilities between France and England at this time. The journalist refers to the *Wealth of Nations* as "this excellent book" but notes that it did not achieve immediately the high reputation it enjoyed later (549).[18] He also questions Smith's originality, maintaining that his theory of political economy did not differ in essentials from those of Verri, Tucker, and Hume. He further observes that Smith made extensive use of a French collection on the arts and trades,[19] and concludes with the observation that Smith's "plan belongs to him, and as he has developed his doctrine more than others, and has put forward more extensive proofs than any of his predecessors, he has the same rights to the glory, or to the reproach, of having propagated a system that tends to confuse the wealth of nations with their prosperity" (549–50). It appears, then, that even so progressive a periodical as the *Journal Encyclopédique*, while taking note of the importance of Smith's economic theory, was far from accepting it without reservation.[20]

The absence of a review of the *Wealth of Nations* in the *Année Littéraire* is problematic. Perhaps the death of Fréron in 1776 prevented the journal from treating the book when it first appeared, but this cannot account for its failure to relate to subsequent editions or translations. Nor is it fair to assume that the literary character of Fréron's journal precluded its treating works in political theory or economics. Indeed, in these categories the *Année Littéraire* does not differ significantly from the *Journal Encyclopédique*.[21] While it is tempting to posit that interest in a work of liberal economic theory would appeal more to a reputedly progressive periodical such as the *Journal Encyclopédique* than to a more avowedly traditionalist one such as the *Année Littéraire*, this hardly appears to be the case. Fréron and his successors showed no reticence in reviewing works of thinkers such as Montesquieu, Voltaire, Rousseau, and Hume, while the government controlled and solidly establishment *Journal des Savants* greeted the first English edition of the *Wealth of Nations* with high praise.[22] Moreover, a periodical so outspokenly supportive of the philosophes, and one that did not have to meet the censor's approval because it was originally distributed as a manuscript newsletter, namely the *Correspondance Littéraire*, discusses the *Theory of Moral Sentiments* but makes no reference to the *Wealth of Nations*.[23] Pending further research, it is difficult to avoid the conclusion that, during his own lifetime, Smith was better known in France for his book on ethics than for his monumental contribution to economic theory.[24] If this was so, it calls for some explanation.

There is, first, evidence that the *Wealth of Nations* did not circulate freely in France before the Revolution. It should be noted that while French translations of the *Theory of Moral Sentiments* were published without hindrance in prerevolutionary France, French translations of the *Wealth of Nations* before 1789 all bore foreign imprints.[25] While the *Wealth of Nations* certainly cannot be construed as belonging to the category of "mauvais livres" which the French government sought to suppress, it was nevertheless unwelcome to at least a significant portion of the administration.[26] Robert Darnton in particular has shown the importance of French language publishing outside France during the Old Regime, and that the core of this enterprise dealt in books that were not acceptable or welcome to the authorities.[27]

Beyond such indirect evidence, we have the words of the anonymous critic of Roucher's translation of Smith's book in 1790, that "an academician distinguished by his extensive knowledge of political economy" had translated the first three books of the *Wealth of Nations* and written a commentary on them, but was then unable to find a publisher for his work (*JE*, 1790, 7: 394).[28] It would appear that the academician in question was Morellet. In his memoirs he recalls receiving a presentation copy of the *Wealth of Nations* from Smith, and beginning a translation of it. Unfortunately for Morellet, the abbé Blavet finished a piecemeal translation before him, and a publisher having picked it up, Morellet found himself unable to sell his manuscript. Indeed, nor could he find a publisher who would accept the manuscript gratis, or raise the money to publish it himself.[29] In his correspondence, Morellet goes further, and states that he was refused permission by the authorities to publish his translation of a chapter of Smith's book.[30] There is no reason to doubt Morellet on this point, which further helps to establish the hostility of the authorities to Smith's weighty and learned study of economic theory. The question is, what was the basis of this hostility?

In French domestic politics, the years 1771 to 1774 saw the attempt at a far-reaching reform of the legal system that, but for the untimely death of Louis XV, might well have succeeded.[31] In an attempt to restore the popularity of the monarchy, the newly crowned Louis XVI called the philosophe, physiocrat, and experienced administrator Turgot to the finance portfolio. Among his many progressive measures were the abolition of guilds and the liberalization of the grain trade. The translation of the chapter of the *Wealth of Nations* that Morellet was refused police permission to publish was the one on prices and wages (bk. 1, chap.

10), which contains criticism of English guilds. Morellet was eager to publish it because he saw in it "an apology, and a very disinterested one" for the abolition of guilds in France, a measure included among Turgot's Six Edicts of January 1776.[32] As guardian of the established order, the Parlement of Paris opposed this measure, as it did the abolition of the *corvée*. Apparently sympathetic to the position of the parlement, the keeper of the seals, who was also charged with supervision of the book trade, intervened to prevent publication of Morellet's translation of the portion in question of Smith's book,[33] frustrating Morellet's attempt to draft Smith in the cause of liberal reform in France. Thus, Smith's book at its first appearance in France became involved in conflicts between different levels of government. With the fall of Turgot, one of its potentially most powerful protectors was lost, and official attitudes toward it came to be determined by those hostile to it.

Smith's views on deregulating trade were to find no more favor with powerful forces in government and the sovereign courts than had his criticism of guilds. Going against both a long-standing policy of government regulation and tenacious popular adherence to a "moral economy," and coming at a time of poor harvests, and thus reduced supplies of wheat, the liberalization of the grain trade precipitated widespread riots known as the "Flour War" during the spring of 1775.[34] In these circumstances it is not surprising that the French government would not have been inclined to facilitate the circulation of a work at whose heart lay the doctrine of unregulated trade. From the perspective of the developed western economies of the twentieth century it is difficult to appreciate the precariousness of the existence of large portions of the populations of preindustrial societies. While free trade promised greater prosperity and plenty in the long run, many working people had no means of surviving protracted periods of high grain prices or unemployment. For them the long run did not exist, and their response to what they perceived as artificially induced subsistence crises was often violent. To this the government was sensitive, and laid its policy accordingly. Unfortunately for the propagation of the teachings of the *Wealth of Nations* in France, the work appeared in circumstances in which its economic theory bore highly charged political and administrative implications.

Hume's publishing history is more complicated than Smith's. Whereas Smith published two large books during his lifetime that both achieved prominence, Hume published a variety of philosophical works, essays, and history that appeared in different forms from 1739 to his death, and beyond. Moreover, from the point of view of a study based on the *Année Littéraire* and the *Journal Encyclopédique*, it is unfortunate that all Hume's major philosophical works—*A Treatise of Human Nature* (1739–40), *An Enquiry Concerning Human Understanding* (1748), and *An Enquiry Concerning the Principles of Morals* (1751)—appeared before these two periodicals existed. The same is true of the *Essays, Moral and Political* (1741–42) and the *Political Discourses* (1752). The potentially serious consequences of the early publication of many of Hume's most important works for our study is offset, however, by the fact that the first extensive French translation of Hume's works appeared only in 1758–60, by which time both periodicals were well established.[35] Extensive translations of Hume's *Essays* did not appear until 1767. The publication of Hume's *History of England* began in 1754, the same year the *Année Littéraire* was founded, and two years before the *Journal Encyclopédique* appeared, but it was not completed until 1762. Thus, the lag in translation to French of Hume's earlier works, and the existence of our two periodicals when the later ones appeared, provide a reasonably full basis for an examination of the reception of his work in the two journals.[36]

Considering for the moment only reviews of works written by Hume, we find that the *Année Littéraire* devoted just under 180 pages to commenting on the writings of the Scottish philosopher, the *Journal Encyclopédique* just over 330 pages (see table 1). Since the *Journal Encyclopédique* published roughly 4,000 pages of reviews and articles a year, and the *Année Littéraire* roughly 2,700, the two journals seem to have given roughly proportional space to Hume's works.[37]

Despite an inevitable element of arbitrariness, for purposes of analysis Hume's works will be divided into three main categories: philosophy (the *Treatise* and *Enquiries*), essays and dissertations, and history. Comparing the allocation of space in the two periodicals for each of these categories, table 1 demonstrates striking similarities. Both periodicals devote between four and five percent of their reviews of Hume's works to his philosophy; both give just over a quarter of their review space to the essays

## Table 1: Space Devoted to Reviews of Smith and Hume in the *Année Littéraire* and *Journal Encyclopédique**

### SMITH

|       | AL            |         | JE            |         |
|-------|---------------|---------|---------------|---------|
| *TMS* | 59.50 pages   |         | 24.00 pages   |         |
| *WN*  |               |         | 61.00         |         |
|       | 59.50         |         | 85.00         |         |

### HUME

|                        | AL          |          | JE          |          |
|------------------------|-------------|----------|-------------|----------|
| Philosophy             |             |          |             |          |
| *Treatise*             | —           |          | —           |          |
| *Enquiries*            | 8.00 pages  | 4.52%    | 14.50 pages | 4.36%    |
| Essays and             |             |          |             |          |
| Dissertations          | 42.50 pages | 24.01%   | 90.75 pages | 27.29%   |
| History                | 126.50      | 71.47%   | 227.50      | 68.35%   |
|                        | 177.00      | 100.00%  | 332.75      | 100.00%  |

*Source: *Anneé Littéraire* and *Journal Encyclopédique*

and dissertations; and both devote close to seventy percent to his *History*.[38] To the degree that these periodicals are representative, it would appear that during the second half of the eighteenth century Hume was known in France primarily as an historian, secondarily as an essayist concerned with economic, political, moral, and literary questions, and only incidentally as a philosopher. Further, neither the *Année Littéraire* nor the *Journal Encyclopédique* mentions Hume's masterpiece, the *Treatise of Human Nature,* and while both treat the *Enquiry Concerning Human Understanding*, neither reviews the *Enquiry Concerning the Principles of Morals*. The reasons for the neglect of the *Treatise* are not far to seek. Hume himself described it as having *"fallen deadborn from the press,"*[39] and there was no French translation of the work in the eighteenth century.[40] For both the *Année Littéraire* and the *Journal Encyclopédique,* then, Hume was primarily a gifted stylist, essayist, and historian. It now remains to be seen whether the two periodicals agree in their evaluations of Hume's work.

Given Hume's epistemological skepticism and radical critique of religion, Fréron's treatment of him is remarkably restrained. In 1759 he offers a criticism of the *Natural History of Religion* that takes up Hume's thesis and meets it on its own grounds (*AL*, 1759, 7: 73–82). He states fairly that Hume sees polytheism as the primal form of religion, that it originates from the passions of man, and that theism derives gradually by a process of abstraction from polytheism. Hume's conclusion amounts to "a kind of skepticism" (78). To this Fréron responds that by limiting himself to classical sources, Hume accepted their polytheistic bias, and his failure to use the Bible—understandable enough on Hume's part—led him to overlook the early case of Hebrew theism (monotheism), and wrongly to take Christianity as the first monotheistic religion (78–80). Having established the antiquity of Hebrew monotheism, Fréron proceeds, in the best Enlightenment fashion, to assert the primacy of fact over theory, and to deny the validity of any "speculation" or "conjecture" that comes into conflict with the facts (80–81). Fréron further points out Hume's inconsistency in sometimes praising the toleration of polytheism, sometimes showing it to have been guilty of the worst excesses (81). Fréron acknowledges that the *Natural History of Religion* is well written and well thought out, and concludes: "For the rest, this Treatise is not without merit, and with the exception of one or two places, you will read it with pleasure. It is the reverie of a profound Philosopher" (82).[41]

In an earlier review of Hume's *Essays*, published in 1754, Fréron had been broadly favorable. He pointed out that the work enjoyed an extremely high reputation in England, and that its object was "to improve the Government, to make the country rich and the People happy" (*AL*, 1754, 5: 73). The work in question is a translation of twelve of Hume's essays, and is entitled *Discours politiques*. Fréron provides an objective summary, often with favorable comments, on Hume's essays on commerce, society, and politics. In his conclusion, Fréron calls Hume "without doubt a man of genius, but something of a skeptic [*un peu sceptique*]," and finds in his work profundity, originality, "and as in all English works, many irregularities [*inégalités*]." By making this translation available to the French public, Fréron observes, the translator has "rendered a true service to his fatherland" ( 97).[42]

Though the *Journal Encyclopédique* published two reviews of

the *Natural History of Religion*, in 1757 (*JE*, 1757, 3–ii: 35, 39) and
1759 (*JE*, 1759, 5–iii: 23–40), and a further review of the essays
in its French edition of 1759 (6–i: 3–22), it was not more sympathetic toward this work than the *Année Littéraire*. The journalist
of the *Journal Encyclopédique* begins the brief 1757 review of the
English edition of the *Natural History of Religion* with the observation that "the duty to make known new works of great writers
does not oblige us to accept their opinions, especially when
these opinions are excessively bold" (*JE*, 1757, 3–ii: 35). The reviewer admires Hume as a writer and thinker but objects to his
implied criticisms of religion. In a subsequent review of the
French edition of the work in 1759, the journalist's criticisms
become more pointed. Hume's essay is characterized "by the
boldness of its paradoxes," which reflect the abuse of the author's powers of reasoning (*JE*, 1759, 5–iii: 23). Hume maintains
that polytheism is tolerant, monotheism intolerant; and in
adopting a purely rational approach to Christianity, he strips it
of its mystery (33, 37). The reviewer of the *Journal Encyclopédique*
expresses reservations about Hume's essay in concluding: "Such
is the arrogant system that modern incredulity does not fear to
oppose to revelation. This fragile edifice has so little consistency
in the foundations that M. Hume gives it, that it would be easy
for us to overturn it entirely" (40). The appeal to revelation, to
which, interestingly enough, Fréron did not have recourse,
holds a central place in the refutation of Hume's attempts at the
anthropology and psychology of religion printed with the
French translation of the work—the anonymous *Examen de
l'histoire naturelle de la Religion*. While calling Hume "one of the
finest geniuses of England," the reviewer of the *Examen de l'histoire naturelle* in 1759 also sees in him a representative of modern incredulity attempting to overthrow the authority of
revelation (*JE*, 1759, 6-i: 3). After following the author of the *Examen* in his criticism of Hume's use of sources, contradictions,
and positing of hypotheses,[43] the reviewer of the *Journal Encyclopédique* concludes:

> All these contradictions are the result less of defective powers of rea-
> soning, than of the desire to form a system independent of Revela-
> tion. There is the reef upon which will founder all those who seek
> to escape its empire; for revelation is, despite all the clamors raised
> against it, the central point of meeting at which all truths necessar-
> ily concur. (*JE*, 1759, 6-i: 22)

These are views that we might have expected to find in the *Année Littéraire*. That they occur in a periodical generally regarded as more progressive and liberal than Fréron's suggests that the distance between the *Journal Encyclopédique* and *Année Littéraire* may be less than has been thought.

In their evaluations of Hume's *History of England*, the *Année Littéraire* and the *Journal Encyclopédique* are broadly similar. The reviews in the *Année Littéraire* seem to be by different hands. The reviewer of the Stuart and Tudor volumes, almost certainly Fréron himself, expresses some reservations about these works, but is generally positive. As author of the Stuart volume, Hume is praised for "wisdom and impartiality" exceeding other English authors who have treated the subject, and he is said to be "a philosophical spectator who recounts the facts as a simple witness" (*AL*, 1760, 4: 3). In the Tudor reviews of 1763, "the celebrated M. David Hume" is again praised for his impartiality, as well as the wisdom and circumspection of his judgments concerning the English Reformation and his careful avoidance of partisanship ("*l'esprit de parti*") (*AL*, 1763, 2: 289, 302). Hume is said to "extend his views and researches farther than other Historians" and to be as devoted as humanly possible to the search for historical truth (*AL*, 1763, 3: 13, 35). Fréron goes so far as to compare Hume to Tacitus in the acuteness of his analyses of politics and of human motivation, and states:

> What distinguishes him above all is the love of truth that consistently leads him; always a Philosopher, never an enthusiast, he praises and blames equally those who seem to him in effect worthy of praise or reproach. He never allows himself to be carried away by the furor of party feeling [*fureur de parti*], which, if one may so express himself, shrinks men and turns them into machines directed by prejudice alone, the leading strings of the rude common people. (39–40)

The main theme of the Tudor reviews, which both Hume and the *Année Littéraire* journalist would have been familiar with from the works of Montesquieu, and on which they appear to have been in close agreement, was the evil of absolute or despotic power. In an English context, Fréron indulged freely in the antidespotism rhetoric so common in France during the second half of the eighteenth century.[44] Toward the end of his review of the Tudor volume, Fréron praises Hume for the fairness of his treatment of the French and their religion: "He has the unique glory of being the first English author to have rendered justice to our nation and to the ministers of our religion, when he believed the truth was favorable to them" (40).

The review of the Plantaganet volume in 1766 is written from an altogether different, even contradictory, point of view.[45] Hume is criticized sharply and repeatedly for precisely those things for which he was praised so highly in the earlier reviews. A large portion of the Plantagenet volume is said to consist in unwarranted criticisms of, and declamations against, the Roman Catholic Church and its clergy (AL, 1762, 2: 4). For example, Hume is said to use "injurious epithets" and to indulge in "outrageous invectives" against Thomas à Becket (16, 20). The reviewer also finds an anti-French bias in Hume's tendency to criticize French kings, and accuses the Scottish author of directing "gross insults" against Louis VII (24, 23). Not content with challenging the objectivity and fairness of Hume's treatment of the Catholic Church and of France, the reviewer questions Hume's competence as a historian. He brings attention to numerous factual inaccuracies (12–13, 14, 16–17, 18), and states that

> the author has sometimes neglected the most essential duty of a historian, that of discussing the facts before presenting them. One finds that too often he has recourse to probability [vraisemblance] and conjecture to render the facts he puts forward plausible. A historian makes things much easier by giving himself this license, and saves himself much research; but he runs the risk of giving his own opinion for certain truths. (27–28)

It is not, the reviewer continues, Hume's ability as a historian that had made his work so popular, but his style, his penetrating analyses of institutions, and his powers of exposition. This constitutes a curious reversal of the judgments of the Année Littéraire on the Tudor and Stuart volumes.[46]

In its reviews of the first volume of the History of England, the Journal Encyclopédique tends to emphasize different aspects of Hume's work, but its tone remains close to the Année Littéraire. The second part of the English edition is described in 1757 as well written, accurate, and lively, and is generally regarded as worthy of Hume's reputation (*JE*, 1757, 2–ii: 84). Commenting in 1760 on the social, economic, and cultural sections of the Prévost translation of the Stuart volumes, the *Journal Encyclopédique* reviewer writes admiringly: "One sees there a Philosopher who weighs all things with a strict impartiality, and whose views are as broad as they are fair" (*JE*, 1760, 4–ii:18).[47] In a later review, the journal praises Hume for his style, clarity, precision, and impartiality, qualities that make his work "infinitely precious" (*JE*, 1760, 5-i: 48). Yet the *Journal Encyclopédique* does not admire Hume uncritically. It notes with disapproval that sections of the first volume on the Stuarts were perceived as attacking religion, and cites Hume's response at length (*JE*, 1757, 2–ii: 61–65). It further complains that the distinguished author has "too independent a mind on all manner of things" (*JE*, 1760, 5–i:48). The *Journal Encyclopédique* also points out rare errors of fact or attribution in the *History,* and beyond this qualifies its praise of Hume's impartiality with the charge that he sometimes adopts British prejudices, as in his unsympathetic treatment of Ireland (*JE*, 1760, 4–ii: 7–8, 14, and iii: 25). Hume's predilection for republicanism is also said to have caused him to overlook the better qualities of certain monarchs (*JE*, 1760, 5–i: 48). Thus, like the *Année Littéraire,* Pierre Rousseau's periodical offers a highly favorable appreciation of Hume as historian, though it also expresses a range of reservations about his work.

Reviews of his books aside, Hume is also mentioned in other contexts in the *Année Littéraire* and the *Journal Encyclopédique*.[48] Of seven such instances in Fréron's journal, five relate to the celebrated quarrel between Hume and Rousseau in 1766, which precipitated a flurry of pamphlets and lively interest in large sections of the literate public.[49] While a legitimate subject for journalism, the quarrel provided Fréron with an opportunity for bringing attention to dissension among the philosophes. The *Journal Encyclopédique*, by contrast, was far more discreet on this subject. It printed only three items on the quarrel, but had eight others on properly literary subjects. Most of these were letters to the editor or reviews of other works that discuss Hume's *History of England.* While it is difficult to find significant differences of tone or content in the way the two periodicals under consideration treated the works of Smith and Hume, there is considerable variation in the attention they give to one of the great literary quarrels of the day.

By way of conclusion, I would like to make three points that summarize the findings of this study. The first concerns the way these two periodicals selected and evaluated the works of Smith and Hume. We have seen that the *Journal Encyclopédique* had a somewhat more varied format and a tendency to review more works in foreign languages than the *Année Littéraire*, so that its reviews of the works of our two Scots authors often preceded those of its Parisian rival. With the sole exception of the failure of Fréron's paper to review the *Wealth of Nations*, however, the two journals chose to review and to neglect the same works of Smith and Hume. Both, for example, devoted several reviews to the *Natural History of Religion*, while passing over in silence the *Dialogues concerning Natural Religion*, which were published posthumously in 1779, and of which a French translation appeared the same year. Moreover, both periodicals devoted roughly proportional space to the different genres in which Hume wrote, so that he is reflected in their pages primarily as a historian, secondarily as an essayist, and only incidentally as a philosopher. Even more importantly, in their evaluations of Hume and Smith, the *Année Littéraire* and the *Journal Encyclopédique* are in substantial agreement. Both praise the *Theory of Moral Sentiments* for providing a theory of ethics that avoids positing the radical egoism of Enlightenment liberalism, which also troubled writers such as Rousseau and Diderot,[50] and both express admiration for Hume's style and erudition, as well as serious reservations about his treatment of religion. It appears, therefore, that it is more appropriate to view the *Année Littéraire* and the *Journal Encyclopédique* as two foci within a broad consensus of enlightened opinion than to see one standing for, and the other against, basic Enlightenment values.

Secondly, the *Année Littéraire* and the *Journal Encyclopédique* present the two Scottish thinkers in ways that may seem strange to us today. The *Année Littéraire*, especially, in giving us Adam Smith without the *Wealth of Nations*, might as well have given us *Pamela* without Mr. B, *Jacques le fataliste* without his master, or *Tristram Shandy* without Uncle Toby. The *Journal Encyclopédique*, for reasons that have been suggested above, and may be more tactical than substantial, provides, for our taste today, a properly balanced picture of Smith. Both journals, however, chose to emphasize the historical component of Hume's work to the point that his properly philosophical books were almost overlooked or—in the cases of the *Treatise* and the *Enquiry Concerning the Principles of Morals* —altogether ignored. Rather than ascribing these choices to the ideological or intellectual limitations of our journalists or to pressure from the authorities, the appropriate conclusion is more likely that perceptions and evaluations of Hume and Smith during the Enlightenment were different from ours.

The final point I wish to make about the treatment of Hume and Smith in the *Année Littéraire* and the *Journal Encyclopédique* concerns the different ways in which these two Enlightenment periodicals perceived these two eminent Scottish writers, and the way they are perceived today. For scholars who now study the eighteenth century, Hume and Smith are the brightest jewels in the crown of the Scottish Enlightenment. Both are taken as models of sociability, and Hume also of affability. Both are rightly ascribed important places in the liberal tradition, Smith as the founding father of liberal economics. For many historians, British empiricism and liberalism are implicitly contrasted to French rationalism and extremism, and the eminently gentlemanly qualities of Hume and Smith have contributed to their reputations for moderation. It is precisely in this respect that the representation of these Scottish thinkers in these two French Enlightenment periodicals takes on added significance. They are presented not as eminent elder statesmen of the Enlightenment, whose battles have been fought and won, but rather as thinkers working at the cutting edge of the movement, whose views on economics and social organization in Smith's case, epistemology and religion in Hume's, were so daring as to require careful, critical treatment. It is precisely this sense of daring and excitement in the writings of Hume and Smith that is restored to us in considering the way in which the *Année Littéraire* and the *Journal Encyclopédique* treated the works of two of the most respected and respectable figures of eighteenth-century letters.

## NOTES

1. References to these journals will be abbreviated as *AL* and *JE*. Translations are my own unless otherwise indicated.

2. Subscriptions to these journals varied between roughly one thousand and two thousand. For a treatment of subscription figures for periodicals of

the Old Regime, see Harvey Chisick, *The Production, Distribution and Readership of a Conservative Journal of the Early French Revolution: The* Ami du Roi *of the Abbé Royou* (Philadelphia, 1992), 17–21.

3. Rémy G. Saisselin, *The Literary Enterprise in Eighteenth-Century France* (Detroit, 1979), 105–15; Jean Balcou, *Fréron contre les philosophes* (Geneva, 1975).

4. Harvey Chisick, "The Disappearance of a Great Enlightenment Periodical: The *Année Littéraire*, 1789–90," *Studies on Voltaire and the Eighteenth Century* 287 (1991): 119–30.

5. Balcou, *Fréron contre les philosophes*, 6, 94, 154–55, 160, 190; Jean de Viguerie, *Histoire et dictionnaire du temps des lumières, 1715–1789* (Paris, 1995), 292, 1001.

6. The basic study of the *Journal Encyclopédique* is Raymond Birn, *Pierre Rousseau et les philosophes de Bouillon*, in *Studies on Voltaire and the Eighteenth Century* 29 (1964).

7. Paul Van Tieghem, *L'Année Littéraire (1754–1790) comme intermédiaire en France des littératures étrangères* (1914; reprint, Geneva, 1966), 6–8. Of the foreign works reviewed in Fréron's journal, 57 percent had originally been published in English, 19 percent in Italian, and 17 percent in German.

8. Van Tieghem, *L'Année Littéraire*, 6.

9. After Fréron's death in 1776, this proportion increased, especially during the 1780s. See Chisick, "Disappearance," 123–26.

10. The attribution is by Barbier, in *Dictionnaire des anonymes*.

11. *Catalogue de la Bibliothèque Nationale*. There is no evidence that Condorcet's notes were ever published. The attribution is by Barbier, in *Dictionnaire des anonymes*. This edition appeared under the imprint of Yverdon. In a solid early treatment of the *Wealth of Nations* in France, David Murray pointed out that the early and little-known 1778/79 La Haye translation of the *Wealth of Nations*—which was the first translation of the work in French—differs significantly from Blavet's translation. David Murray, *French Translations of the Wealth of Nations* (Glasgow, 1905), 9–13. British Library, 11907.AA2. Ian Ross, however, attributed the La Haye translation to Blavet. *The Life of Adam Smith* (Oxford, 1995), 362.

12. The *Journal Encyclopédique* also published a short obituary of Smith in 1793 (*JE*, 1793, 2: 547–50), which expresses less than unqualified approval of his work.

13. The journalist of the *Journal Encyclopédique* in 1759 compares Smith's concept of sympathy as the basis of virtue to Cumberland's notion of universal benevolence and to Hutcheson's concept of an internal sense of the good, and finds all three similar in the important respect that they provide an objective and permanent basis for ethics (*JE*, 1759, 7–ii: 4).

14. For a broader treatment of the *Theory of Moral Sentiments*, see Takaho Ando, "The Introduction of Adam Smith's Moral Philosophy into France," in *Adam Smith: International Perspectives*, ed. Hiroshi Mizuta and Chuhe Sugiyama (London, 1993), 199–211. Ando is primarily concerned to place Smith's moral thought in the context of French ethical theory, of which the works of Helvétius are taken as representative. He also puts considerable emphasis on the translation of the *Theory of Moral Sentiments* by Sophie de Grouchy, Condor-

cet's wife. This translation, which Ando regards as the best, did not appear until 1798. For further discussion of Sophie de Grouchy's translation and critique of the *Theory of Moral Sentiments,* see Deidre Dawson's essay in the current volume.

15. In effect, the *Journal Encyclopédique* simply divided its 1776 and 1790–91 reviews in two in order to keep the length of reviews in line with its normal practice. It is unusual to find a review longer than fifteen pages in the *Journal Encyclopédique,* but a single work, if deemed important enough, could be given an extremely long review, broken down into two, three, or more sections, published in series. In this way, the editor retained variety in any single issue of the journal.

16. Richard F. Teichgraeber has found that the *Wealth of Nations* received generally favorable but rather superficial reviews in the English periodical press when it appeared. "'Less Abused than I had Reason to Expect': The Reception of *The Wealth of Nations* in Britain, 1776–90," *The Historical Journal,* 30 (1987), 341–43.

17. Murray, too, found Roucher's translation to be "of no great merit" (*French Translations of* The Wealth of Nations), 5.

18. Salim Rashid has argued convincingly that the *Wealth of Nations* had not achieved the status and influence by the time of Smith's death that it was to enjoy in the nineteenth century. See his article, "Adam Smith's Rise to Fame: A Reexamination of the Evidence," *The Eighteenth Century: Theory and Interpretation* 23 (1982): 64–85. This view is confirmed and impressively elaborated by Teichgraeber, "Less Abused." Takaho Ando, "Introduction of Smith's Moral Philosophy," 199, also sees Smith's economic thought having an influence in France only after the outbreak of the French Revolution. Daniel Diaktine, on the other hand, finds in the number of early translations of the *Wealth of Nations* evidence for the success of the work. "A French Reading of *The Wealth of Nations* in 1789," in Mizuta and Sugiyama, *Adam Smith,* 213–23. Diaktine argues, however, that Smith was fundamentally misunderstood in France at this time.

19. The reference is probably to the *Encyclopédie ou Dictionnaire raisonné des Sciences, des Arts et des Métiers* of Diderot, d'Alembert, Jaucourt, and their many collaborators. Possibly, however, the journalist had in mind the *Description des Arts et Métiers* produced under the auspices of the Academy of Sciences, the designs and plates of which the *Encyclopédie* was itself accused of appropriating. See John Lough, *The Encyclopédie* (London, 1971), 86–88.

20. Basing himself on an analysis of a summary of the *Wealth of Nations* of over two hundred pages in the *Bibliothèque de l'homme publique,* which he believes Condorcet to have been responsible for, Daniel Diaktine argues that Smith's book was "unintelligible" and "completely misunderstood" ("French Reading," 216, 220). He arrives at this conclusion by considering the omission by the editor(s) of the analytical core of the work in bk. 1, chaps. 5–9, and their failure to appreciate the market mechanism. Indeed, Diaktine maintains that "the role of the market and competition had no meaning for the French reader of *The Wealth of Nations*" (218). This is a bold and forceful argument. It does not sit well, however, with the view of the Enlightenment that sees the attempt to apply the Newtonian paradigm of science to society as one of the

distinctive features of the movement. See, for example, Peter Gay, *The Enlight-enment: An Interpretation*, 2 vols. (New York, 1966–69), 2:174–87, 319–68. Nor does it find confirmation in the *Journal Encyclopédique* reviews of the book which, while less than enthusiastic, do seem to reflect a reasonable grasp of what Smith was about.

21. During 1773 and 1774 the *Année Littéraire* devoted 6.98 percent of its reviews and 5.05 percent of its space to works on economics, while for the *Journal Encyclopédique* the corresponding figures for the same period are 5.66 and 5.68. This information is part of a more extensive study of the two jour-nals that I have undertaken.

22. *The Wealth of Nations* is called "this great work, which reflects the supe-rior genius and talent of the author of the *Theory of Moral Sentiments*". *Journal des Savants*, February 1777, in-quarto edition, 81.

23. Grimm, Diderot, Raynal, Meister, et al., *Correspondance littéraire, philo-sophique et critique,* ed. Maurice Tourneux, 16 vols. (Paris, 1877–82), 6:143–44. The author of this comment, writing in 1764, observes that the *Theory of Moral Sentiments* did not enjoy as much success in France as in England, and blames this on the quality of the translation. Curiously, there is no mention whatever of Smith in another important manuscript newsletter of the period, the *Mém-oires secrets pour servir à l'histoire de la république des lettres en France depuis 1762,* which covers the period down to 1787, and was published at London in thirty-six volumes between 1777 and 1789.

24. This finding is congruent with Salim Rashid's demonstration of the rel-ative lack of influence of the *Wealth of Nations* during the eighteenth century in his article, "Adam Smith's Rise to Fame." Teichgraeber also emphasizes the slow growth of appreciation for the *Wealth of Nations* (see "Less Abused").

25. The 1788 edition bears the imprints of both London and Paris. Ian Ross asserts that there was a Paris as well as an Yverdon edition of Blavet's 1781 translation (*Smith*, 362). The catalogue of the Bibliothèque Nationale, how-ever, shows no Paris edition of the *Wealth of Nations* in 1781.

26. On the French book trade under the Old Regime, see David Thomas Pottinger, *The French Book Trade in the Ancien Régime* (Cambridge, Mass., 1951); François Furet et al., *Livre et Société dans la France du XVIIIe siècle*, 2 vols. (Paris and La Haye, 1965–70); Robert Darnton, *The Literary Underground of the Old Regime* (Cambridge, Mass., 1982); and Elizabeth L. Eisenstein, *Grub Street Abroad: Aspects of the French Cosmopolitan Press from the Age of Louis XIV to the French Revolution* (Oxford, 1992), chap. 1.

27. Robert Darnton, *The Forbidden Bestsellers of Pre-Revolutionary France* (New York, 1995), xx–xxi. Morellet appealed for a subsidy to translate the *Wealth of Nations* when it first appeared on the grounds that "the work seems to me so useful that it deserves this encouragement without which it will, in effect, not be translated at all, or will be translated in Holland by some hack." Letter to Turgot, 22 February 1776, in *Lettres d'André Morellet,* ed. Dorothy Medlin, Jean-Claude David, and Paul Leclerc, 3 vols. (Oxford, 1991–96), 1:310.

28. It is worth noting in this respect the observation of the *Journal des Sa-vants* shortly after the appearance of the first English edition of the *Wealth of Nations* that "Some of our own men of letters who had read the book had de-cided that it was not suitable for translation into our language." The reason

given was that it would be unlikely to find a publisher. *Journal des Savants*, February 1777, 81.

29. André Morellet, *Mémoires de l'abbé Morellet de l'Académie française sur le dix-huitième siècle et sur la Révolution*, ed. Jean-Pierre Guicciardi (Paris, 1988), 207. Morellet had a low opinion of both the Blavet and Roucher translations of the *Wealth of Nations*. Smith, on the other hand, expressed approval of, and appreciation for, Blavet's translation in a letter to Blavet of 23 July 1782, in *The Correspondence of Adam Smith*, ed. Ernest Campbell Mossner and Ian Simpson Ross (Oxford, 1977), 259–60. But this did not prevent Smith from later expressing a lively interest in seeing the translation he had heard Morellet had prepared (279).

30. *Lettres d'André Morellet*, 1:329–30. He alleges that magistrates of the Parlement of Paris were behind the hostility to the *Wealth of Nations*. Given the consistent opposition of the magistrates to Turgot's policies and their inclination to pose as defenders of the people, this claim seems plausible.

31. The Maupeou reforms have recently become the object of considerable interest among students of the Old Regime. In addition to the older study of Jules Gustave Flammermont, *Le Chancelier Maupeou et les Parlements* (Paris, 1885), see Durand Echeverria, *The Maupeou Revolution: A Study in the History of Libertarianism, France, 1770–1774* (Baton Rouge, La., 1985) and *The Maupeou Revolution: The Transformation of Politics at the End of the Old Regime*, ed. Keith Baker, in *Historical Reflections/Réflexions Historiques* 18 (1992).

32. Morellet to Turgot, 9 March 1776, in *Lettres d'André Morellet*, 1: 324.

33. Morellet to Turgot, 30 March 1776, ibid., 1: 329–30.

34. On this subject, see Steven L. Kaplan, *Bread, Politics and Political Economy in the Reign of Louis XV*, 2 vols. (The Hague, 1976), chaps. 11–13; V. S. Ljublinski, *La Guerre de farines: Contribution à la lutte des classes en France, à la veille de la Révolution*, trans. F. Adiba and J. Radiguet (Grenoble, 1979); Cynthia A. Bouton, *The Flour War: Gender, Class and Community in Late Ancien Régime French Society* (University Park, Pa., 1994), and the fundamental article of E. P. Thompson, "The Moral Economy of the English Crowd in the Eighteenth Century," *Past and Present*, no. 50 (1971).

35. This is a five-volume octavo edition, translated by J. B. Merian and J. B. R. Robinet and published in Amsterdam. It includes the two *Enquiries* and the four *Dissertations*. Robinet, in addition to editing an important encyclopedia, also worked as a journalist on the *Journal Encyclopédique*.

36. The reception of Hume's work in France was the subject of two doctoral dissertations in the 1950s, one by Paul H. Meyer at Columbia University, and the other by Laurence Bongie for the University of Paris. Bongie's findings with respect to Hume's history are capably presented in the first chapter of his study, *David Hume: Prophet of the Counter-revolution* (Oxford, 1965). Recently Mark G. Spencer has produced a doctoral dissertation on "The Reception of David Hume's Political Thought in Eighteenth-Century America" (University of Western Ontario, 2 vols., 2001).

37. The format of both periodicals is duodecimo. While the *Année Littéraire* tends to use a uniform and fairly large type, the *Journal Encyclopédique* is more variable and uses smaller typefaces.

38. History played a significant role in eighteenth-century publishing. Be-

tween 10 and 20 percent of books published with state approval at this time were histories (François Furet, "La 'librairie' du royaume de France au 18e siècle," in *Livre et société*, 1:19–21). Further, in two important periodicals, reviews of works on history accounted for as much as 30 percent of all reviews, and seldom fell below 15 percent (Jean Ehrard et Jacques Roger, "Deux périodiques français au 18e siècle: le *Journal des Savants* et les *Mémoires de Trévoux*," in *Livre et Société*, 1:40–41, 48, 54–55).

39. Hume, "My Own Life," in *Essays Moral, Political, and Literary*, ed. Eugene F. Miller (Indianapolis, 1985), xiv.

40. Hume received only one favorable and three unfavorable reviews of the *Treatise* upon its appearance. See Ernest Campbell Mossner, *The Life of David Hume* (Oxford, 1954), 119–30. Neither the *Année Littéraire* nor the *Journal Encyclopédique* contributed to what Mossner calls the "roar" directed against the *Treatise* in the 1770s (116). See also Mossner's article, "The Continental Reception of Hume's *Treatise*," *Mind* 56 (1947): 31–43.

41. At the outset of his review, Fréron asserts that Hume's "system" had to be fought (*AL*, 1759, 7, 73). He also notes that this edition of the *Natural History of Religion* was accompanied by a refutation of the work by the translator (ibid., 82).

42. By the time Hume's *Enquiries* were translated in 1767, his works were regarded as dangerous and were forbidden in France. The writings of Hume collected under the title *Pensées philosophiques, morales, critiques, littéraires et politiques de M. Hume* (Londres [i.e., Paris], 1767) were edited so they would contain only such views as were "in conformity with Christian morality; all dangerous details have been suppressed."

43. If these points recall the review of the *Année Littéraire*, it is in part because they draw on the same source. Fréron acknowledges having used some of the *Examen* in formulating his criticism of Hume's essay (*AL*, 1759, 6: 82).

44. Hume described the condition of Englishmen under the Tudors as comparable to oriental slaves, while Fréron observes in 1763: "Nothing can be compared to the absolute power of this monarch [Henry VIII], if not the enormous abuse he made of it during the greater part of his reign" (*AL*, 1763, 2: 318, 314; 3: 9–10, 31, 41–42). Fréron's clear and consistent criticism of absolutism and despotism here raises questions about the traditional portrayal of him as an uncompromising spokesman of throne and altar.

45. This had been recognized by Bongie, *David Hume*, 21–23.

46. One way of explaining this change over a period of less than three years is to posit a different reviewer for the Plantagenet volume. Not only the differences of judgment, but also those of approach recommend this possibility. The later review relies much more heavily than the earlier ones on erudition that brings factual errors to light. It is also less inclined to recount striking incidents or to describe unusual personalities. On the other hand, the Plantagenet volume focuses on a period for which the Enlightenment had little sympathy, but orthodox Catholics a great deal.

47. He also asserts that Hume comes close to the impartiality of the ideal philosopher-historian (*JE*, 1760, 4-ii:6).

48. There is only one such mention for Smith: his obituary notice in the *Journal Encyclopédique*.

49. On this quarrel, see Mossner, *Life of Hume,* chap. 35, and Jean Guéhenno, *Jean-Jacques Rousseau,* trans. John and Doreen Weightman, 2 vols. (New York, 1966), 2: chap. 6.

50. See, for example, Rousseau's view on pity in the state of nature in the *Discourse on the Origins of Inequality,* and Diderot's handling of the problem in the *Encyclopédie* article "Political Authority," as well as in *Rameau's Nephew,* which can be read as a *reductio ad absurdum* of the basic Enlightenment value of self-interest.

# From Moral Philosophy to Public Policy: Sophie de Grouchy's Translation and Critique of Smith's *Theory of Moral Sentiments*

DEIDRE DAWSON

IN 1793, AS THE TERROR WAS RAGING IN PARIS AND THE STREETS WERE being bloodied by the guillotine, Sophie de Grouchy, marquise de Condorcet, was writing her response to Adam Smith's *Theory of Moral Sentiments*, entitled *Lettres à Cabanis sur la sympathie*. Both she and her husband, Jean Antoine Nicolas de Caritat de Condorcet, were under attack by Jacobin extremists; de Grouchy had almost emigrated to America with their daughter, Eliza, and Condorcet would soon go into hiding in a vain attempt to escape imprisonment and execution. In spite of the worsening turn of events, de Grouchy kept working on the *Lettres* throughout the Terror and after her husband's death. As Alain Pons has pointed out, to translate a book on moral sentiments and to write in praise of sympathy at such a time was either an act of blindness and escapism or a noble attempt to remain faithful to the ideals of human capacity for reason, compassion, and progress, for "the *Lettres sur la sympathie* can be considered one of the ultimate and most perfect testimonies to the thought and sensibility of the Age of Enlightenment."[1] It seemed as if Robespierre's tyranny only reinforced the Condorcets' belief in progress and reform through education and social equality.

At the urging of his wife, whom he considered an equal partner in his intellectual endeavors, Condorcet set about completing his ambitious *Esquisse d'un tableau historique des progrès de l'esprit humain* / [Sketch for a Historical Picture of the Progress of the Human Mind] while he was in hiding from July 1793 to

March 1794. During this time he also wrote a touching and illuminating essay addressed to his daughter Eliza, which contains advice on how to lead a happy and moral life. In his will, written during the same period, Condorcet stipulated that de Grouchy's writings should also be studied by Eliza as part of her education: "When the moment of justice has come, she will find help in my writings. The advice I have written for her, and her mother's letters on friendship will provide a moral education. Other writings by her mother give very useful viewpoints on the same subject."[2] Clearly, the Condorcets shared the view that moral sentiments are not contrary to human nature and can be channeled into virtuous actions when properly nurtured. "Virtue consists in following the penchants of nature, but in knowing how to use them to the fullest and direct them," Condorcet wrote in his *Esquisse*.[3] As Jean-Paul de Lagrave notes, Condorcet was echoing similar sentiments expressed by Sophie de Grouchy in her *Lettres sur la sympathie*: "Where is the individual who, instead of looking beyond nature for a new way to enjoy or abuse his blessings, finds every day a new pleasure in changing all the bonds of duty and servitude around him into relationships of charity, good faith, and kindness . . . ?" (*Lettres*, 8, 183). De Lagrave has quite aptly caracterized de Grouchy's concept of society as presented in her *Lettres sur la sympathie* as "a society of happiness."[4]

Sophie de Grouchy and the marquis de Condorcet had been interested in Adam Smith's work for many years. Condorcet, twenty years older than his wife, had met Smith in the mid-1760s while the Scot was being fêted by Parisian society. As a supporter of Turgot's ideas on the liberalization of commerce and the establishment of a free grain market in France, Condorcet, like Turgot, would later be a great admirer of the *Wealth of Nations*. Indeed, Condorcet wrote a commentary on the *Wealth of Nations* that was meant to be published shortly after Antoine Roucher's 1790 French translation, but these plans were interrupted by the violent events of the Revolution. Sophie de Grouchy was only two years old in 1766, when Adam Smith frequented the Parisian salons of the duchesse d'Enville and Julie de l'Espinasse and dined with Helvétius, d'Alembert, and d'Holbach, but she was one day to be a *grande dame* of the philosophic movement in her own right, setting up a salon in the Hotel de

Monnaies, where she and Condorcet resided after their marriage in 1786.

De Grouchy and Condorcet had been drawn together by a common interest in the plight of three victims of judiciary error, the *roués de Chaumont,* whose cause was taken up by de Grouchy's uncle, Charles Dupaty, president of the parliament of Bordeaux. In this notorious miscarriage of justice, three peasants, Bradier, Simare, and Lardoise, were accused of having assaulted and robbed a couple. Even though there had been no examination of physical evidence or questioning of witnesses, the men were initially condemned to life in the galleys, and then to death by execution on the wheel. Thanks to his connections with government officials, Dupaty obtained permission for a retrial, caught up with the three accused as they were being taken to Chaumont for execution, and later proved their innocence. Condorcet helped Dupaty prepare the defense of the peasants, and this is how he first came into contact with Dupaty's niece, Sophie.[5]

Both de Grouchy and Condorcet were committed to bringing about major judicial and political reform in France. In 1791, along with Thomas Paine, the Condorcets founded *la Société républicaine,* the first republican society in France, which included only two other members. [6] Paine also frequented de Grouchy's salon, as did Thomas Jefferson, Benjamin Franklin's grandson, and Benjamin Constant. De Grouchy translated into French Paine's speeches to the National Assembly, including his inflammatory speech of 1 July 1791, which was the first public call for the creation of a French Republic. When *la Société républicaine* launched its journal *Le Républicain ou défenseur du gouvernent représentatif,* de Grouchy again lent her linguistic skills to the republican cause through translating Paine's prose into French. In a strange way, Paine owed a debt to Adam Smith, for it was de Grouchy's interest in reading and understanding the *Theory of Moral Sentiments* that prompted her to master the English language well enough to become a very adept translator.

Three French editions of Adam Smith's *Theory of Moral Sentiments* appeared before 1800. The first London edition of 1759 was translated into French by Marc-Antoine Eidous and published in 1764 as *Métaphysique de l'âme.* The *Correspondance littéraire* noted that if Smith's work had created less of a sensation in France than in Britain, this was partly owing to the poor quality of the first translation, which did not do justice to the original.[7] This explains why, when Smith arrived in France in 1764, he found that most of the philosophes and literary figures who were familiar with his work had read the original English edition, in spite of the availability of a French edition. The third edition of the *Theory of Moral Sentiments*, published in London in 1767, was taken up by a new translator, the Abbé Blavet, between 1774 and 1775, but this translation was found lacking as well. Sophie de Grouchy reports that she had heard of Smith's work but had put off reading it for several years because "I had heard bad things about the French translation of this work, and I did not [yet] know English well enough to read it in the original" (*Lettres*, 1, 69). Twenty years later de Grouchy began her own translation of the seventh edition of the *Theory of Moral Sentiments*, which had appeared in London in 1792. It was published in Paris in 1798, along with her translation of Smith's essay on the origin of languages, which had been appended to all British editions of the *Theory of Moral Sentiments* since the third.[8] For two centuries de Grouchy's was the "definitive" French translation of the *Theory of Moral Sentiments*. The translators of the first new French translation in over two hundred years acknowledge that the elegance of de Grouchy's prose is still without equal: "the translation of the Marquise de Condorcet, is complete and perhaps the most elegant in its style. Undeniably, she provides the reader with the pleasure of a refined language, which in addition has the immense advantage of being contemporary with Smith's."[9]

A comparison of a passage from Eidous's 1764 translation of the *Theory of Moral Sentiments* to de Grouchy's 1798 translation reveals why the latter stood the test of time for so long. In chapter 1 of part 4, "Of the Effect of Utility Upon the Sentiment of Approbation," in which Smith presents his famous metaphor of the invisible hand, he writes, "They [the rich] are led by an invisible hand to make nearly the same distribution of the necessaries of life, which would have been made, had the earth been divided into equal portions among all its inhabitants, and thus without intending it, without knowing it, advance the interest of the society, and afford means of the multiplication of the species" (*TMS*, 185). Eidous's translation is awkward and imprecise: "Une main invisible les force à faire des choses nécessaires à la vie, à peu près la même distribution que si la terre eût été divisée par égales parts entre tous ceux qui l'habitent; & c'est ainsi que, sans en avoir l'intention, & même à leur insçu, ils contribuent au bien être de la Société, & fournissent à la subsistance de plusieurs milliers d'hommes"[10] [An invisible hand forces them to do the things that are necessary to life, in more or less the same distribution as if the earth had been divided into equal parts between those who inhabit it; and it is thus that, without intending it, and without even their own knowledge, they contribute to the subsistence of several thousands of men]. De Grouchy renders the same passage into French thus: " Une main invisible semble les forcer à concourir à la même distribution des choses nécessaires à la vie qui aurait lieu si la terre eût été donné en égale portion à chacun de ses habitants; et ainsi, sans en avoir l'intention, sans même le savoir, le riche sert l'intérêt social et la multiplication de l'espèce"[11] [An invisible hand seems to force them to contribute to the same distribution of the necessities of life that would occur if the earth had been given in equal portion to each of its inhabitants; and thus, without intending it, without even knowing it, the rich man serves the interest of society and the multiplication of the species].

In the "invisible hand" extract as in other passages, de Grouchy's 1798 translation, while not always literal, captures eloquently Smith's meaning. Chapter 1 of the *Theory of Moral Sentiments*, on sympathy, contains a short but crucial paragraph in which Smith first presents his definition of sympathy to the reader: "Pity and compassion are words appropriated to signify our fellow-feeling with the sorrow of others. Sympathy, though its meaning was, originally, the same, may now, however, without much impropriety, be made use of to denote our fellow-feeling with any passion whatever" (*TMS*, 10). De Grouchy translates: "On se sert des mots de pitié et de compassion pour exprimer le sentiment que les souffrances des autres nous font éprouver: quoique le mot de sympathie fût originellement borné à cette signification, cependant on peut, sans impropriété, l'employer pour exprimer la faculté de partager les passions des autres, quelles qu'elles soient."[12] In some ways the elegant French of de Grouchy conveys Smith's ideas better than Smith himself, for his broad definition of sympathy as "our fellow-feeling with any passion whatsoever" led some readers to misunderstand his meaning and to identify sympathy with benevolence (*TMS*, 10–11n. 1). De Grouchy's rendering of this definition, which can be retranslated into English as "our ability to share the passions of others, whatever they may be," approximates more closely Smith's actual concept of sympathy, and is less likely to be misinterpreted. However de Grouchy's translation of Smith's phrase "our fellow-feeling with any passion" as "our *ability* to share the passions of others" reveals that she had some reservations about how readily this fellow-feeling might actually be put into practice.

For this reason, de Grouchy felt compelled to add to her translation of the *Theory of Moral Sentiments* a critique of Smith's theory entitled *Lettres à Cabanis sur la sympathie*. To enhance its persuasive tone, she used the rhetorical mode of eight philosophical letters addressed to a single reader, Georges Cabanis, a physician and philosopher who was married to her sister and was a close friend of the Condorcets. *Lettres à Cabanis sur la sympathie* constitutes both a reinforcement and a criticism of Smith's moral philosophy, and it was always included when her translation was reprinted in 1820, 1830, and 1860.[13] In his notes to the 1860 edition, Henri Joseph Léon Baudrillart (1821–1892), an eminent political economist and professor in the Collège de France, commented that the philosophical theory upon which *Lettres sur la sympathie* is based does not differ significantly from that of Smith, and that "the points of dissent with Smith manifested by the author all refer to secondary points. [The letters] are, above all, an ingenious commentary of Smith's work."[14] Baudrillart seems to underestimate the significance of de Grouchy's critique of the *Theory of Moral Sentiments*. While de Grouchy does take issue with Smith on some specific points that could be considered minor, she goes beyond Smith's theory of sympathy and develops her own theory as to the origins of our fellow-feelings for others. Furthermore, she uses this theory as the basis for the ambitious program of education and social reform that she and her husband Condorcet had formulated and promoted during the crucial years between the taking of the Bastille and the Terror, when the future of France for the next two centuries was at stake.

An important point on which de Grouchy diverged from Smith is in her translation of Smith's definition of sympathy, and her interpretation of this concept. As we have seen, de Grouchy translated Smith's definition of sympathy, "our fellow-feeling with any passion whatever" (*TMS*, 9), as "la faculté de partager les passions des autres, qu'elles quelles soient" [the ability to share the passions of others, whatever they may be]. In the first letter in her *Lettres sur la sympathie*, she offers her own definition: "La sympathie est la disposition que nous avons à sentir d'une manière semblable à celle d'autrui" [sympathy is the tendency we have to feel in a manner similar to the way others feel] (*Lettres*, 1, 70). This is an important distinction, for a tendency is not an immediate reaction to the spectacle of the suffering of others, but rather an inclination or predisposition to empathize with others that may or may not function when such a situation arises. Whereas Smith had declared that "the greatest ruffian, the most hardened violator of the laws of society, is not altogether without it" (*TMS*, 9), Sophie de Grouchy believed that sympathy is dependent on sensibility, a faculty that must be cultivated through education and constant application. "It hardly seems necessary to prove that the more sensibility is practiced, the more intense it becomes . . . a sensibility that is not put into practice weakens, and can no longer be excited except by very strong impressions" (*Lettres*, 1, 75).

In the second letter, de Grouchy concurs with Smith that sympathy is an essential component of humanity, of what it means to be human. She compares this "sentiment of humanity" to "a grain planted deep in the heart of man by nature, which the faculty of reflection will fertilize and develop" (*Lettres*, 2, 81). It is the responsibility of adults to teach children how to react sympathetically to the world around them. The first letter on sympathy contains an emotional plea to the reader: "Fathers, mothers, teachers, the destiny of the generation who will follow you is virtually in your hands! Guilty you will be, if you let miscarry in your children the precious seeds of sensibility, which await, for their development, the sight of pain, the example of compassion, the tears of gratitude, and an enlightened hand to kindle them and stir them up" (*Lettres*, 1, 76). What de Grouchy suggests quite clearly is that pity, compassion, gratitude, and other moral sentiments are not innate, but must be learned by example.

Sophie de Grouchy was in fact skeptical that sympathy, which is triggered by sensory perceptions and enhanced by our sensibility and imagination, could constitute a system of ethics without the guidance of reason. "It is reflection which, coming to the aid of our natural volatility, forces our compassion to be active, in reminding it of objects which had made only a momentary impression," she writes; ". . . it is reflection which, at the sight of pain, reminds us that we are subject to this tyrannical destructor of life . . . it is reflection, finally, that, through the habits it creates in our sensibility, makes humanity become an active and permanent sentiment in our souls" (*Lettres*, 2:80). Although de Grouchy concedes that as fellow humans we experience a spontaneous emotional reaction to certain spectacles that arouse our compassion or indignation, she considers Smith's notion of sympathy too idealistic because it assumes that all persons feel it to the same degree. The *Theory of Moral Sentiments* opens with the famous passage that reveals Smith's very positive view of human nature: "How selfish soever man may be supposed, there are evidently some principles in his nature, which interest him in the fortunes of others, and render their happiness necessary to him, though he derives nothing from it except the pleasure of seeing it. Of this kind is pity or compassion, the emotion which we feel for the misery of others, when we either see it, or are made to conceive it in a very lively manner" (*TMS*, 9).

While the major focus of the *Theory of Moral Sentiments* is the analysis of such moral sentiments and the role they play in social relationships, Smith never really explains how such sentiments are cultivated in the first place. To reformers like Condorcet and de Grouchy, whose proposals for social and political change were considered radical in an era when radical thinking was far from unusual, Smith's theory underestimated the power of the family, the state, and its institutions to mold a moral and sensitive individual capable of sympathy. De Grouchy makes the observation that "inhabitants of the countryside, and in general those people whose occupations involve them most directly in menial tasks that do not permit any reflection, are less capable of compassion than other men."[15] For de Grouchy, since the capacity to experience a sympathetic reaction to the situation of others could be altered by external social and material conditions, a theory of moral sentiments which identifies sympathy as the very core of moral sentiments must also address the issue of how to create social conditions necessary for sympathy. Freedom from want is not sufficient to guarantee that an individual will be capable of sympathy. Indulgence in selfish pleasures and vain pursuits is as much a hindrance to the development of moral sentiments as extreme poverty and hardship:

> In a class that is freer and richer, in a more elevated rank, does not one also see men more or less human, in proportion to their being more or less capable of sentiment and above all, reflection? Are they not always without humanity, as they are without compassion, those beings preoccupied by exclusive passions that originate in their selfishness or in vanity, and that leave no room for attention except to the object of their desire, no time for reflection except for ways to obtain it?[16]

In the little space he devotes to the role of education in the formation of character, Smith emphasizes self-control more than the more general considerations of "humanity." Children must eventually leave the "indulgent partiality" they enjoy at home and must face the outside world, the "great school of self-command" (TMS, 145). Smith takes it for granted that moral character is developed by active participation in the life of the community, and he says very little about the education process itself in his work on moral philosophy.

Smith, however, probably would not have disagreed with Sophie de Grouchy's distinction between a capacity for sympathy shared by all human beings and a more active use of sympathy, which requires some effort to develop, and he shared her view that a child's moral education must begin at home:

> Do you wish to educate your children to be dutiful to their parents, to be kind and affectionate to their brothers and sisters? put them under the necessity of being dutiful children, of being kind and affectionate brothers and sisters: educate them in your own house. . . . Domestic education is the institution of nature; public education, the contrivance of man. It is surely unnecessary to say, which is likely to be the wisest. (TMS, 222)

In this respect, Smith holds views in common with Rousseau, whose fictional pupil Emile is educated as far away as possible from the educational institutions of the day. In Rousseau's opinion, those institutions only reinforce class differences and cultivate vices such as arrogance and selfishness. Sophie de Grouchy agrees with Smith and Rousseau that a moral education must begin in the early years of childhood, but she does not believe that a whole country full of Emiles and their private tutors constitutes a practical solution.

Furthermore, Rousseau's insistence on educating girls and boys separately was anathema to the Condorcets, whose advocacy of complete political and economic equality of men and women entailed full participation of both sexes in the public sphere. Rather than reject the notion of public education, de Grouchy helped Condorcet formulate his proposals to reform the education system of the Ancien Régime. Upon his election to the Legislative Assembly in 1791, Condorcet was given the task of drafting a report of public education, in which he called for the abolition of the monopoly of the clergy over education, the creation of public schools for both girls and boys, the right of women to be admitted to colleges and learned societies, the necessity of training more doctors, midwives, and veterinarians to meet the needs of people in the city and the countryside, and the availability of practical training in various skills for people of all classes. Moral education should not be left in the hands of the church, and should begin at home, with parents taking special care to develop the child's ability to reflect upon her actions and feelings. "It is not a question of giving [children] principles of conduct or about teaching them truths, but about making them able to reflect upon their sentiments, and preparing them for the moral ideas that must one day spring forth from these reflections," he writes in his *Second Mémoire sur l'instruction publique*.[17]

Although Smith made few references to education in the *Theory of Moral Sentiments*, he strongly advocated the necessity of public instruction in the *Wealth of Nations*. In her comparative study of Smith and Condorcet, Emma Rothschild draws several parallels between the two philosophers' views on this subject. In a passage that closely resembles passages from the writings of both Condorcet and de Grouchy, Smith argues in the *Wealth of Nations* that laborers forced to perform monotonous, mindless tasks will eventually become emotionally and mentally incapacitated: "The torpor of his mind renders him, not only incapable of relishing or bearing a part in any rational conversation, but of conceiving any generous, noble, or tender sentiment, and consequently of forming any just judgment concerning many even of the ordinary duties of private life."[18] Rothschild further notes that Condorcet makes direct references to the passages on education from the *Wealth of Nations* in his proposals for public instruction dating from the early 1790s.[19] Given the close collaboration between de Grouchy and Condorcet, as stressed in Jean-Paul de Lagrave's article on the influence of de Grouchy on Condorcet's thought,[20] and given that Condorcet actually wrote a commentary on the *Wealth of Nations* for the 1790 French translation, as noted earlier, it seems surprising that in her *Lettres sur la sympathie,* drafted between 1793 and 1794 and published in 1798, de Grouchy makes no mention whatsoever of Smith's arguments in favor of public education, which so closely approximate her own. It is important to bear in mind, however, that de Grouchy intended her *Lettres* to be a response to the *Theory of Moral Sentiments*, and not an analysis of Smith's entire oeuvre. At the beginning of her commentary, she describes the process through which she began drafting the *Lettres sur la sympathie*: "rather than follow the ideas of the Edinburgh philosopher, I let myself follow my own. As I read his chapters on sympathy, I drafted others on the same subject: I will write them to you in succession, so that you can judge me; I do not say so that you can judge us, for I am far from claiming to parallel [Smith]" (*Lettres*, 1, 70). This passage suggests that de Grouchy made notes as she was reading the *Theory of Moral Sentiments*, and that the acts of reading Smith's work and writing her own thoughts were almost simultaneous. She further explains that Smith's identification of sympathy as the force behind our moral feelings and actions prompted her to investigate the origins and formation of sympathy, which she found lacking in Smith's theory. From this perspective, it makes sense that de Grouchy did not refer to Smith's emphasis on public education in the *Wealth of Nations*, for she felt that this point should have been made in the *Theory of Moral Sentiments*.

De Grouchy takes issue with Smith on several other important points. As the passages above indicate, she wishes to go beyond Smith's analysis of how sympathy works by explaining how sympathy can be molded and used to build a better world. Like her husband, she is preoccupied with the role of education in forming responsible citizens. Indeed, Condorcet asserts that there could be no citizenship without equal educational opportunities for both men and women, and he firmly believes that social justice and equality are the prerequisites of a moral society. In order for Smith's spectator to react sympathetically to the suffering of his fellow human being, he must be freed from the constant concern for his own survival that characterized the life of most peasants and laborers, especially in France, where the medieval system of forced labor was still in effect. This could only be achieved through a radical redistribution of wealth. "One of the principal objectives of our laws," writes Sophie de Grouchy, "should be to create and maintain an equality of fortune among citizens, which would result in a degree of comfort for each of them, without exception, so that the preoccupation caused by the constant worry about providing for the necessities of life would not render them incapable of the degree of reflection necessary to perform all the natural sentiments, particularly that of humanity."[21] De Grouchy's views on the judiciary system under the Ancien Régime can be aligned with those of Voltaire and Beccaria, in that she stresses that any punishment must be proportionate to the severity of the crime. However, in her seventh letter on sympathy, de Grouchy emphasizes the legal ramifications of economic inequality: "Criminal laws, by their severity, and civil laws, when they favor inequality, are the cause of the impunity of lesser crimes; and they can also be considered the cause of greater crimes, because the impunity of the former is the sole encouragement to commit the others" (*Lettres*, 7, 173).

In the most recent biography of Sophie de Grouchy, Thierry Boissel points out that de Grouchy's criticism of legal institutions as perpetuators of social and judicial inequality is far more radical than the writings of other philosophes concerned with judicial reform, including Condorcet himself. Boissel cites the following passage from de Grouchy's seventh letter to support her case: "If laws were clear, they would warn all men equally. If they were just, they would allow no exceptions. If they were precise, they would leave no room for corruption and dishonesty . . . laws should be a supplement to the conscience of the citizen . . . too often, they are nothing but oppressive chains" (*Lettres*, 7, 161 ).[22] De Grouchy believed that most laws had become so distorted in favor of those who held money and privileges that it would be preferable to start from scratch: "let all the vice-ridden institutions be abolished from one end of the earth to the other, so that only necessary and reasonable laws remain, let the arbitrary power that reduces its victims to ignorance and credulity through plunging them in misery and servitude disappear forever, and human reason, sound and vigorous, will rise up from under its chains, will prevail in all classes and will itself form public opinion. . . . the current order of society of all peoples whose government does not have as its foundation natural rights of men, is the sole cause of the obstacles that ambition and vanity throw in the way of the movements of conscience" (*Lettres*, 7, 163–64).

De Grouchy's strong egalitarian principles cause her to disagree with some of the examples Smith uses to illustrate the various kinds of sympathy, such as his claim that we feel greater compassion for a dethroned monarch than for an ordinary person who suffers a change in social status because we naturally sympathize with and admire the happiness and fortune enjoyed by royalty. In book 1, chapter 2 of the *Theory of Moral Sentiments*, entitled "On the origin of Ambition, and the distinction of Ranks," Smith explains that the misfortunes of kings and lovers constitute the bulk of tragic literature, and arouse the sympathy of the spectators, because "in spite of all that reason and experience can tell us to the contrary, the prejudices of the imagination attach to these two states a happiness superior to any other. To disturb, or to put an end to such perfect enjoyment, seems to be the most atrocious of all injuries" (*TMS*, 52). This statement is based on two premises that Smith puts forth earlier in the same chapter: that "mankind are disposed to sympathize more entirely with our joy than with our sorrow" (*TMS*, 50), and that it is natural to feel reverence and respect for our political and social superiors. "That kings are the servants of the people, to be obeyed, resisted, deposed, or punished, as the public conveniency may require, is the doctrine of reason and philosophy," Smith states; "but it is not the doctrine of Nature. Nature would teach us to submit to them for their own sake. . . . The strongest motives, the most furious passions, fear, hatred, and resentment, are scarce sufficient to balance this natural disposition to respect them" (*TMS*, 53). While Smith maintains that the "distinction of ranks and the order of society" are founded upon this disposition inherent in human nature, Sophie de Grouchy sees distinctions of rank and fortune as contrary to the natural order of things. In response to Smith's passage on our reaction to the misfortunes of kings, she writes in her fourth letter: "It is at least certain that this is absolutely opposed to the sentiment of natural equality that makes us contemplate with jealousy or at least severity all that is beyond our reach" (*Lettres*, 4, 108). De Grouchy concedes that "we feel more compassion for their misfortunes than for those of other men" but explains that "it is only because kings seem to us to be preserved from such misfortunes by their lofty rank, that we feel they must be more sensitive to them." In the sixth edition of the *Theory of Moral Sentiments*, in which Smith places greater emphasis on self-command, he upholds his earlier idea that "this disposition to admire, and almost to worship, the rich and powerful, and to despise, or, at least to neglect persons of poor and mean condition" is "necessary both to establish and to maintain the distinction of ranks and the order of society," but admits that this same disposition is "the great and most universal cause of the corruption of our moral sentiments" (*TMS*, 61). De Grouchy certainly agrees with the latter point, but she disputes the notion that a disposition to admire the rich is natural, and insists that such values are socially determined and politically legislated. "The civilized man," she writes, using the Rousseauian, pejorative definition of civilized, "if he is governed by prejudices and by bad laws, is therefore naturally envious and jealous, and he is increasingly so in proportion to the extent to which the vices of social institutions draw him further away from nature, corrupt his reason and make his happiness depend on the satisfaction of a larger amount of needs" (*Lettres*, 4, 113).

In the sixth part of the *Theory of Moral Sentiments*, which Smith added to the 1790 edition, the virtue of self-command, along with the critical gaze of the impartial spectator, is presented as an element that can temper the corrupting predispositions inherent in our nature. "Self-command is not only itself a great virtue," writes Smith, "but from it all the other virtues seem to derive their principal lustre" (*TMS*, 241). Writing from a feminist perspective, de Grouchy finds little relevance in the "masculine" virtues of self-command and self-control that Smith emphasizes. Smith's infelicitous use of the adjective "womanish" to characterize the vocalization of pain did not help his argument. "We esteem the man who supports pain and even torture with manhood and firmness; and we can have little regard for him who sinks under them, and abandons himself to useless outcries and womanish lamentations" (*TMS*, 244). In de Grouchy's analysis, people endure pain with as much resignation as they can because they are aware that some pain is unavoidable and even necessary, and that moaning will bring them no relief. Extreme restraint in the face of intense physical or moral suffering stems from a desire to be admired by others, or from personal satisfaction at having conquered pain, rather than from magnanimity or courage. "It is absolutely false that the principle of firmness or courage in the face of physical pain derives from the little sympathy that such suffering inspires in others . . . such firmness comes, either from the desire to be admired, or from a kind of contentment with oneself for possessing great courage. . . ." (*Lettres,* 4, 110)

De Grouchy refutes other examples used by Smith, but the greatest fault she finds with Smith's explanation of morals through the mechanism of sympathy is that it relies very little on reflection, or reason, in the forming of moral judgments. Of course, this was deliberate on Smith's part; like Hume, Smith was antirationalist, in the sense that he believed that our assessment of what constitutes a moral or immoral action derives not from reason, but rather from a complex interaction of emotional and psychological factors. Hume elaborates upon this point at the beginning of the third book of *A Treatise of Human Nature*, in a section entitled *Moral distinctions not deriv'd from Reason*:

> Since morals, therefore, have an influence on the actions and affections, it follows, that they cannot be deriv'd from reason; and that because reason alone, as we have already prov'd, can never have any such influence. Morals excite passions, and produce or prevent actions. Reason of itself is utterly impotent in this particular. The rules of morality, therefore, are not conclusions of our reason.[23]

In part 7 of the *Theory of Moral Sentiments,* Smith states:

> But though reason is undoubtedly the source of the general rules of morality, and of all the moral judgments which we form by means of them; it is altogether absurd and unintelligible to suppose that the first perceptions of right and wrong can be derived from reason. . . . These first perceptions, as well as all other experiments upon which any general rules are founded, cannot be the object of reason, but of immediate senses and feeling. . . . reason cannot render any particular object either agreeable or disagreeable to the mind for its own sake. Reason may show that this object is the means of obtain-

ing some other which is naturally either pleasing or displeasing, and in this manner may render it either agreeable or disagreeable for the sake of something else. (*TMS*, 320)

Rousseau had been even more emphatic in separating reason from morality, asserting in his *Second Discourse on the Origins of Inequality* (1755) that man's natural capacity for pity and compassion progressively weakens as his reason leads him to calculate how to assert his independence and authority over other individuals once he enters into a social setting: "It is reason that engenders self-love, and it is reflection that strengthens it; It is reason that turns man back on himself and that separates him from all that annoys and afflicts him. It is philosophy that isolates him; it is philosophy that allows him to say privately, at the sight of a suffering man, 'Perish if you will, I am safe.'"[24]

Sophie de Grouchy, a great admirer of both Rousseau and Smith, diverges significantly from them in her view of the role that reason plays in the formation of our moral judgments. She believed, as we have seen, that sympathy functions best under the best of circumstances, when poverty and hardship, or decadence and self-indulgence, have not dulled the natural sensibility that human beings are endowed with from birth. This natural sensibility is itself enhanced by the capacity for reflection: "But it is in observing man himself that one recognizes more easily that he owes the greatest part of his humanity to the faculty of reflection: in effect, he is human to the extent that he is sensitive and reflective."[25] While our senses and feelings might trigger our initial reaction to the sight of a suffering person, "reflection prolongs the ideas initiated by our senses, it extends and conserves in us the effect of the sight of pain and one can say that it is reflection that make us really human" (*Lettres*, 2, 80). For de Grouchy, then, sympathy is a combination of the "immediate senses and feelings" that Smith maintains are at the base of our moral judgments and our ability to think and reflect upon these feelings. And here lies the crux of the problem for de Grouchy. If our immediate senses and feelings are determined in part by external social and economic factors, which have created, in her view, "a mass of people who have become nearly insensitive to everything that is not directly linked to their existence and their happiness" (*Lettres*, 3, 91), then the capacity of the masses to reflect upon their feelings is even more limited. In such circumstances, the ability to make moral judgments is not only subjective, but also extremely tenuous. On the surface, de Grouchy and Condorcet, like their fellow combatants in the war against what Voltaire aptly named *l'infâme* (ignorance, religious superstition, prejudice, and opposition to progress) seem to share the overly idealistic faith in reason as the remedy to all social and moral ills. However, as we have seen throughout this chapter, de Grouchy was in fact quite pragmatic, in that she recognized the magnitude of the task facing the generation that had come of age during the Revolution: "What immense work remains to be done in the area of education, not to develop or direct nature, but simply to conserve in nature the inclinations towards goodness, so that they won't be smothered by those prejudices which are so common and widely accepted that they corrupt at the very source sentiments of humanity and equality, sentiments which are as essential to the moral happiness of each individual as to the maintenance of equity and security in all of the links of the social order" (*Lettres*, 4, 114).

It is clear that for Sophie de Grouchy our predisposition to feel for and with our fellow human beings is not sufficient to guarantee that such feelings will be able to surface when a situation necessitating a sympathetic reaction presents itself. De Grouchy uses the metaphor of a seed, which must be planted in fertile soil and carefully tended before it can sprout and bear fruit, to illustrate how dependent our innate capacity for sympathy is on external conditions. While it is fair to say that the Condorcets were progressive, in the sense that they believed that tangible progress in improving humanity and the plight of humankind was possible, they were not optimistic that such change would come about naturally without equal educational opportunities for people of all classes and complete social and political equality of the sexes. Without a just society, the natural mechanism of sympathy, so minutely dissected and eloquently described by Smith, could not function.

Another common view of de Grouchy and Condorcet is that philosophers have a moral obligation to advocate change. Catherine Kintzler highlights this idea as crucial for understanding Condorcet: "Like Socrates, Condorcet thinks that truth is accessible to common reason, and that it cannot be unjust; like him, he believes that the role of the philosopher is in the public arena, that it is in these places where opinion triumphs in principle that reason must speak in reality."[26] Upon reading de Grouchy's *Lettres sur la sympathie*, one has the impression that the thing she regrets most about Smith is that he does not occupy enough of the public space, that he did not evolve from a moral philosopher into a social reformer. In a sense, *Lettres sur la sympathie* is an attempt by de Grouchy to complete this task, for through her commentary on Smith she advocates reforms that will allow all individuals to realize their moral, intellectual, and social potential.

The fact that *Lettres à Cabanis sur la sympathie* was always included in nineteenth-century editions of her translation of the *Theory of Moral Sentiments* underscores the tremendous impact of de Grouchy's commentary on the reception of Smith's book from 1798 onward. If Smith's moral philosophy was perceived as having relevance to the social and political issues of the day during the century in which France experienced two more revolutions, in 1830 and 1848, and saw the rise of a new generation of social reformers, it is partly thanks to Sophie de Grouchy, whose commentary on Smith emphasized the fundamental role that political and educational institutions play in creating a socioeconomic environment conducive to the moral development of the individual. An English translation of *Lettres sur la sympathie* is long overdue, for Sophie de Grouchy's work is important not only for its impact on the reception of Smith's book in France, but also because it constitutes a major contribution to moral philosophy in its own right.

## NOTES

1. Alain Pons, preface to Sophie de Grouchy, marquise de Condorcet, *Lettres sur la sympathie; suivies des Lettres d'amour*, ed. Jean-Paul de Lagrave (Montréal, 1994), 7 (cited hereafter as *Lettres*). English translations are mine.

2. "Testament," in *Condorcet: Foundations of Social Choice and Political Theory*, ed. and trans. Ian McLean and Fiona Hewitt (Aldershot, U.K., and Brookfield, Vt., 1994), 290.

3. Jean-Antoine-Nicolas de Caritat, marquis de Condorcet, *Esquisse d'un tableau historique des progrès de l'esprit humain* (Paris, 1972), 138–39, cited in Jean-Paul de Lagrave, "L'Influence de Sophie de Grouchy sur la pensée de Condorcet," in *Condorcet: mathématicien, économiste, philosophe, homme politique*, ed. Crépel and Gilain (Paris, 1989), 438.

4. Jean-Paul de Lagrave, "Thomas Paine et les Condorcet," in *Thomas Paine ou la République sans frontières*, ed. B. Vincent (Nancy, 1993), 61.

5. For a detailed account of this case, see Elisabeth Badinter and Robert Badinter, *Condorcet (1743–1794): Un intellectuel en politique* (Paris, 1988), 229–35.

6. Scholars of the French Revolution are not in total agreement about the identity of the two other members of the very exclusive but influential *Société républicaine* founded by Paine and the Condorcets. Paine names Achille Duchâtelet, Revolutionary officer and grandson of Emilie du Châtelet, the famous physicist and mistress of Voltaire, as one of the founding members. The fifth member was either Nicolas de Bonneville, journalist and cofounder with Condorcet of *Le Cercle social*, or Brissot, director of *Le Patriote français*. See Jean-Paul de Lagrave, "Thomas Paine et les Condorcet," in *Thomas Paine*, 58, and Bernard Vincent, *Thomas Paine ou la Religion de la liberté* (Saint-Amand-Montrond, 1987), 209.

7. Cited in the introduction to Adam Smith, *The Theory of Moral Sentiments*, ed. D. D. Raphael and A. L. Macfie (Oxford, 1976), 30 (cited hereafter as *TMS*). On the reception of Smith's works in the *Année Littéraire* and the *Journal Encyclopédique*, see the chapter by Harvey Chisick in this volume.

8. *Théorie des Sentimens Moraux, ou Essai Analytique, sur les Principes des Jugemens que portent naturellement les Hommes, d'abord sur les Actions des autres, et ensuite sur leurs propres Actions: Suivi d'une Dissertation sur l'Origine des Langues; par Adam Smith; Traduit de l'Anglais, sur la septième et dernière Edition, par S. de Grouchy Veuve Condorcet. Elle y a joint huit Lettres sur la Sympathie*, 2 vols. (Paris, An 6 de la République [1798]).

9. Adam Smith, *Théorie des Sentiments Moraux*, trans. Michaël Biziou, Claude Gautier, and Jean-François Pradeau (Paris, 1999), 10. These translators praise the 1798 translation for its readability and its fidelity to Smith's meaning, but at the same time they note that "the roughness, the repetitions, the awkwardness of Smith's style" were smoothed over perhaps a bit too much by de Grouchy's stylistic elegance. They propose a more literal, if perhaps less literary, translation in order to restore the "didactic dimension" of Smith's text, which, having originated in public lectures, inevitably contained a certain amount of deliberate repetition for rhetorical effect.

10. *Métaphysique de l'Ame, ou Théorie des sentiments moraux, traduite de l'anglois de M. Adam Smith, Professeur de Philosophie Morale, dans l'Université de Glasgow, par M. ***,* 2 vols. (Paris, 1764), 2:111.

11. Adam Smith, *Théorie des Sentiments Moraux*, ed. Henri Baudrillart; trans. Sophie de Grouchy, marquise de Condorcet (Paris, 1860), 212.

12. Ibid., 4.

13. The only twentieth-century edition of de Grouchy's translation of the *Theory of Moral Sentiments* appeared in 1982, in a series appropriately called "Les Introuvables" [The Impossible to Find].

14. Smith, *Théorie des Sentiments Moraux* (1860 ed.), 434 n. 1. Baudrillart was the author of over thirty works covering the fields of political economy, political and social history, moral philosophy, and economics, including titles such as *Etudes de philosophie morale et d'économie politique* (1858), *L'argent et ses critiques* (1867), *Des rapports de l'économie politique et de la morale* (1883), and *Essai sur le mouvement social et intellectuel en France depuis 1789* (1902).

15. Sophie De Grouchy, "Lettres à Cabanis sur la Sympathie," in Smith,

*Théorie des Sentiments Moraux* (1860 ed.), 2:443. This passage has been omitted from de Lagrave's recent edition of the *Lettres*.

16. Ibid., 2:444.

17. Condorcet, *Second Mémoire sur l'instruction publique,* quoted in Catherine Kintzler, *Condorcet: L'instruction publique et la Naissance du Citoyen* (Paris, 1984), 95.

18. Quoted in Emma Rothschild, *Economic Sentiments: Adam Smith, Condorcet and the Enlightenment* (Cambridge, Mass. and London, 2001), 225.

19. Ibid., 225.

20. Cited in note 4 above.

21. De Grouchy, "Lettres à Cabanis sur la sympathie," in Smith, *Théorie des Sentiments Moraux* (1860 ed.), 2:443.

22. Thierry Boissel, *Sophie de Condorcet: Femme des lumières (1764–1822)* (Paris, 1988), 209.

23. David Hume, *A Treatise of Human Nature,* ed. L. A. Selby-Bigge (Oxford, 1968), 457.

24. Jean-Jacques Rousseau, *Discourse on Inequality in Rousseau's Political Writings,* ed. Bondanella and Ritter; trans. Bondanella (New York and London, 1988), 29.

25. De Grouchy, "Lettres à Cabanis sur la sympathie," in Smith, *Théorie des Sentiments Moraux* (1860 ed.), 2:443.

26. Kintzler, *Condorcet,* 17.

# Enlightenment and Its Discontents: Robert Wallace and Rousseau on the Republic of Virtue

### B. Barnett Cochran

Jean-Jacques Rousseau, citizen of Geneva, was the great voice of provincial protest against the project of French Enlightenment and modernity. That protest was never more clearly or succinctly expressed than in his first celebrated essay, his dissenting response to the self-patronizing question from Dijon: "Whether the Restoration of the Sciences and the Arts Has Contributed to the Purification of Morals." Rousseau's *First Discourse* did not so much condemn learning as the modern world of opulence, power, inequality, injustice, and vice. Learning in such a context merely reflects and furthers corruption. Only in a republic, such as Sparta or Rome, could men be citizens, and be virtuous. The Enlightenment of the French salon can only accentuate the corruption of manners and morals. On such a foundation, what good can Enlightenment produce?

Though sounded in Paris, this was the doctrine of a Genevan, ironically, or fittingly, issued in the twilight of that republic's sovereign life. By 1750, when the *First Discourse* appeared, two centuries of Genevan independence from France, maintained by a balance of competing political aspirations between France and Savoy, had effectively ended. Rousseau may have been largely unaware of the details of this struggle,[1] and of course among his travels he found other republican resources to marshal against the great tyrannical monarchies. Yet he habitually read his republican idealism back into Geneva, of which he continued to consider himself a "citizen."

Like Rousseau, Robert Wallace of Edinburgh (1697–1771) represents a voice of provincial protest against an increasingly imposing urban, courtly, and enlightened culture. Nicholas

Phillipson has reminded us to consider Edinburgh's Enlightenment in the context of provincial culture.[2] What role might Edinburgh play in the modern world of wealth and power? The Scottish response was a movement toward developing the languages, concepts, and institutions that could comprehend and legitimate the emerging modernity of large, centrally controlled, aristocratically led, commercially driven states. The Scots sought to show how Scotland could remain virtuous while participating in such an enterprise as subordinate partners to the urban, urbane, court culture of London.[3] In the midst of this process, Wallace stands out as a voice of dissent. In the spirit of Rousseau's *Discourses*, he laments the loss of virtue, radical inequality, the effects of commercialization on personality, and the death of citizenship in the modern world. Wallace and Rousseau should therefore be seen as cobelligerents in a tragic, futile protest against Enlightenment and modernity.

It is perhaps not surprising that Wallace has not been remembered this way. His résumé is not that of a radical, and his situation in life does not suggest the sort of profound social alienation that marked Rousseau's. Wallace was a popular and respected Church of Scotland minister in Edinburgh, quite near the epicenter of the Edinburgh literati, whose project was to make room for Scotland in the modern world and room in Scotland for polite learning. He was a social insider and a joiner, a founding or early member of the Rankenian Club, the Philosophical Society, and the Select Society. He has traditionally been cast as a model and early leader of the group of moderate clergymen led by William Robertson, who did so much to create intellectual space and distinction within the Kirk in the second half of the century.[4] His ecclesiastical career was made largely by crown patronage.[5] During the brief Tweeddale administration of Scotland in the 1740s, Wallace was the manager of church offices in the gift of the crown. His prestige and success are symbolically captured in his honorary titles: royal chaplain for George II and George III.[6]

Wallace was a creative, eccentric writer whose literary corpus presents the modern scholar with some formidable interpretive challenges, further complicated by the fact that the private Wallace was sometimes at variance with the public.[7] He is best remembered today for *A Dissertation on the Numbers of Mankind in Antient and Modern Times*, which was published in Edinburgh in

1753 as part of a celebrated debate with David Hume on the history of world population. He is also recalled as the under-acknowledged author of a population calculus later developed and elaborated by Robert Malthus in his *Essay on the Principle of Population* (1798); Wallace's computations are found in his *Various Prospects of Mankind, Nature, and Providence*, which appeared in London in 1761. He also published two individual sermons and other works, including *Characteristics of the Present Political State of Great Britain* (1758), a polemical response to John Brown's popular, civic humanist condemnation of the British state, *Estimate of the Manners and Principles of the Times* (1757–58).

Historians have been at a loss about just what to do with this enigmatic minister from Edinburgh. Perhaps closest to the mark, Caroline Robbins more than forty years ago placed him in the tradition of British liberal "commonwealthmen,"[8] though not without missteps. Conversely, in H. T. Dickinson's mapping of the British ideological landscape, Wallace turns up, on the strength of his *Characteristics*, among the conservative "Court" or "Establishment" whigs who defended the post-Revolution settlement against those who criticized Walpoleon politics with a view to an ancient constitutional tradition.[9] Norah Smith, whose previously cited dissertation is the essential biographical source, presents Wallace as a theologically innovative social critic and reformer, a prophetic voice echoing the Enlightenment's vision of social progress, very much in the spirit of the French philosophe Condorcet, though without his "revolutionary zeal."[10] While there is something to be said for this interpretation of Wallace's complex and paradoxical literary career, the comparison with Condorcet distorts more than it reveals about Wallace's outlook. For Wallace was singing in a different key, which was much closer to that of his Genevan contemporary, the rather less optimistic Rousseau, who often preferred the past to the present or the future. Writing in the 1750s, Rousseau and Wallace marshalled resources embedded in the classical republican tradition to argue for the ancients against the moderns in a struggle that had largely lost its relevance for Condorcet's generation.[11] In the 1750s it was not yet clear that the day belonged to the moderns, or at least it was no clearer to Wallace than it was to Rousseau. Appealing to the ancient foundation, both men demolished the modern superstructure. And when they considered rebuilding an alternative political and moral order, they engaged the common problem of finding a viable place for a virtuous republic in a world of absolutism and commercial empire.

Rousseau shared a basic belief with the French philosophes that nature was a grand order that encompassed human beings. The character of his dissent was in his insistence that modern society had deviated too far from the natural moral order of things.[12] In the *First Discourse* (1750), corruption has come at the hands of modern learning. The ideal order is that of ancient Sparta and Republican Rome, where men were citizens, possessing martial valor, a simple austerity, and moral virtue. There the virtues thrived because they were nurtured and rewarded. With science, and with the arts, came social distinction, inequality, and vice.

> Where do all these abuses arise [martial & moral corruption] if not in the fatal inequality introduced among men by the distinction of talents and the disparagement of the virtues? This is the most obvious effect of all our studies, and the most dangerous of all their consequences. . . . The wise man does not run after fortune; but he is not insensitive to glory; and when he sees it so badly distributed his virtue, which a little emulation would have animated and turned to the advantage of society, languishes and dies in misery and oblivion.[13]

The modern world is rich in inequality and unrestrained vice. Men are no longer citizens. Modern society rewards selfish ambition. Martial valor languishes.

> What will become of virtue when one has to get rich at all cost? The ancient political thinkers forever spoke of morals and of virtue; ours speak only of commerce and of money. One will tell you that . . . a man is worth to the state only what he consumes in it. By that token one Sybarite would easily have been worth thirty Lacedaemonians. Try to guess, then, which of the two Republics, Sparta or Sybaris, was subdued by a handful of peasants, and which caused Asia to tremble. (16)

This critique of modernity was continued in Rousseau's *Second Discourse* (1755), though from a different point of view. The ideal moral order, if one excepts the dedicatory letter to the Republic of Geneva, is no longer drawn from the image of the ancient republic. To answer the Academy of Dijon's question, "What is the Origin of Inequality Among Men, and is it Authorized by the Natural Law?" one must first know what a man is, Rousseau asserts. Others have failed to strip away what is natural to man only in society and to have reached what is truly natural. Natural man was largely alone, guided by desires rather than reason, and free, because he was not dependent on any other human. Natural inequalities in the precivil, presocial state amounted to little. Only when small, family-based settled communities developed, with quickening desires and the appropriation of tools (including language) to satisfy them, did natural inequalities begin to be augmented.[14] Still, this was the stage of society that must have been most endearing and most enduring, as long as tools were directed toward goals that an individual could attain alone. But when cooperation of labor set in, when men began to need the aid of others, "equality disappeared, property came into existence, labor became necessary" (51). In the *Second Discourse*, Rousseau strikes the crowning blow in that rhetorically captivating moment when humans entered the tragic age of true inequality:

> The first person who, having enclosed a plot of land, took it into his head to say *this is mine* and found people simple enough to believe him, was the true founder of civil society. What crimes, wars, murders, what miseries and horrors would the human race have been spared, had someone pulled up the stakes or filled in the ditch and cried out to his fellow men: "Do not listen to this impostor. You are lost if you forget that the fruits of the earth belong to all and the earth to no one!" (44)

Just as Rousseau was being celebrated and denounced for these compelling arguments, Robert Wallace was developing his version of dissent in a dialogue with David Hume that was also to be prominent in learned discourse: the population debate. Sometime between 1737 and 1745 Wallace had presented a paper on the history of world population at the Philosophical Society in Edinburgh.[15] Inspired in part by Montesquieu, Wallace argued for the superior populousness of the ancients. He continued to revise and expand the treatise, and when Hume entered the society in 1751, Wallace asked him to read it. As it happened, Hume was also in the advanced stages of an essay on population, which he then gave to Wallace. This essay, published in Hume's *Political Discourses* in 1752, argued for a greater population in the modern age.[16] Hume included a deferential preface, acknowledging a debt to Wallace's treatise, and urging its publication, "which will serve to give great light into the present question."[17] Wallace's *Dissertation on the Numbers of Mankind* was published in Edinburgh the next year, and the debate became celebrated in European polite society as a model of civility and enlightenment.[18] Ostensibly about the relative population of the world in ancient and modern times, the debate actually engaged both participant's fundamental ideological commitments,[19] as Hume made clear when he observed that "if everything else be equal, it seems natural to expect, that wherever there are most happiness and virtue, and the wisest institutions, there will also be most people" (*Philosophical Works*, 3:384).

It is worth noting that, in more senses than the merely chronological, Wallace's *Dissertation on the Numbers of Mankind* was situated between the *First Discourse* and *Second Discourse* of Rousseau. The *Dissertation* opens with an exercise in political arithmetic, a calculation of theoretical world population based on a hypothetical equation for human rates of reproduction. Wallace observes that any such equation, however conservative, would produce a present world population far in excess of what it actually could be. Hence the problem is to explain the moral and natural causes for mankind's reproductive failure. This he addresses much as Rousseau tried to explain the failure of modern society to make men happy in the *Second Discourse*, by recalling the natural stages of social development from mankind's most primitive state. That is, Wallace develops a conjectural history, that genre of analysis soon to flourish in France and to become a defining characteristic of Scottish social inquiry. Interestingly, while the form of the *Dissertation* is that of Rousseau's *Second Discourse*, its substance is much like the *First Discourse*, even though the bulk of the work, except for the long appendix answering Hume, had been written before Rousseau published anything. Wallace used a conjectural scheme to present the ancient republic of virtue as a superior form of life and to expose the false pretensions of the modern world.

According to the *Dissertation*, the natural history of man is marked by three distinct stages of economic, social, and political development. The defining characteristics of each stage are its mode of production and a complementary cultural ethos or system of tastes and propriety. The earliest human societies were "savage" or "barbaric," terms likely appropriated from Montesquieu to denote economic systems based on the "spontaneous" acquisition of subsistence through hunting and fishing.[20] Manners were "rude." In time, improvements in agricultural methods led to settled life typified by the small family farm. Commerce tended to be carried out on a limited and local scale. The corresponding cultural ethos featured "simplicity" in tastes and manners. The political form of Wallace's second stage in the *Dissertation* is the republic; Rome is paradigmatic. In time the ancient republics evolved, or devolved, into large commercial states with complex economic relations and cultural conventions, the foremost of which were luxury, social inequality, and a "false" sense of "refinement." This shift in material and moral structures was accompanied by the rise of imperial despotism. This natural social development was driven by a range of human desires, particularly an appetite for improvement deeply rooted in human nature.

Unlike Rousseau, Wallace did not attempt to push back the limits of our ignorance of earliest man via conjecture, at least not in the *Dissertation*. But he returned to the question in 1761 in his *Various Prospects of Mankind, Nature, and Providence*, where he reviewed Rousseau's scheme in the *Second Discourse*. There he expresses horror at the image of that isolated, savage, and nonrational natural man (111–12), a reaction echoed in a chorus of Scottish voices.[21] For Wallace, the earliest man was man in society, though a barbaric society not worth emulating. At the same time, Wallace expresses sympathy with Rousseau's attack on property as the seed from which so much human distress has sprouted (111). This communal inclination was already strongly present in the *Dissertation*, but for Wallace it was in mankind's second phase, rather than the first, that society was marked by material equality.

Clearly, Rome performed the same role for Wallace that Sparta did for Rousseau: both provided an ideal image of a model community built on citizenship, simplicity, and virtuosity. In Wallace's lively, neostoic historical imagination, Rome before Caesar had a constitution in which human tastes and desires were harmonized with the providential ordering of nature. Just as Rousseau gloried in the constitution of Lycurgus, so Wallace attributed this wise balance to the lawgiver Romulus, whose great insight was to establish equality in the distribution of land among Rome's leading citizens. While much of the modern world is materially organized around the principle of primogeniture, the ancient republics rested on an entirely different foundation, the result of wise, intentional planning and deliberation.

Hume's essay challenged the assumption of ancient calculating lawgivers, just as he tended to picture ancient republics as generally politically turbulent, unstable, and riddled with factionalism. Wallace answered Hume in the appendix of the *Dissertation* with a closely reasoned analysis of the Roman constitution in order to demonstrate the care with which it had been crafted. Wallace's republican Romans understood the general interest of the city to be grounded upon equality, which in turn rested on laws regulating property ownership and preventing its accumulation. Romulus originally divided the modest expanse of his city by studying the principles of "mediocrity," and the laws of succession that would preserve it:

> And, mediocrity being absolutely necessary for the well-being and subsistence of his little state, it was necessary to regulate the order of succession, so as to preserve it among the citizens, and to hinder any particular person from acquiring so great wealth, as would give him either superior eminence or greater influence than the rest of his fellows. . . . for the partition of the lands, and the preservation of mediocrity among the citizens, seem to have been the true cause and original of all those rules of succession, which were in force till the time of the Decemvirs. (234)

In order to prevent an estate from passing out of one family and being united with that of another, succession was limited to heirs by the male line, though the heirs themselves could be either male or female. No citizen possessed the power of "testament," that is, the power to designate an heir through a written will. Citizens held the right of testament as a public trust. Only by act of public legislation could a citizen designate an heir not in adherence to this prescription. Such a bill would only be passed if the proposed inheritance was perceived to be in the

public interest. The citizens understood that without such a policy the fundamental nature of their political existence would be
altered. They were therefore extremely careful about enacting
bills of testament. "For these were times of virtue," Wallace
writes in the appendix, "in which it would always be first considered, whether any bill was or was not *e republica*" (238–39).
Although Wallace had to admit in response to Hume that the
Twelve Tables had indeed altered this set by strengthening the
power of the paternal head to dispose of the estate as he was
inclined, he nevertheless maintained that the old ways continued long in practice, virtue sustaining what law no longer pro-
tected.[22] Where the skeptical Hume had found chaos and
instability, Wallace could detect a golden age of republican virtue and social equality. And consistent with the neo-Harring-
tonian view of inheritance, he argues in the appendix that the
rise of Caesar and imperial despotism was precipitated by the
eventual shift in property relations:

> By consequence, the legal succession usually took place, and the
> custom of making testaments did not grow common for a great
> number of years; so that still an equality of fortune was preserved,
> and the most eminent citizens were possessed of only a little spot.
> However, testaments did at last become frequent; and, of course,
> that mediocrity of fortune, which is the basis of republican govern-
> ment, was soon destroyed. Some citizens became poor, others ac-
> quired immense possessions; ideas of riches and poverty became
> familiar, and cries for agrarian and sumptuary laws became violent.
> But the evil was become both so universal and so virulent, as to
> admit of no remedy. The republic was at last destroyed. (240)

It is not hard to see why Hume and Wallace disagreed about
the stability of the ancient republics. Hume's *Political Discourses*
were intended to present modern commercial regimes as having
fundamentally improved upon the ancient republics. In his
view, modern states are founded on a truer reflection of human
nature. Ancient republics sought political stability through cur-
bing natural human passions for acquisition and comfort. They
imposed an unnatural morality of self-denial and ascetic citizenship. In so doing, they hampered the development of an integrated social structure with a large, politically responsible
middle class. The result was a turbulent political system and a
militaristic culture. Modern commercial states, built as they are

on a more realistic understanding of human nature, allow for a greater range of self-interest, greater wealth production, a broader tax base, and hence greater capacity for defense. A healthy social structure will, in time, put more political power in the hands of a growing middle class, whose wealth, rather than public spiritedness, will qualify them for public service. A moral transformation will take place as greater wealth produces refinement, moderation, and improvement. More people will have the resources to be fulfilled and happy. And while such citizens will naturally be prone to factionalism and self-interest in politics, a wise jurisprudential division of powers among society's various orders will ensure that the conflict of passionate groups will produce the public good.[23] While Hume still had a foot in classical republicanism, his gaze was directed forward, toward a new world that was soon to emerge with James Madison.

Neither Wallace nor Rousseau could abide such a modernity. Wallace was convinced that Hume's analysis of human nature was a product of the corrupt tastes of a corrupt age, just as Rousseau was certain that neither Hobbes nor Locke had really found man in his "original state" of nature. Believing, like Rousseau, in a natural moral order, Wallace was convinced that humans most nearly lived in conformity with that order in their simple agrarian-republican stage of development. Wallace was therefore at odds with one of the main trajectories of Scottish social thought. It is now customary to associate the development of Scottish conjectural history with the need to make sense out of the modern world of commerce. In Adam Smith's fourth stage of society, for instance, it is clear that Machiavellian *fortuna* has been transcended. Commerce is not corruption or decay. Yet Wallace's conjectural account, which predates the earliest published four-stage theories, is designed rather to historicize *fortuna* than to defeat it. In the *Dissertation*, modern commercial states create boundless desires, transforming luxuries into necessities (25). The pressure to sustain such lifestyles delays and limits marriage, resulting in population decline and national weakness (23). Thus, modern forms of life are less viable, as well as less virtuous, than the form of life embedded in the fabric of the ancient republics.

And like Rome in the later Republic, the modern world is yielding to despotism in the form of the absolute monarchs.

Wallace sees this shift in political power reflected in the false tastes, sensibilities, and "overrefinement" of modern court and aristocratic circles. The loss of simplicity of taste was most evident in the abandoning of agrarian values and occupations. Wallace decried British landlords who racked their rents, took no interest in land improvement or usage, and frittered away the fruits of peasant labor on an ostentatious life in London and luxurious opulence in the country. While this critique of modern life as corrupt and pernicious to the poor was peripheral to his population thesis in the *Dissertation*, from the pulpit Wallace spoke more directly to the issue, as in a sermon preached in Edinburgh during the Jacobite uprising of 1745:

> Alas! how false are many of our ideas of magnificence and refinement? There have been times when these manufactures, which are left to the lowest and poorest of the people, and are so much despised by the rich and great, who rather chuse to spend their time in an inglorious ease and idleness, or in trifling and pernicious gaming, or in the foolish and silly pomp of visiting and show, worse than idleness itself; I say, there have been times when these manufactures, and especially agriculture, and the most useful Arts of spinning and weaving, were in the highest honour, nor despised by the rich and great. In ancient times the greatest sages and lawgivers delighted in the plainest and most simple methods of living, and the most eminent generals have been taken from the plow, and after doing the most signal service to their country, and gaining the most glorious victories over its enemies, have returned with the highest satisfaction and contentment to their peaceful labours.[24]

With such strokes we find Wallace alongside Rousseau in the 1750s striking a blow for the ancients in the old battle for the books in order to expose the corruption and injustice of modern life. In the 1760s both men began to explore what promise the ideals undergirding the republic of virtue might hold for the modern world. Could civic virtue be restored to the age of Enlightenment and modernity? This was a formidable challenge. By mid-century it was becoming clear to many that the independent republic was not capable of competing in the European international arena.[25] Montesquieu had gone to the heart of the matter with his portrayal of the British constitution in *The Spirit of the Laws*: the British had transcended the limitations of the past by creating a form of government unlike any other, in that its guiding spirit was not virtue, honor, or moderation, but liberty. There the citizen's interests are secured by a balanced constitution. Citizens are free to pursue commercial interests within a constitutional framework that establishes justice and preserves the public good. British constitutional liberty has made ancient concepts of civic virtue obsolete.[26] It is helpful to think of Wallace and Rousseau as having taken up Montesquieu's gauntlet to find, if possible, a place for ancient virtue in the modern world.[27] Both men sought a constitutional solution that would harmonize the legitimate private interests of citizens with the public good.

Rousseau's *Second Discourse* presented the onset of private property as the greatest source and symbol of social inequality and modern slavery. In the *Social Contract*, Rousseau did not attempt to establish liberty and equality by undoing this civilizing moment. To live in society may not be natural, but property is natural to society. Property is now within the realm of legitimate private interest. But those interests must be secured from the encroachments of powerful and ambitious men. All private, particular wills, moreover, must be harmonized with the "General Will." This Rousseau proposed to accomplish via legalistic mechanisms, and above all, through a theory of popular sovereignty.[28] A great lawgiver, a modern day Lycurgus, can create a legal order in which the true private interests of citizens are harmonized with the public good. In and through the assembly there is equality among citizens. No individual is subject to any other, but only to the law, which is of the citizen's own creation, and represents the "General Will." Hence, it is critical that citizens vote with the best interests of the public in view. While this situation cannot be guaranteed, laws against factionalism have such a purpose in view. The promotion of civil religion and the use of censorship to mold public opinion are also critical. The opinions and customs of the people must be such that only virtue is rewarded. Therefore, ambitious men will seek virtue rather than wealth or power. If the citizen's values become corrupted, the law will cease to embody the General Will, and liberty will be lost.

Wallace took up the question of an ideal political order in *Various Prospects,* in the course of examining the various causes for mankind's disappointing level of progress. Among these are the jealousies that exist among the great, the violent ambitions of kings, poverty, indolence, and an unjust distribution of labor. These problems appear to be the result of four basic components of human nature, which make the task of creating a virtuous social order difficult. These might be summarized as ambitiousness, covetousness, indolence, and a love of personal liberty (75–76). Following both the logic of Wallace's historical interpretation in the *Dissertation* and the spirit of Rousseau's *Second Discourse, Various Prospects* concludes that the only political order capable of harmonizing these passions in a just, equitable manner is one founded on absolute material equality. No theory of sovereignty, division of powers, or other legalistic solution can bring real social harmony to the private passions of men. Romulus's basic insight must be perfected, that is, carried to its logical conclusion.

The pattern that Wallace presents for such a society in *Various Prospects* is roughly that of Thomas More's *Utopia*. Following Harrington's principle that power ultimately follows property, only material equality will produce social equality. It follows that the constitutional details of such a polity might vary with little consequence, so long as a few basic principles are observed:

> "That there should be no private property. That every one should work for the public, and be supported by the public. That all should be on a level, and that the fruits of every one's labour should be common for the comfortable subsistence of all the members of the society. And, lastly, that every one should be obliged to do something, yet none should be burdened with severe labor." (46)

Under such an arrangement, the currently disruptive aspects of human nature would be brought into a peaceful social equilibrium. Ambition would be redirected toward the public good by eliminating social distinctions based on property and wealth. Forms of labor would be esteemed for their usefulness to the public. Prejudices against agriculture would fade. Social forces that now lead to opulence and display would be redirected toward practical, useful arts, and toward the attainment of learning, wisdom, and virtue. In such a world, covetousness would naturally cease because men's interests would no longer be in opposition to each other. Citizens would experience joy as naturally at the sight of general happiness as they do now for their own private good fortune. Natural indolence would be overcome by various social mechanisms: social contempt for those who rob the public of labor, a strong sense of patriotism inspired by such a polity, the examples of patriotic labor, and the aesthetic charm that such a system of perfect equality would produce (75–86).

But what of liberty? More's communitarian project was designed to radically reduce the private sphere for the sake of the public. In what sense could citizens in Wallace's ideal state be considered free? Liberty, in his scheme, is not constituted by the mechanism of a popular assembly, by which citizens rule themselves.[29] Nor is liberty secured through a constitutional separation of powers, the "balanced government" that Montesquieu had taught the British to admire about themselves. To discuss liberty in *Various Prospects*, Wallace, like Rousseau, turned to a theory of socialization. He considered how the passion for individual autonomy would be socially reconstructed in a society secured on a foundation of material equality. As he reminded the reader, "we may be convinced, that the ideas of men who have been born and educated under an equal government, must be very different from the idle conceits which have grown up among us, through the licentiousness of our manners" (82). The concept of liberty in the modern world is itself corrupt, emerging as it does in the context of an unnatural, corrupt social and political order.

Remarkably, this observation holds as much for balanced constitutional governments as for absolutist monarchies. The real problem with absolutism is not the deprivation of individual liberty, though that may often occur. Rather, it is that absolutists substitute their own private interest for that of the public. Hence, a prince may often indulge his subjects in the liberty "to be as wicked and wretched as they please," so long as his own interests are secured (91). Where the power of kings has been limited by a constitutional distribution of power, the result has not been true liberty but something more on the order of a legally established license.

There is a radical edge to this critique that Wallace's interpreters have often failed to appreciate, in part because Wallace himself typically blunted that edge with caveats to the effect that the British constitution generally secured the "lives, liberties and property" of its citizens better than any other system. In fact, Wallace was an articulate defender of these "Principles of

1688" in times of national emergency, such as the dark days of the Seven Years' War when he wrote his *Characteristics*; at such times, he believed, the defense of Britain was simply the duty of virtue, understood as patriotism. This tension within his published works derives from the fact that he came of age intellectually among the first generation of Edinburgh University students after the Union with England in 1707, which joined the Scots to the constitutional principles following from the English Revolution of 1688. In that environment, Presbyterians were the leading defenders of the Revolution Settlement, and criticism of the principles of 1688 or the Union was generally linked with Jacobite desires to see a return of the Stuarts.[30] Hume wonderfully encapsulated this situation with his observation that in Scotland there were no Tories, only Jacobites.[31] Or to put it another way, Rousseau wrote the *Discourses* and the *Social Contract* from Paris, while Wallace wrote as a British citizen in Edinburgh. Rousseau's social theorizing was unencumbered by the ebb and flow of republican Geneva or Venice. He had very little personally at stake. As a minister of the Presbytery of Edinburgh, however, Wallace felt keenly the burden of professional and national responsibilities. In short, while Rousseau and Wallace both came to believe that maintaining the civic virtue of the citizenry was the critical element in preserving liberty, only Wallace was in a position to practice what he preached.[32] Rousseau, as a citizen of the world, was unfettered by any such entanglements.

So it is that in his *Various Prospects*, despite a perfunctory caveat, Wallace argues that a society arranged in accordance with nature and reason cannot be secured with balanced government or representative institutions. Under modern, "free" governments, he writes,

the people in general are not laid under such proper and wholesome restraints, as are equally profitable to themselves, and are necessary to make them co-operate towards the general good. The ancients did too little in this way, but the moderns much less; and now, under the very best governments, rich men are allowed to spend their time and their money, to do something or nothing, to marry, or to abstain from marriage, and to educate their children as they please. About all these things, though of the greatest importance, even free governments seem to be too little anxious; leaving the people to be idle, lewd, and voluptuous; to contract all kinds of bad habits, to gratify all their whims and fancies, though infinitely pernicious both to themselves and the public; provided only they do not invade property, nor give any disturbance to others, in indulging in the same boasted but dangerous liberty.

Under the Utopian government, such destructive liberty is not allowed, but licentiousness is curbed with the strictest care. However, real liberty, or the liberty of indulging ourselves freely in every thing agreeable to nature and reason, no where flourishes with such security. Where such an equality is preserved, scarce can we suppose liberty to be in danger. Nor can the highest love of liberty ever be supposed dangerous, under such an equitable constitution. (93–95)

In the ideal society, "liberty" is effectively redefined in terms of equality and virtuous public-mindedness, a state of mind produced by socialization and education within a materially egalitarian society.

By demonstrating what must be done to create a virtuous political order, Rousseau and Wallace denounced the injustices of modern life and exposed the inadequacies of the modernizing, Enlightenment project. That entire undertaking was founded on a perverse inequality that made justice unattainable, and in some sense even unintelligible. But of what use are virtuous republics to the modern world? Rousseau might write a constitution for Corsica, but what of France? In his *Dissertation*, Wallace offered a reform program for rural Scotland based on the concept of the small planned agricultural village (149–61). But Britain could not be Utopia. Both men offered their models less as social blueprints than as an additional layer of social critique. Even the order of the *Social Contract* cannot escape the wheel of fortune. Deterioration is at work even here, and the best that one can hope for is to slow the process of decay.[33] In Judith Shklar's apt judgment, the *Social Contract* is a "yardstick" for measuring all existing governments rather than a pattern for creating better ones,[34] and the same is true for Wallace. A system based on community of property is possible and might even have come about through historical contingency. But it could not last. Such an order of moral perfection would be victimized by its own success. Were the governments of the world so patterned, Wallace argues in *Various Prospects*, population would naturally expand beyond the resources of the earth, and confusion and disorder would then reign (114).

This is why Wallace's career should be understood in the context of Rousseau's critique of modernity, rather than as an endorsement of a future golden age, on the order of Condorcet. Indeed, when Condorcet imagined a future of freedom, equality, and enlightenment, he encountered this same seemingly relentless relationship of population, food supply, and happiness that Wallace developed in his *Dissertation* and *Various Prospects*. But Condorcet resolved the dilemma. With the coming of institutional and moral perfection, people will realize that what they owe the next generation is not existence, but happiness, and they will limit the size of families accordingly:

> By then men will know that, if they have a duty towards those who are not yet born, that duty is not to give them existence but to give them happiness; their aim should be to promote the general welfare of the human race or of the society in which they live or of the family to which they belong, rather than foolishly to encumber the world with useless and wretched beings.[35]

Wallace was an imaginative fellow who might have developed a similar path around the obstacle of his population calculus. But there was no need. Moral perfection, virtue, equality, and justice are concepts that do not belong to this realm. They had a shadowy existence in the distant past, and they expose the vain pretentiousness of the present. But the better state they promise lies not within space and time, but beyond it. *Various Prospects* is, finally, a Christian-Platonist defense of providence and a future state of perfection. We have a "clear and distinct" idea of moral perfection, which nevertheless cannot exist in history. It must belong to another realm. What greater answer could there be to the freethinking Hume's doubts about the existence of a wise providence?[36]

It is here that Wallace's thought differs most significantly from Rousseau's. Rousseau sought, so far as it might be possible, to defeat Machiavellian *fortuna,* in part by subordinating religion to the ends of the state. Wallace the churchman, on the other hand, in what is really a most unexpected and charming twist in the history of ideas, embraces *fortuna* as a defense of Divine Providence. Even here the divergence of thought is by no means complete. There is at least an echo in the somber, private reflections of Rousseau, who sensed the paradoxes in his own thought and despaired of a just moral order for this world:

The whole of nature is my witness. It is not in contradiction with itself; I see in nature an admirable physical order always consistent with itself. The moral order should be the same. Yet my life's experience has been the apparent breakdown of this order, and so it will begin after my death.[37]

In a sense, neither man found an entirely adequate answer to the dilemma posed by Montesquieu: what place can virtue have in the modern world? France could not be Corsica; Britain could not be Utopia. The achievement of both men lay in peeling away the veneer of confidence and self-assurance that the project of Enlightenment and modernity was ushering in a morally superior age. Wallace once observed that Rousseau's *First Discourse*, which developed this theme so cogently, was the only modern work to have surpassed the eloquence and beauty of Cicero and Demosthenes.[38] The seemingly great achievements of modern, enlightened society are ephemeral, because they have not led to moral progress, but have rather accentuated a long history of inequality and injustice. Against the growing spirit of self-assurance, commercial expansion, dispassionate inquiry, and moral progress, Rousseau and Wallace registered reasoned and impassioned dissent.

## NOTES

1. Linda Kirk, "Genevan Republicanism," in *Republicanism, Liberty, and Commerical Society, 1649–1776*, ed. David Wootton (Stanford, 1994), 287–88.

2. Nicholas Phillipson, "Culture and Society in the Eighteenth-Century Provinces," in *The University in Society*, ed. Lawrence Stone (Princeton, 1975), 407–88.

3. See also Nicholas Phillipson, "The Scottish Enlightenment," in *The Enlightenment in National Context*, ed. Roy Porter and Mikuláš Teich (Cambridge, 1981), 19–40.

4. See, for example, John Ramsay, *Scotland and Scotsmen in the Eighteenth Century*, 2 vols., ed. Alexander Allardyce, (Edinburgh and London, 1888), 1:247. Ernest Campbell Mossner, *The Forgotten Hume: Le Bon David* (New York, 1943), 106, follows Ramsay. Norah Smith casts some doubt on this relationship in "The Literary Career and Achievement of Robert Wallace" (Ph.D. dissertation, Edinburgh University, 1973), 418.

5. Henry R. Sefton, "Rev. Robert Wallace: An Early Moderate," *Records of the Scottish Church History Society* 16 (1969): 2.

6. George Wallace, "Memoirs of Dr. Wallace of Edinburgh," *Scots Magazine* 33 (1771): 343.

7. Most of Wallace's unpublished material is in the Laing Collection in Edinburgh University Library.

8. Caroline Robbins, *The Eighteenth-Century Commonwealthman* (Cambridge, Mass., 1959), esp. 14, 202–11.

9. H. T. Dickinson, *Liberty and Property: Political Ideology in Eighteenth-Century Britain* (London, 1977), 141–42, 151n.

10. This general view was expounded earlier by Robbins, who writes of Wallace having "an ebullient belief in progress typical of his age" (*Eighteenth-Century Commonwealthman*, 205). For Smith's account, stressing the parallel between Wallace's and Condorcet's visions of an enlightened and perfected future of rationalized human relations, see "Literary Career," 352–63.

11. Ernest Campbell Mossner has very ably and correctly put Wallace in this context in *Forgotten Hume*, 111–17, and "Hume and the Ancient-Modern Controversy, 1725–1752: A Study in Creative Skepticism," *University of Texas Studies in English* 28 (1949): 149.

12. Norman Hampson, "The Enlightenment in France," in Porter and Teich, *The Enlightenment in National Context*, 49.

13. Jean-Jacques Rousseau, "Discourse on the Sciences and Arts," in *The First and Second Discourses Together with the Replies to Critics and Essay on the Origin of Languages*, trans. Victor Gourevitch (New York, 1986), 22.

14. Jean-Jacques Rousseau, *Discourse on the Origin of Inequality*, trans. Donald A. Cress (Indianapolis and Cambridge, 1992), 47–48. This summary is also indebted to James Miller's fine introduction, v–xviii.

15. The best account of this society is in R. L. Emerson, "The Philosophical Society of Edinburgh, 1737–1747," *British Journal for the History of Science* 12 (1979): 155–70.

16. "Of the Populousness of Ancient Nations," in *The Philosophical Works of David Hume*, 4 vols. (Edinburgh, 1826), 3:421–508. Robert Luehrs, "Population and Utopia in the Thought of Robert Wallace," *Eighteenth-Century Studies* 20 (Spring, 1987): 325, argues that Hume's essay was a response to Wallace, whereas Smith, "Literary Career," 191–92, contends that Hume was entering into the continental debate of Montesquieu and Voltaire, among others. However, Mossner, "Hume and the Ancient-Modern Controversy," 141, shows that Hume's concern with the question of ancient populousness, and his generally skeptical approach to the issue, dates at least from the 1730s, that the population question was central to Hume's "science of man" as a whole, and that, for these reasons, the essay would likely have existed in some form apart from Wallace or the continental debate.

17. Cited in F. H. Heinemann, *David Hume: The Man and his Science of Man* (Paris, 1940), 11.

18. Mossner, *Forgotten Hume*, 105, and chap. 5 generally. Mossner's account is the most thorough retelling of the debate, and forms the basis of this paragraph.

19. Frederick Whelan, "Population and Ideology in the Enlightenment," *History of Political Thought* 12 (1991): 45–53, puts this debate squarely in its ideological context, by usefully summarizing population discourse in the second half of the eighteenth century.

20. Montesquieu distinguishes between "savage" societies of hunters and

"barbarous" ones founded on herding, *Spirit of the Laws,* two vols. in one, trans. Thomas Nugent, (New York, 1949), i:276. Wallace draws no such distinction. It should also be noted that, as Ronald Meek has shown in *Social Science and the Ignoble Savage* (Cambridge, 1976), 31–35, Montesquieu does not place these societies in time, in an account of social development.

21. See Peter France, "Primitivism and Enlightenment: Rousseau and the Scots," *Yearbook of English Studies* 15 (1985): 72–79, for an account of Scottish social thinkers engaging Rousseau's primitivism.

22. On this question, Wallace writes in the *Dissertation* that "we must not conclude, that they immediately made free use of this power. It was much otherwise; the people at that time had a love of the republic, and, of course, of mediocrity of fortune. Their virtue did all, and the love of it hindered the people from counteracting the public law, and opposing the public good, by overturning those rules of succession, which were so necessary for preserving equality among the citizens, and harmony in the commonwealth" (240).

23. See John Robertson, "The Scottish Enlightenment at the Limits of the Civic Tradition," in *Wealth and Virtue: The Shaping of Political Economy in the Scottish Enlightenment,* ed. Istvan Hont and Michael Ignatieff (Cambridge, 1983), 154–60.

24. Robert Wallace, *Ignorance and Superstition a Source of Violence and Cruelty, and in Particular the Cause of the Present Rebellion. A Sermon Preached in the High Church of Edinburgh, Monday January 6, 1745–6* (1746), 24–25.

25. Franco Venturi, *Utopia and Reform in the Enlightenment* (Cambridge, 1971), 41.

26. M. M. Goldsmith, "Liberty, Virtue, and the Rule of Law, 1689–1770," in *Republicanism, Liberty, and Commercial Society,* ed. Wootton, 225.

27. Goldsmith has put Rousseau in this context in "Liberty, Virtue, and the Rule of Law," 227–32.

28. Maurizio Viroli, "The Concept of Order and the Language of Classical Republicanism in Jean-Jacques Rousseau," in *The Languages of Political Theory in Early Modern Europe,* ed. Anthony Padgen (Cambridge, 1987), 169–70. My understanding of the *Social Contract* is heavily indebted to Viroli's interpretation. See also his *Jean-Jacques Rousseau and the "Well-Ordered Society,"* trans. Derek Hanson (Cambridge, 1988).

29. Wallace seems relatively uninterested in working out the details of the political machinery. He notes simply that those who govern should be few in number and should not be distinguished from the rest of society by ostentation or pomp. His brevity reinforces the supposition that power ultimately follows property.

30. Wallace occasionally acknowledged this tension explicitly, as when he criticized the Presbytery of Edinburgh for its stringent denunciation of the staging of John Home's tragedy *Douglas* in 1757: decrying the times as evil and corrupt opens the door to disaffection that feeds Jacobite sympathies. Nevertheless, Wallace viewed the reopening of the Edinburgh playhouse as a function of cultural and moral corruption, much as Rousseau viewed the theater in Geneva. See "An address to the Reverend the Clergy . . . on occasion of composing acting and publishing the Tragedy called *Douglass,*" Edinburgh University Library, La.2.620:2, 51–52.

31. Hume, "Of the Parties of Great Britain," in *Philosophical Works*, 3:79.

32. Wallace discussed his understanding of a minister's civic responsibilities in an unpublished sermon of September 1740 that was a thinly veiled attack on Walpole's regime (Edinburgh University Library, La.2.620:22). That understanding was civic humanist in origin: the patriotic minister, like the magistrate, must set private interest aside, shun factionalism, and pursue the public good.

33. Judith Shklar, *Men and Citizens: A Study of Rousseau's Social Theory* (Cambridge, 1969) 208–9. See also Bertrand de Jouvenel, "Rousseau the Pessimistic Evolutionist," *Yale French Studies* 28 (1961–62), 83–96.

34. Shklar, *Men and Citizens*, 17, 208.

35. Antoine-Nicolas de Condorcet, *Sketch for a Historical Picture of the Progress of the Human Mind*, trans. June Barraclough (London, 1955), 189.

36. Cf. *First Discourse*, 16, where Rousseau rails at philosophers who employ their talents to undermine the foundations of religion and virtue.

37. Rousseau to Moutou, 14 February 1769, cited in Viroli, *Jean-Jacques Rousseau*, 15.

38. Wallace, "Treatise on Taste," Edinburgh University Library, Dc.1.55, 580.

# Beccaria, Voltaire, and the Scots on Capital Punishment: A Comparative View of the Legal Enlightenment

Ferenc Hörcher

Gentleness reigns in moderate governments.

—Montesquieu

Mercy to the guilty is cruelty to the innocent.

—Adam Smith

It is widely accepted in Scottish enlightenment scholarship that jurisprudence played a crucial role in Scottish moral and political philosophy, and that natural jurisprudence was one of its dominant discourses. Yet the eighteenth-century debate on capital punishment, and on the reform of criminal law generally, is more often discussed by legal historians than by historians of moral and political thought.[1] Indeed, I am unaware of any modern monograph by a historian of ideas dedicated to this rather delicate issue. What follows is an attempt to revisit this debate with a focus on its moral, political, and philosophical consequences rather than on its strictly criminal jurisprudential ones. I shall demonstrate that the European reception of Beccaria's famous book on crime and punishment was far from homogeneous, and that disagreement with its basic principles did not necessarily make one an ardent opponent of social progress. My claim is that a view of capital punishment depended far less on one's degree of "enlightenment," or on basic convictions in criminal theory, than on one's choice of strategy to justify the idea of social justice. It is revealing to consider the possibility that adherence to the social contract theory prevented Beccaria from finding a place for capital punishment in his system, and thus led him to the brave new idea of the unjustifiability of capital punishment. Lord Kames and Adam Smith followed the opposite strategy: a fear of the socially dangerous outcome of the social contract theory gave them the impetus to work out their criminal theories more precisely, relying more heavily on their own special social and moral "theory of sentiments."

The main protagonists in this debate on capital punishment are Voltaire, Allan Ramsay, Kames, and Smith. All of them came to be interested in the subject as a result of reading Beccaria, who was in turn influenced by Montesquieu. Even though I shall confine myself to the more important dissimilarities in their criminal theories, I am aware that there are also striking similarities in their approaches, and I do not offer this essay as an argument against the underlying unity of the European Enlightenment.[2] In measuring the distance between the enlightened reformism of eighteenth-century France and Scotland, with a cursory glance at Italy, I contend not that the ideas and arguments analyzed here were the only ones available to European contemporaries but that the dissimilarity of the theoretical positions says a great deal about the relevance of the national cultural inheritances within the shared intellectual tradition of the legal enlightenment.

The story begins with the publication in Liverno in summer 1764 of the *Treatise on Crimes and Punishments* (*Dei delitti e delle pene*) by Cesare Beccaria, who was then only twenty-six years old. Although there are those who think that the young Milanese's little book did not achieve much more than to assemble the available radical opinions about the most urgent tasks that needed to be done if contemporary criminal law were to become less outrageous and barbaric, Becarria's concepts were so radical, and his arguments so daring, that the *Treatise* instantly provoked a debate throughout Europe on the possible directions of criminal law reform.[3]

Since we can only interpret Beccaria from our own vantage point, we cannot fully appreciate today the novelty and freshness of his voice, or the radically egalitarian, almost proto-communist tone of his rhetoric. The most obvious and unproblematic approach to his work takes his achievement as a large step in the irresistible march of humanity toward the perfect realization of human potential. Voltaire called Beccaria a "humane author" and a "lover of humanity."[4] Even Kant, a forceful opponent, wrote about his "motives of compassionate sentimentality and affected humanity."[5] But there is another possible reading of Beccaria's project. Keeping in mind that, in the period before the French Revolution, the boundaries between conservatives and radicals were not sharply drawn, I shall argue that there existed at the time other alternatives within the reformist camp of the Enlightenment. By sketching Beccaria's position and comparing it with that of Voltaire and the Scots, I will show that a preference for a regime of criminal law more moderate than the existing one did not necessitate a point of view as contractarian as Beccaria's.

In his famous chapter 28 on "The Death Penalty," Beccaria introduces a rather "modern" conception of the origin and structure of civil society. He explains sovereignty (and, in a somewhat embarrassing way, the laws) as "nothing but the sum of the smallest portions of each man's own freedom; they represent the general will which is the aggregate of the individual wills."[6] Obviously, this is an alternative to the "general will" of his intellectual master, Rousseau. It is less obvious that by founding his criminal law theory on a theory of sovereignty in this way, Beccaria turns the problem of criminal jurisprudence (that is, the question of capital punishment) into a political battlefield, and into a debate over the nature of the relationship between the state and its subjects. Beccaria assumes a radical position in this battle. When he writes that "the death penalty . . . is an act of war on the part of society against the citizen," he excludes in advance the possibility that capital punishment may be just. For who can legitimize the war of the state against its own citizens? But Beccaria does not stop there. "Who has ever willingly given up to others the authority to kill him?" he asks. When reading these lines, some of his contemporary opponents began to fear that he was trying to make criminal law into a bargain that could be negotiated, contradicting all the traditional beliefs of eighteenth-century Europe.

In Italy, it was Ferdinando Facchinei, a Benedictine monk, who gave the first thoroughgoing criticism of Beccaria in his *Notes and Observations (Note ed osservazioni sul libro intitolato Dei delitti e delle pene)* of 1765. Although the literature on Beccaria usually regards Facchinei as the spokesman of Roman Catholic reaction, others recognize in him a proto-Burkean figure, whose criticism originated in a different understanding of his own age. Facchinei, the author of a book on Newton, criticized Beccaria for his exclusion of religious considerations from his reflections on criminal law, and for his contractarianism, egalitarianism, and libertarianism. From our point of view, his position is fascinating, because it foreshadows some of the elements of the Scottish criticisms of Beccaria.

We have to bear in mind that, at the time of writing his book, Beccaria was a motivated young man who possessed all the liberty of an independent intellectual within the natural barriers of the freedom of thought in an absolutist state. No wonder his achievement was a kind of legal utopia, as the perspicacious Allan Ramsay observed. It is interesting to see how this utopia confronted reality.

It was in Paris salons that the spectacular intellectual reception of Beccaria's work was prepared and perfected. By 1766 the book was already translated into French, and at the same time transformed. The considerably older and less naive Voltaire was among those who tried to utilize some of the novelties of the work of this remarkable provincial talent.[7] He undoubtedly found the book suitable for theoretically buttressing his "entirely pragmatic" struggle to rescue some innocent victims of the brutal machinery of contemporary French criminal law,[8] and considered it a way to create the model of reform in criminal law, both for his enlightened friends in Paris and on the thrones of the European monarchies.

Yet why did Voltaire not fully accept Beccaria's theoretical position on the question of capital punishment?[9] Why did Beccaria not join the Frenchman's campaign for the Chevalier de La Barre? And what was the real cause behind the fact that, after his first visit to Paris, Beccaria was no longer inclined to mingle with the radical representatives of the French—that is, Parisian—Enlightenment? These are not questions of mere biographical importance. When the best-known figure of the Enlightenment is an enthusiastic admirer of an unknown provincial thinker, who does not return these gestures as one would have expected, we are entitled to ask why. Although this essay cannot solve this mystery, it attempts to throw light on the matter by first casting a glance at Voltaire's commentary on Beccaria and then turning to the Scottish critics of Beccaria, who were more explicit on this issue.

Although his most powerful critic was a monk, and the orthodoxy of his faith was challenged by many of his critics, Beccaria did not see the church as his primary opponent, the way Voltaire did. When dealing with criminal law, Voltaire believed he was dealing with "priestcraft," as Hume would call it. When Voltaire was studying the original Italian edition of Beccaria's work in 1765, he had already been fully engaged in his legal controversies. Furthermore, the issue of capital punishment was to stay with Voltaire until the end of his life, as part of his campaign against the contemporary legal practice of the Church. This is important because Voltaire's aims decided his strategy, which in turn determined the arguments he used. Voltaire attributed most of the faults of legal practice to "the intrusion of the ecclesiastical powers into areas that are properly the concern of civil governments alone."[10]

When we read Voltaire's arguments against ecclesiastical intrusions through the eyes of the Scots, they appear very Hobbesian. It was Hobbes who first tried to separate the power of the sword and the crosier.[11] Voltaire was very keen on this post-revolutionary British experience. In his *Commentary on the Book On Crimes and Punishments*, he dwells on Roman examples to show that the legal sphere should not be occupied by religion: "[blasphemies] . . . had no effect whatsoever on the government of the state; because they disturbed no institution [of the State], no religious ceremony" (253). With the Romans, it was evident that "offences against the gods are a matter only for the gods." But not so with the Scots. This provides a clue as to why the latter opposed Voltaire's views: Hobbesian viewpoints constituted a red flag in eighteenth-century Scotland, instantly provoking reactions.

Yet Voltaire's characteristic figure recalls not only Hobbes but also the more sympathetic figure of Montesquieu, who was something of a hero in Scottish intellectual circles. They liked the civilization thesis, which Voltaire had taken from Montesquieu and articulated in his *Commentary* in sentences like these: "It was tyranny in particular that was the first form of government to order the death penalty for those who had a few differences in matters of dogma" (246); or, "Everywhere men forget that they are brothers, and they persecute each other to death" (257); or again, "this part of the world looks like a huge scaffold covered with executioners and their victims, surrounded by judges, sbirros, and spectators" (258). These are statements praising the civilized peace and harmony of society, a thesis that was appreciated by most of the Scots, even though some of them confronted it with their republican convictions of moral corruption and martial virtues. Even Kames failed to reconcile the contradiction between these two poles of his thought: the ideas of the progress of society and of moral purity. He would surely have refused to answer affirmatively Voltaire's provocative question: "Will those nations which pride themselves on being civilized not pride themselves also on being humane?" (261).

As to the political philosophy latent in the *Commentary*, it is also important to mention Voltaire's own hesitation between a natural law theory and a theory of public interest. It is perhaps in this essay that Voltaire appears to be closest to natural law theory. He gives an explicit definition of what he means by this term:

> I call natural laws those laws that nature points to in all ages to all men for the maintenance of that sense of justice which nature . . . has engraved in our hearts. Everywhere theft, violence, murder, ingratitude towards benevolent parents, perjury committed in order to harm rather than help an innocent person, plotting against one's country are all obvious crimes that are curbed with various degress of severity, but always justly. (263)

This is another idea very much in tune with a specific line of thought of the Scottish Enlightenment. Kames and Smith must have rejoiced when reading expressions like "the sense of justice . . . engraved in our hearts," or when they came to meditate on the proposition that natural laws are pointed to in all ages and among all men in a comparable fashion. Voltaire's position also resembles that of the Scots in that he too combined natural jurisprudence with an ardent sensitivity toward the infinite varieties of the phenomenon of law: "There are as many legal systems as there are towns, and in the same parliament the maxim of one court is not that of the court of next door" (278). But with Voltaire, unlike the Scots, this was less than a compliment.

On the other hand, Voltaire's thought contains a pragmatic component that may have been viewed suspiciously by some of the Scots. They would have found the following call in Voltaire's *Commentary* less than sufficient: "Chain to the State all the subjects of the State with self-interest" (249). Of course, self-interest was present in the Scottish discourse, as represented by Hume and some of his followers, above all Smith and Millar, who took Mandeville seriously enough. But with the Scots, self-interest should not contradict sympathy and the universal sense of justice. Smith would not have natural laws so definitely separated from political laws, while for Voltaire political laws are "those laws that are made for reasons of short term need, either to consolidate power or in anticipation of misfortune" (263). Neither would Smith have been likely to share the democratic, Lockean overtones of the following argument by Voltaire: "It is not only up to legal experts, but to all men, to declare whether or not the spirit of the law had been twisted" (266). Finally, Smith did not trust in man's reason as much as Voltaire. That is to say, Smith, following Hume, did not share with Voltaire that fundamental and still naive trust in man's intellectual capacity, which at the end of the century was so vehemently and painfully refuted by the political and military upheaval of the whole continent. The essence of the Scottish position can be given in a shorthand, negative way by pointing out that the Scots did not cherish hopes about Voltaire's concluding remark: "We are seeking to perfect everything in this century; so let us seek to perfect the laws on which our lives and fortunes depend!" (279).

Others have shown how far the Scottish thinkers preferred the wisdom of the unintended consequences of the natural development of law to the intensive activity of individual legislators. In what follows, therefore, I take as my starting point the difference between the activist jurisprudence of Beccaria and Voltaire and the Kames-Smith variant of moderate and retiring reformism. I shall concentrate on some less obvious aspects of the Scottish reaction to the new challenge of the criminal law reform movement, and explore the role attributed to the "moral sense" and the concept of sympathy in the respective theories of the Scots, as well as the importance they assigned to the theological basis of the theory of justice.

One other distinction has to be made concerning the Scottish reception of natural law theory. A great deal of research has been conducted recently about the origins of the modern natural law tradition, as represented by such Continental thinkers as Grotius, Pufendorf, and Barbeyrac, in addition to British thinkers, such as Hobbes and Locke. Despite other differences among them, most of the recent commentators agree that these writers

originated a conception of justice in which utility plays a determining role, as the force behind all sorts of political action. But
this idea is the diametrical opposite of the sort of Scottish jurisprudence with which this essay is concerned. I see a fine line of
demarcation between Hume and his contemporaries, because I
think the relation to the natural law tradition is one of the key
issues separating Hume's theory from most of the other Scottish
thinkers of his age, including Smith, to whom the idea of commercial society as built up of self-interested individuals is so
often attributed. It is important to see that Kames and Smith
himself explicitly rejected the natural law concept of the function of law, as developed by theorists from Grotius to Pufendorf.

According to Grotius, who is often regarded as the originator
of modern natural law, man in the state of nature has a natural
right to punish. In making this claim, Grotius is referring to Cicero and to Biblical examples of justified individual retribution.[12]
The individual right of punishment, however, is handed over to
the ruler at the moment of the creation of the state. The right of
the political authority to punish arises as a result of the fact that
the "atomic individuals" give up their own right to punish.
Criminal justice originally belonged to the individual but "the
State has a Power to prohibit the unlimited Use of that right
towards every other Person; for maintaining publick Peace and
good Order" (1.4.2). Justice, therefore, should be subordinated
to social utility.

Selden, an ardent follower as well as a critic of Grotius, similarly held "a strong form of the Grotian position on the origin
and nature of political authority."[13] His originality lay in the
fact that he tried to extirpate the natural law roots of the social
contract. He insisted that the contractors were free to bargain
on the terms of the contract; for him "the only definite rule was
that whatever a contract specified had to be performed, on pain
of divine punishment." Punishment was divine as far as its
status was concerned and not as far as the sanctions and the justification were concerned. Selden drifted so far away from the
original natural law account that he insisted that "there were
clearly no common principles of morality accessible to all men
by the light of their natural reason."[14] It was only on the most
general terms that "legitimacy for human powers depended
upon their being in accordance with natural law"; otherwise,

"every law is a contract between the king and the people, and therefore to be kept."[15]

Hobbes refines this theory by stating that the authority of the magistrate is not a "gift of the subjects" but rather comes from the subjects' surrendering their respective natural rights to punishment, while the sovereign does not do so. Although the right itself is of divine origin, it is not used for divine but rather for earthly purposes: "The aym of Punishment is not revenge, but terrour."[16] Locke, supposedly also contributing to the Hobbesian discussion, did accept that in the state of nature an individual surrendered his rights to punishment, but only for retribution ". . . proportionate to his transgression, which is so much as may serve for Reparation and Restraint. For these two are the only reasons, why one Man may lawfully do harm to another, which is that we call punishment."[17] As for the purpose and proportion of punishment, Locke says the following: "Each transgression may be punished to that degree and with so much severity as will suffice to make it an ill bargain to the offender" (293, 13). So again, the main purpose of punishment is deference. And again, it is this right which, having belonged to him as an individual, remains to be reserved for the magistrate after the emergence of civil society. Locke's refusal to invest the government with much extra power is also made clear in the following remark: "Remember that Absolute Monarchs are but Men" (293, 13).

Finally, Samuel Pufendorf makes explicit the analytical distinction between the right of the magistrate to punish, belonging to him as to any other individual through the law of nature, and the right (or duty) to defend the state: "The sovereign civil authority has a twofold right over the citizens' lives: a direct right in the suppression of crime, and an indirect right in defence of the state."[18] As far as the direct right is concerned, "executing its right directly the sovereign power may take away citizens' lives for atrocious crimes and as a punishment" (158). After society had been established, however, a new element comes into play: the interest of the society. This is when the magistrate receives the indirect right of punishment. But since punishment is of divine origin, and the magistrate human, Pufendorf is ready to assert that "when human beings inflict punishments they have to consider not only what evil was done, but also what good may come from its punishment" (159).

When "determining" "the precise kind and amount of punishment to be inflicted in individual cases," the "only object" of
the "supreme civil authority" must be "the good of the country" (161). This is the utility principle (36), which is to overcome in this system the aspect of vengeance taken for the
individual damage caused by the offender. Eventually, what the
magistrate executes as punishment is "public and open punishment designed to strike terror into others."[19] When proportion-
ing punishment, it is not the injury committed by the offender
which detemines the degree of punishment, but the passions of
the offender: "penalties . . . should be adequate to curb the passion by which men are driven to the crime for which the penalty provides." Natural law and the notion of punishment as
belonging to God's authority are in fact only indirectly present:
"social life has been imposed upon men by God's authority,"
and "He has enjoined the human race to observe as laws those
dictates of reason which He has Himself promulgated by the
force of the innate light" (36). Besides this justificational function, the reference to natural law comes into the picture when
dealing with "the usefulness of religion" itself: "fear of temporal
punishment would certainly not suffice to keep the citizens to
their duty" (43).

Thus, the theory of punishment in the Grotian heritage of
natural law is distinguished by the following characteristics.
First, the right of punishment belongs to individuals as their
natural right, enabling them to preserve their lives in the state
of nature. Second, according to the social contract, magistrates
are charged with preserving the peace and safety of society, and
punishment in civil society belongs to the magistrate and has
the exclusive function of defending the interest of the state. As
we shall see below, the Kames-Smith version of the moral sense
theory of punishment is just as much opposed to the modern
school of natural law as it is to the Beccarian concept of punishment as determined by the social contract.

The ideas of Allan Ramsay, the Scottish painter and writer,
constitute an interesting interlude in the story of the debate initiated by Beccaria. Ramsay connects the Parisian scene with the
Scottish background, provides a model of how Beccarian ideas
could infiltrate Scottish intellectual milieus, and foreshadows
the type of reaction it could provoke. His thought is discussed

here as a model of one type of Scottish response to Beccaria's work.

Ramsay reflected upon *On Crimes and Punishments* in a letter to Diderot of January 1766. As Franco Venturi explains, he "despised its egalitarian spirit, and dismissed the idea of a social contract."[20] In a pamphlet entitled *Thoughts on the Origin and Nature of Government. Occasioned by the Late Disputes between Great Britain and Her American Colonies,* written in 1766 and published in London in 1769, Ramsay refuses to accept the principle "frequently laid down . . . that all men in their natural state are free and independent" (8). The basis for his refusal is, first, that he cannot accept that "a natural state" ever existed, and second, that in his opinion the principle of equal right to liberty—which can hardly be separated from the principle of "an equal right to property"— "has never been actually acknowledged by any but the very lowest class of men; who have been easily persuaded to embrace so flattering a doctrine from the mouth of a Wat Tyler" (8). Neither does he accept the theory of a voluntary social contract as the basis of legitimizing a government:

> The rights of government are built upon something much more certain and permanent than any voluntary human contract, real and imaginary; for they are built upon the weakness and necessities of mankind. The natural weakness of man in a solitary state prompts him to fly for protection to whoever is able to afford it, that is to some one more powerful than himself; while the more powerful standing in need of his service, readily receives it in return for the protection he gives . . . from this is derived all the relations of master and servant, patron and client, king and subject. (10)

That is, instead of a voluntary association, Ramsay prefers to speak about a "reciprocal obligation of protection and service" (11). But he was perhaps even more annoyed by Beccaria's frame of mind:

> Political questions cannot be treated by means of geometrical and mathematical abstractions. Laws do not take shape *a priori* from general principles drawn from human nature. Everywhere laws have arisen from the particular needs and circumstances of individual societies.

In a Humean fashion, Ramsay is suspicious of "theoretical philosophers, witty intellectuals, cold examiners of human nature," the more so because "the idle dreams of metaphysicians, uncountenanced by fact and experience . . . carry, upon certain occasions; some confused resemblance on reality" (9).

Ramsay and the Scots generally did not oppose reforms as such, but they viewed the whole issue of progress or regress at least partly from the perspective of the republican tradition. Although reason may help to civilize manners, the cost to be paid is corruption. Civilization points directly at luxury. For Ramsay, as for Hume and for Kames, liberty and security are strongly, if inversely, connected concepts: too much individual liberty may damage public security, for "those who advocate the suppression of torture, the wheel, impalement, the rack, as well as arbitrary imprisonments and executions, would deprive themselves of their surest means of security and would abandon the state to the mercy of the first bunch of rebels who like better to command than to obey."[21]

It is not only for this age-old historiographical reason that Ramsay is so keen to retain the idea of severe punishment. According to the concept of power in his *Thoughts on the Origin and Nature of Government*, the ability of the state to punish its subjects is a sign of its controlling the highest power: "A law without a penalty is no more than an advice; and a penalty without a power to inflict it would be ridiculous / and this is so consonant to common sense and common language, that there is probably no language in the world in which to prevail and to give law are not synonymous" (17). Ramsay was obviously utilizing ideas that were current in the Scotland of his day but were not always popular in other European intellectual circles. We shall later see how far his denial of the existence of a social contract, or his convictions about the impossibility of human equality or the necessity of reciprocal obligations, resemble the jurisprudence of Kames and Smith. There is a sign, however, that shows his real alliance more clearly than any of these doctrines. When Ramsay mentions "the immediate impulse of man" as the source of judging which acts are against nature, and which are not, this sounds like a variant of the doctrine of the moral sense so characteristic of the Scottish school, and opposed by Hume. This naturalistic approach to moral sensibility was very powerfully expressed in the theory of Lord Kames.

In "Scottish Echoes," Franco Venturi tries to introduce Beccaria as someone who stood very close to the intellectual disposition of Kames. He refers to an observation of Beccaria's French translator, Morellet, who, after having read the translation of a work of Lord Kames, exclaimed that "Kames is Beccaria's brother." In what follows, I shall argue that Morellet did not read Kames thoroughly enough, and that the opinion of Kames's translator, Mathieu-Antoine Bouchaud, is more to the point, when he states: "Mr. Beccaria is a philosopher who deals with his subject from the most useful point of view for humanity. My Scot is no more than a jurist who describes with a feeble and sometimes insecure hand the progressive evolution of law in most nations."[22] Unlike Venturi, I do not believe that a close resemblance between Beccaria and Kames can be established merely because both men attempted to construct a general history of human development based on economics and law. This element, after all, is present in a number of thinkers of the age.

Moreover, an appendix to the biography of Lord Kames by Alexander Fraser Tytler, Lord Woodhouselee provides indirect evidence for setting them against each other. Entitled "On the Principles of Criminal Justice, as Unfolded in Lord Kames's *Essay on the History of the Criminal Law*: with an Examination of the Theory of Montesquieu and Beccaria, Relative to Crimes and Punishments," Woodhouselee's appendix shows how Beccaria and Voltaire, with their opposition to capital punishment, refuted the established way of thought of other lawyers, politicians, and philosophers who were for it, "on the score of justice, wisdom, and the most enlarged humanity."[23] Before considering the main arguments of this small essay, however, it is necessary to examine the best-known direct evidence of Lord Kames's theory of criminal law: his essay on the "History of Criminal Law" in his 1758 book, *Historical Law-Tracts*.[24]

That moral sense plays a major role in Kames's understanding of the nature of punishment is exemplified by the following phrase at the beginning of the essay, which is reminiscent of the Voltairean definition of natural law, cited above: "In the breast of man a Tribunal is erected for Conscience" (3). Moral sense or conscience is a "natural restraint" on man initiated by the "dread of punishment." It is an internalized version of natural reason, a kind of natural sentiment or passion. It is implanted by God into the hearts of offenders as well as victims, and as a result of it, "the criminal submits naturally to the punishment," which he considers as a "debt" on his own part (21). The debt is materialized in the form of a personal revenge on the part of the victim, to whom it belongs "by the law of nature." Only at a certain stage of social progress can revenge be transferred to the public, that is, to the legal authority (20). When this is achieved, the purposes of human punishments will become, first, to add weight to those which nature has provided, and second, to "enforce municipal regulations" (73). By then, the peace of society is considered as in many ways more important than that of individuals. Authority is transferred from the individual conscience to the external tribunal, the legal authority: "After public authority is firmly rooted in the minds of the people, punishments more rigorous may be ventured upon" (72). As this idea of the "socialization of revenge" shows, authority (that is, the legitimation to use the instrument of criminal punishment against the criminal) is not obtained from some sort of social contract but rather is a natural result of the evolution of civil society. However, as it is ideologically transformed into a theory of saving the peace of the community, it in fact can turn out to be more severe than it would have been if it had remained in the hands of the victim. By now punishment (very often capital punishment) is backed up by "reason of state." It takes a long time, and the intellectual evolution of subjects, to accept human (that is, civil) authority, even if it is not so eager to show its power when the system of punishments becomes more sophisticated and less in need of proving its authority. It is only "when a people become altogether tame and submissive" (72) that capital punishments are avoided as much as possible and in their place punishments are chosen, which, "equally with death; restrain the delinquent from committing a like crime a second time" (76).

This account of the progress of criminal law was formulated by Kames before the appearance of Beccaria's famous book. It is interesting to note that most phases of its development coincide with the Beccarian vision. The difference lies in the terms used and in the respective views of how far society can be manipulated by laws, as well as in the function attributed to law. In Kames's theory, punishment has a sacred function: it is a means to keep up the balance of the moral equilibrium in society. The students of law, Kames writes in the preface to *Historical Law-*

*Tracts*, "must pry into the secret recesses of the human heart and become well acquainted with the whole moral world, that they may discover the abstract reasons of all laws."[25] One of his best recent interpreters also refers to this attribute of his theory: "Man discerned the moral character of action through his *'moral sense* or *conscience*,' and the dictates of this moral sense could be construed as laws of nature, which for Kames includes notions of divine purposes and final causes."[26] On the other hand, this moral sense, which he conceives as an innate faculty of man, is inflexible only as far as its most general notions of justice are concerned, and is capable of improvement in many other respects: "The moral sense is born within us . . . [but] re-quire[s] much cultivation."[27] So Kames's theory is no less "pro-gressive" than that of Beccaria; and due to his professional legal experience, his attitude to the nature of legal change is more de-tailed and professional than Beccaria's. It is the characteristic double-sidedness of his theory—viewing moral sense both as an innate capacity and as culturally acquired—that makes it unac-ceptable to Hume. Hume's hostility to the naturalistic account is a clear indication of the difference between Humean and Smithian jurisprudence, and a reason why Beccaria was so fond of Hume's philosophy.

It is worthwhile comparing these views with a later account of Kames's ideas, given by his friend and former protegé, Lord Woodhouselee.[28] The starting point here is Kames's dissatisfac-tion with the status quo of criminal jurisprudence: "It is a mat-ter of equal regret to the politician and to the moralist, that the science of Criminal Jurisprudence, on which the good govern-ment and peace of society most materially depend, should, in this enlightened period, remarkable for its advancement in many of the branches of political economy, as well as of the phi-losophy of morals, remain in a state of great imperfection" (73). This is, of course, a reformist argument, which expresses discon-tent with the jurisprudence of its own time. Furthermore, it has a utilitarian bent, since Kames speaks about good government and the peace of society, as one might expect an eighteenth-century British thinker to do. Yet very soon one realizes that criminal law is here founded on a principle which simple utili-tarian considerations cannot establish. In opposition to Joseph Priestley's theory of criminal law, which presents as the objects of criminal law, first, to lessen the number of future crimes, and second, to give a sense of personal security, and which claims that the "punishment has no reference to the degree of moral turpitude in the criminal" (79, quoting Priestley's *Lectures on General Policy*), Woodhouselee's account of Kamesian criminal jurisprudence refers to the "decision of the moral sense" in the formation of criminal law sentences, and—using words that relate to the Voltairean definition of natural law almost word for word—to

> that natural feeling of justice which is implanted in the human breast. . . . To lessen the number of crimes in future, is undoubtedly an important object of the criminal law: but it is neither its sole, nor even its primary object. The primary object of the criminal law, is the accomplishment of justice, by the proper punishment of crimes that have actually been committed. (79)

Criminal law is here again founded on a theory of human nature, yet in a more sophisticated manner than in the original version in *Historical Law-Tracts*. According to this theory, we have a "beautiful sympathetic frame of nature," which enables us to "feel delight and satisfaction from every act of benevolence or of virtue," and "pain and indignation from every deed of malice or of vice" (80). This is certainly and avowedly Adam Smith, as a quotation from the *Theory of Moral Sentiments* soon makes clear (81–82n.). Again, the personal moral sense becomes vested in the state as society grows more complex, and through this development a criminal act grows into an "outrage against society," with the following explanation: "He who commits an injury against society, incurs an obligation, and contracts a debt to society, of which the creditor is entitled to exact the payment" (83). This argument is directed against Beccaria's claim that the state, founded on a social contract, cannot have the right to take the life of its citizens. This would only be true if political expediency were "the sole foundation of the right of punishment," but according to this later version of Kamesian theory, "its true foundation [is] the principle of revenge" (84). As Woodhouselee sums up Kames's view,

> The Marquis de Beccaria, whose *Essay on Crimes and Punishments* breathes a very amiable spirit of humanity, has founded all his reasonings on that mistaken idea of Montesquieu, which makes the prevention of crimes the sole end of punishment, and therefore the

principle of Criminal Justice. The arguments which he employs, and the conclusions which he draws, are such as may be expected from the assumption of false premises. (88)

This is the point upon which I established my claim that the main difference between Beccarian and Kamesian jurisprudence lies not so much in their actual legal doctrines as in their premises.

According to Woodhouselee, it is also a false proposition "that laws are the sum of the smallest portions of the private liberty of each individual" (89, quoting Beccaria). "The right of punishment," Kames believes, "is not formed out of any portions, great or small, of the liberty of individuals, voluntarily given up by them to the State" (90). The reason for this denial is simple: criminal law would become impossible if we thought it to be in need of the individual's consent, for "who ever gave his consent to be whipped, or pilloried, or banished?" (90). Quite the contrary, it is more proper to say that the right arises from the criminal action itself. "[The criminal] subjects himself to vengeance or to punishment by the very act;" and: "The question, therefore, with regard to the right of the State to inflict capital punishments, will come to this short issue, 'Are there any crimes, which, in justice, deserve the punishment of death?'" (91). Thanks to the moral-sense foundation of his theory, Kames is in a position to argue that "there must be no just criterion of right and wrong in the mind of that man, who does not instantly acknowledge, that there are crimes of that degree of atrocity, to which no other punishment than death is an adequate retribution" (91). Therefore, capital punishment is warranted by "our moral feelings" (92).

The result is clear: "Let the sword of justice be unsheathed, and injured nature have her full revenge" (94). This statement amounts to a full attack on the Beccarian revolution in jurisprudence: "It is the vice of the present age," writes Woodhouselee, "and the sickly cast of its morality, to have substituted a species of metaphysical sentiment for genuine feeling" (94). This "genuine feeling" is partly an offshoot of the sentimental moral universe of eighteenth-century theories of art (and Kames was an influential theorist in that field, too), but it is more closely related to the Smithian version of moral sense theory, as expressed in a term that also came originally from art theory: the "impartial spectator."

Yet Kames also strives to lend a political underpinning to his own position, which would also legitimize it before practical politicians. Making use of a Hobbesian idea, he presents the counterpart of the feeling of revenge—the fear of death as a suitable vehicle—in the hands of tactful politicians, for the maintenance of the peaceful order of society: "The preservation of life is the first concern of man; the fear of losing life is the greatest of all fears; this fear is, of consequence, the greatest of all restraints on the commission of such actions as are punishable by the loss of life" (99). In Kames's view, man is open to all sorts of moral turpitude, and his theory therefore does not require the kind of universal benevolence present in many contemporary systems: "Universal benevolence is indeed not required of man. . . . But for promoting the general good, everything is required of him that he can accomplish."[29] However, this is still very far from a purely utilitarian theory of criminal jurisprudence.

Adam Smith's jurisprudence, as put forward in the *Theory of Moral Sentiments* and the *Lectures on Jurisprudence*, represents another variant of pro-capital punishment criminal law theory in eighteenth-century Scotland, one less bellicose but no less severe than that of Kames. Although it is also a reformist theory, it cannot accept even the direction to which Beccaria's ideas turn. In part 2 of the *Theory of Moral Sentiments*, entitled "Of Merit and Demerit; or, of the Objects of Reward and Punishment," Smith reflects on the theory of punishment. Like Woodhouselee, Smith traces reward and punishment to the sentiments of gratitude and resentment, which deem them proper when the "impartial spectator entirely sympathizes with them."[30] Now it is generally accepted in Smith scholarship that the concept of the impartial spectator is one of the most important notions of Smith's moral theory. It is rarely noticed, however, that this concept helps Smith to establish his theory of just punishment on a foundation that is connected to natural law but that avoids the parallel danger of accepting either the social contract of Rousseau and Beccaria or the utility principle of the Grotian natural law tradition, which was also utilized by Beccaria. In what follows, I shall first show how far the concept of the impartial spectator is still within a general natural law framework and then analyze Smith's rejection of the concepts of social contract and utility.

Smith presents his concept of the impartial spectator at the beginning of the *Theory of Moral Sentiments*. It is the viewpoint of human affairs available to someone who is not directly involved in them but sufficiently humane to be capable of "changing places in fancy with the sufferer" (*TMS*,10). This meaning is clarified by the concept of sympathy which, unlike in present-day usage, is meant "to denote our fellow-feeling with any passion whatever" (*TMS*,10). The impartial spectator, or the man within, is the viewpoint from which each individual can judge the propriety of his own or other persons' behavior: if the impartial spectator can sympathize with an action, it is proper. The capacity of the individual to step back into the position of the impartial spectator is made possible by the moral sense:

> Upon whatever we suppose that our moral faculties are founded, whether upon a certain modification of reason, upon an original instinct, called a moral sense, or upon some other principle of our nature, it cannot be doubted, that they were given us for the direction of our conduct in this life. . . . The very words, right, wrong, fit, improper, graceful, unbecoming, mean only what pleases or displeases those faculties. (*TMS*, 164–65)

These faculties are available to man as a result of being human, which is to say, sociable, but without being always and universally benevolent.

If the impartial spectator is a category of moral theory, it is for Smith also a guide to arrive at the justification of punishment. His criminal jurisprudence is in many ways part of a natural jurisprudence, as the viewpoint of the impartial spectator shows; it is the stance of "every reasonable man" (*TMS*, 69–70). As a number of scholars have noted, natural jurisprudence is vital for Smith. He regards it as "of all sciences by far the most important, but hitherto, perhaps, the least cultivated" (*TMS*, 218). Yet his understanding of natural jurisprudence is in a way more orthodox than that of the other representatives of the modem school of natural law, for he sees a more direct interplay between the laws of God and those of nature. By this I mean that with the concept of the impartial spectator, Smith preserves the self-condemning character of traditional Augustinian morality, and does not allow it to be overtaken by the utility principle. With the concept of the impartial spectator, Smith puts a strict and quasi-objective judge behind each of us, and so makes our moral equilibrium dependent on an internalized external viewpoint.

At the same time, Smith is returning to the Old Testament idea of retributive justice, which does not allow the utility principle to overturn the internal structure of the analytics of punishment. As a result, his moral principles are embedded in principles of divine authority that are available to each individual by taking the viewpoint of the impartial spectator. This makes it possible for the individual to transform moral principles into principles of punishment. Through the impartial spectator, each of us is directly linked to an external viewpoint of our actions. This offers Smith the chance to work out his elaborate system of self-criticism, establishing a close link between morally wrong actions and their punishments (a point that is also recommended by Beccaria). But this link in Smith's system is nothing less than natural, and is only in need of reinforcement by the social institutions of punishment. The mechanism of punishment is internalized and follows a pattern almost as solid as the laws of nature. To sum up these points, in Smith's theory of punishment, divine punishments overlap with the punishments of the moral consciousness and criminal punishments:

> What is agreeable to our moral faculties, is fit, and right, and proper to be done; the contrary wrong, unfit, and improper. . . . Since [the moral faculties], therefore, were plainly intended to be the governing principles of human nature, the rules which they prescribe are to be regarded as the commands and laws of the Deity, promulgated by those vice-gerents which he has thus set up within us. . . . But those general rules which our moral faculties observe in approving or condemning whatever sentiment or action is subjected to their examination . . . have a much greater resemblance to what are properly called laws, those general rules which the sovereign lays down to direct the conduct of his subjects. (*TMS*, 165–66)

In his *Lectures on Jurisprudence,* Smith explicitly refers to Grotius when criticizing the reference to public interest in the justification of public punishment: "That which Grotius and other writers commonly alledge as the original measure of punishments, viz the consideration of the publick good, will not sufficiently account for the constitution of punishments."

Therefore, "in those crimes which are punished chiefly from a view to the publick good the punishment enacted by law and that which we can readily enter into is very different."[31] This means that it is the concept of the impartial spectator which prevents Smith from accepting the principle of public interest as the sole foundation of public punishment. Instead, making use of his historical investigations into the social development and institutionalization of punishment, he affirms that "the revenge of the injured . . . is the real source of the punishment of crimes" (104). The atavistic sentiment of revenge is still a sure guide for the most civilized impartial spectator, for "that action must . . . surely appear to deserve punishment, which every body who hears of it is angry with, and upon that account rejoices to see punished" (*TMS*, 70).

In addition to impartial spectators, there are also partial spectators who are responsible for the peace of the community: civil magistrates. But even the magistrate should not simply regard what the public wants as the principle of punishment: we have seen that moral principles work like the "laws of the deity," and that punishment has a function of actualizing otherwise internally felt necessities. The magistrate bears the responsibility to let the external laws of society reflect this inner and higher reality: "If the murderer should escape from punishment . . . [the victim] would call upon God to avenge, in another world, that crime which the injustice of mankind had neglected to chastise upon earth" (*TMS*, 91).

This is the source of the magistrate's entitlement for the use of power. The magistrate has a natural superiority over others: "There is the same propriety in submitting to them as to a father, as all of those in authority are either naturally or by the will of the state who lend them their power placed far above you" (318). It is interesting to see how what appears at one point as Smith's conception of authority resembles what at another locus is labeled the Tory principle and contrasted with the Whig principle of utility, which in its turn is connected to the social contract:

The principle of authority is that of the Tories, as that of utility is followd by the Whigs. They say . . . that [the rulers] have no authority unless what they derive from the people. This is their principle, tho they do not explain it very distinctly, endeavouring to reconcile it to the notion of a contract. . . . The Tories pretend that the kingly authority is of divine institution, that the kings derive their authority immediately from God, and that . . . he has as it were a patriarchall authority and is a sort of father to his people. (319–20)

I do not want to claim that Smith argues in favor of either of the political parties, but it is certainly not incidental that the editors of the *Lectures* notice that, in the sixth and final edition of the *Theory of Moral Sentiments* of 1790, "Smith writes with approval of 'the divine maxim of Plato, never to use violence to [one's] country no more than to his parents'" (320n. 77), which one can legitimately interpret as a sign of his position on the eve of the French Revolution. In this reading, Smith stands quite near to a Burkean type of old Whiggism, sharing the assumption that liberty should always be ordered, and that no argument is strong enough to count as a pretext for starting a civil war.

While the entitlement may come from a higher authority, it is necessity that makes us approve of the enforcement of the laws of justice "by the punishment of those who violated them." But again, besides political necessity (or the necessity of police), another element plays a part here: the concept of sociability, which Smith calls "a natural love for society" (*TMS*, 88). The priority of society over the individual is here again established by way of a natural inclination that dwells within the breast of the individual, who "has an abhorrence at whatever can tend to destroy society." "Hence it is, they say, that he often approves of the enforcement of the laws of justice even by the capital punishment of those who violate them. The disturber of the public peace is hereby removed out of the world, and others are terrified by his fate from imitating his example" (*TMS*, 88).

After Smith's understanding of authority, necessity, and sociability, we have to consider yet another element that contributed, in his opinion, to the creation of society without any social contract. This is natural progress, which allows societies to use the sociable capacities of individuals in order to improve their personal lot. Sociability is a natural inclination of man, which is assisted by the natural allegiance to authority and the calculations of self-interest to arrange the conditions for human society to develop. It is social development which enables man to polish his moral sense, to listen to the silent voice of conscience and society in order to build up a very strict criminal regime at first, which becomes milder as the people become mentally aware of their own respective responsibilities and adopt more civilized habits.

Then it will appear that there are natural reasons for the individual to take part in the preservation of society. Punishment is not so much a determining factor in this process. On the other hand, it is still in need of a justification, and possibly by more natural reasons. But as we have seen, it has its own independent rationale in revenge or resentment. In the *Lectures on Jurisprudence,* Smith makes this point clear:

> Injury naturaly excites the resentment of the spectator, and the punishment of the offender is reasonable as far as the indifferent spectator can go along with it. This is the natural measure of punishment. It is to be observed that our first approbation of punishment is not founded upon the regard to public utility which is commonly taken to be the foundation of it. It is our sympathy with the resentment of the sufferer which is the real principle. (475)

Although Smith is referring to the natural sentiments of man concerning crimes and punishments, he realizes the danger of relying too heavily on these very sentiments, for "when [the criminal] ceases to be an object of fear, with the generous and humane he begins to be an object of pity" (*TMS*, 88). But Smith is skeptical enough about human capacities and realizes that few men act upon the dictates of reason; they are not animated by their reflections on the causes and effects of their behavior, and "few men have reflected upon the necessity of justice to the existence of society" (*TMS*, 89). What motivates our reactions to a wrongdoing is not so much "the general interest of society" but "a concern for that very individual who has been injured" (*TMS*, 90). This, however, is not a personalized relationship between the observer and the victim, but rather compassion initiated by sympathy and the judgment of the impartial spectator: "The concern . . . is no more than the general fellow-feeling which we have with every man merely because he is our fellow-creature" (*TMS*, 90). So in Smith's thought, the sense of criminal justice is an innate sense and an interindividual affair, which connects the observer and the victim (and the offender, as shown below) to the larger society. "A man of humanity . . . applauds with ardour . . . the just retaliation which seems due to such detestable crimes" (*TMS*, 90–91).

Thus, Smithian theory represents a return to strict Augustinian morality, that is to say, to a conviction that punishments are authorized by a sacred law, albeit prompted by the innate moral sense of the impartial spectator. Natural law and natural religion join together here in a last great effort to reunite legal theory with theology and natural law. Understanding this point helps us to see the notable change in the last edition of the *Theory of Moral Sentiments* in 1790. Here a longer, traditional rhetorical sequence is replaced by a dry and indeed Humean sentence at the end of Smith's paragraph on punishments. The new version is the following: "In every religion, and in every superstition that the world has ever beheld, accordingly, there has been a Tartarus as well as an Elysium; a place provided for the punishment of the wicked, as well as one for the reward of the just" (*TMS*, 91). I interpret this passage not as a sign that Smith was distancing himself from the traditional role of religion in a theory of punishments, as is commonly thought, but rather as a sign that he remained within the framework of the religious approach to crimes—an approach detestable to Voltaire and presumably also to Beccaria.

To conclude, punishments in these theories preserve their by now long-forgotten significance and find their own role in satisfying man's moral sense, as well as society's needs for balance and justice. They also show that even within the general movement of Enlightenment, it was possible to hold views which today may sound antiquated or unenlightened. That is because some of the pro-capital punishment theories of criminal jurisprudence in the Enlightenment were founded upon theories of the origin and the aim of civil society as well as upon general theories of morality and natural moral theology.

On the basis of what has been said, the following three patterns may be distinguished among Enlightenment authors. First, there is the position of those, like Beccaria, who accept a theory of the social contract as the foundation of society and therefore cannot accept capital punishment in their legal theory. Second, there are those, such as Voltaire, who call for legal reform on the basis of political (and antireligious) convictions, but who do not support the abolition of capital punishment because they do not consider it politically useful. Finally, there is the approach of the Scots (except for Hume), who support capital punishment because of a concept of justice based on a naturalistic theory of moral sense.[32] These three attitudes, however, are actually intertwined in a number of ways, due to influences and counterinfluences, and therefore should not be taken as isolated, ideal positions. Their relationships are family resemblances, both similar to and different from each other. In that sense, views on capital punishment are examples of the pluralism of Enlightenment social thought.

## NOTES

I am grateful to Istvan Hont, James Moore, and John Robertson for comments on earlier versions of this paper.

1. See, for example, the recent exchange between Alan Norrie, "Punishment and Justice in Adam Smith," *Ratio Juris* 2 (1989): 227–39 and Eric Miller, "Sympathetic Exchange, Adam Smith and Punishment," *Ratio Juris* 6 (1996): 182–97.

2. My position is near to Franco Venturi's in his *Utopia and Reform in the Enlightenment* (Cambridge, 1971), where he writes about reading Voltaire after Beccaria: "By doing so, what the men of the Enlightenment had in common and the ways in which they differed in the mid-sixties becomes clear" (108).

3. On the reception of Beccaria's book, see Franco Venturi, "Cesare Beccaria and Legal Reform," in his *Italy and the Enlightenment: Studies in a Cosmopolitan Century*, ed. Stuart Woolf; trans. Susan Corsi (New York, 1972), 154–64, as well as other writings by the same author.

4. Voltaire, *Commentary on the Book On Crimes and Punishments, by a Provincial Lawyer* (*Commentaire sur le livre des délits et des peines*, 1766), in Voltaire, *Political Writings*, ed. David Williams (Cambridge, 1994), 244–79, esp. 245, 261.

5. Immanual Kant, *The Metaphysics of Morals*, in Kant, *Political Writings*, ed. G. H. Reiss, trans. H. B. Nisbet (Cambridge, 1970), 131–76, quoting 157.

6. Cesare Beccaria, *On Crimes and Punishments, and Other Writings*, ed. Richard Bellamy; trans. Richard Davies with Virginia Cox and Richard Bellamy (Cambridge, 1995), 66. Other quotations in this paragraph refer to the same source.

7. On the French reception of the book, see Venturi's notes in *Cesare Beccaria, Dei delitti e delle pene. Con une racilta di lettere e documenti relativi all nascita dell'opera e alla sua fortuna nell'Europa del Settecento*, ed. Franco Venturi (Turin, 1973).

8. See David Williams, introduction to Voltaire, *Political Writings*, xxiv.

9. On this dissimilarity, see Venturi, *Utopia and Reform*, 108.

10. Williams, Introduction to Voltaire, *Political Writings*, xxvi.

11. See, for example, J. G. A. Pocock, "Conservative Enlightenment and Democratic Revolutions: The American and French Cases in British Perspective," in *Government and Opposition* 24 (1989): 81–106.

12. Richard Tuck, *Natural Rights Theories* (Cambridge, 1979).

13. Ibid., 96.

14. Quoted in Richard Tuck, *Philosophy and Government, 1572–1651* (Cambridge, 1993) 195.

15. Ibid., 215.

16. Thomas Hobbes, *Leviathan* (London, 1984), 355.

17. John Locke, *Two Treatises on Government* (Cambridge, 1970), 289, 8.

18. Samuel Pufendorf, *On the Duty of Man and Citizen According to Natural Law,* ed. James Tully; trans. Michael Silverthorne (Cambridge, 1991), 158. All quotations in this paragraph are drawn from this source.

19. Cf. Hobbes's use of the same expression in note 17 above.

20. Franco Venturi, "Scottish Echoes in Eighteenth-Century Italy," in *Wealth and Virtue: The Shaping of Political Economy in the Scottish Enlightenment,* ed. Istvan Hont and Michael Ignatieff (Cambridge, 1983), 345–62, quoting 346.

21. Quoted in Venturi, "Scottish Echoes," 346.

22. Quoted by Venturi, ibid., 348. It is important to note that Lord Woodhouselee contrasted Beccaria's and Voltaire's views with those of lawyers, politicians, and philosophers. See Alexander Fraser Tytler, Lord Woodhouselee, *Memoirs of the Life and Writings of the Honourable Henry Home of Kames,* 2 vols. (Edinburgh, 1807), 1:53.

23. Woodhouselee, "On the Principles of Criminal Justice," in his *Memoirs of Kames,* appendix 10, 1:73–103, quoting 74.

24. Henry Home, Lord Kames, *Historical Law-Tracts,* 2 vols. (Edinburgh, 1758), 1:1–88. The citations in the following paragraph are drawn from this, the first edition of Kames's book.

25. Kames, *Historical Law-Tracts,* 2nd ed. (Edinburgh, 1761), xl.

26. Lieberman, *Province of Legislation Determined,* 153.

27. Henry Home, Lord Kames, *Sketches of the History of Man,* 4th ed., 4 vols. (Edinburgh, 1788), 1:196–97, quoted in Lieberman, *Province of Legislation Determined,* 152.

28. Unless otherwise noted, the citations that follow refer to Woodhouselee's essay "On the Principles of Criminal Justice," cited in note 24 above.

29. Kames, *Sketches of the History of Man,* 4:46.

30. Adam Smith, *The Theory of Moral Sentiments,* ed. D. D. Raphael and A. L. Macfie (Oxford, 1976), 69 (hereafter *TMS*). Kames himself also utilized the Smithian concepts of sympathy and the "impartial spectator."

31. Adam Smith, *Lectures on Jurisprudence,* ed. R. L. Meek, D. D. Raphael, and P. G. Stein (Oxford, 1978), 104. Unless otherwise noted, the citations that follow are drawn from this source.

32. An alternative version of this third position is put forward in Kant's *Metaphysics of Morals* (155–58), which also supports capital punishment on the basis of a concept of justice but does so by giving greater weight to an idea of punishment grounded in eternal or "categorical" principles of morality and religion. It is worth noting that some of Kant's arguments against Beccaria parallel those of Kames and Smith, and that his position against capital punishment cannot simply be reduced to reactionary or unenlightened political thinking.

# Contributors to *Scotland and France in the Enlightenment*

PAUL-GABRIEL BOUCÉ has been Professor of English Language and Literature at the Sorbonne since 1971. Most of his research bears on Fielding, Sterne, and especially Smollett, whose first and third novels (*Roderick Random* and *Ferdinand Count Fathom*) he edited. Boucé's most recent publications include *Sexuality in Eighteenth-Century Britain* and *Guerre et Paix: La Grande Bretagne au Dix-huitième siècle,* of which he is editor and contributor, and a number of articles on sexual mentalities and mores. A Norman, he is a former Naval Reserve Officer and Visiting fellow of Wolfson College, Cambridge.

PIERRE CARBONI graduated from the Ecole Normale Supérieure in Paris and is Assistant Professor of English at the University of Nantes, France, where he teaches Eighteenth-Century and Scottish cultural history and literature. He studied the relevance of Belles-Lettres in the Scottish Enlightenment's cultural refoundation and published several articles on the theme of literature and the nation in Scotland after the Union. His current research is on James Thomson's identity as a Scot and poet. The French government has recently appointed him to the National Council of Universities.

HARVEY CHISICK is the author of *The Limits of Reform in the Enlightenment: Attitudes toward the Education of the Lower Classes in Eighteenth-Century France* (1980), *L'Éducation élémentaire dans un contexte urbain sous l'Ancien Régime: Amiens au XVIIe et XVIIIe siècles* (1982), *The Production, Distribution and Readership of a Conservative Journal of the Early French Revolution: The Ami du Roi of the Abbe Royou* (1992), and of a number of articles on the social and intellectual history of eighteenth-century France and Scotland.

B. Barnett Cochran is Associate Professor of History at Mount Vernon Nazarene University in Ohio. A recent recipient of an Emory University Ph.D., his thesis on Robert Wallace and George Turnbull explored the problem of Scottish national identity in the Enlightenment period.

Deidre Dawson is Associate Professor of French at Michigan State University. She is the author of a book on Voltaire's correspondence and has recently co-edited a collection of essays entitled *Progrès et violence au XVIIIe siècle*. Dawson has written about the French sources of Adam Smith's *Theory of Moral Sentiments* and the impact of this work on French painters and writers at the end of the eighteenth century. The French government made Dawson a *Chevalier dans l'ordre des palmes académiques* in 1997 for her services to French culture.

Kathleen Hardesty Doig is Associate Professor of French at Georgia State University. She is the author of a book on the *Supplement* to the *Encyclopédie*, co-author of a study on the *Encyclopedie méthodique*, and one of the co-authors of a book being edited by Frank A. Kafker, on the early editions of the *Encyclopaedia Britannica*. She has written articles on the history of eighteenth-century encyclopedism, including the Yverdon *Encyclopédie*.

Andrew Hook is Emeritus Bradley Professor of English Literature at the University of Glasgow. His most recent publications include *From Goosecreek to Gandercleugh: Studies in Scottish-American Literary and Cultural History*, and *F. Scott Fitzgerald: A Literary Life*. He edited the eighteenth-century volume in the Aberdeen *History of Scottish Literature* . He is a member of the Advisory Board of the Edinburgh Edition of the *Waverley Novels* and co-edited *The Fair Maid of Perth* for that edition. Professor Hook is a past president of the Eighteenth Century Scottish Studies Society, and was recently elected Fellow of both the Royal Society of Edinburgh and the British Academy.

Ferenc Hörcher is Associate Professor of Aesthetics at the Faculty of Arts and of the Theory of State at the Faculty of Law of Pázmány Péter Catholic University, Hungary. He was a fellow of the Institute for Advanced Studies in the Humanities, Edinburgh for the academic year 1999–2000. His publications include a book on The Scottish Enlightenment, of which he is editor and translator of original sources into Hungarian, and *A Cambridge View on Early Modern Political Thought* (in Hungarian). Hörcher has published essays on the history of moral philosophy in Scotland, as well as a comparison of Hume's and Wittgenstein's philosophy of common life. Hörcher's most recent book, *Towards a Pragmatic Theory of Natural Law* is in press.

FRANK A. KAFKER is Professor Emeritus of History at the University of Cincinnati. He is the author of *The Encylopedists as a Group: A Collective Biography of the Authors of the Encyclopédie* and the co-author of *The Encyclopedists as Individuals: A Biographical Dictionary of the Authors of the Encyclopédie*. He has also edited two books on eighteenth-century encyclopedias. He was the co-editor of the journal *French Historical Studies* from 1985 to 1992 and the President of the Society for Eighteenth-Century French Studies from 1995 to 1997. His current research is centered on the eighteenth-century editions of the *Encyclopaedia Britannica*.

SYLVIE KLEIMAN-LAFON is Maître de Conférences in Eighteenth Century English Literature and History of Ideas at Amiens University. A graduate from the Ecole Normale Supérieure, she is the author of several articles dealing with Scottish literature and Scottish thinkers, more particularly on questions related to the debate on Æsthetics in the Eighteenth Century. She is currently working on the notion of translation in Eighteenth Century Britain and France.

JEFF LOVELAND is Associate Professor of French at the University of Cincinnati. He is the author of a book entitled *Rhetoric and Natural History: Buffon in Polemical and Literary Context* and has contributed sections to a forthcoming book on the first three editions of the *Encyclopaedia Britannica*.

DUNCAN MACMILLAN, art historian and art critic, is Professor Emeritus of the History of Scottish Art in the University of Edinburgh. His books include *Painting in Scotland the Golden Age 1707–1843*, *Scottish Art in the Twentieth Century* and a number of monographs. His major work *Scottish Art 1460–1990* was greeted as definitive when it was published in 1990 and a new edition has recently appeared under the title *Scottish Art 1460–2000*. Professor Macmillan is an Honorary Member of the Royal Scottish Academy and a Fellow of the Royal Society of Arts.

Susan Manning is Grierson Professor of English Literature at the University of Edinburgh. Her primary research interests lie in the field of Scottish-American literary relations, the subject of her books *The Puritan-Provincial Vision* (1990), and *Fragments of Union: Making Connections in Scottish and American Writing* (2002). Her editions of Scottish Enlightenment authors include Scott's *Quentin Durward*, and Henry Mackenzie's *Julia de Roubigné* published in 1999. She has also published articles on Burns, Boswell, and Hume.

Pierre Morère is Professor of English and Scottish literature and was vice-president of the University Stendhal (Grenoble, France) from 1996 to 2000. He is co-director of the Scottish Studies Centre in Grenoble. He edited a volume on Eighteenth-Century Scotland in 1997 and published recently in French reviews several articles on Kames, Hume, Godwin, Addison and Steele, Walter Scott and Mary Wollestonecraft. He is co-editor of the yearly review *Études Écossaises* and member of the editorial board of *Études Anglaises*.

A. E. Pitson is Lecturer in Philosophy at the University of Stirling. He has published various articles on the philosophy of the Scottish Enlightenment and, in particular, on David Hume. He has also contributed papers on numerous occasions to meetings of the Hume Society. In 1999 he was elected to the Executive Board of the Hume Society and was also appointed Book Reviews Editor for the journal *Hume Studies*. His book *Hume's Philosophy of the Self* was published in 2002.

# Index

335